W9-AUR-391

Accelerated VB 2008

Guy Fouché and Trey Nash

Apress®

Accelerated VB 2008

Copyright © 2008 by Guy Fouché and Trey Nash

All rights reserved. No part of this work may be reproduced or transmitted in any form or by any means, electronic or mechanical, including photocopying, recording, or by any information storage or retrieval system, without the prior written permission of the copyright owner and the publisher.

ISBN-13 (pbk): 978-1-59059-874-0

ISBN-10 (pbk): 1-59059-874-1

ISBN-13 (electronic): 978-1-4302-0339-1

ISBN-10 (electronic): 1-4302-0339-0

Printed and bound in the United States of America 9 8 7 6 5 4 3 2 1

Trademarked names may appear in this book. Rather than use a trademark symbol with every occurrence of a trademarked name, we use the names only in an editorial fashion and to the benefit of the trademark owner, with no intention of infringement of the trademark.

Lead Editor: Dominic Shakeshaft
Technical Reviewers: Tim Patrick, Fabio Claudio Ferracchiati
Editorial Board: Clay Andres, Steve Anglin, Ewan Buckingham, Tony Campbell, Gary Cornell,
    Jonathan Gennick, Kevin Goff, Matthew Moodie, Joseph Ottinger, Jeffrey Pepper, Frank Pohlmann,
    Ben Renow-Clarke, Dominic Shakeshaft, Matt Wade, Tom Welsh
Project Manager: Sofia Marchant
Copy Editor: Kim Benbow
Assistant Production Director: Kari Brooks-Copony
Production Editor: Kelly Gunther
Compositor: Lynn L'Heureux
Proofreader: Elizabeth Welch
Indexer: Present Day Indexing
Cover Designer: Kurt Krames
Manufacturing Director: Tom Debolski
Distributed to the book trade worldwide by Springer-Verlag New York, Inc., 233 Spring Street, 6th Floor, New York, NY 10013. Phone 1-800-SPRINGER, fax 201-348-4505, e-mail orders-ny@springer-sbm.com, or visit http://www.springeronline.com.

For information on translations, please contact Apress directly at 2855 Telegraph Avenue, Suite 600, Berkeley, CA 94705. Phone 510-549-5930, fax 510-549-5939, e-mail info@apress.com, or visit http://www.apress.com.

Apress and friends of ED books may be purchased in bulk for academic, corporate, or promotional use. eBook versions and licenses are also available for most titles. For more information, reference our Special Bulk Sales—eBook Licensing web page at http://www.apress.com/info/bulksales.

The information in this book is distributed on an "as is" basis, without warranty. Although every precaution has been taken in the preparation of this work, neither the author(s) nor Apress shall have any liability to any person or entity with respect to any loss or damage caused or alleged to be caused directly or indirectly by the information contained in this work.

The source code for this book is available to readers at http://www.apress.com.

To Jim and Kay Liegl for their friendship and the jaunts in the Jeep
To Charlotte Fouché for her laughter and her compassion toward others
To Gaston Fouché Sr. for his cuisine and sharing the art of the meal
To Frank Reed for the music and trumpet duets after my lessons were long over
To Jodi Fouché for her poetry, being my biggest fan, and unequivocal love
—Guy Fouché

Contents at a Glance

Contents

About the Authors

GUY FOUCHÉ is a business intelligence and decision support system consultant in the Dallas, Texas, area. He has developed a large number of Visual Basic systems in a variety of industries, supporting companies of all shapes and sizes. His VB programming experience dates back to Version 1. Yes, Version 1. Guy spends his evenings playing one of his eight trumpets and expanding his composition skills using the current generation of music technologies. On the weekend, he puts as many miles as he can on his bright yellow Honda F4i sport motorcycle. Guy and Jodi enjoy taking nine-day trips in their Jeep 4 × 4, taking photographs and writing travelogues along the way. You can view their photography at `http://photography.fouche.ws`.

TREY NASH is a principal software engineer working on security solutions at a market-leading security software company. Prior to that, he developed Bluetooth solutions for the release of Microsoft Vista, and he called Macromedia Inc. home for five years before that. At Macromedia, he worked on a cross-product engineering team for several years, designing solutions for a wide range of products throughout the company, including Flash and Fireworks. He specialized in COM/DCOM using C/C++/ATL until the .NET revolution. He's been glued to computers ever since he scored his first, a TI-99/4A, when he was a mere 13 years old. He astounded his parents by turning a childhood obsession into a decently paying career, much to their dismay. Trey received his bachelor of science and his master of engineering degrees in electrical engineering from Texas A&M University. When he's not sitting in front of a computer, you can find him working in his garage, playing his piano, brushing up on a foreign language (Russian and Icelandic are the current favorites), or playing ice hockey.

About the Technical Reviewers

TIM PATRICK has been working professionally as a software architect and developer for nearly 25 years. By day he develops custom business applications in Visual Basic for small to medium-sized organizations. He is a Microsoft Certified Solution Developer (MCSD). In April 2007, Microsoft awarded Tim with its Most Valuable Professional (MVP) award for his work in supporting and promoting Visual Basic and its community of users. Tim received his undergraduate degree in computer science from Seattle Pacific University. You can contact him through his web site, www.timaki.com.

FABIO CLAUDIO FERRACCHIATI is a senior developer for Brain Force (www.brainforce.com). A prolific writer on leading-edge technologies, he's contributed to more than a dozen books on .NET, C#, Visual Basic, and ASP.NET. He's a .NET MCSD and lives in Milan, Italy.

Acknowledgments

We offer a huge thank you to everyone at Apress who has had input into these pages!

Guy Fouché and Trey Nash

In addition, a note of my appreciation goes to the following people:

Kim Benbow and Kelly Gunther for many a well-chosen edit and making these pages look their best.

Tim Patrick and Fabio Ferracchiati: their insights have added a great deal to this book.

Sofia Marchant for managing countless revisions and keeping us all on track.

Dominic Shakeshaft for his knowledgeable, experienced guidance throughout this edition.

Guy Fouché

Introduction

Visual Basic 2008 (VB 2008) is relatively easy to learn for anyone familiar with another object-oriented language. Even someone familiar with Visual Basic 6.0 who is looking for an object-oriented language will find VB 2008 easy to pick up. However, though VB 2008, coupled with .NET, provides a quick path for creating simple applications, you still must know a wealth of information and understand how to use it correctly in order to produce sophisticated, robust, fault-tolerant applications. We teach you what you need to know and explain how best to use your knowledge so that you can quickly develop true VB 2008 expertise.

Idioms and design patterns are invaluable for developing and applying expertise, and we show you how to use many of them to create applications that are efficient, robust, fault-tolerant, and exception-safe. Although many are familiar to C++ and Java programmers, some are unique to .NET and the Common Language Runtime (CLR). We show you how to apply these indispensable idioms and design techniques to seamlessly integrate your VB 2008 applications with the .NET runtime, focusing on the new capabilities of VB 2008.

Design patterns document best practices in application design that many different programmers have discovered and rediscovered over time. In fact, .NET itself implements many well-known design patterns. You will see these practices detailed throughout this book. Also, it is important to note that the invaluable tool chest of techniques is evolving constantly.

.NET 3.5 provides a unique and stable cross-platform execution environment. VB 2008 is only one of the languages that target this powerful runtime. You will find that many of the techniques explored in this book are also applicable to any language that targets the .NET runtime.

As you'll see, it doesn't take years of trial-and-error experience to become a VB 2008 expert. You simply need to learn about the right tools and the correct ways to use them. That's why we wrote this book for you.

About This Book

We assume that you already have a working knowledge of some object-oriented programming language, such as C++, Java, or Visual Basic. If you already know some VB 2005 or VB 2008, you may find yourself skimming Chapters 1 and 2.

Chapter 1, "VB 2008 Overview," gives a quick glimpse of what a simple VB 2008 application looks like.

Chapter 2, "VB 2008 Syntax," introduces the VB 2008 language syntax. We introduce you to the two fundamental kinds of types within the CLR: value types and reference types. We also describe namespaces and how you can use them to logically partition types and functionality within your applications.

Chapter 3, "Classes and Structures," provides details about defining types in VB 2008. You'll learn more about value types and reference types in the CLR. We also discuss the inefficiencies inherent in boxing and discuss object creation, initialization, and destruction.

Chapter 4, "Methods, Properties, and Fields," discusses using methods to add behavior to your types, using properties to enforce encapsulation, and using fields to represent the state of your object. You'll explore method parameter types, overloading, property modifiers, and field initializers.

Chapter 5, "VB 2008 and the CLR," expands on Chapter 1 and quickly explores the managed environment within which VB 2008 applications run. We introduce you to assemblies, which are the basic building blocks of applications into which VB 2008 code files are compiled. Additionally, you'll see how metadata makes assemblies self-describing.

Chapter 6, "Interfaces," details interfaces and the role they play in the VB 2008 language. Interfaces provide a functionality contract that types may choose to implement. You'll learn the various ways that a type may implement an interface, as well as how the runtime chooses which methods to call when an interface method is called.

Chapter 7, "Operator Overloading," details how you may provide custom functionality for the built-in operators of the VB 2008 language when applied to your own defined types. You'll see how to overload operators responsibly, since not all managed languages that compile code for the CLR are able to use overloaded operators.

Chapter 8, "Exception Handling," shows you the exception-handling capabilities of the VB 2008 language and the CLR. Creating exception-safe and exception-neutral code is tricky in VB 2008, and you'll see that creating fault-tolerant, exception-safe code doesn't require the use of Try, Catch, or Finally constructs at all. We also describe some of the capabilities within the .NET runtime that allow you to create more fault-tolerant code.

Chapter 9, "Working with Strings," describes how strings are a first-class type in the CLR and how to use them effectively in VB 2008. A large portion of the chapter covers the string-formatting capabilities of various types in the .NET Framework and how to make your defined types behave similarly by implementing IFormattable. Additionally, we introduce you to the globalization capabilities of the framework and show you how to create custom CultureInfo instances for cultures and regions that the .NET Framework doesn't already know about.

Chapter 10, "Arrays and Collections," covers the various array and collection types available in VB 2008. You can create two types of multidimensional arrays, as well as your own collection types, while utilizing collection-utility classes. You'll also learn how to implement IEnumerable so that your collection types will work well with For . . . Each statements.

Chapter 11, "Delegates and Events," shows you the mechanisms used within VB 2008 to provide callbacks. Historically, all viable frameworks have always provided a mechanism to implement callbacks. VB 2008 goes one step further and encapsulates callbacks into callable objects called *delegates*. Also, you'll see how the .NET Framework builds upon delegates to provide a publish-subscribe event-notification mechanism, allowing your design to decouple the source of the event from the consumer of the event.

Chapter 12, "Generics," introduces you to probably the most exciting feature added to VB 2008 and the CLR. Using generics, you can provide a shell of functionality within which to define more specific types at run time. Generics are most useful with collection types and provide great efficiency compared to the collections of previous .NET versions.

Chapter 13, "Threading," covers the tasks required in creating multithreaded applications in the VB 2008 managed virtual execution environment. You'll see how delegates, through use of the "I owe you" (IOU) pattern, provide an excellent gateway into the process thread pool. Arguably, synchronization is the most important concept when getting multiple threads to run concurrently. This chapter covers the various synchronization facilities available to your applications.

Chapter 14, "VB 2008 Best Practices," is a dissertation on the best design practices for defining new types and how to make them so you can use them naturally and so consumers won't abuse them inadvertently. We touch upon some of these topics in other chapters, but discuss them in detail in this chapter. This chapter concludes with a checklist of items to consider when defining new types using VB 2008.

Chapter 15, "LINQ with VB 2008," explores a new set of technologies built into the .NET 3.5 Framework. LINQ provides a common object model and syntax to consume data with your VB 2008 applications. This chapter covers LINQ to Objects, LINQ to XML, and LINQ to SQL, showing you how to query in-memory objects, XML documents, and relational databases with these technologies. We also discuss several technologies that support LINQ, including type inference, anonymous types, extension methods, and Lambda expressions.

CHAPTER 1

■■■

VB 2008 Overview

This book is for experienced object-oriented developers. In this overview, we will take a look at some of the major language differences between Visual Basic 2008 (VB 2008), C# 3.0, and Visual Basic 6.0 (VB6). Functionally, VB 2008 and C# 3.0 are nearly identical, and you can use either language to create stable, high-performance applications in the .NET environment. You'll see the biggest differences in the syntax, which is completely different between the two languages. VB 2008 and VB6 are also vastly different from each other, and we will look at some of the overreaching differences between the two languages. Next, we will review a simple VB 2008 program to get an idea of the programmatic structure in .NET 3.5 and wrap up with a summary of what's new for current VB programmers in this latest and greatest version, VB 2008.

Differences Between VB 2008, C# 3.0, and VB6

This new version of VB has been specifically designed to target the new programming model provided by .NET 3.5. Both C# 3.0 and VB 2008 are designed to write programs that work with the .NET runtime. Whereas C# 3.0 was designed with C and C++ programmers in mind, VB 2008 is designed to be more accessible to the large base of existing VB programmers. The new language targets the .NET 3.5 programming model and is derived from previous versions of VB, but you'll find that it's quite different. The language changes are due to the fact that in order to support the framework, VB 2008 must provide more object-oriented features as well as type safety.

.NET Runtime

To understand VB development in the .NET environment, you first need to understand some components of the .NET environment and how they interact. This section summarizes how VB programs are compiled and run in .NET. The execution engine of .NET is known as the common language runtime (CLR). The CLR is primarily responsible for loading and executing code, as well as memory management, security, and handling of types.

At the top level is the VB language itself, or any language that targets the CLR, that is used to create code. The VB compiler takes the written code and generates intermediate language (IL). For example, a DLL or EXE contains IL that is understood by the CLR. Any code written to run in the CLR is known as *managed code*, because it runs under the control of the CLR. Managed code is an IL because it is halfway between the high-level language (VB) and the lowest-level language (assembly/machine code).

At run time, the CLR compiles the IL into native code on the fly by using the just-in-time (JIT) compiler. The JIT compiler creates native code that is CPU-specific, so you could take the IL for a program and compile it on computers with different architectures. JIT compiling comes with its pros and cons. It may seem that an obvious disadvantage is the inefficiency of compiling code at run time. However, the JIT compiler doesn't convert all the IL into native code; rather, it converts only the code that's executing into native code to be run. At the same time, it creates stubs to any methods not executing so that when those methods are called, the JIT compiler will compile and execute the necessary code.

An advantage of JIT compiling is that the working set of the application is reduced because the memory footprint of intermediate code is smaller. During the execution of the application, only the needed code is JIT-compiled. Unused code, such as printing code if the user never prints a document, is never JIT-compiled. Moreover, the CLR can optimize the program's execution on the fly at run time. For example, on the Windows platform, the CLR may determine a way to reduce page faults in the memory manager by rearranging compiled code in memory, and it could do all this at run time. That said, there are times when JIT compilation can be a performance drawback. In this case, you can use native image generation (NGen) to precompile IL on the machine where it's running.

The CLR replaces the traditional VB runtime and also eliminates the use of COM, DCOM, MTS, or COM+. VB applications now run in the context of the CLR, so there's no more need for the host of distributed technologies that were once so prevalent. Of course, you can still access COM components if you need to through the interop layer provided by .NET.

■**Note** If you wish, you could actually code a program in raw IL while building it with the Microsoft Intermediate Language (MSIL) Assembler. Of course, that would be a very inefficient way to write programs, but the fact that you could do it demonstrates the cross-platform capabilities of .NET. You can convert any language that supports .NET into IL, and the CLR can understand IL from any language. From there, you can JIT-compiled the IL into native code for the particular CPU architecture on which it's running.

VB 2008 and C# 3.0

VB 2008 and C# 3.0 are nearly identical in what you can accomplish with them; you can use either language to access all the classes and functions provided by the .NET Framework. Essentially, you can do everything in VB 2008 that you can do in C# 3.0, although one language may provide a more streamlined approach than the other, depending on what you're trying to accomplish.

When discussing VB 2008 and C# 3.0, it's easier to talk about their differences than their similarities. In the latest release, both languages add new language extensions, including Language-Integrated Query (LINQ), query comprehensions, anonymous types, lambda expressions, and extension methods. Later chapters cover each of these topics extensively.

The only real differences are that currently C# 3.0 provides the ability to write unsafe code, and VB 2008 provides late binding. Unsafe code in C# 3.0 is that which uses pointers to manage and access memory directly. You might need to use unsafe code for performance reasons or to write low-level Win32 API calls, to the ReadFile function, for example. Unsafe code may be warranted at times, but it isn't recommended because it cannot be verified to be safe and creates objects in memory that cannot be removed by garbage collection. Late binding was kept in the VB language to maintain compatibility with previous versions. Late binding allows you to create a variable as a type of Object and then later assign it to a variable either implicitly by assigning it to an object instance or using the `CreateObject` function. Early binding is preferred over late binding because late binding incurs a performance hit, and the compiler can't report errors at compilation time, which means you'll receive them at run time instead.

VB 2008 and VB6

The Visual Basic language, beginning with VB .NET 2002, was completely overhauled to support the CLR, so it bears only a passing resemblance to VB6. This results in a steep learning curve for many developers, but the trade-off is a whole new programming model that, when applied correctly, provides a better development environment and better software. In addition to a whole new compilation model, the CLR provides improved memory management, an object-oriented environment, and type safety. One of the biggest changes to the VB language is that it is now truly object-oriented. This means that each and every object (including data types) derive from `System.Object`. Instead of the VB runtime and the Win32 API, you now have the entire Base Class Library (BCL) of objects to work with. The challenge for programmers new to .NET is navigating this vast library and knowing where to find the classes they need. Becoming familiar with the .NET Framework will make you a better and faster programmer. The BCL is a subset of the .NET Framework and provides types that can be utilized by any code written to run in the CLR. The BCL includes the `System.Collections`, `System.Diagnostics`, `System.IO`, `System.Registry`, `System.Globalization`, `System.Reflection`, `System.Text`, and `System.Drawing` namespaces, to name a few.

CLR Garbage Collection

One of the key facilities in the CLR is the garbage collector (GC). In the managed runtime environment, the GC heap is responsible for managing all objects. It monitors an object's lifetime and frees it from memory when no part of the program references the object. The GC doesn't remove an object from memory as soon as there are no references to it. Rather, it runs periodically and releases objects from memory when necessary. There may be a delay from the time that all references to an object are released to the time that it's destroyed by the GC. Objects have a `Finalize` destructor (it's implicitly created at run time if you don't have it explicitly defined) that's called by the GC. However, the `Finalize` destructor doesn't fire immediately when an object loses scope. The automatic nature of the GC means that object lifetimes are nondeterministic in the .NET environment.

The GC does not remove all resource-handling burdens from your plate. For example, a file handle is a resource that must be freed when the consumer is finished with it. The GC only handles memory resources directly. To handle resources other than memory, such as database connections and file handles, you can use the `Finalize` destructor to free resources when the GC notifies you that your object is being destroyed. You can also implement the `IDisposable` interface in your classes to release resources immediately. Chapter 4 covers both of these topics in more detail.

Common Type System

In order to support multiple programming languages, the CLR implements the common type system (CTS) to ensure that data types in each language mean the same thing and are handled in the same way. The CTS means that a variable defined as a 32-bit signed integer (`Int32`) in VB is the same as an Int32 variable in C# or COBOL.NET. The CTS provides a framework for all type definitions that ensures consistency and type safety in each .NET language. Another benefit of the CTS is that it provides an object-oriented model for type definition so that all types are handled as objects.

The CTS contains two categories of types: value types and reference types. Value types are often referred to as primitives or built-in types and directly contain their data. Examples of value types are Integer, Boolean, and Float. An Enum is another kind of value type that declares a set of related integer values, and there are also user-defined value types. Value types are very efficient and take up little memory. A value type variable always has a value. When value type variables are passed in memory, the actual value of the variable is passed. Here's an example that illustrates the nature of value types:

```
Public Class EntryPoint
    Shared Sub Main()
        Dim Value1 As Integer = 0
        Dim Value2 As Integer = Value1

        Value2 = 123

        Console.WriteLine("Values:  {0}, {1}", Value1.ToString, Value2.ToString)
    End Sub
End Class
```

Here's the output from the preceding example:

```
Values:  0, 123
```

This demonstrates that you can set the value of a value type to that of another value type, but no reference exists between the two types. On the other hand, reference types store a reference to the memory address of its value, which is an instance of the reference type. For example, let's say you declare a variable of type Dataset with the command Dim ds As New DataSet. The value of ds is actually a pointer (or reference) to the dataset that resides somewhere in memory. Reference type variables are not tied to their value and can have a null reference. When you pass a reference type—let's use the ds variable as an example—a copy is made of the reference to the dataset; the entire dataset is not copied. If the ds variable is passed into a function and a change is made to it, that change would be seen in the dataset in the calling code as well. This snippet of code illustrates the nature of reference types:

```
Class Class1
    Public Value As Integer = 0
End Class

Public Class EntryPoint
    Shared Sub Main()
        Dim Reference1 As New Class1()
        Dim Reference2 As Class1 = Reference1

        Reference2.Value = 123
```

```
        Console.WriteLine("Values:  {0}, {1}", Reference1.Value, Reference2.Value)
    End Sub
End Class
```

Here's the output from the previous code:

```
Values:  123, 123
```

The value of the variable `Reference2` is a reference to variable `Reference1` (an instance of `Class1`). So any changes to `Reference2` will be reflected in `Reference1`.

A Simple VB 2008 Program

Now let's take a look at a VB 2008 program from 50,000 feet and consider the ubiquitous Hello World! program. Here's what the code and output look like:

```
Public Class EntryPoint
    Shared Sub Main()
        System.Console.WriteLine("Hello World!")
    End Sub
End Class
```

```
Hello World!
```

Note the structure of the program. It declares a type (a class named `EntryPoint`) and a member of that type (a method named `Main`). `Main` calls `Console.WriteLine` to display "Hello World!" in a Command Prompt window. When you run this program in debug mode, the compiler creates a `HelloWorld.exe` in the `\obj\Debug` directory of your project.

Every program requires an entry point, and in the case of VB, it is usually the `Main` method. You declare the `Main` method inside of a class (in this case, named `EntryPoint`). The return type for the `Main` method is an optional `Integer`. In the example, `Main` has no parameters, but if you need access to command-line parameters, you can retrieve them via the `My.Application.CommandLineArgs.Item` method. The `My` namespace makes it easier to find classes you will use often for application tasks, file I/O, local computer hardware access, and network access to name a few. A few of the `My` namespaces include `My.Application`, `My.Computer`, `My.Forms`, `My.Settings`, and `My.User`. To illustrate VB's platform independence, if you happen to have a Linux OS running (with the Mono VES installed on it), you can copy this `HelloWorld.exe` directly over in its binary form and it will run as expected, assuming everything is set up correctly on the Linux box.

What's New in VB 2008

The latest version of VB features a host of enhancements and new features for VB programmers. These include improvements to the .NET Framework, Visual Studio Integrated Development Environment (IDE) improvements, and changes to the VB language itself. Specific enhancements to the VB language that will be of interest to programmers include query comprehensions, LINQ support, anonymous types, lambda expressions, and extension methods.

Query Comprehensions

Query comprehensions are very similar to SQL queries in syntax. They are comprised of the familiar Select, From, and Where clauses, named *query operators*. You combine query operator clauses to form *query expressions*. These expressions can then be used to return a data set from various sources, such as XML and collections. An example statement would look like this:

```
Dim SmallCapStocks = From Stock In AllStocks _
    Where Stock.Price < 10.0 _
    Select Stock
```

This code snippet will create SmallCapStocks and populate it with stocks priced less than $10.00 from AllStocks.

Implicitly Typed Local Variables

Implicitly typed local variables provide a shortcut in declaring your variables. In VB 2005, you would initialize variables in one of the following ways:

```
Dim CompanyName As String = "ABC Company"
Dim OutstandingShares As Integer = 10000
Dim Capitalization As Double = 3000000.0
```

In VB 2008, these can now be written in this manner:

```
Dim CompanyName = "ABC Company"
Dim OutstandingShares = 10000
Dim Capitalization = 3000000.0
```

Declaring local variables this way causes the type of each variable to be inferred from the right-hand expression. In earlier releases of VB, such statements would have caused these variables to be declared as the generic Object data type, but VB 2008 now enforces strong data types on these declarations.

Object Initializers

Object initializers allow combining creation of an object and the initialization of its fields into one statement. Consider the following code, written in VB 2005:

```
Dim WidgetCo As New Stock

With WidgetCo
    .Ticker = "WC"
    .Name = "Widget Corp."
    .Price = 25.0
End With
```

In VB 2008, this can now be written like this:

```
Dim WidgetCo = New Stock With { _
    .Ticker = "WC", _
    .Name = "Widget Corp.", _
    .Price = 25.0 _
}
```

Array Initializers

Array initializer expressions can create and initialize an array and infer its element types at the point of declaration. This example creates an array of U.S. Stocks and populates it with three new Stock elements:

```
Dim USStocks() = { _
    New Stock With { _
        .Ticker = "US1", _
        .Name = "Western Company", _
        .Price = 15.75}, _
    New Stock With { _
        .Ticker = "US2", _
        .Name = "Eastern Company", _
        .Price = 17.0}, _
    New Stock With { _
        .Ticker = "US3", _
        .Name = "Midwest Company", _
        .Price = 8.0} _
}
```

LINQ to XML

LINQ to XML is an in-memory API that allows you to read, write, and create XML. XML can be treated as a built-in data type in VB 2008. You can also create XML using *XML Literals* and query *XML documents* using *XML Properties*.

A simple XML document can be created with the following code snippet:

```
Dim Stocks As XElement = _
    <Stocks>
        <Stock StockID="1">
            <Ticker>S1</Ticker>
            <Company>Company 1</Company>
            <PriceQuote>25.00</PriceQuote>
        </Stock>
        <Stock StockID="2">
            <Ticker>S2</Ticker>
            <Company>Company 2</Company>
            <PriceQuote>8.00</PriceQuote>
        </Stock>
    </Stocks>
```

LINQ to Objects

LINQ to Objects allows you execute SQL-like queries over your arrays and collections. Executing these queries, you are able to filter your collection for more specific processing. The following example executes a simple query against an array of integers:

```
Imports System
Imports System.Linq

Public Class EntryPoint
    Shared Sub Main()
        Dim someNumbers As Integer() = {5, 4, 3, 2, 1, 0}

        Dim query = From x In someNumbers _
                Where x >= 3 _
                Select x

        For Each item In query
            Console.WriteLine("{0} is >= 3", item)
        Next
    End Sub
End Sub
```

This code filters someNumbers to create query, and query will contain the three integers, which are those greater than or equal to 3. The For Each . . . Next statement will loop through query and produce the following results:

```
5 is >= 3
4 is >= 3
3 is >= 3
```

Lambda Expressions (Inline Functions)

Lambda expressions provide you with a way to create inline, anonymous methods. The functions you create do not need to be typed, as they infer their types at run time. Creating a VB method to determine even numbers might look like the following:

```
Shared Function IsEven(ByVal x As Integer) As Boolean
    If x Mod 2 = 0 Then
        Return True
    Else
        Return False
    End If
End Function
```

Using an inline function, you can reduce the amount of code needed to accomplish the same purpose, as in the following code snippet:

```
Function(n) n Mod 2 = 0
```

Extension Methods

Extension methods allow you to add methods to an existing CLR type. This enables you to expand the functionality of a type without needing to create a subclass. The following example shows the syntax for an extension method:

```
<Extension()> _
Public Function IsTickerValid(ByVal aTicker As String) As Boolean
    Dim ValidTicker As Boolean = True

    If aTicker.Length > 4 Then
        ValidTicker = False
    End If

    Return ValidTicker
End Function
```

Extension methods avoid the need to create a separate class, with a shared method, to validate the ticker symbol.

Anonymous Types

Using anonymous types, you are able to declare, define, and use types that the VB compiler will generate for you in the background. Anonymous types are able to infer field names and will create properties for these fields as well. This example shows an anonymous type declared in VB:

```
Dim anAnonymous = New With {.FirstName = "Jodi", .LastName = "Fouche"}
```

IntelliSense Everywhere

When using extension methods and anonymous types, you will find that the VB IDE is aware of these types and methods. As such, it includes your extension methods with the extended type's methods in all IntelliSense lists while coding. Anonymous types will show their compiler-generated properties in IntelliSense lists while coding.

Nullable Types, Enhanced in VB 2008

Nullable type syntax is enhanced in VB 2008. A new type modifier (?) allows you to define your types as nullable. The following code snippet demonstrates the current syntax and the new shortcut.

```
Dim x As Nullable(Of Integer)
Dim y As Nullable(Of Integer)

Dim x As Integer?
Dim y As Integer?
```

Relaxed Delegates, Enhanced in VB 2008

Relaxed delegates extend and enhance the VB's implicit conversions to delegate types. Using relaxed delegates allows you to omit arguments from event handlers. For example, the following code statements are now valid in VB:

```
Sub OnClick(sender As Object, e As Object) Handles aButton.Click
Sub OnClick Handles aButton.Click
```

Option Infer

Using `Option Infer` lets you specify whether VB should enforce type declarations for your types. While setting `Option Infer On` may allow for quicker development, it may lead to maintenance challenges down the road.

`Option Infer On` is the default setting for new projects in VB 2008 and can be changed via Project Properties ➤ Compile.

Summary

In this chapter, we've touched upon the high-level characteristics of programs written in VB 2008. That is, all code is compiled into IL rather than the native instructions for a specific platform. Additionally, the CLR implements a garbage collection system to manage raw memory allocation and de-allocation, freeing you from having to worry about one of the most common errors in software development: improper memory management.

Next, we explored the CTS with a couple of simple examples to compare value types to reference types. Our first VB program gave us a simple class with a `Main` procedure, which simply echoed "Hello World!" to the Command Prompt.

Finally, we looked at some of the new features that are now a part of VB, including LINQ, object and array initializers, extension methods, anonymous types, and `Option Infer`.

In the next chapter, we'll dive into VB syntax, explore VB namespaces, and discuss control flow.

■ ■ ■

CHAPTER 2

VB 2008 Syntax

This chapter is an introduction to the syntax of the Visual Basic (VB) language. The topics covered here are the glue that binds programs together. We'll take a close look at types and variables, as the common type system (CTS) is a key component of the .NET common language runtime (CLR).

We'll also look at *namespaces*: a .NET concept you'll put into practice as soon as you write your first program. Understanding namespaces not only helps you navigate VB classes and other types to find the features you need, but it also helps you to organize your own types in a logical manner. We'll wrap up with an overview of VB control flow statements, which may differ in syntax from other languages but are the same in concept.

Types and Variables

Types in VB can be either value types or reference types. Value types, such as structures and built-in types, live in memory reserved by your application: the *stack*. When your program executes a method, it places (*pushes*) all declared variables onto the stack. These variables will be freed (*popped*) from the stack and memory returned to your application when your function completes. A memory area called the *heap* is where data for your reference types, such as classes and arrays, are stored. A *reference* to this data location is stored on the stack. As an object can have multiple references to it at any given moment, its memory is not freed from the heap until all references to it are freed.

As we progress through this chapter, we'll discuss types and variables in more detail. Chapters 3 and 4 will continue the discussion in greater depth.

Strong Typing

VB is a strongly typed language. Well, to be more precise, VB *can* be a strongly typed language. *Strong typing* means that every variable and object instance that's declared must be of a well-defined type. A strongly typed language provides rules for how variables of different types can interact with each other. Strongly typed variables enable the compiler to check that the operations being performed on variables and objects are valid. For example, suppose you have a method that computes the average of two integers and returns the result. The method is declared in VB as follows:

```
Function ComputeAvg(ByVal Param1 As Integer, ByVal Param2 As Integer) As Double
    Return (Param1 + Param2) / 2
End Function
```

This method accepts two integers and returns a double. Therefore, if you attempt to call this method and pass in two Customer objects, you'll receive a compile-time error. Now, let's write the method slightly differently:

```
Function ComputeAvg(ByVal Param1 As Object, ByVal Param2 As Object) As Object
    Return (Convert.ToInt32(Param1) + Convert.ToInt32(Param2)) / 2
End Function
```

The second version of ComputeAvg() is still valid, but you have forcefully stripped away the type information. Because all type instances in .NET eventually derive from System.Object, you could pass in String, Boolean, or Customer objects to this method, and you wouldn't receive an error until run time when the function attempts to convert the parameters. The Object keyword in VB is an alias for the class System.Object, and it is perfectly valid to declare parameters as type Object; however, Object is not a numeric type. In order to perform the calculation, you must first "cast" the objects into integers. The result is also returned as an instance of type Object. If you attempt to pass two Customer objects, the compiler won't return an error because those objects both derive from System.Object, as every other class does. Although this version of the method seems more flexible, this flexibility comes at the price of type safety and performance.

Needless to say, it's always best to find bugs at compile time rather than run time. If you were to use the first version of ComputeAvg() and try to pass in anything other than integers, you wouldn't be able to compile the application. Type safety is one of the tenets of development in .NET, and the language is designed to support it.

The reason we say that VB *can* be strongly typed is that, in contrast to C#, it supports undeclared and untyped variables. *Undeclared* means you can reference a variable without first declaring it with a Dim, Private, or Public declaration. *Untyped* means that even if you declare a variable using statements such as Dim, you are not required to identify its type. VB will create any undeclared or untyped variables as type Object. The two settings that affect strong typing and variable declaration in VB are Option Explicit and Option Strict.

Option Explicit: This setting enforces the declaration of variables. When Option Explicit is set to On within a file, any variable must be explicitly declared. If Option Explicit is On and you have an undeclared variable, you'll receive a compiler error. If Option Explicit isn't specified in the file, the compiler default is On. In the following snippet, you'll receive a compiler error on the last line because the variable VarUndeclared is not declared anywhere. If Option Explicit was Off, both the variables VarDeclared and VarUndeclared would be valid. When this code compiles, VB will define VarUndeclared as type Object until it's assigned, at which point it will implicitly convert it to a Double because of its data assignment:

```
Option Explicit On
. . .
Dim VarDeclared As Double

VarDeclared = ComputeAvg(108, 7933)
VarUndeclared = ComputeAvg(108, 7933)
```

Option Strict: The Option Strict setting is related to any implicit data conversions that VB performs on variables. When Option Strict is On, VB will only allow your variables to be converted from one data type into another where no data loss will occur. This is known as a *widening conversion*. If you attempt to convert a variable to a type that has less precision, or a smaller capacity, VB will generate an error. Converting variables this way is known as a *narrowing conversion*.

Option Strict also disallows late binding. If Option Strict isn't specified, the compiler default is Off. Using the second ComputeAvg function shown previously, you can see that the code will fail at compile time because Option Strict won't allow an implicit conversion from Object to Double. If Option Strict was Off, this code would compile and run:

```
Option Strict On
. . .
Dim x As Double = 0.0

x = ComputeAvg(108, 7933)

Function ComputeAvg(ByVal Param1 As Object, ByVal Param2 As Object) As Object
    Return (Convert.ToInt32(Param1) + Convert.ToInt32(Param2)) / 2
End Function
```

You can set Option Explicit and Option Strict in your project properties on the Compile tab in the Compile Options area. We recommend you keep both Option Explicit and Option Strict set to On in your applications, primarily because you'll avoid is having to debug some devious errors that only appear at run time. This practice also ensures that your code is strongly typed and is consistent with the type safety of other .NET languages.

Type Categories

Every entity in a VB program is an object that lives in memory on either the stack or the managed heap. Where an entity is allocated depends on whether it's a value type or a reference type. Every method is defined in a class or module declaration (which is really a class under the hood). Even the built-in value types, such as Integer, Long, and Double, implicitly have methods associated with them. In VB, it's perfectly valid to write a statement such as this:

```
Console.WriteLine(108.ToString())
```

This statement returns the string value "108". This syntax emphasizes how everything in VB is an object, even down to the most basic types. In fact, the keywords for the built-in types in VB are actually aliases that are mapped directly into types in the System namespace. You can elect not to use the built-in VB types and explicitly use the types in the System namespace, but this practice is discouraged as a matter of style. Table 2-1 lists the built-in types with their size and corresponding types in the System namespace.

Table 2-1. *VB Intrinsic Types*

VB Type	Size in Bytes	System Type	CLS-Compliant
Boolean	N/A	System.Boolean	Yes
Byte	1	System.Byte	Yes
Char	2	System.Char	Yes
Date	8	System.Datetime	Yes
Decimal	16	System.Decimal	Yes
Double	8	System.Double	Yes
Integer	4	System.Int32	Yes
Long	8	System.Int64	Yes
Object	4	System.Object	Yes
SByte	1	System.SByte	No
Short	2	System.Int16	Yes
Single	32	System.Single	Yes
String	N/A	System.String	Yes
UInteger	4	System.Uint32	No
ULong	8	System.UInt64	No
UShort	2	System.Uint16	No

For each entry in the table, the last column indicates whether the type is compliant with the Common Language Specification (CLS). The CLS is defined as part of the Common Language Infrastructure (CLI) standard to facilitate language interoperability. The CLS is a subset of the CTS and is designed to foster language interoperability by defining the features that are standard across each language. This is needed because, even though the CLR supports a rich set of built-in types, not all languages that create managed code support all other language types. For example, in the past, VB didn't support unsigned types, whereas C# did. So the designers of the CLI defined the CLS to standardize types and facilitate interoperability between the languages.

If your application will be entirely VB-based and won't create any components consumed from another language, then you don't need to adhere to the strict guidelines of the CLS. But if you work in a project that builds components using various languages, or you know there's a chance that your components will be called from other languages in the future, then conforming to the CLS is much more of a consideration.

Value Types

Value types typically reside in the memory stack and are commonly used when you need to represent data that is generally small in its memory footprint. Value types are efficient, and when a value type variable goes out of scope, it's immediately removed from the stack. The most common value types are the built-in data types such an Integer, Boolean, and Double. The following code snippet demonstrates creating a value type and passing it to the Console.Writeline method:

```
Dim TheAnswer As Integer = 42
Console.WriteLine(TheAnswer.ToString)
```

In the first code line, TheAnswer is created and initialized with a value of 42. The second code line passes a copy of TheAnswer to Console.WriteLine().

You can create user-defined value types in VB by using the Structure keyword, as shown in the following snippet. User-defined value types behave in the same way that the built-in value types do:

```
Public Structure Coordinate 'This is a value type
    Dim x As Integer
    Dim y As Integer
End Structure
```

Value types can live on the managed heap, but not by themselves. One way this can happen is if a reference type contains a value type. Even though a value type inside of an object lives on the managed heap, it still behaves the same as a value type on the stack when it comes to passing it into a method. Any changes made to the value instance are only local changes to the copy, unless the value was passed by reference. The following code illustrates these concepts:

```
Public Structure Coordinate 'this is a value type
    Dim x As Integer
    Dim y As Integer
End Structure

Public Class EntryPoint 'this is a reference type
    Public Function AttemptToModifyCoord(ByVal Coord As Coordinate) As Boolean
        Coord.x = 1
        Coord.y = 3
        Return True
    End Function

    Public Function ModifyCoord(ByRef Coord As Coordinate) As Boolean
        Coord.x = 10
        Coord.y = 10
        Return True
    End Function

    Shared Sub Main()
        Dim Location As New Coordinate
        Dim EP As New EntryPoint

        Location.x = 50
        Location.y = 50

        EP.AttemptToModifyCoord(Location)
        System.Console.WriteLine("( {0}, {1} )", Location.x, Location.y)
```

```
        EP.ModifyCoord(Location)
        System.Console.WriteLine("( {0}, {1} )", Location.x, Location.y)
    End Sub
End Class
```

The output from the example is as follows:

```
( 50, 50 )
( 10, 10 )
```

In the Main method, the call to AttemptToModifyCoord actually does nothing to the Location.x and Location.y values. This is because in the AttemptToModifyCoord method, the Location parameter is passed by value and the method modifies a local copy of the structure that was made when the method was called. On the contrary, the Location parameter is passed by reference to the ModifyCoord method. Thus any changes made in the ModifyCoord method are actually made on the Location value in the calling scope.

Enumerations

Enumerations (Enum) make coding easier by allowing you to create a structure of constants. For example, let's say you're working with a customer service application, and there are four customer types of Individual, Home Business, Corporate, and Federal. Each of these types is represented by an ID value of 1, 2, 3, or 4. Instead of having to remember the ID values of the customer types throughout your code, you can create an Enum and map the customer type ID to a name like this:

```
Enum CustomerType As Integer
    Individual = 1
    Corporate = 2
    HomeBusiness = 3
    Federal = 4
End Enum
```

Note that the values don't have to be in any sequential order. Each constant that's defined in the enumeration must be defined with a value within the range of the underlying type. If a value is not specified for an enumeration constant, it takes the default value of 0 (if it's the first constant in the enumeration) or the value of the previous constant plus 1. This example is an enumeration based upon a Long:

```
Enum Color As Long
    Red
    Green = 50
    Blue
End Enum
```

In the preceding example, if you had left off the Long keyword after the Color type identifier, the enumeration would have been of type Integer. In this Enum, the value for Red is 0, the value for Green is 50, and the value for Blue is 51. The following code uses this enumeration:

```
Public Class EntryPoint
    Enum Color As Long
        Red
        Green = 50
        Blue
    End Enum

    Shared Sub Main()
        Dim SystemColor As Color = Color.Red

        System.Console.WriteLine("Color is {0}", SystemColor.ToString)
    End Sub
End Class
```

If you run this code, you'll see the following output:

```
Color is Red
```

This code actually uses the name of the enumeration rather than the ordinal value 0. This magic is done by the System.Enum type's implementation of the ToString method, which returns the color's name.

▓Note The underlying type of the Enum must be an integral type that is one of the following: Byte, SByte, Short, UShort, Integer, UInteger, Long, or ULong.

When referring to Enum members, you precede the member name with the Enum name. However, as a syntactical shortcut, you can use the Imports statement with your Enum. Then you are able to refer to your Enum members without their fully qualified names, like this:

```
Imports ConsoleApplication1.Color
Dim SystemColor As Color = Red
```

Reference Types

In contrast to value types, reference types are allocated on the managed heap. They are initialized by calling the New constructor on an object defined with the Class keyword. When a reference type variable goes out of scope, it's not just removed from the heap but must be torn down by calling the appropriate class destructors. This is the job of the garbage collector (GC). The GC manages the placement of all objects in memory. At any time, objects can be moved to a different location in memory, and the GC ensures that variables that reference those objects are updated.

Reference types can also be initialized by assignment from another variable of a compatible type, as in the following code snippet, which creates two reference type variables:

```
Public Class Coordinate
        Dim x As Integer
        Dim y As Integer
End Class
. . .
Dim Point1 As Coordinate = New Coordinate
Dim Point2 As Coordinate = Point1
```

In the example, the values of Point1 and Point2 are pointers to the Coordinate object allocated on the heap. If you passed Point1 into a function that updated x and y, you would see those changes in Point2 as well.

■**Note** Conventionally, the term *object* refers to an instance of a reference type, and the term *value* refers to an instance of a value type. Regardless of what you call them, all instances of any type derive from type System.Object.

In the managed environment of the CLR, the GC automatically handles all memory-management tasks, including the creation and destruction of objects. This frees you from having to worry about explicitly deleting objects and minimizes memory leaks. At any point in time, the GC determines how many references exist to a particular object on the heap. If it determines there are none, it starts the process of destroying the object on the heap. The previous code snippet contains two references to the same object. The first one, Point1, is initialized by creating a new Coordinate object. The second one, Point2, is initialized from Point1. The GC won't collect the Coordinate object on the heap until both of these references are outside any usable scope. Table 2-2 provides a summary of the differences between value types and reference types.

Table 2-2. *Comparison of Value Types and Reference Types*

Value Type	Reference Type
Represents simple values.	Represents more complex data structures.
Declared using a Dim, Private, or Public statement.	Declared calling a class constructor.
Initialized to 0 or empty value by default.	Initialized to Nothing by default.
Allocated on the stack.	Allocated on the managed heap.
Must always have a value.	Can have Nothing as a value.
Value contains an actual value.	Value is a pointer to an object in memory.
When Passed as a ByVal Parameter	
A copy of the value is made.	A copy of the reference to the memory location is made.
Garbage Collection	
Removed from the stack by the garbage collector (GC) when it goes out of scope.	Destructors are called by the GC, and the object is removed from the heap by the GC when it goes out of scope.

Type Conversion

Now that you have a good understanding of types in the .NET world, let's take a look at converting instances of one type to another. In some cases, this conversion is done implicitly by the compiler when the value being converted won't lose any precision or magnitude. As you saw in the discussion of Option Strict, this is known as a widening conversion. In the following code snippet, the ComputeAvg function expects two Integer parameters, but when you pass in parameters of type Short, there's no compiler error. The compiler automatically converts Param1 and Param2 to integers because there's no danger that the value of a Short (with a maximum value of 32,767) will be too large to fit in an Integer (with a maximum value of 2,147,483,647):

```
Function ComputeAvg(ByVal Param1 As Integer, ByVal Param2 As Integer) As Double
      Return (Param1 + Param2) / 2
End Function

Dim Param1 As Short = 108
Dim Param2 As Short = 123
Dim ComputedAverage As Double

ComputedAverage = ComputeAvg(Param1, Param2)
```

In cases where precision could be lost, an explicit conversion is required. In VB, you have two options when performing an explicit conversion: you can use the VB conversion functions such as CStr or the System.Convert class functions such as Convert.ToString. Table 2-3 lists the functions available for explicit conversions.

Table 2-3. *Data Type Conversion Functions*

VB Function	Convert Function	Description
N/A	ToBase64CharArray	Converts an array of unsigned integers to an array of Unicode characters
N/A	ToBase64String	Converts an array of unsigned integers to a string
CBool	ToBoolean	Converts an expression to a Boolean value
CByte	ToByte	Converts an expression to a Byte value
CChar	ToChar	Converts the first character of a string to a Char value
CDate	ToDateTime	Converts an expression to a DateTime value
CDbl	ToDouble	Converts a numeric expression to a double precision floating point value (Double)
CDec	ToDecimal	Converts a numeric expression to a Decimal value
CInt	ToInt32	Converts a numeric expression to an Integer value
CLng	ToInt64	Converts a numeric expression to a Long value
CObj	N/A	Converts an expression to an Object
CSByte	ToSByte	Converts a numeric expression to an SByte value
CShort	ToInt16	Converts a numeric expression to a Short value

continued

Table 2-3. *Continued*

VB Function	Convert Function	Description
CSng	ToSingle	Converts a numeric expression to single precision floating point value (Single)
CStr	ToString	Converts an expression to a string
CUInt	ToUInt32	Converts a numeric expression to an unsigned integer value (UInteger)
CULng	ToUInt64	Converts a numeric expression to an unsigned long value (ULong)
CUShort	ToUInt16	Converts a numeric expression to an unsigned short value (UShort)

Casting variables with either of these methods is pretty straightforward, as this code snippet shows:

```
Dim StringValue As String = "123"
Dim IntegerValue As Integer

IntegerValue = CInt(StringValue)
```

Deciding whether to use the conversion functions or the Convert class methods is strictly a matter of style. The Convert class makes code more consistent with data type conversions in C#, which doesn't have functions such as CStr. The Convert class is found in the System namespace, and the methods are called like this:

```
Dim StringValue As String = "123"
Dim IntegerValue As Integer

IntegerValue = Convert.ToInt32(StringValue)
```

If the conversion causes a loss in magnitude, the conversion may throw an exception at run time. For example, if you tried to convert the string "746475959658567" to an Integer, you would receive an overflow error because that value exceeds the maximum value that an Integer can contain.

CType

Another common need is to convert reference types from one type to another. CType converts an expression to the specified data type, object, structure, class, or interface, and the syntax is as follows:

```
CType(expression, typename)
```

A base class must be explicitly cast to a derived type because the derived type inherits from the base class. However, a derived class can be implicitly cast to a base type using the CType function.

Consider a Coordinate class and a GraphCoordinate class that inherits from and extends the Coordinate class. You also have a PrintCoordinates function that sends the x and y values to the console:

```
Public Class Coordinate
        Public x As Integer
        Public y As Integer
End Class

Public Class GraphCoordinate
        Inherits Coordinate

        Public PointDesc As String
End Class

Public Function PrintCoordinates(ByVal Coord As Coordinate) As Boolean
        System.Console.WriteLine("( {0}, {1} )", Coord.x, Coord.y)

        Return True
End Function
```

As we said before, a derived type can always be cast to a base type. The following code snippet won't cause any errors:

```
Dim Coord As New Coordinate
Coord.x = 10
Coord.y = 50

Dim oCoord As Object = New Coordinate
```

Now let's define the GraphCoordinate instance and then attempt to call the PrintCoordinates function:

```
Dim GraphCoord As New GraphCoordinate
GraphCoord.x = 50
GraphCoord.y = 50
GraphCoord.PointDesc = "This is the graph point"

PrintCoordinates(Coord)
PrintCoordinates(GraphCoord)
PrintCoordinates(oCoord)
```

The first two calls to the PrintCoordinates function succeed because any object that derives from the Coordinate class can be passed as a parameter. However, with Option Strict On, the third call results in a compiler error, disallowing the implicit conversion of oCoord to the Coordinate class. In order to pass oCoord as a parameter, you must "cast it" to the Coordinate type, like this:

```
PrintCoordinates(CType(oCoord, Coordinate))
```

Another keyword related to reference type conversion is TypeOf. Use TypeOf before using CType to determine if you can successfully convert the object. Prior to calling the PrintCoordinates method, you could check the type of the oCoord variable and then call the method:

```
If TypeOf (oCoord) Is Coordinate Then
    PrintCoordinates(CType(oCoord, Coordinate))
End If
```

DirectCast and TryCast

Two VB keywords related to casting reference types are DirectCast and TryCast. The DirectCast function is used to cast reference types just like CType and has a similar syntax:

```
DirectCast(expression, Type)
```

However, DirectCast offers better performance because it directly attempts to convert the specified type, and if it can't, it throws an exception. The command var = CType("123", Integer) attempts to convert "123" even though it's a string, and this statement succeeds because VB will implicitly cast "123" to an Integer. But the command var = DirectCast("123", Integer) will fail because the compiler won't try any implicit conversions and attempts to directly convert a string to an Integer. It's recommended to use DirectCast when you know a reference type conversion will work and you need the extra performance benefit. Another difference between CType and DirectCast is that you can only use DirectCast on types that have an inheritance relationship. Therefore, you can't use DirectCast on value types, including structures.

The TryCast function has the same syntax as DirectCast and performs the same reference type conversion. However, if the cast fails, the function returns Nothing instead of throwing an error. So instead of handling errors from CType or DirectCast, you can use TryCast and check for Nothing. In this code snippet, TryCast attempts to convert reference type x to a type of EntryPoint. This conversion would normally cause an exception, but with TryCast, you simply check for the result of the conversion:

```
Dim y As Object = TryCast(x, EntryPoint)
If y Is Nothing Then
    'Do something here, for failed cast
Else
    'Do something here, for successful cast
End If
```

Boxing

Another common type of conversion is a *boxing* conversion. Boxing is required when a value type must be assigned to a variable as a reference type. To accomplish this type of conversion, simply declare an object and set its value to that of the value type variable. When you do this, an object is allocated dynamically on the heap that contains the value of the value type. Chapter 3 covers boxing in VB extensively. The following code demonstrates boxing:

```
Public Class EntryPoint
    Shared Sub Main()
        Dim EmployeeID As Integer = 303
        Dim BoxedID As Object = EmployeeID
        Dim UnboxedID As Integer = CInt(BoxedID)
```

```
        EmployeeID = 404

        System.Console.WriteLine(EmployeeID.ToString())
        System.Console.WriteLine(UnboxedID.ToString())
    End Sub
End Class
```

Running the preceding code will display the following in the console window:

```
404
303
```

Boxing occurs when the Object variable BoxedID is assigned the Integer variable EmployeeID. A heap-based object is created, and the value of EmployeeID is copied into it. This is how the gap is bridged between the value type and the reference type worlds within the CLR. The BoxedID object actually contains a copy of the EmployeeID value. This point is demonstrated in the snippet when the original EmployeeID value is printed after the boxing operation. Before printing out the values, you unbox the value and copy the value contained in the object on the heap back into another Integer on the stack. Unboxing is the opposite action to boxing and is the process of converting the reference type variable back to a value type variable on the stack.

Reference Type Operators

VB includes operators that are helpful specifically when working with reference types. Given the fact that explicit conversions can fail and throw exceptions, times arise when you want to test the type of a variable first instead of performing a cast and seeing whether or not it fails. The Is operator in conjunction with the TypeOf keyword returns a Boolean that determines if you can convert the given expression to the given type as either a reference conversion or a boxing or unboxing operation. For example, consider the following code:

```
Public Class EntryPoint
    Public Class BaseType
        Public x As Integer
        Public y As Integer
    End Class

    Public Class DerivedType
        Inherits BaseType

        Public DT1 As Long
        Public Description As String
    End Class

    Shared Sub Main()
        Dim DerivedObj As DerivedType = New DerivedType()
        Dim BaseObj1 As BaseType = New BaseType()
        Dim BaseObj2 = DerivedObj
```

```
            If TypeOf BaseObj2 Is DerivedType Then
                Console.WriteLine("BaseObj2 {0} DerivedType", "is")
            Else
                Console.WriteLine("BaseObj2 {0} DerivedType", "isnot")
            End If

            If TypeOf BaseObj1 Is DerivedType Then
                Console.WriteLine("BaseObj1 {0} DerivedType", "is")
            Else
                Console.WriteLine("BaseObj1 {0} DerivedType", "isnot")
            End If

            If TypeOf DerivedObj Is BaseType Then
                Console.WriteLine("DerivedObj {0} BaseType", "is")
            Else
                Console.WriteLine("DerivedObj {0} BaseType", "isnot")
            End If

            Dim j As Integer = 123
            Dim Boxed As Object = j
            Dim Obj As Object = New Object()

            If TypeOf Boxed Is Integer Then
                Console.WriteLine("Boxed {0} Integer", "is")
            Else
                Console.WriteLine("Boxed {0} Integer", "isnot")
            End If

            If TypeOf Obj Is Integer Then
                Console.WriteLine("Obj {0} Integer", "is")
            Else
                Console.WriteLine("Obj {0} Integer", "isnot")
            End If

            If TypeOf Boxed Is ValueType Then
                Console.WriteLine("Boxed {0} System.ValueType", "is")
            Else
                Console.WriteLine("Boxed {0} System.ValueType", "isnot")
            End If
        End Sub
End Class
```

The output from this code is as follows:

```
BaseObj2 is DerivedType
BaseObj1 isnot DerivedType
DerivedObj is BaseType
Boxed is Integer
Obj isnot Integer
Boxed is System.ValueType
```

Two related operators that are useful when working with reference types are Is and IsNot. The syntax for these operators looks like this:

```
BooleanResult = Object1 Is Object2
```

These two operators return a Boolean value after comparing the first object to see if it refers to the same object as the second. The Is and IsNot operators only consider reference types, and VB will generate a compiler error if you try to use Is or IsNot with value types. Here's a code snippet using the Is operator:

```
Dim ObjectA As New Object
Dim ObjectB As New Object
Dim ObjectC As New Object
Dim ObjectD As New Object
Dim IsObject As Boolean

ObjectA = ObjectC
ObjectB = ObjectC

IsObject = ObjectA Is ObjectC
IsObject = ObjectB Is ObjectC
IsObject = ObjectB Is ObjectA
IsObject = ObjectC Is ObjectD
```

The first three comparisons result in True because ObjectA and ObjectB both refer to ObjectC. The third comparison is the most interesting because, even though ObjectA and ObjectB have no relationship to each other through direct assignment, they both refer to ObjectC and therefore are the same as each other. The final comparison results in False because ObjectD is not assigned anywhere.

Namespaces

Namespaces are used to organize your types within an assembly and help you avoid naming collisions between your identifiers. Using namespaces, you define all of your types such that their identifiers are qualified by the namespace that they belong to. You've already seen namespaces in action in many of the code snippets so far. For instance, in the Hello World! example from Chapter 1, you saw the use of the Console class, which lives in the .NET Framework Class Library's System namespace and whose fully qualified name is System.Console. It's a good practice to organize your components with namespaces, and the general recommendation is to use some sort of identifier, such as your organization's name as the top-level namespace and then more specific library identifiers as nested namespaces.

Namespaces provide an excellent mechanism for making your types more discoverable, especially if you're designing libraries meant for consumption by others. For example, you can create a general namespace such as `MyCompany.Widgets` where you put the most commonly used types of widgets. Then you can create a `MyCompany.Widgets.Advanced` namespace where you place all of the less commonly used, advanced types. Sure, you could place them all in one namespace. However, it's much easier for consumers of your libraries to see the types logically arranged with the commonly used ones separated from the less commonly used types.

Note Within a namespace, you can define "container" items, such as modules, interfaces, classes, delegates, enumerations, structures, and nested namespaces. You cannot have properties, procedures, variables, or events within a namespace.

Defining Namespaces

The syntax for declaring a namespace is simple. The following code shows how to declare a namespace called `Acme`:

```
Namespace Acme
    Public Class Class1

    End Class
End Namespace
```

A namespace can span multiple VB files, and you can have multiple namespaces in a single VB source file. When all the code in a project is compiled, the set of identifiers included in the namespace is a union of all of the identifiers in each of the namespace declarations. In fact, this union spans across assemblies. If multiple assemblies contain types defined in the same namespace, the total namespace consists of all of the identifiers across all the assemblies that define the types. It's possible to nest namespace declarations, and this can be done in one of two ways. The first way is straightforward:

```
Namespace Acme
    Namespace Utilities
        Public Class Class1

        End Class
    End Namespace
End Namespace
```

By default, each executable contains a namespace with the same name as your project. Given this example, to access the `Class1` class using its fully qualified name, you must identify it as `HelloWorld.Acme.Utilities.Class1`. However, if you're working in the `HelloWorld` project, the `HelloWorld` namespace is assumed, and you could also use `Acme.Utilities.Class1` as the fully qualified name. The following example demonstrates an alternate way of defining nested namespaces:

```
Namespace Acme

End Namespace

Namespace Acme.Utilities
    Public Class Class1

    End Class
End Namespace
```

The effect of this code is the exact same as the previous code. In fact, you may omit the first empty namespace declaration for the `Acme` namespace. It's only left there to point out that the `Utilities` namespace declaration is not physically nested within the `Acme` namespace declaration. Any types that you declare outside of a namespace become part of the global namespace.

Using Namespaces

Now let's take a look at how to use namespaces. We'll examine some code that uses the `Class1` class that was defined in the previous section:

```
Dim c As Acme.Utilities.Class1 = New Acme.Utilities.Class1
```

Using the fully qualified name is rather verbose and might eventually lead to a bad case of carpal tunnel syndrome. The `Imports` statement avoids this. The `Imports` statement creates a sort of alias that tells the compiler that you're using an entire namespace or an individual class in a namespace. In this case, `Imports` creates an implicit naming alias for the fully qualified name. Most of the time, developers bring in the entire namespace, as in the following example:

```
Imports Acme.Utilities
Dim c As Class1 = New Class1
```

The code is now easier to deal with and easier to read. You can only refer to a namespace in an assembly that your project has a reference to. So if you want to use a type in the `System.XML` namespace, you must first add a reference to `System.Xml.dll` because that's the assembly in which the namespace is declared. Another namespace issue you might run into is having two namespaces that each contain a class with the same name. This is perfectly legal because their fully qualified names are unique. Let's say, for example, you have your own data access types defined in a namespace called `Acme.Data` with a `DataTable` class, and you also use the `System.Data` namespace that has a `DataTable` class:

```
Namespace Acme.Data
    Public Class DataTable

    End Class
End Namespace
```

If you use the `DataTable` class, the compiler won't know which namespace you're referring to and will throw an ambiguous name exception. In a case like this, you have two options. The first is to use the fully qualified namespace name. The second is to assign an explicit alias to a namespace, like this:

```
Imports System.Data
Imports db = Acme.Data
```

Anywhere you want to use the `DataTable` class in your own namespace, you just prefix the class name with db, like this:

```
Dim c As db.DataTable = New db.DataTable
```

Object Browser

A handy tool for browsing and locating namespaces in VB is the Object Browser. Access this utility in Visual Basic Express (VBE) or the Visual Studio IDE by selecting View ➤ Object Browser. You'll see a tree view of all the referenced components in your project, as in Figure 2-1.

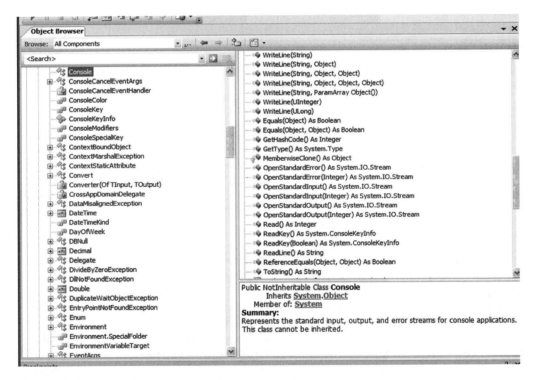

Figure 2-1. *The Object Browser, displaying the Console class*

In the Object Browser, you can see each namespace in your project as well as each type defined in the namespace and the type members.

Statements

Lines of code in VB are terminated with a carriage return/line feed (CRLF). Unlike C#, VB has no logical line-termination character. A statement can only span multiple lines with a line-continuation character, which is an underscore preceded by a space. If you have a long function name or statement and you want to make it more readable, just break it into multiple lines like this example:

```
Function ComputeAvg(ByVal Param1 As Integer, _
    ByVal Param2 As Integer) As Double

    Return (Param1 + Param2) / 2
End Function
```

Conversely, you can put multiple statements on one line using the colon. You have probably already seen multiple variable declarations on the same line if the variables are all the same type:

```
Dim x, y, z As Integer
```

You can put multiple variable declarations of different types on the same line like this:

```
Dim x, y, z As Integer : Dim a, b, c As String
```

You can also write multiple statements on the same line using the colon:

```
x = 0 : y = 1 : z = 2
```

Although VB provides the ability to put multiple statements on one line, this is rarely used, as it makes code less readable and more difficult to maintain.

Control Flow Constructs

You may be familiar with VB language elements, such as If . . . Then . . . Else, that are used to control the flow of your program. This section is an overview of those constructs.

If . . . Then . . . Else

The conditional construct If . . . Then . . . Else first checks an expression that must resolve to a Boolean value. Then based on that value, the statements that you specify are executed. The general syntax of this construct is

```
If condition Then
    statements
ElseIf elseifcondition Then
    elseifstatements
Else
    elsestatements
End If
```

Here's an If statement in its simplest form with an If condition, statements, and an End If:

```
If x = 0 Then
    y = 1
End If
```

You can also write this on a single line, although from a stylistic point of view, it is less readable, and as soon as you need to add more statements, you'll need a corresponding End If:

```
If x = 0 Then y = 1
```

If the first If condition evaluates to False, the program flow will go to the first ElseIf condition and evaluate it. If conditions evaluate to False, execution continues to each subsequent ElseIf and then the Else statement:

```
If x = 0 Then
    y = 1
ElseIf x = 1 Then
    y = 10
End If
```

Select . . . Case

VB also offers another conditional construct called Select . . . Case. This statement offers a flexible method for evaluating many known choices:

```
Select Case expression
    Case expressionevaluation
        statements
    Case Else
        elsestatements
End Select
```

You must always close a Select . . . Case statement with End Select. There are many options for evaluating Case expressions. You can check for a single value, a range of values, or multiple values:

```
Select Case x
    Case Is <= 0
        y = 1
    Case 1 - 5
        y = 10
    Case 6, 7, 8
        y = 100
    Case 10
        y = 20
End Select
```

You can also use Case Is with an operator (like <=) to evaluate the expression. The Is keyword in a Select . . . Case statement is not related to the Is operator used to evaluate reference types. As soon as a Case is evaluated to be true, the statements following it are executed, and then flow control moves to the statement after End Select.

Iteration and Looping Constructs

VB is no different than other languages in that it provides constructs for iterating and looping over items until a condition is met. Let's take a quick tour of these statements.

For Each . . . Next

The For Each . . . Next statement allows you to iterate over a collection of objects and execute statements for each element in the collection. The For Each . . . Next syntax looks like this:

```
For Each element As datatype In collection
    statements
    Exit For
Next element
```

If you have an array (or any other type of collection) of strings, for example, you could iterate over each string using the following code:

```
Dim StringArray(1) As String
StringArray(0) = "Cat"
StringArray(1) = "Dog"

For Each Item As String In StringArray
    Console.WriteLine("{0}", Item)
Next
```

Within the first line of the For Each . . . Next loop, you declare the type of your iterator variable. In this example, it's a string. Following the declaration of the iterator type is the identifier for the collection to iterate over. You can use the For Each . . . Next loop with any object that implements the IEnumerable interface, making it perfect for actions such as looping over rows in an ADO DataTable or elements in an ArrayList.

The elements within the collection used in a For Each . . . Next statement must be able to be converted to the iterator type. If the value being evaluated can be converted to the iterator type, VB performs the conversion implicitly. If the conversion fails, the For Each . . . Next statement throws an InvalidCastException at run time. For example, this modification to the previous example causes an OverflowException runtime error on the second array element because VB implicitly tries to convert it from Long to Integer:

```
Dim anArray(1) As Long
    anArray(0) = 2
    anArray(1) = 3473928374736

For Each Item As Integer In anArray
    Console.WriteLine("{0}", Item.ToString())
Next
```

▆**Note** Modifying an iterator variable, or passing it to a method, can make your code difficult to read and debug. You should treat the iterator variable as read-only.

Finally, the Exit For statement is used if you reach a condition in which you want to terminate execution of the loop early. Control then passes to the statement following the Next statement.

For . . . Next

The For . . . Next construct is used to loop over items in a group, and you define the number of times the loop iterates by use of an expression. The basic For . . . Next syntax looks like this:

```
For counter As datatype  = start To end
    statements
    Exit For
Next counter
```

You can declare the counter variable inline, which is a nice feature comparable with C#. The For counter expression evaluates to a Boolean, and each time it's true, the subsequent statements are executed. If you want to exit the loop before the expression evaluates to False, use the Exit For statement:

```
For i As Integer = 0 To 10
    Console.WriteLine("{0}", i.ToString)
Next i
```

Do While and Do Until

While the For . . . Next statement iterates based on a known number of times or a number derived from a count of something, Do While and Do Until execute statements until a certain condition is either true or false. Here's the basic Do syntax:

```
Do While | Until condition
    statements
    Exit Do
Loop
```

The Do While executes the statements *while* the defined condition is True. On the other hand, Do Until executes the statements *until* the defined condition is True. Do loops are useful when you don't know the number of times you'll need to execute a statement. In this example, the code loops through the array of integers while the value of the array element is less than or equal to 5:

```
Dim MyArray() As Integer = {1, 2, 3, 4, 5, 6, 7, 8, 9, 10}
Dim rnd As Random = New Random
Dim i As Integer = rnd.Next(0, 9)

Do While MyArray(i) <= 9
    Console.WriteLine("{0}", MyArray(i).ToString)
    i += 1
Loop
```

The result will be the numbers between the random number and 10 appearing on the console. If you want to accomplish the same thing using the Do Until construct, it would perform the statements until the evaluated expression was true, and it would look like this:

```
Do Until MyArray(i) > 9
    Console.WriteLine("{0}", MyArray(i).ToString)
    i += 1
Loop
```

Continue

The Continue statement allows you to skip to the next iteration of a loop without processing the rest of the loop body. For example, in this code, if Counter is 6 or 7, execution goes to the Next line. If Counter is 1, 2, 3, 4, 5, 8, 9, or 10, the number is written to the console and normal execution goes to the Next line.

```
For Counter As Integer = 1 To 10
    Select Case Counter
        Case 1 To 5, 8 To 10
            Console.WriteLine("{0}", Counter.ToString)
        Case 6, 7
            Continue For
End Select
```

You can use the Continue command with Do While, Do Until, and For looping constructs (Continue Do, Continue While, and Continue For).

Summary

In this chapter, we discussed the differences between value types and reference types and some of the issues involved in converting the two. We also covered some of the highlights of the VB syntax and some control flow statements. Now we're ready to dive into the core of VB development—classes and structures.

CHAPTER 3

■ ■ ■

Classes and Structures

Everything in Visual Basic (VB) is an object. As VB is an object-oriented language, the objects that you create through class definitions have all the same capabilities of the other predefined objects in the system. In fact, keywords such as `Integer` and `Boolean` are merely aliases to predefined value types within the `System` namespace, `System.Int32`, and `System.Boolean`, respectively.

The ability to invent your own types is an integral part of object-oriented systems. The cool thing is that, since even the built-in types of the language are plain-old common language runtime (CLR) objects, the objects you create are on a level playing field with the built-in types. In other words, the built-in types don't have special powers that you cannot muster. The cornerstone for creating these types is the *class definition*. Class definitions, using the `Class` keyword, define the internal state and the behaviors associated with the objects of that class's type.

Along with classes, the VB language supports the definition of new *value types* through the `Structure` keyword. A `Structure` is a lightweight object that cannot inherit from another class or `Structure`, nor can another `Structure` or class inherit from them.

VB, along with the Visual Studio Integrated Development Environment (IDE), is an excellent tool to facilitate rapid application development. While the CLR can be daunting at first, you can put together reasonable applications without knowing every single detailed behavior of the language. As you build applications and gain understanding of the VB language and the CLR, the more effective you'll become at developing and designing robust applications.

Class Definitions

Let's go ahead and have a look at a simple class now so you can get a feel for things:

```
Public Class Customer
    'Fields/Members
    Private mName As String
    Private mCustomerID As Integer

    'Constructor
    Public Sub New()
        MyBase.New()
    End Sub
```

```
    'Properties
    Public Property Name() As String
        Get
            Return mName
        End Get
        Set(ByVal value As String)
            mName = value
        End Set
    End Property

    Public Property CustomerID() As Integer
        Get
            Return mCustomerID
        End Get
        Set(ByVal value As Integer)
            mCustomerID = value
        End Set
    End Property

    'Methods
    Public Function SaveCustomerToDB() As Boolean
        'Put code for this function here.
        'For now, return success
        Return True
    End Function
End Class
```

This class declaration defines a `Customer` class. The *access modifier* in front of the `Class` keyword, in this case `Public`, controls the visibility of the type from inside and outside of the assembly. The class `Customer` is publicly accessible, which means that you can create instances of this class. The `Customer` class contains two fields, a constructor, two properties, and one function. The property methods allow read/write access to the fields, and the function is used to save the customer to a database.

Constructors

Constructors are called when an object is created. There are two types of constructors: *default constructors* and *instance constructors*. A class can have only one default constructor, and it can have no parameters. The name of the default constructor is `New()`.

Instance constructors, on the other hand, are called when an instance of a class is created. They typically set up the state of the object by initializing the fields to a desired predefined state. You can also do any other type of initialization work, such as connecting to a database and opening a file. A class can have multiple instance constructors that can be *overloaded*.

Instance constructors can execute parent and self-constructors via `MyBase.New()` and `Me.New()`, as in the following snippets:

```
Public Sub New()
    MyBase.New()
End Sub
```

```
Public Sub New(ByVal aString as String)
    Me.New()
End Sub
```

Accessibility

Access modifiers can be used on just about any defined entity in a VB program, including classes and any member within the class. Access modifiers applied to a class affect its visibility from inside and outside the containing assembly. Access modifiers applied to class members, including methods, fields, properties, and events affect the visibility of the member from outside of the class. Table 3-1 describes the various access modifiers available.

Table 3-1. *Access Modifiers in VB*

Access Modifier	Meaning
Public	Member is completely visible outside both the defining scope and the internal scope. Access to a public member is not restricted at all.
Protected	Member is visible only to the defining class and any class that derives from the defining class.
Friend	Member is visible anywhere inside the containing assembly. This includes the defining class and any scope within the assembly that is outside the defining class.
Protected Friend	Member is visible within the defining class and anywhere else inside the assembly. This modifier combines Protected and Friend using a Boolean OR operation. The member is also visible to any class that derives from the defining class, whether it's in the same assembly or not.
Private	Member is visible only within the defining class, with no exceptions. This is the strictest form of access.

Properties can have mixed access modifiers. A Property getter can be Public, while a Property setter can be declared as a Friend. This allows every consumer read access, but only the containing assembly can update the field. In the following example, notice the Friend modifier on the setter:

```
Public Property CustomerID() As Integer
    Get
        Return mCustomerID
    End Get
    Friend Set(ByVal value As Integer)
        mCustomerID = value
    End Set
End Property
```

Class members can use all five variants of the access modifiers. The default access of the class members, in the absence of any modifiers at all, is Public. Classes can only have one of two access modifiers. Classes can either be Public or Friend. By default, they are Friend.

You can apply only Public, Private, and Friend to Structure member definitions. We cover Structure definitions in greater detail later in the chapter in the section titled "Value

Type Definitions." Notice the absence of `Protected` and `Protected Friend`. This is due to the fact that structures are implicitly sealed, meaning they cannot be base classes. We cover the `NotInheritable` modifier in more detail in the section titled "NotInheritable Classes."

Interfaces are implicitly `Public`, as they define a set of operations, or contract, that a class can implement. It makes no sense for an interface to have any restricted access members, since restricted access members are normally associated with a class implementation, and interfaces, by their definition, contain no implementation. The same applies to enumerations (`Enum`), as they are normally used as a named collection of constants and have no internal implementation. Finally, a `Namespace` is also implicitly `Public`, and cannot have any access modifiers applied to it.

Interfaces

Even though much of Chapter 6 is devoted to the topic of interfaces, it is worth introducing interfaces at this point for the purposes of discussion in the rest of this chapter. Generally speaking, an *interface* is a definition of a contract. Classes can choose to implement various interfaces, and by doing so, they guarantee to adhere to the rules of the contract. When a class inherits from an interface, it is required to implement the methods of that interface. A class can implement as many interfaces as it wants by listing them in the interface list of the class definition.

In general terms, an interface's syntax closely resembles that of a class. However, each member is implicitly `Public`. Interfaces can only contain instance methods; therefore, you can't include any `Shared` methods in the definition. Interfaces don't include an implementation; interfaces don't contain any internal code, so they are semantically abstract in nature.

The members of an interface can only consist of members that ultimately boil down to methods in the CLR. This includes methods, properties, and events. The following code shows an example of an interface and a class that implements the interface:

```
'NOTE: Standard practice is that you preface Interface with a capital "I"
Public Interface IMusician
    Sub PlayMusic()
End Interface

Public Class TalentedPerson
    Implements IMusician

    Public Sub PlayMusic() Implements IMusician.PlayMusic

    End Sub

    Public Sub DoALittleDance()

    End Sub
End Class

Public Class EntryPoint
    Shared Sub Main()
        Dim Dude As New TalentedPerson()
        Dim Musician As IMusician = Dude
```

```
        Musician.PlayMusic()
        Dude.PlayMusic()
        Dude.DoALittleDance()
    End Sub
End Class
```

The previous example defines an interface named IMusician. A class, TalentedPerson, indicates that it wants to support the IMusician interface through the Implements keyword. The class declaration is basically saying, "I would like to enter into a contract to support the IMusician interface, and I guarantee to support all the methods defined by that interface." The requirement of that interface is merely to support the PlayMusic method, which the TalentedPerson class does so faithfully. It is customary to name an interface type with a leading uppercase I. When reading code, this stands as a marker to indicate that the type in question is, in fact, an interface.

Now, clients can access the PlayMusic method in one of two ways. They can either call it through the object instance directly, or they can obtain an interface reference onto the object instance and call the method through it. Because the TalentedPerson class supports the IMusician interface, references to objects of that class are implicitly convertible to references of IMusician. The code inside the Main method in the previous example shows how to call the method both ways.

The topic of interfaces is broad enough to justify devoting an entire chapter to them, which we do in Chapter 6. However, the information regarding interfaces covered in this section is enough to facilitate the discussions in the rest of this chapter.

MyBase and MyClass Keywords

When you derive from a class—a process also referred to as *inheritance*—oftentimes you need to call a method or access a field, property, or method on the base class from within a method on the derived class. The MyBase keyword exists for this purpose; MyBase is like an object variable that always refers to the base class from which the current instance class was derived. You can use the MyBase keyword just like any other instance variable, but you can use it only within the block of an instance constructor, instance method, or instance property accessor. You cannot use it in Shared methods because MyBase allows access to base class implementations of an instance, much like Me allows access to the instance owning the method. Let's look at the following code block:

```
Public Class A
    Private x As Integer

    Public Sub New(ByVal var As Integer)
        Me.x = var
    End Sub

    Public Overridable Sub DoSomething()
        System.Console.WriteLine("A.DoSomething")
    End Sub
End Class
```

```
Public Class B
    Inherits A

    Public Sub New()
        MyBase.New(123)

        'Constructor code here
    End Sub

    Public Overloads Overrides Sub DoSomething()
        System.Console.WriteLine("B.DoSomething")
        MyBase.DoSomething()
    End Sub
End Class

Public Class EntryPoint
    Shared Sub Main()
        Dim b As B = New B()

        b.DoSomething()
    End Sub
End Class
```

Here's the output from the preceding code:

```
B.DoSomething
A.DoSomething
```

In the preceding example, you can see two uses of the MyBase keyword. The first use is in the constructor for Class B. As a derived class doesn't inherit instance constructors, when initializing the object, it is sometimes necessary to explicitly call one of the base class constructors during initialization of the derived class. This syntax is in the Class B instance constructor. The base class initialization occurs after the declaration of the derived class constructor's parameter list but before the constructor code block. The section titled "Creating Objects" discusses the ordering of constructor calls and object initialization.

The second use of the MyBase keyword is in the B.DoSomething() implementation. In our implementation of Class B, we borrow the DoSomething() implementation in Class A while implementing B.DoSomething(). We do this by calling the A.DoSomething() implementation directly from within B.DoSomething(), using the MyBase keyword.

MyClass is like an object variable that always refers to the current instance of a class as it was implemented. The MyClass keyword executes its call as if the method or property had been marked NotOverridable. The following code demonstrates:

```
Public Class A
    Private x As Integer
```

```vbnet
    Public Sub New(ByVal var As Integer)
        Me.x = var
    End Sub

    Public Overridable Sub DoSomething()
        System.Console.WriteLine("A.DoSomething")
    End Sub

    Public Sub UseMe()
        Me.DoSomething()
    End Sub

    Public Sub UseMyClass()
        MyClass.DoSomething()
    End Sub
End Class

Public Class B
    Inherits A

    Public Sub New()
        MyBase.New(123)
    End Sub

    Public Overloads Overrides Sub DoSomething()
        System.Console.WriteLine("B.DoSomething")
        MyBase.DoSomething()
    End Sub
End Class

Public Class EntryPoint
    Shared Sub Main()
        Dim b As B = New B()

        b.UseMe()
        b.UseMyClass()
    End Sub
End Class
```

Here's the output from the preceding code:

```
B.DoSomething
A.DoSomething
A.DoSomething
```

The b.UseMyClass method call executes the A.DoSomething method. This is because even though the UseMyClass method is called from an instance of Class B, the method uses the

MyClass keyword, causing it to call the DoSomething method in Class A. The MyClass keyword ensures that the Overridable method implemented in your base class is called, not the over-ridden method in your derived class.

NotInheritable Classes

When you create a new class, you may design it with the express intent for it to serve as a base class or to allow for specialization. VB offers the NotInheritable keyword for those occasions when you want to prohibit a class from ever being derived from. At first, you might think that you should rarely use the NotInheritable keyword. However, the contrary may be a better practice, as inheritance can be tricky. For a class to serve as a good base class, you must design it with that goal in mind. If not, you should mark it NotInheritable. Now you may be thinking, "Shouldn't I leave it inheritable so that someone can possibly derive from it in the future, thus retaining maximum flexibility?" The answer is usually no. A class that is meant to serve as a base class should be designed with that in mind from the start.

MustInherit Classes

On the exact opposite end of the spectrum from NotInheritable classes are MustInherit classes. Sometimes, you need to design a class whose only purpose is to serve as a base class. You mark classes such as these with the MustInherit keyword.

The MustInherit keyword tells the compiler that this class is meant to be used only as a base class, and therefore it does not allow code to create instances of that class. Let's look at an example:

```
Public MustInherit Class GeometricShape
    Public Overridable Sub Draw()
    End Sub
End Class

Public Class Circle
    Inherits GeometricShape

    Public Overrides Sub Draw()
        'Do some drawing.
    End Sub
End Class

Public Class EntryPoint
    Shared Sub Main()
        Dim Circle As New Circle

        'This will not work!
        'Dim shape2 As New GeometricShape

        Circle.Draw()
    End Sub
End Class
```

It makes no sense to create a GeometricShape object all by itself because it's so abstract. Typically, you'd want to create a type of geometric shape, such as a circle, triangle, or square. To enforce this, you mark the GeometricShape class as MustInherit. Therefore, if the code in Main() attempts to create an instance of GeometricShape, a compiler error will be emitted. Using the MustInherit keyword is a way of saying to the compiler that the deriving classes must override the methods. Since the method must be overridden by the derived classes, it makes no sense for the GeometricShape.Draw() member to have an implementation when you can't ever create an instance of GeometricShape anyway.

Designing a base class this way creates a template of behavior by providing an implementation to inherit. Your derived classes can then inherit from this base template and implement the details.

Nested Classes

You define nested classes within the scope of another class definition. Classes that are defined within the scope of a namespace, but not inside the scope of another class, are called *non-nested classes*. Nested classes have some special capabilities and lend themselves well to situations where you need a helper class that works on behalf of the containing class.

For example, a container class might maintain a collection of objects. Imagine that you need some facility to iterate over those contained objects and also allow external users who are doing the iteration to maintain a marker, or iterator of sorts, representing their place during the iteration. Using nested classes this way is a common design technique that prevents users from holding onto direct references to the contained objects, and it gives you greater flexibility to change the internal behavior of the container class without breaking the code that uses the container class.

Nested classes have access to all of the members that are visible to the containing class, even if they're private. Consider the following code, which represents a container class that contains instances of GeometricShape:

```
Imports System.Collections

Public MustInherit Class GeometricShape
    Public MustOverride Sub Draw()
End Class

Public Class Rectangle
    Inherits GeometricShape

    Public Overrides Sub Draw()
        System.Console.WriteLine("Rectangle.Draw")
    End Sub
End Class

Public Class Circle
    Inherits GeometricShape
```

```vb
        Public Overrides Sub Draw()
            System.Console.WriteLine("Circle.Draw")
        End Sub
End Class

Public Class Drawing
    Implements IEnumerable

    Private Shapes As ArrayList

    Public Sub New()
        Shapes = New ArrayList()
    End Sub
    Public Function GetEnumerator() As IEnumerator _
        Implements Collections.IEnumerable.GetEnumerator

        Return New Iterator(Me)
    End Function
    Public Sub Add(ByVal Shape As GeometricShape)
        Shapes.Add(Shape)
    End Sub

    Private Class Iterator
        Implements IEnumerator

        Private Position As Integer
        Private Drawing As Drawing

        Public Sub New(ByVal Drawing As Drawing)
            Me.Drawing = Drawing
            Me.Position = -1
        End Sub

        Public Sub Iterator(ByVal Drawing As Drawing)
            Me.Drawing = Drawing
            Me.Position = -1
        End Sub
        Public Sub Reset() Implements Collections.IEnumerator.Reset
            Position = -1
        End Sub

        Public Function MoveNext() As Boolean _
            Implements Collections.IEnumerator.MoveNext
```

```
                Position += 1
                Return (Position < Drawing.Shapes.Count)
            End Function
            Public ReadOnly Property Current() As Object _
                Implements Collections.IEnumerator.Current

                Get
                    Return Drawing.Shapes(Position)
                End Get
            End Property
        End Class
End Class

Public Class EntryPoint
    Shared Sub Main()
        Dim Rectangle As New Rectangle
        Dim Circle As New Circle
        Dim Drawing As New Drawing

        Drawing.Add(Rectangle)
        Drawing.Add(Circle)

        For Each Shape As GeometricShape In Drawing
            Shape.Draw()
        Next
    End Sub
End Class
```

This example introduces a few new concepts, such as the IEnumerable and IEnumerator interfaces, which Chapter 10 covers. For now, let's focus primarily on the nested class usage. As you can see, the Drawing class supports a method called GetEnumerator(), which is part of the IEnumerable implementation. It creates an instance of the nested Iterator class and returns it.

The Iterator class takes a reference to an instance of the containing class, Drawing, as a parameter to its constructor. It then stores away this instance for later use so that it can get at the Shapes collection within the Drawing object. However, the Shapes collection in the Drawing class is Private. It doesn't matter, since nested classes have access to the containing class's private members.

Also, notice that the Iterator class itself is declared Private. Non-nested classes can only be declared as either Public or Friend, and they default to Friend. You can apply the same access modifiers to nested classes as you can to any other member of the class. In this case, you declare the Iterator class as Private so that external code, such as in the Main() routine, cannot create instances of the Iterator directly. Only the Drawing class itself can create instances of Iterator. It doesn't make sense for a class other than Drawing. GetEnumerator() to be able to create an Iterator instance because this nested class acts on its containing class.

Nested classes that are declared public can be instantiated by code external to the containing class. The notation for addressing the nested class is similar to that of namespace qualification. In the following example, you can see how to create an instance of a nested class:

```
Public Class A
    Public Class B

    End Class
End Class

Public Class EntryPoint
    Shared Sub Main()
        Dim B As New A.B()
    End Sub
End Class
```

Item Property Indexers

Indexers allow you to treat an object instance as if it were an array. This allows for a more natural usage of objects that are meant to behave as a collection, such as instances of the Drawing class from the previous section. Indexers in VB are implemented via an Item default property, and may not be Private or Shared.

Conceptually, the indexer is similar to a method in that it can take a parameter when used, and you can apply many of the same modifiers to the indexer as you can to a method. However, it also behaves like a property, as you define the accessors with a similar syntax. Following the parameter list in the indexer declaration is the code block for the indexer, which is just like a property code block in its syntax. The main difference is that the accessors for the indexer can access the parameter passed, whereas the accessors of a property don't have user-defined parameters. Let's add an indexer to the Drawing object and see how you can use it:

```
Imports System.Collections

Public MustInherit Class GeometricShape
    Public MustOverride Sub Draw()
End Class

Public Class Rectangle
    Inherits GeometricShape

    Public Overrides Sub Draw()
        System.Console.WriteLine("Rectangle.Draw")
    End Sub
End Class

Public Class Circle
    Inherits GeometricShape
```

```vbnet
        Public Overrides Sub Draw()
            System.Console.WriteLine("Circle.Draw")
        End Sub
End Class


Public Class Drawing
    Private Shapes As ArrayList

    Public Sub New()
        Shapes = New ArrayList
    End Sub

    Public ReadOnly Property Count() As Integer
        Get
            Return Shapes.Count
        End Get
    End Property

    Default Public ReadOnly Property Item(ByVal Index As Integer) As GeometricShape
        Get
            Return CType(Shapes(Index), GeometricShape)
        End Get
    End Property

    Public Sub Add(ByVal Shape As GeometricShape)
        Shapes.Add(Shape)
    End Sub
End Class

Public Class EntryPoint
    Shared Sub Main()
        Dim Rectangle As Rectangle = New Rectangle()
        Dim Circle As Circle = New Circle()
        Dim Drawing As Drawing = New Drawing()
        Dim i As Integer = 0

        Drawing.Add(Rectangle)
        Drawing.Add(Circle)

        For i = 0 To Drawing.Count - 1 Step 1
            Dim Shape As GeometricShape = Drawing(i)

            Shape.Draw()
        Next
    End Sub
End Class
```

As shown, you can access the elements of the `Drawing` object in the `Main()` routine as if they were inside a normal array. Also, since this indexer only has a `Get` accessor, it is read-only. Keep in mind that if the collection holds onto references to objects, the client code can still change the state of the contained object through that reference. But since the indexer is read-only, the client code cannot swap out the object reference at a specific index with a reference to a completely different object.

One difference is worth noting between a real array and the indexer. You cannot pass the results of calling an indexer on an object as a `ByRef` parameter to a method as you can do with a real array. This is similar to the same restriction placed on properties.

Partial Classes

Partial classes were added in VB 2005. So far, you've seen how to define classes in one single file, and until VB 2005, it was impossible to split the definition of a class across multiple files. At first, such a convenience may not seem worthwhile. After all, if a class has become so large that the file is hard to manage, that may be an indication of poor design. But arguably, the main reason partial classes were introduced is to support code-generation tools.

Normally, when you work within the confines of the IDE, the IDE tries to help you out by generating some code for you. For example, a wizard generates helpful `DataSet` derived classes when using ADO.NET facilities. The classic problem has always been editing the resulting code generated by the tool. It was always a dangerous proposition to edit the output from the tool because any time the parameters to the tool change, the tool regenerates the code, thus overwriting any changes made. This is definitely not desired. Previously, the only way to work around this was to use some form of reuse, such as inheritance or containment, thus inheriting a class from the class produced by the code-generation tool. Many times these were not natural solutions to the problem, and the code generated was not designed to take inheritance into consideration.

Now, you can slip the `Partial` keyword into the class definition right before the `Class` keyword, and voilà, you can split the class definition across multiple files. One requirement is that one file that contains part of the partial class must use the `Partial` keyword, and you must define all of the partial pieces within the same namespace. Now, with the addition of the `Partial` keyword, the code generated from the code-generation tool can live in a separate file from the additions to that generated class, and when the tool regenerates the code, you don't lose your changes.

You should know some things about the process the compiler goes through to assemble partial classes into a whole class. You must compile all the partial pieces of a class together at once so the compiler can find all of the pieces. For the most part, all of the members and aspects of the class are merged together using a union operation. Therefore, they must coexist together as if you had declared and defined them all in the same file. Base interface lists are unioned together. However, since a class can have one base class at most, if the partial pieces list a base class, they must all list the same base class. Other than those restrictions, you'll probably agree that partial classes are a welcome addition.

Value Type Definitions

A value type is a lightweight type that is allocated on the stack instead of on the heap. The only exception to this rule is a value type that is a field in an object that lives on the heap. Value types include the VB numeric data types, such as `Integer`, `Enum`, and `Structure`. A value type is a type that behaves with value semantics. That is, when you assign a value type variable to another value type variable, the contents of the source are copied into the destination and a full copy of the instance is made. This is in contrast to reference types, or object instances, where the result of copying a reference type variable to another is that there is now a new reference to the same object. Also, when you pass a value type as a parameter to a method, the method body receives a local copy of the value, unless the parameter was declared as a `ByRef` parameter. In VB, you declare a structure using the `Structure` keyword rather than the `Class` keyword.

On the whole, the syntax of defining a structure is the same as a class, with some notable exceptions. A structure cannot declare a base class. Also, a structure is implicitly sealed. That means that nothing else can derive from a structure. Internally, a structure derives from `System.ValueType`, which in turn extends `System.Object`. This is so that `ValueType` can provide implementations of `Equals()` and `GetHashCode()`, among others, which are meaningful for value types. The section titled "System.Object" covers the nuances involved with implementing the methods inherited from `System.Object` for a value type. Like classes, you can declare structures in partial pieces, and the same rules for partial pieces apply to structures as they do to classes.

Constructors

Types defined as structures can have default constructors just like classes. Structures can also have instance constructors, with one notable exception. They cannot have a user-defined default, parameterless constructor, nor can they have instance field initializers in the structure definition. Static field initializers are permitted, though. Parameterless constructors are not necessary for value types, since the system provides one, which simply sets the fields of the value to their default values. In all cases, that amounts to setting the bits of the field's storage to 0. So if a structure contains an `Integer`, the default value will be 0. If a structure contains a reference type field, the default value will be `Nothing`. Each structure gets this implicit, parameterless constructor that takes care of this initialization. It's all part of the language's endeavors to create verifiably type-safe code. The following code shows the use of the default constructor:

```
Imports System

Public Structure Square
    Private mWidth As Integer
    Private mHeight As Integer

    Public Property Width() As Integer
        Get
            Return mWidth
        End Get
        Set(ByVal Value As Integer)
            mWidth = Value
        End Set
    End Property
```

```
    Public Property Height() As Integer
        Get
            Return mHeight
        End Get
        Set(ByVal Value As Integer)
            mHeight = Value
        End Set
    End Property
End Structure

Public Class EntryPoint
    Shared Sub Main()
        Dim sq As New Square()

        Console.WriteLine("{0} x {1}", sq.Width, sq.Height)

        sq.Width = 1
        sq.Height = 2

        Console.WriteLine("{0} x {1}", sq.Width, sq.Height)
    End Sub
End Class
```

Running this example yields the following results:

```
0 x 0
1 x 2
```

The first result demonstrates that the system-provided constructor has initialized the fields to the default value of 0, while the second result displays the assignment of these fields in the code.

The Meaning of Me

The Me keyword within class methods behaves as a constant, read-only value that contains a reference to the current object instance. Even though instance constructors in structure value types cannot use the MyBase keyword to call base class constructors, they can have an initializer. It is valid for the initializer to use the Me keyword to call other constructors on the same structure during initialization, as in the following example:

```
Public Structure ComplexNumber
    Private Real As Double
    Private Imaginary As Double

    Public Sub New(ByVal Real As Double, ByVal Imaginary As Double)
        Me.Real = Real
        Me.Imaginary = Imaginary
    End Sub
```

```
    Public Sub New(ByVal Real As Double)
        Me.New(Real, 0)
    End Sub
End Structure

Public Class EntryPoint
    Shared Sub Main()
        Dim valA As ComplexNumber = New ComplexNumber(1)
    End Sub
End Class
```

The previous code introduces an initializer that calls the first constructor from the second one, which only assigns the Real value. When an instance constructor contains an initializer, the Me keyword behaves as a ByRef parameter in that constructor's body. And, since it is a ByRef parameter, the compiler can assume that the value has been initialized properly before entry into the method's code block. In essence, the initialization burden is deferred to the first constructor whose duty it is to make sure it initializes all fields of the value.

One last note to consider is that even though the system generates a default, parameterless initializer, you can't call it using the Me keyword.

Finalizers

Value types are not allowed to have a finalizer and are removed from the stack as soon as they go out of scope. The concept of finalization, or nondeterministic destruction, is reserved for instances of classes, or objects, because that is how management of the heap works. If structures had finalizers, the runtime would have to manage the calling of the finalizer each time the value goes out of scope.

Be careful when initializing resources within structure constructors. Consider a value type that has a field, which is a handle to some sort of low-level system resource. Suppose this low-level resource is allocated, or acquired, in a special constructor that accepts parameters. You now have a couple of problems to deal with. Since you cannot create a default, parameterless constructor, how can you possibly acquire the resource when the user creates an instance of the value without using one of the custom constructors? The answer is, you cannot. The second problem is that you have no automatic trigger to clean up and release the resource, since you have no destructor.

Interfaces

Although it's illegal for a structure to derive from another class, it can still implement interfaces. Supported interfaces are listed in the same way as they are for classes, in a base interface list after the structure identifier. Generally, supporting interfaces for structures is the same as supporting interfaces for classes. Chapter 6 covers interfaces in detail. Implementing interfaces on structures has performance implications; specifically, it incurs a boxing operation to call methods through an interface reference on the structure value instances.

Boxing and Unboxing

All types within the CLR fall into one of two categories: reference types (objects) or value types (values). You define objects using classes, and you define values using structures. A clear divide exists between these two. Objects live on the memory heap and are managed by the garbage collector. Values normally live in temporary storage spaces, such as on the stack. The one notable exception already mentioned is that a value type can live on the heap as long as it is contained as a field within an object. However, it is not autonomous, and the GC doesn't control its lifetime directly. Consider the following code:

```
Public Class EntryPoint
    Shared Sub Print(ByVal obj As Object)
        System.Console.WriteLine("{0}", obj.ToString())
    End Sub

    Shared Sub Main()
        Dim x As Integer = 42

        Print(x)
    End Sub
End Class
```

It looks simple enough. In Main(), there is an Integer, which is an alias for System.Int32, and it is a value type. You could have just as well declared x as type System.Int32. The space allocated for x is on the local stack. You then pass it as a parameter to the Print() method. The Print() method takes an object reference and simply sends the results of calling ToString() on that object to the console. Let's analyze this. Print() accepts an object reference, which is a reference to a heap-based object. Yet you're passing a value type to the method. How is this possible?

The key is a concept called *boxing*. At the point where a value type is defined, the CLR creates a runtime-created wrapper class to contain the value type. Instances of the wrapper live on the heap and are commonly called *boxing objects*. This is the CLR's way of bridging the gap between value types and reference types.

The boxing object behaves just like any other reference type in the CLR. Also note that the boxing type implements the interfaces of the contained value type. The boxing type is a class type that is generated internally by the virtual execution system of the CLR at the point where the contained value type is defined. The CLR then uses this internal class type when it performs boxing operations as needed.

The most important thing to keep in mind with boxing is that the boxed value is a copy of the original. Therefore, any changes made to the value inside the box are not propagated back to the original value. For example, consider this slight modification to the previous code:

```
Public Class EntryPoint
    Shared Sub PrintAndModify(ByVal obj As Object)
        System.Console.WriteLine("{0}", obj.ToString())
```

```
        Dim x As Integer = CType(obj, Integer)
        x = 21
    End Sub
    Shared Sub Main()
        Dim x As Integer = 42

        PrintAndModify(x)
        PrintAndModify(x)
    End Sub
End Class
```

This output from the preceding code might surprise you:

```
42
42
```

You might expect the second value sent to the console to be 21, but the fact is, the original value, x, declared and initialized in Main(), is never changed. As you pass it to the PrintAndModify method, it is boxed, since the PrintAndModify method takes an object as its parameter. Even though PrintAndModify() takes a reference to an object that you can modify, the object it receives is a boxing object that contains a copy of the original value. The preceding code also introduces another operation called *unboxing* in the PrintAndModify method. Since the value is boxed inside of an instance of an object on the heap, you can't change the value because the only methods supported by that object are methods that System.Object implements. Technically, it also supports the same interfaces that System.Int32 supports. Therefore, you need a way to get the value out of the box. You can accomplish this syntactically with casting by using the CType function. Notice that you cast the object instance back into an Integer, and the compiler is smart enough to know that what you're really doing is unboxing the value type.

The operation of unboxing a value is the exact opposite of boxing. The value in the box is copied into an instance of the value on the local stack. Again, any changes made to this unboxed copy are not propagated back to the value contained in the box. Now you can see how boxing and unboxing can really become confusing. As shown, the code's behavior is not obvious to the casual observer who is unfamiliar with the fact that boxing and unboxing are going on. What's worse is that two copies of the Integer are created between the time the call to PrintAndModify() is initiated and the time that the Integer is manipulated in the method. The first copy is the one put into the box. The second copy is the one created when the boxed value is copied out of the box.

Technically, it's possible to modify the value that is contained within the box. However, you must do this through an interface. The runtime-generated box that contains the value also implements the interfaces that the value type implements and forwards the calls to the contained value. So, you could do the following:

```
Public Interface IModifyMyValue
    Property X() As Integer
End Interface
```

```
Public Structure MyValue
        Implements IModifyMyValue
        Public _x As Integer

        Public Property X() As Integer Implements IModifyMyValue.X
            Get
                Return _x
            End Get
            Set(ByVal Value As Integer)
                _x = Value
            End Set
        End Property

        Public Overloads Overrides Function ToString() As String
            Dim output As System.Text.StringBuilder = New System.Text.StringBuilder

            output.AppendFormat("{0}", _x)
            Return output.ToString
        End Function
    End Structure

    Public Class EntryPoint
        Shared Sub Main()
            Dim MyVal As MyValue = New MyValue
            MyVal.X = 123

            Dim obj As Object = MyVal
            System.Console.WriteLine("{0}", obj.ToString)

            Dim IFace As IModifyMyValue = CType(obj, IModifyMyValue)
            IFace.X = 456
            System.Console.WriteLine("{0}", obj.ToString)

            Dim NewVal As MyValue = CType(obj, MyValue)
            System.Console.WriteLine("{0}", NewVal.ToString)
        End Sub
    End Class
```

You can see that the output from the code is as follows:

```
123
456
456
```

As expected, you're able to modify the value inside the box using the interface named IModifyMyValue. It's not the most straightforward process, however, as before you can obtain an interface reference to a value type, you must box it. This makes sense if you think about the fact that references to interfaces are object reference types.

When Boxing Occurs

Since boxing is handled implicitly for you, it's important to know the instances when VB boxes a value. Basically, a value gets boxed when one of the following conversions occur:

- Conversion from a value type to an object reference

- Conversion from a value type to a System.ValueType reference

- Conversion from a value type to a reference to an interface implemented by the value type

- Conversion from an enum type to a System.Enum reference

In each case, the conversion normally takes the form of an assignment expression. The first two cases are fairly obvious, since the CLR is bridging the gap by turning a value type instance into a reference type. The third one can be a little surprising. Any time you implicitly cast your value into an interface that it supports, you incur the penalty of boxing. Consider the following code:

```
Public Interface IPrint
    Sub Print()
End Interface

Public Structure MyValue
    Implements IPrint
    Public x As Integer

    Public Sub Print() Implements IPrint.Print
        System.Console.WriteLine("{0}", x)
    End Sub
End Structure

Public Class EntryPoint
    Shared Sub Main()
        Dim MyVal As MyValue = New MyValue

        MyVal.x = 123

        'No Boxing
        MyVal.Print()

        'Boxing occurs
        Dim Printer As IPrint = MyVal
        Printer.Print()
    End Sub
End Class
```

The first call to Print() is done through the value reference, which doesn't incur boxing. However, the second call to Print() is done through an interface. The boxing takes place at the point where you obtain the interface. At first, it looks like you can easily sidestep the boxing operation by not acquiring an explicit reference typed on the interface type. This is true in this case, since `Print()` is also part of the public contract of `MyValue`. However, had you implemented the `Print()` method as an explicit interface, then the only way to call the method would be through the interface reference type. So it's important to note that any time you implement an interface on a value type explicitly, you force the clients of your value type to box it before calling through that interface. The following example demonstrates this:

```
Public Interface IPrint
    Sub Print()
End Interface

Public Structure MyValue
    Implements IPrint
    Public x As Integer

    Sub Print() Implements IPrint.Print
        System.Console.WriteLine("{0}", x)
    End Sub
End Structure

Public Class EntryPoint
    Shared Sub Main()
        Dim MyVal As MyValue = New MyValue

        MyVal.x = 123

        'Must box the value
        Dim Printer As IPrint = MyVal

        Printer.Print()
    End Sub
End Class
```

Efficiency and Confusion

As you might expect, boxing and unboxing are not the most efficient operations in the world. What's worse is that the compiler silently does the boxing for you. You really must take care to know when boxing is occurring. Unboxing is usually more explicit, since you typically must do a cast operation to extract the value from the box, but there is an implicit case we'll cover soon. Either way, you must pay attention to the efficiency aspect of things. For example, consider a container type, such as a `System.Collections.ArrayList`. It contains all of its values as references to type `Object`. If you were to insert a bunch of value types into it, they would all be boxed. Thankfully, generics, which is covered in Chapter 12, can solve this inefficiency for you. Boxing is inefficient, and you should avoid it as much as possible. Since boxing is an implicit operation, it takes a keen eye to find all of the cases of boxing. The best tool to use to determine whether boxing is occurring is the IL Disassembler (IL DASM). Using the IL Disassembler, you can examine the intermediate language (IL) code generated for your methods, and the box operations will be clearly identifiable. You can run the disassembler by navigating to All Programs ➤ Microsoft Windows SDK for Visual Studio ➤ Tools ➤ IL Disassembler.

As mentioned previously, unboxing is normally an explicit operation introduced by a cast from the boxing object reference to a value of the boxed type. However, unboxing is implicit in one notable case. Remember the differences of the Me reference within methods of classes vs. methods of structures? The main difference is that, for value types, the Me reference acts as a ByRef parameter. So when you call a method on a value type, the hidden Me parameter within the method must be a managed pointer rather than a reference. The compiler handles this easily when you call directly through a value type instance. However, when calling a virtual method or interface method through a boxed instance—thus through an object—the CLR must unbox the value instance so that it can obtain the managed pointer to the value type contained within the box. After passing the managed pointer to the contained value type's method as the Me pointer, the method can modify the fields through the Me pointer, and it will apply the changes to the value contained within the box. Be aware of hidden unboxing operations if you're calling methods on a value through a box object. Unboxing operations in the CLR are not inefficient in and of themselves. The inefficiency stems from the fact that VB typically combines that unboxing operation with a copy of the value.

System.Object

Every object in the CLR derives from System.Object. Object is the base type of every type, and the VB Object keyword is an alias for System.Object. It's convenient that every type in the CLR and in VB derives from Object. For example, you can treat a collection of instances of multiple types homogenously simply by casting them to Object references.

Even System.ValueType derives from Object. However, some special rules govern obtaining an Object reference. On reference types, you can turn a reference of Class A into a reference of class Object with a simple implicit conversion. Going the other direction and setting an object of type System.Object to an object of type A requires a runtime type check and an explicit cast using the cast syntax of CType(A, Object).

Obtaining an Object reference directly on a value type is, technically, impossible. Semantically, this makes sense because value types live on the stack. It can be dangerous for you to obtain a reference to a transient value instance and store it away for later use if, potentially, the value instance is gone by the time you finally use the stored reference. For this reason, obtaining an Object reference on a value type instance involves a boxing operation, as described in the previous section.

Object provides several useful and generic methods, including a GetType method that obtains the runtime type of any object running in the CLR. Such a capability is extremely handy when coupled with reflection—the capability to examine types in the system at run time. GetType() returns an object of type Type, which represents the real, or concrete, type of the object. Using this object, you can determine everything about the type of the object on which GetType() is called. Also, given two references of type Object, you can compare the result of calling GetType() on both of them to find out if they're actually instances of the same concrete type.

System.Object contains a method named MemberwiseClone(), which returns a shallow copy of the object. Chapter 14 talks more about this method. When creating the copy, all value type fields are copied on a bit-by-bit basis, whereas all fields that are references are simply copied, such that the new copy and the original both contain references to the same object. When you want to make a copy of an object, you may or may not desire this behavior. Therefore, if objects support copying, you should consider supporting the ICloneable interface and do the correct thing in the implementation of that interface. This method is declared as protected so that only the class for the object being copied can call it, since MemberwiseClone() can create an object without calling its instance constructor. Such behavior could potentially be destabilizing if it were made public.

The Equals(), GetHashCode(), and ToString methods of System.Object are Overridable, and if the default implementations of the methods inside System.Object are not appropriate, you should override them. ToString() is useful when generating textual, or human-readable, output and a string representing the object is required. For example, during development, you may need the ability to trace an object out to a debug output at run time. In such cases, it makes sense to override ToString() so that it provides detailed information about the objects and its internal state. The default version of ToString() simply calls the ToString() implementation on the Type object returned from a call to GetType(), thus providing the name of the type of the object.[1]

The Finalize method deserves special mention. VB 2008 doesn't allow you to explicitly override this method on structure types. If you override this method for a class, the garbage collector will execute your finalizer before destroying your object.

Creating Objects

Object creation is a topic that looks simple on the surface, but in reality is relatively complex under the hood. You need to be intimately familiar with what operations take place during the creation of a new object instance or value instance in order to write constructor code effectively and use field initializers effectively. Also, in the CLR, not only do object instances have constructors, but so do the types they're based on. These constructors are represented by a shared constructor definition. Constructors allow you to get work done at the point the type is loaded and initialized into the application domain.

The New Keyword

The New keyword lets you create new instances of objects or values. However, it behaves slightly differently when used with value types as opposed to object types. For example, New doesn't always allocate space on the heap. Let's discuss what it does with value types first.

Using New with Value Types

The New keyword is only required for value types when you need to invoke one of the constructors for the type. Otherwise, value types simply have space reserved on the stack for them, and the client code must initialize them fully before you can use them. The "Value Type Definitions" section on constructors in value types covered this.

---

1. Be sure to read Chapter 9, which gives reasons why Object.ToString() is not what you want when creating software for localization to various locales and cultures.

Using New with Reference Types

You use the New operator to create reference type objects. In this case, the New operator allocates space on the heap for the object being created. If this fails, it will throw an exception of type System.OutOfMemoryException, thus aborting the rest of the object-creation process.

After it allocates the space, all of the fields of the object are initialized to their default values. This is similar to what the compiler-generated default constructor does for value types. For reference type fields, they are set to null. For value type fields, their underlying memory slots are filled with all zeros. The net effect is that all fields in the new object are initialized to either null or 0. Once this is done, the CLR calls the appropriate constructor for the object instance, based upon the parameters given. The New operator also sets up the hidden Me parameter for the constructor, which is a read-only reference to the new object created on the heap, and that reference's type is the same as the class type. Consider the following example:

```
Public Class A
    Public x As Integer
    Public y As Integer

    Sub New(ByVal x As Integer, ByVal y As Integer)
        Me.x = x
        Me.y = y
    End Sub
End Class

Public Class EntryPoint
    Shared Sub Main()
        'We can't do this!
        'Dim objA As New A()

        Dim objA As New A(1, 2)
        System.Console.WriteLine("objA.x = {0}; objA.y = {1}", objA.x, objA.y)
    End Sub
End Class
```

This example will display the following results to the console:

```
objA.x = 1; objA.y = 2
```

In the Main method, you cannot create a new instance of A by calling the default constructor, as the class constructor is expecting two parameters. The compiler doesn't create a default constructor for a class unless no other constructors are defined. However, you could create your own New constructor with no parameters. The rest of the code creates a new instance of A, and then outputs its values to the console.

Shared Constructor

A class can have at most one Shared constructor, and that constructor cannot accept any parameters. You can never invoke Shared constructors directly. Instead, the CLR invokes them when it needs to initialize the type for a given application domain. The Shared constructor is called before an instance of the given class is first created or before some other Shared fields on the class are referenced.

```
Imports System

Public Class A
    Private y As Integer = InitY()
    Private x As Integer = InitX()
    Private Shared a As Integer = InitA()
    Private Shared b As Integer = InitB()

    Shared Sub New()
        Console.WriteLine("Shared A::A()")
    End Sub

    Private Shared Function InitX() As Integer
        Console.WriteLine("A.InitX()")
        Return 1
    End Function

    Private Shared Function InitY() As Integer
        Console.WriteLine("A.InitY()")
        Return 2
    End Function

    Private Shared Function InitA() As Integer
        Console.WriteLine("A.InitA()")
        Return 3
    End Function

    Private Shared Function InitB() As Integer
        Console.WriteLine("A.InitB()")
        Return 4
    End Function
End Class

Public Class EntryPoint
    Shared Sub Main()
        Dim objA As A = New A
    End Sub
End Class
```

The output from the code is as follows:

```
A.InitA()
A.InitB()
Shared A::A()
A.InitY()
A.InitX()
```

The shared constructor was called before an instance of the class was created. However, notice the important ordering that occurs. The shared field initializers are executed before the body of the shared constructor executes. This ensures that the instance fields are initialized properly before possibly being referenced within the shared constructor body.

It is the default behavior of the CLR to call the type initializer before any member of the type is accessed. This means that the type initializer will execute before any code accesses a field or a method on the class or before an object is created from the class.

Instance Constructor and Creation Ordering

Instance constructors follow a lot of the same rules as shared constructors, except they're more flexible and powerful, so they have some added rules of their own. Let's examine those rules.

Instance constructors can have what's called an *initializer expression*. An initializer expression allows instance constructors to defer some of their work to other instance constructors within the class, or more importantly, to base class constructors during object initialization. This is important if you rely on the base class instance constructors to initialize the inherited members. Constructors are never inherited, so you must go through explicit means such as this in order to call the base class constructors during initialization if you need to.

If your class doesn't implement an instance constructor at all, the compiler will generate a default parameterless instance constructor for you, which really only does one thing: it calls the base class default constructor through the MyBase keyword. If the base class doesn't have an accessible default constructor, a compiler error will be generated. For example, the following code doesn't compile:

```
Public Class A
    Private x As Integer

    Public Sub New(ByVal x As Integer)
        Me.x = x
    End Sub
End Class

Public Class B
    Inherits A
End Class

Public Class EntryPoint
    Shared Sub Main()
        Dim objB As B = New B()
    End Sub
End Class
```

The problem is that a class with no explicit constructors is given a default parameterless constructor by the compiler that merely calls the base class parameterless constructor, which is exactly what the compiler tries to do for Class B. However, since Class A does have an explicit instance constructor defined, the compiler doesn't produce a default constructor for Class A. So there is no accessible default constructor available on Class A for Class B's compiler-provided default constructor to call. In order for the previous example to compile, either you need to explicitly provide a default constructor for Class A, or Class B needs an explicit constructor.

Destroying Objects

The CLR environment contains a garbage collector, which manages memory on your behalf. You can create new objects all day long, but you never have to worry about freeing their memory explicitly. Garbage collection eliminates bugs and application crashes that come from memory allocation/deallocation mismatches, otherwise known as memory leaks. Garbage collection is a technique meant to avoid those types of bugs, since the execution environment now handles the tracking of object references and destroys the object instances when they're no longer in use.

The CLR tracks every managed object reference in the system. Once the CLR realizes that an object is no longer reachable via a reference, it flags the object for deletion. The next time the garbage collector compacts the heap, these flagged objects either have their memory reclaimed or are moved over into a queue for deletion if they have a finalizer. It is the responsibility of another thread, the finalizer thread, to iterate over this queue of objects and call their finalizers before freeing their memory. Once the finalizers have completed, the memory for the object is freed on the next collection pass and the object is destroyed.

Finalizers

Like the constructor New(), the destructor Finalize() is created implicitly when you create an object and, by default, doesn't do anything. When used flagrantly and unnecessarily, finalizers can degrade the performance of the CLR because finalizable objects live longer than their nonfinalizable counterparts. Even allocating finalizable objects is more costly. Finalizers are difficult to write because you cannot make any assumptions about the state other objects in the system are in. When the finalization thread iterates through the objects in the finalization queue, it calls the Finalize() method on each object. The Finalize() method has no return type and accepts no parameters.

Although the garbage collector now handles the task of cleaning up memory so that you don't have to worry about it, you have a whole new host of concerns to deal with when it comes to the destruction of objects. A short while ago, we mentioned that finalizers run on a separate thread in the CLR. Therefore, whatever objects you use inside your destructor must be thread-safe. You should not use other objects in your finalizer, as they may have already been finalized or destroyed. This includes objects that are fields of the class that contains the finalizer. You have no guaranteed way of knowing exactly when the garbage collector will call your finalizer or in what order the finalizer will be called between two independent objects. This is one more reason why you shouldn't introduce interdependencies on objects in the destructor code block. After all this dust has settled, it starts to become clear that you shouldn't do much inside a finalizer except basic housecleaning, if anything.

There are times when you should explicitly create a finalizer. For example, you should create a finalizer when your object manages some sort of unmanaged resource. Finally, any object that has a finalizer should implement the Disposable pattern, which the upcoming section titled "Disposable Objects" covers.

Exception Handling

In VB, the runtime will treat an exception thrown in a finalizer that leaves the block uncaught as an unhandled exception, and by default, the process will terminate after notifying you of the exception.

Disposable Objects

Any object that has a finalizer must implement the IDisposable interface. IDisposable is not a perfect replacement for any type of deterministic finalization, but it does get the job done at the expense of adding complexity to the client of your objects.

The IDisposable Interface

The IDisposable definition is as follows:

```
Public Interface IDisposable
    Sub Dispose()
End Interface
```

Notice that it has only one method, Dispose(), and it is within this method's implementation that the dirty work is done. Thus you should completely clean up your object and release all resources inside Dispose(). Even though the client code rather than the system calls Dispose() automatically, it's the client code's way of saying, "I'm done with this object and don't intend to use it ever again."

Even though the IDisposable pattern provides a form of deterministic destruction, it is not a perfect solution. Using IDisposable, the onus is thrown on the client to ensure that the Dispose method is called. There is no way for the client to rely upon the system, or the compiler, to call it automatically.

When you implement Dispose(), you normally implement the class in such a way that the finalizer code reuses Dispose(). This way, if the client code never calls Dispose(), the finalizer code will take care of it at finalization time. Another factor that makes implementing IDisposable challenging for objects is that you must chain calls of IDisposable if your object contains references to other objects that support IDisposable. This makes designing classes a little more difficult, since you must know whether a class that you use for a field type implements IDisposable; and if it does, you must implement IDisposable, and you must make sure to call its Dispose method inside yours.

Given all of this discussion regarding IDisposable, you can definitely start to see how the garbage collector adds complexity to design, even though it reduces the chance for memory bugs. Let's look at an example implementation of IDisposable:

```vbnet
Imports System

Public Class A
    Implements IDisposable

    Private Disposed As Boolean = False

    Public Sub Dispose(ByVal Disposing As Boolean)
        If Not Disposed Then
            If Disposing Then
                'It is safe to access other objects here.
            End If

            Console.WriteLine("Cleaning up object")
            Disposed = True
        End If
    End Sub

    Public Sub Dispose() Implements System.IDisposable.Dispose
        Dispose(True)
        GC.SuppressFinalize(Me)
    End Sub

    Public Sub DoSomething()
        Console.WriteLine("A.DoSomething()")
    End Sub

    Protected Overrides Sub Finalize()
        Console.WriteLine("Finalizing")
        Dispose(False)
    End Sub
End Class

Public Class EntryPoint
    Shared Sub Main()
        Dim objA As A = New A

        Try
            objA.DoSomething()
        Finally
            objA.Dispose()
        End Try
    End Sub
End Class
```

This example will display the following results to the console:

```
A.DoSomething()
Cleaning up object
```

The first thing to notice in the class is an internal Boolean field that registers whether or not the object has been disposed. It's there because it's perfectly legal for client code to call `Dispose()` multiple times. Therefore, you need some way to know that you've done the work already.

You'll also see that the code implements the finalizer in terms of the `Dispose()` implementation. It contains two overloads of `Dispose()`. This lets you know inside the `Dispose(Boolean)` method whether you've got here through `IDisposable.Dispose()` or through the destructor. It tells you whether you can safely access contained objects inside the method.

The `Dispose` method makes a call to `GC.SuppressFinalize()`. This method on the garbage collector allows you to keep the garbage collector from finalizing an object. If the client code calls `Dispose()`, and if the `Dispose` method completely cleans up all resources, including all the work a finalizer would have done, then there is no need for this object to ever be finalized. You can call `SuppressFinalize()` to keep this object from being finalized. This handy optimization helps the garbage collector get rid of your object in a timely manner when all references to it cease to exist.

Now, let's take a look at how to use this disposable object. Notice the `Try/Finally` block within the `Main` method. The `Try/Finally` construct is a way of guaranteeing that certain code will be executed no matter how a code block exits.[2] Regardless of how the execution flow leaves the `Try` block—whether it be normally, through a return statement, or even by exception—the code in the `Finally` block will execute. View the `Finally` block as a sort of safety net. It is within this `Finally` block that you call `Dispose()` on the object. No matter what, `Dispose()` will get called.

This is a perfect example of how nondeterministic finalization throws the onus on the client code, or the user, to clean up the object, whereas deterministic finalization doesn't require the use of `Try/Finally` blocks or to call `Dispose()`. The designers of VB have tried to lessen this load by overloading the `Using` keyword. Although it lessens the load, it doesn't remove the burden put on the client code altogether.

The Using Keyword

The `Using` keyword was added to support the `IDisposable` pattern. The general idea is that the `Using` statement acquires the resources following the `Using` keyword, while the scope of these local variables is confined to the `Using` block. Implementing the `Using` keyword guarantees that the `Dispose` method will be called after the statements in the `Using` block are executed, even if an unhandled error occurs.

Let's take a look at a modified form of the previous example:

```
Imports System

Public Class A
    Implements IDisposable
```

2. Chapter 8 discusses the `Try/Finally` construct in detail.

```vbnet
        Private Disposed As Boolean = False

        Public Sub Dispose(ByVal Disposing As Boolean)
            If Not Disposed Then
                If Disposing Then
                    'It is safe to access other objects here.
                End If

                Console.WriteLine("Cleaning up object")
                Disposed = True
            End If
        End Sub

        Public Sub Dispose() Implements System.IDisposable.Dispose
            Dispose(True)
            GC.SuppressFinalize(Me)
        End Sub

        Public Sub DoSomething()
            Console.WriteLine("A.DoSomething()")
        End Sub

        Protected Overrides Sub Finalize()
            Console.WriteLine("Finalizing")
            Dispose(False)
        End Sub
    End Class

    Public Class EntryPoint
        Shared Sub Main()
            Using objA As A = New A()
                objA.DoSomething()
            End Using

            Using objA As A = New A(), b As A = New A()
                objA.DoSomething()
                b.DoSomething()
            End Using
        End Sub
    End Class
```

Running this code will display the following to the console:

```
A.DoSomething()
Cleaning up object
A.DoSomething()
A.DoSomething()
Cleaning up object
Cleaning up object
```

The meat of the changes is in the Main method. Notice that you replace the Try/Finally construct with the cleaner Using statement. Behind the scenes, the Using statement expands to the Try/Finally construct you already had. While this code is much easier to read and understand, it still doesn't remove the burden from the client code of having to remember to use the Using statement in the first place.

The Using statement requires that all resources acquired in the acquisition process implement IDisposable. If they don't, you'll see a compiler warning.

Summary

This chapter covered the important points regarding the VB type system, which allows you to create new types that have all of the capabilities of implicit types defined by the runtime. We started out by covering class definitions used to define new reference types, then we followed that with structure definitions used to create instances of new value types within the CLR, and we described the major differences between the two. Related to the topic of value types is that of boxing and unboxing, which we showed can introduce unintended inefficiencies when you don't understand all of the places that the compiler can introduce boxing.

We then turned our attention to the complex topics of object creation and initialization, as well as object destruction. Destruction is a rather tricky topic in the CLR, since your reference types can support either deterministic destruction or nondeterministic destruction.

Chapter 4 will begin by exploring how methods are implemented in VB. After methods, we'll cover properties and fields, which allow you to control the state of your objects.

■ ■ ■

Methods, Properties, and Fields

A *method* defines a function or procedure that you can perform on an object or class. Methods are used to define an object's behavior and responsibilities. Methods can also be used to enforce business rules or operational logic.

Properties enable you to enforce encapsulation by controlling access to the internal state of your objects. Using properties, you can create specific implementations for each data member in your class, including validation logic. You can also enforce whether your properties are updatable or read-only.

Fields represent the actual data members of your class. Fields can represent private data, for use internally by your object, or accessible data. Fields that are meant to be accessible should be placed inside a property to control access to their values.

Methods

Methods come in two flavors: *shared* and *instance*. If the method is an instance method, you can call it on an object. If the method is a shared method, you can call it only on the class. The difference is that instance methods have access to the instance fields of the object instance, whereas shared methods don't have access to instance fields or methods. Shared methods can only access shared class members.

Methods can have metadata attributes attached to them, and they can also have optional modifiers attached. We discuss them throughout this chapter. These modifiers control the accessibility of the methods, as well as facets of the methods that are germane to inheritance. Every method may have a return type or parameters.

Shared Methods

You call shared methods on the class rather than on instances of the class. Shared methods only have access to the shared members of the class. You declare a method as shared by using the Shared modifier, as in the following example:

```
Public Class A
    Public Shared Sub SomeFunction()
        System.Console.WriteLine("SomeFunction() called")
    End Sub
```

```
    Shared Sub Main()
        A.SomeFunction()
        SomeFunction()
    End Sub
End Class
```

Running the preceding code example displays the following:

```
SomeFunction() called
SomeFunction() called
```

Notice that both methods in this example are shared. In the Main method, you first access the SomeFunction method using the class name. You then call the shared method without qualifying it. This is because the Main and SomeFunction methods are both defined in the same class and are both shared methods. Had SomeFunction() been in another class, say Class B, then you would have had no choice but to reference the method as B.SomeFunction.

Instance Methods

Instance methods operate on objects. In order to call an instance method, you need a reference to an instance of the class that defines the method. The following example shows the use of an instance method:

```
Public Class A
    Public x As Integer
    Public y As Integer
    Public Shared z As Integer

    Public Sub SomeOperation()
        x = 1
        Me.y = 2
        A.z = 3
    End Sub
End Class

Public Class EntryPoint
    Shared Sub Main()
        Dim obj As A = New A()

        obj.SomeOperation()
        System.Console.WriteLine("x = {0}, y = {1}, z = {2}", obj.x, obj.y, A.z)
    End Sub
End Class
```

Running the preceding code displays the following result:

```
x = 1, y = 2, z = 3
```

In the Main method, you create a new instance of Class A and then call the SomeOperation method through the instance of that class. Within the method body of SomeOperation(), you have access to the instance (x, y) and shared (z) fields of the class, and you can assign to them simply by using their identifiers. Even though the SomeOperation method can assign the shared field z without qualifying it, it makes for more readable code if the assignment of shared fields is qualified by the class name, even in the methods of the same class. Doing so is helpful for that special someone who comes after you and has to maintain your code. And that special someone could be you!

Notice that when you assign to y, you do so through the Me identifier. You should note a few important things about Me when used within an instance method body. It is treated as a read-only reference whose type is that of the class. Using Me, you can access the fields of the instance, as the previous example shows when assigning the value of y. Because Me is a read-only value, you may not assign it. If you try to do so, VB will display a "'Me' cannot be the target of an assignment" error.

Method Parameter Types

Method parameters declare a variable identifier that is valid for the duration and scope of the method itself. Unless the parameter is declared as a ByRef parameter, such reassignment will remain local to the method. Arguments, by default, are passed by value.

ByVal Arguments

Parameters passed to methods are value arguments, unless you attach the ByRef or ParamArray keywords to them. A ByVal parameter is in scope within the method block following the parameter list, and the method receives a copy of the passed variable at invocation time. Be careful by what this means, though. If the passed variable is a structure or value type, then the method will receive a copy of the value. The caller does not see any changes made locally to the value.

ByRef Arguments

If the passed variable is a reference to an object on the heap, as any variable for a class instance is, then the method will receive a copy of the *reference*. Thus the caller of the method sees any changes made to the object through the reference. Placing the ByRef modifier ahead of the parameter type in the parameter list for the method indicates passing parameters by reference. When a variable is passed by reference, a new copy of the variable is not made, and the caller's variable is directly affected by any actions within the method. As is usually the case in the common language runtime (CLR), this means two slightly different things, depending on whether the variable is an instance of a value type (structure) or an object (class).

When a value or object instance is passed by reference, no copy of the variable is made, which means that a new reference to the object on the heap is not created. Additionally, the verifier ensures that the variable referenced by the ByRef parameter has been definitely assigned before the method call. Let's take a look at some examples to put the entire notion of ByRef parameters into perspective:

```vbnet
Imports System

Public Structure MyStruct
    Public val As Integer
End Structure

Public Class EntryPoint
    Shared Sub Main()
        Dim myValue As MyStruct = New MyStruct()

        myValue.val = 10
        PassByValue(myValue)
        Console.WriteLine("Result of PassByValue: myValue.val = {0}", myValue.val)

        PassByRef(myValue)
        Console.WriteLine("Result of PassByRef: myValue.val = {0}", myValue.val)
    End Sub

    Shared Sub PassByValue(ByVal myValue As MyStruct)
        myValue.val = 50
    End Sub

    Shared Sub PassByRef(ByRef myValue As MyStruct)
        myValue.val = 42
    End Sub
End Class
```

The previous example contains two methods: PassByValue() and PassByRef(). Both methods modify a field of the value type instance passed in. However, as the following output shows, the PassByValue method modifies a local copy, whereas the PassByRef method modifies the caller's instance as you would expect:

```
Result of PassByValue: myValue.val = 10
Result of PassByRef: myValue.val = 42
```

The ByRef keyword is required at the point of call into the PassByRef method. The ByRef keyword at the point of call also makes the code easier to read. When others read the code at the point of call, they know that the method could make some changes to the object being passed by ByRef.

Now, let's consider an example that uses an object rather than a value type:

```vbnet
Imports System

Public Class EntryPoint
    Shared Sub Main()
        Dim myObject As Object = New Object()
```

```
        Console.WriteLine("myObject.GetHashCode() == {0}", myObject.GetHashCode())
        PassByRef(myObject)
        Console.WriteLine("myObject.GetHashCode() == {0}", myObject.GetHashCode())
    End Sub

    Shared Sub PassByRef(ByRef myObject As Object)
        'Assign a new instance to the variable.
        myObject = New Object()
    End Sub
End Class
```

In this case, the variable passed by a reference is a reference type. Instead of the method receiving a copy of the reference, thus creating a new reference to the same object, the original reference is referenced instead. Yes, this can be confusing. In the PassByRef method, the reference passed in is reassigned with a new object instance. The original object is left with no references to it, so it is now available for garbage collection. To illustrate that the myObject variable references two different instances between the point before it is called and the point after it is called, we sent the results of myObject.GetHashCode(), which returns the hash code for each instance, to the console to demonstrate.

ParamArray

VB makes it a snap to pass a variable list of parameters. Simply declare the last parameter in your parameter list as an array type and precede the array type with the ParamArray keyword. Now, if the method is invoked with a variable number of parameters, those parameters are passed to the method in the form of an array that you can easily iterate through, and the array type that you use can be based on any valid type. Here's a short example:

```
Imports System

Public Class EntryPoint
    Shared Sub Main()
        VarArgs(42)
        VarArgs(42, 43, 44)
        VarArgs(44, 56, 23, 234, 45, 123)
    End Sub

    Shared Sub VarArgs(ByVal val1 As Integer, ByVal ParamArray vals As Integer())
        Console.WriteLine("val1: {0}", val1)

        For Each i As Integer In vals
            Console.WriteLine("vals[]: {0}", i)
        Next

        Console.WriteLine()
    End Sub
End Class
```

Here are the results from the previous example:

```
val1: 42

val1: 42
vals[]: 43
vals[]: 44

val1: 44
vals[]: 56
vals[]: 23
vals[]: 234
vals[]: 45
vals[]: 123
```

In each case, VarArgs() is called successfully, but also in each case, the array referenced by the vals parameter is a different size. As you can see, referencing a variable number of parameters is pretty easy. You can code an efficient Add method to a container type using parameter arrays where you need only one call to add a variable number of items.

Method Overloading

VB method overloading is a compile-time technique in which, at a call point, the compiler chooses a method from a set of methods with the same name. The compiler uses the argument list of the method to choose the method that fits best. Methods without variable-length parameter arrays get preference over those with such arrays. The method return type is part of the signature as well, but the return type cannot be the only difference. If the compiler gets to a point where multiple methods are ambiguous with regard to overloading, it stops with an error.

Method overloading cannot cause runtime exceptions because the entire algorithm is applied at compile time. When the compiler fails to find an exact match based on the parameters given, it then starts hunting for a best match based on implicit convertibility of the instances in the parameter list. Thus if a single parameter method accepts an object of type A, and you have passed an object of type B that is derived from type A, in the absence of a method that accepts type B, the compiler will implicitly convert your instance into a type A reference to satisfy the method call. Depending on the situation and the size of the overloaded method set, the selection process can still be a tricky one. It's usually best to minimize too many confusing overloads where implicit conversion is necessary to satisfy the resolution. Too many implicit conversions can make code difficult to follow, requiring you to actually execute it in a debugger to see what happens. That's not to say that implicit conversion is bad during overload resolution; just use it judiciously and sparingly.

Overridable and MustOverride Methods

VB implements the notion of Overridable (virtual) and MustOverride (abstract) methods, just as other object-oriented (OO) languages do. That's no surprise at all, since VB is an object-oriented language, and overridable methods are the primary mechanism for implementing dynamic polymorphism.

You declare an overridable method using the Overridable or MustOverride modifiers on the method at the point of declaration. They both introduce the method into the declaration space as one that a deriving class can override. The difference between the two is that MustOverride methods are required to be overridden, whereas Overridable methods are not. Overridable methods, in contrast to MustOverride methods, are required to have an implementation associated with them. Overridable methods, along with interfaces, are the only means of implementing polymorphism within VB.

Overrides and Shadows

To override a method in a derived class, you must tag the method with the Overrides modifier. If you don't, you'll get a compiler warning telling you that you need to provide either the Shadows modifier or the Overrides modifier in the derived method declaration. This requirement enhances code clarity. The following code illustrates this requirement:

```
Imports System

Public Class A
    Public Overridable Sub SomeMethod()
        Console.WriteLine("A.SomeMethod")
    End Sub
End Class

Public Class B
    Inherits A

    Public Sub SomeMethod()
        Console.WriteLine("B.SomeMethod")
    End Sub
End Class

Public Class EntryPoint
    Shared Sub Main()
        Dim objB As B = New B()
        Dim objA As A = objB

        objA.SomeMethod()
    End Sub
End Class
```

This code will run, but not without the following warning:

```
sub 'SomeMethod' shadows an overridable method in the base class 'A'.
To override the base method, this method must be declared 'Overrides'.
```

When the code is executed, A.SomeMethod() gets called. So what does the Shadows keyword do? It breaks the virtual chain at that point in the hierarchy. When calling an overridable method through an object reference, the method called is determined from a method lookup table at run time. If a method is overridable, the runtime searches down through the hierarchy looking for the most derived version of the method, and then it calls that one. However, during the search, if it encounters a method marked with the Shadows modifier, it backs up to the method of the previous class in the hierarchy and uses that one instead. That is why A.SomeMethod() is the method that gets called. Had B.SomeMethod() been marked as Overrides, then the code would have called B.SomeMethod() instead.

As VB defaults to using the Shadows modifier when no modifiers are present, it throws off the warning to get your attention. Finally, the Shadows modifier is in conflict with the Overridable modifier in meaning, in the sense that the method marked Shadows could either also be overridable or not. In the previous example, you did not also attach the Overridable modifier to B.SomeMethod(), so there cannot be a Class C derived from B that overrides B.SomeMethod(), since it's not overridable. Thus the Shadows keyword not only breaks the virtual chain, but it redefines whether the class and the derived classes from Class B will get an overridable SomeMethod().

Another issue to consider with regard to overriding methods is whether to call the base class version of the method and when. In VB, you call the base class version using the MyBase identifier, as shown:

```
Imports System

Public Class A
    Public Overridable Sub SomeMethod()
        Console.WriteLine("A.SomeMethod")
    End Sub
End Class

Public Class B
    Inherits A

    Public Overrides Sub SomeMethod()
        Console.WriteLine("B.SomeMethod")

        MyBase.SomeMethod()
    End Sub
End Class

Public Class EntryPoint
    Shared Sub Main()
        Dim objB As B = New B
        Dim objA As A = objB

        objA.SomeMethod()
    End Sub
End Class
```

The output of the previous code prints the following:

```
B.SomeMethod
A.SomeMethod
```

Inheritance with overridden methods can increase the amount of documentation that you should provide the consumers of your class. This documentation should include both public and protected methods, the overridable methods, and must clearly state whether the base class should call them and when.

If you follow the Non-Virtual Interface (NVI) pattern described in Chapter 14, the overridable method in question will be protected.

NotInheritable Methods

Reasons stated in the last chapter point out why you should seal your classes by default and only make classes inheritable in well-thought-out circumstances. Inheritance, coupled with overridable methods, can add a great deal of complexity to your classes. Therefore, when designing classes, we recommend that you create NotInheritable classes and document the public interface well. Consumers who need to extend the functionality can still do so, but through containment rather than inheritance. Extension through containment, coupled with interface definitions, is usually more powerful than class inheritance.

In rare instances, when you're deriving from a class with overridable methods, you may want to force the virtual chain for a specific method to end at your override. In other words, you don't want further derived classes to be able to override the overridable method. To do so, you also mark the method with the NotOverridable modifier. As is obvious from the name, it means that no further derived classes can override the method. They can, however, provide a method with the same signature, as long as the method is marked with the Shadows modifier, as discussed in the previous section. In fact, you could mark the shadowed method as overridable, thus starting a new virtual chain in the hierarchy. This is not the same as sealing the entire class, which doesn't even allow a class to derive from this one in the first place. Therefore, if the deriving class is marked as NotInheritable, then marking override methods within that class with NotOverridable is redundant.

A Final Few Words on Overridable Methods

Clearly, VB provides a lot of flexible keywords to make some interesting things happen when it comes to inheritance and overridable methods. However, just because the language provides them does not mean that it's wise to use them.

The Shadows modifier is a quick way to introduce some surprises into a class hierarchy. If you ever find yourself using that modifier on a method, you're most likely using a class in a way that it was not intended to be used. You could be deriving from a class that should have been marked NotInheritable in the first place.

Properties

Properties are one of the nicest mechanisms within VB and the CLR that enable you to enforce encapsulation. In short, you use properties to strictly control access to the internal state of an object.

A property, from the point of view of the client of the object, looks and behaves just like a public field. The notation to access a property is the same as that used to access a public field on the instance. However, a property doesn't have any associated storage space within the object, as a field does. Rather, a property is a shorthand notation for defining *accessors* used to read and write fields. The typical pattern is to provide access to a private field in a class through a public property.

Properties significantly enhance your flexibility as a class designer. For example, if a property represents the amount of table rows in a database table object, the table object can defer the computation of the value until the point where it is queried through a property. It knows when to compute the value because the client will call an accessor when it accesses the property.

Accessors

Accessors allow you to control access to the state of a class. Get accessors allow for read access, while Set accessors allow for write access to your properties. Accessors can provide read-write, read-only, or write-only access to your properties. Beginning with Visual Basic 2005 (VB 2005), Get and Set accessors can have different accessibility levels, provided that the Set accessor is more restrictive.

Get blocks are called when the client of the object reads the property. This accessor must return a value or an object reference that matches the type of the property declaration. It can also return an object that is implicitly convertible to the type of the property declaration. For example, if the property type is a Long and the getter returns an Integer, the Integer will be implicitly converted to a Long without losing precision. Otherwise, the code in this block is just like a parameterless method that returns a value or reference of the same type as the property.

Set accessors are called when the client attempts to write to the property. Setters do not return a value. When you create a property in VB, it creates a variable named value in your setter that is the same type as that of the property declaration. When you write to the property, the value variable will have been set to the value or object reference that the client has attempted to assign to the property. The Set accessor is like a method that takes one parameter of the same type as the property.

Declaring Properties

As with most class members, you can attach metadata attributes to a property. Various modifiers that are valid for properties are similar to ones for methods. Other modifiers include the ability to declare a property as Shared, NotInheritable, Overrides, MustOverride, and so on.

The following code defines a property, Temperature, in Class A:

```
Public Class A
    Private mTemperature As Integer

    Public Property Temperature() As Integer
        Get
            System.Console.WriteLine("Getting value for temperature")
            Return mTemperature
        End Get
```

```
        Set(ByVal value As Integer)
            System.Console.WriteLine("Setting value for temperature")
            mTemperature = value
        End Set
    End Property
End Class

Public Class EntryPoint
    Shared Sub Main()
        Dim obj As A = New A()

        obj.Temperature = 1
        System.Console.WriteLine("obj.Temperature = {0}", obj.Temperature)
    End Sub
End Class
```

Running the previous code displays the following output to the console:

```
Setting value for temperature
Getting value for temperature
obj.Temperature = 1
```

The first thing we did in Class A was to define a property named Temperature, which has a type of Integer. Each property declaration must define the type that the property represents. That type should be visible to the compiler at the point where it is declared in the class, and it should have at least the same accessibility as the property being defined. For instance, if a property is public, the type of the value that the property represents must at least be public.

Temperature is the name clients will refer to when using the property, as if it were a field. The example merely returns the private field mTemperature from the internal state of the object instance.

Read-Only, Write-Only, and Read-Write Properties

If you define a property with only a Get accessor, that property will be read-only. Likewise, if you define a property with only a Set accessor, you'll end up with a write-only property. And lastly, a property with both accessors is a read-write property.

You may be wondering why a read-only property is any better or worse than a read-only public field. At first thought, it may seem that a read-only property is less efficient than a read-only public field. However, the just-in-time (JIT) compiler will optimize the code to access the property. In the case where the property simply returns a private field, this argument of inefficiency does not hold. While writing the code seems to be inefficient, VB can automatically generate the property code for any chosen field.

In most cases, a read-only property is more flexible than a read-only public field. One reason is that you can defer a read-only property's computation until the point where you need it. So, in reality, it could provide for more efficient code, when the property is meant to represent something that takes significant time to compute. If using a read-only public field for this purpose, the computation would have to happen in the block of the constructor. All the necessary data to make the computation may not even be available at that point. Or you may waste time in the constructor computing the value when the user of the object may not ever access the value.

Read-only properties help enforce encapsulation. If you originally had a choice between a read-only property and a read-only public field, and you chose the read-only property, you would have had greater flexibility in future versions of the class to do extra work at the point where the property is accessed without affecting the client. For example, imagine if you wanted to do some sort of logging in debug builds each time the property is accessed. The client would effectively be calling a method implicitly, albeit one of the special property methods, to access the data. The flexibility of things that you can do in that method is almost limitless. Had you accessed the value as a public read-only field, you wouldn't call a method or be able to do anything without switching it over to a property and forcing the client code to recompile.

Fields

Fields are the bread and butter that make up the state of objects. Typically, you declare a new class only if you need to model some new type of object with its own custom internal state, represented by its fields.

You declare fields with a type, just like other variables. The possible field modifiers are as follows:

```
Public
Protected
Friend
Protected Friend
Private
Shared
Const
ReadOnly
```

Many of these are mutually exclusive. Those that are mutually exclusive control the accessibility of the field and consist of the modifiers `Public`, `Protected`, `Friend`, and `Private`.

The `Shared` modifier controls whether a field is static or nonstatic. In the absence of the `Shared` modifier, a field is an *instance* field, and thus each object created from the class has its own copy of the field. This is the default. When decorated with the `Shared` modifier, the field is shared among all objects of a class on a per-application-domain basis.

Shared fields are not included in the memory footprint of the object instances. In other words, objects don't encapsulate the shared fields; rather, classes encapsulate the shared fields. It would be inefficient for all instances of the object to contain a copy of the same shared variable in their memory footprint. And worse than that, the compiler would have to generate some sort of code to make sure that when the shared field is changed for one instance, it would change the field in all instances. For this reason, the shared fields actually belong to the class and not to the object instances. In fact, when a shared field is publicly accessible outside the class, you use the class name and not the object instance variable to access the field.

■Note Shared fields have another important quality: they are global to the application domain within which their containing types are loaded. Application domains are an abstraction that is similar to the process abstraction within an operating system, but it's a lighter-weight mechanism. You can have multiple application domains in one operating system process. If your CLR process contains multiple application domains, each application domain will have a copy of the class's shared fields. A shared field's value in one application domain can be different from the same shared field in another application domain. Unless you create extra application domains yourself, your application will have only one application domain: the default application domain. However, this distinction is important when working in environments such as ASP.NET, where the concept of the application domain is used as the isolation mechanism between two ASP.NET applications.

Another field modifier that comes in handy from time to time is the ReadOnly modifier. As you can guess, it defines the field so you can only read from it. You can write to it only during object creation. You can emulate the same behavior with greater flexibility using a read-only *property*. Shared ReadOnly fields are initialized in a shared constructor, while instance ReadOnly fields are initialized in an instance constructor. Alternatively, you can initialize ReadOnly fields using initializers at the point of their declaration in the class definition, just as you can do with other fields. Only within the constructor can you pass the ReadOnly field as a ByRef parameter to another function. Consider the following example:

```
Public Class A
    Private ReadOnly x As Integer = 123
    Private ReadOnly y As Integer
    Public Const z As Integer = 555

    Public Sub New()
        Me.y = 456
        'We can set y again.
        Me.y = 654

        'Here, we use y as a ByRef parameter.
        SetField(Me.y)
    End Sub

    Private Sub SetField(ByRef val As Integer)
        val = 888
    End Sub

    Shared Sub Main()
        Dim obj As A = New A()

        System.Console.WriteLine("x = {0}, y = {1}, z = {2}", obj.x, obj.y, A.z)
    End Sub
End Class
```

This code example will display the following to the console when run:

```
x = 123, y = 888, z = 555
```

You should note one important nuance in the previous example: the z field is declared using the Const keyword. At first, it may seem that it has the same effect as a ReadOnly field, but it does not. First, a Const field such as this is known and used at compile time. What this means is that the code generated by the compiler in the Main routine can be optimized to where all uses of this variable are replaced with its immediate Const value. The compiler is free to use this performance trick, simply because the value of the field is known at compile time. You access the Const field using the class name rather than the instance name. This is because Const values are implicitly shared and don't affect the memory footprint, or shape, of the object instances. Again, this makes sense because the compiler would optimize away access to that memory slot in the object instance anyway, since it would be the same for all instances of this object.

ReadOnly fields are guaranteed to be computed at run time. Suppose you have one class with both a ReadOnly field and a Const field that lives in assembly A, and code in assembly B creates and uses an instance of that class in assembly A. Now, suppose you rebuild assembly A at a later date, and you modify the field initializers for the ReadOnly field and the Const field. The consumer in assembly B would only see the change in the Const field, unless you recompile the code in assembly B first. This behavior is expected because, when assembly B was built referencing the initial incarnation of assembly A, the compiler optimized the use of the Const values by inserting the literal value into the generated intermediate language (IL) code. Because of this, you need to be careful when deciding whether to use a ReadOnly field or a Const value, and if you choose to use a ReadOnly field, you need to choose carefully between using a ReadOnly field or a read-only property, which the "Properties" section introduced earlier. Properties provide greater design-time and maintenance-time flexibility over ReadOnly fields.

Field Initialization

Initialization of fields can occur during object creation in various ways. One straightforward way of initializing fields is through *initializers*. You use these initializers at the point where you define the field and can use it for both shared or instance fields. For example:

```
Private x As Integer = 789
Private y As Integer
Private z As Integer = A.InitZ()
```

The field x is initialized using an initializer. The notation is rather convenient. Note that this initialization occurs at run time and not at compile time. Therefore, this initialization statement could have used something other than a constant. For example, the variable z is initialized by calling a method, A.InitZ(). At first, this field initialization notation may seem like a great shortcut, saving you from having to initialize all of the fields inside the body of the constructor. However, unless absolutely necessary, you shouldn't initialize instance fields within the instance constructor body. The "Creating Objects" section of Chapter 3 covered shared and instance initialization in detail and demonstrated why initializing fields in the constructor can facilitate code that's easier to maintain and debug. When defining a class, it is sometimes convenient to assign a field a value at the point where the field is declared. The fact is, you can assign a field from any immediate value or any callable method as long as the method is not called on the instance of the object being created. For example, you can initialize fields based upon the return value from a shared method on the same class. Let's look at an example:

```
Imports System

Public Class A
    Private y As Integer = InitY()
    Private x As Integer = InitX()
    Private Shared a As Integer = InitA()
    Private Shared b As Integer = InitB()

    Private Shared Function InitX() As Integer
        Console.WriteLine("A.InitX()")
        Return 1
    End Function

    Private Shared Function InitY() As Integer
        Console.WriteLine("A.InitY()")
        Return 2
    End Function

    Private Shared Function InitA() As Integer
        Console.WriteLine("A.InitA()")
        Return 3
    End Function

    Private Shared Function InitB() As Integer
        Console.WriteLine("A.InitB()")
        Return 4
    End Function
End Class

Public Class EntryPoint
    Shared Sub Main()
        Dim objA As A = New A
    End Sub
End Class
```

The output from the preceding code is as follows:

```
A.InitA()
A.InitB()
A.InitY()
A.InitX()
```

Notice that you're assigning all of the fields using field initializers and setting the fields to the return value from the methods called. All of those methods called during field initialization are shared, which helps reinforce a couple of important points regarding field initialization. Two of the fields, a and b, are shared fields, whereas the fields x and y are instance fields. The runtime initializes the shared fields before the class type is used for the first time in this application domain.

During construction of the instance, the instance field initializers are invoked. As expected, proof of that appears in the console output after the shared field initializers have run. Notice the ordering of the output regarding the instance initializers, and compare that with the ordering of the fields declared in the class itself. You'll see that field initialization, whether it's shared or instance initialization, occurs in the order in which the fields are listed in the class definition. Sometimes this ordering can be important if your shared fields are based on expressions or methods that expect other fields in the same class to be initialized first. If initialization ordering matters, you should consider initializing all of your fields in the body of the shared constructor.

VB has rules about default field initialization that are applied before any field initialization code occurs in the constructor method's code block. By default, VB creates verifiably type-safe code, which is guaranteed not to use uninitialized variables and fields. The compiler goes to great lengths to ensure that this requirement is satisfied. For example, it initializes all fields, whether they're instance or shared fields, to a default value before any of your variable initializers execute. The default value for just about anything can easily be represented by either the value 0 or Nothing. For example, you can initialize an integer or any other similar value type by setting all of the bits in its storage space to 0. For reference types, you set the initial default value to Nothing. Again, this is usually the result of the implementation setting all of the bits of the reference to 0. These default initializations occur before any code executes on the instance or class. Therefore, it's impossible to inspect the uninitialized values of an object or class during initial construction.

Summary

This chapter introduced shared and instance methods, properties as a means to enforce encapsulation, and fields to represent the state of an object. For methods, we explored parameter types and overloading. Turning our attention to properties, we declared properties with their appropriate modifiers and experimented with read-only, write-only, and read-write properties. Finally, we created fields, controlled their accessibility, and used field initializers to set their values.

In Chapter 5, we'll dive into the details of the CLR, how compilation works, and how to program assemblies in VB.

CHAPTER 5

∎ ∎ ∎

VB 2008 and the CLR

In this chapter, we'll look at the .NET runtime, called the common language runtime (CLR), and how it compiles and executes your code. In order to master Visual Basic (VB) development, it is important to understand the components that comprise the CLR and how they work. This helps you write more optimized code that performs better. In addition, understanding how the CLR manages objects in memory helps you troubleshoot any performance issues that may arise. We'll look at how VB is compiled and then how compilation to native code works. Finally, we'll look at the assemblies and metadata—information about those assemblies—which the compiler creates.

VB applications are called *managed applications* because they are managed by the .NET runtime, the CLR. The CLR is an implementation of the Common Language Infrastructure (CLI) standard. The CLI is a specification published by Ecma International, which defines the rules that a development infrastructure must follow in order to provide cross-language compatibility and platform independence. According to the specification, it defines the CLI "in which applications written in multiple high-level languages may be executed in different system environments without the need to rewrite the applications to take into consideration the unique characteristics of those environments."

The CLR is more than just a virtual execution system; it also provides services such as memory management, code safety verification, security, and a strict system of data typing, called the common type system (CTS). The just-in-time (JIT) compiler that translates intermediate language (IL) into CPU-specific assemblies is also part of the CLR.

From VB to IL

The first thing that happens after you write VB code is that the VB compiler, vbc.exe, takes that code and generates IL. These generated files end with the familiar EXE or DLL extension, can be run on multiple platforms, and contain their own metadata. The VB compiler, and any .NET language compiler for that matter, generates IL that must follow certain rules. This is where true language independence begins. Because IL follows certain rules, the CLR can understand IL generated from any high-level language. Hence, the CLR can understand code written in Visual Basic .NET (VB .NET), C# .NET, and even COBOL .NET, once it's compiled into IL.

The .NET Framework SDK comes with a disassembler utility called the IL Disassembler (IL DASM). This utility allows you to peer into your .NET binaries and see the IL that they contain. You can run the disassembler by navigating to All Programs ➤ Microsoft Windows SDK for Visual Studio ➤ Tools ➤ IL Disassembler. Figure 5-1 shows a screenshot of the utility displaying HelloWorld.exe.

Figure 5-1. *"HelloWorld" displayed with the IL Disassembler*

If you run the utility, it displays a tree view of the type data from the assembly. You can also export the IL to a file by performing a dump via the File ➤ Dump menus. As the following code for HelloWorld.exe shows, IL looks similar to assembly language; in essence, it's the assembly language of the CLR:

```
.method /*06000012*/ public static void
        Main() cil managed
{
  .entrypoint
  .custom /*0C000045:0A00001F*/ instance void . . . ( 01 00 00 00 )
  // Code size       14 (0xe)
  .maxstack  8
```

```
// Source File 'C:\ AVB 9.0\HelloWorld\HelloWorld.vb'
//000002:      Shared Sub Main()
   IL_0000:  nop
//000003:          System.Console.WriteLine("Hello World!")
   IL_0001:  ldstr      "Hello World!" /* 70000001 */
   IL_0006:  call       void . . . System.Console::WriteLine(string) /*0A00001E*/
   IL_000b:  nop
//000004:      End Sub
   IL_000c:  nop
   IL_000d:  ret
 } // end of method EntryPoint::Main
```

As you scroll through the IL file, you'll see that it completely describes the program in a low-level manner. The IL for an application written in VB will look very similar to the IL generated by other .NET languages.

From IL to Platform

When your program runs, the CLR must take one more step and translate the IL into platform-specific instructions that can be understood by the particular CPU architecture on which it's running. The process of compiling IL into platform-specific instructions is called *JIT compiling*. The CLR has a JIT compiler for all CPU architectures it supports, so each time you run HelloWorld.exe on a standard Windows computer, the CLR JIT compiler compiles the IL into instructions for the architecture being used. Needless to say, if your code relies on platform-specific libraries or calls any platform-specific APIs, it will only run on that particular architecture.

JIT compiling means a performance hit is incurred each time you run your application. The way JIT works, only the code being executed is compiled, and the loader creates a stub for any unused methods. Then when a previously unused method is called, the stub triggers the JIT compiler to convert that stub into native code. Once code is JIT-compiled, the CLR holds onto it and simply executes the native version the next time it's needed. Although the JIT compilation phase adds some complexity and has an initial runtime performance penalty associated with it, the benefits of a JIT compiler coupled with the CLR can outweigh the time penalty of JIT compiling because

- Managed applications can consume far less memory because, in general, IL code has a smaller footprint than native code. In other words, the "working set" of managed applications is normally smaller than native applications.

- Only code that is called gets JIT-compiled.

- The CLR keeps track of the frequency of calls. If it sees that a JIT-compiled code section has not been called in a long time, it can free the space occupied by it. The code will be recompiled if it's called again.

The CLR may also perform optimizations at run time, unlike native applications, where these optimizations are defined at compile time. Since final compilation occurs at run time in the CLR, optimizations can be applied at any time. If it's the case that the CLR can compile code faster with fewer optimizations, it will default to doing it that way. For code that's called frequently, the CLR can recompile such code with more optimizations turned on, allowing the compiled code to execute faster. For example, the CLR efficiency model can be vastly different depending on how many CPUs exists on the target platform. For native applications, you must do more manual work, either at run time or compile time, to accommodate such a situation. But multi-CPU performance enhancements come for free with the CLR. Additionally, if the CLR determines that different parts of code, scattered all over the application, are called rather frequently, it will move them into memory so that they are located in the same group of memory pages. This minimizes the amount of page faults and increases the cache hits as the application runs.

Understanding Assemblies

An assembly is a self-describing, discrete unit of reusable code within the CLR. Typically, an assembly is an EXE or DLL and is similar in nature to an EXE or DLL in the unmanaged world, but that's where the similarities end. Each assembly in the .NET world consists of the following:

- Header information
- IL
- Metadata
- Manifest

As you saw previously, the primary component of an assembly is IL, which is compiled on the fly by the JIT compiler. Each assembly has a version attached to it, allowing multiple assemblies with the same name but different versions to be separately identifiable. Each assembly must also contain header information that provides information about the assembly to the CLR. The header contains details about versions, entry points, metadata, and other low-level details. You can see the assembly header information if you run the IL Disassembler and select View ➤ Headers. The following shows you abbreviated header information for HelloWorld.exe:

```
----- DOS Header:
Magic:                     0x5a4d
Bytes on last page:        0x0090
Pages in file:             0x0003
. . .
----- PE Optional Header (32 bit):
Magic:                     0x010b
Major linker version:      0x08
Minor linker version:      0x00
Size of code:              0x00002000
. . .
 Image sections:
             .text
             0x00001804 Virtual Size
             0x00002000 Virtual Address
. . .
 Base Relocation Table
             0x00003000 Page RVA
             0x0000000c Block Size
             0x00000002 Number of Entries
```

```
 . . .
 Import Address Table
     DLL : mscoree.dll
               0x00002000 Import Address Table
               0x000037ee Import Name Table
               0          Time Date Stamp
 . . .
 Delay Load Import Address Table
// No data.
 Entry point code:
FF 25 00 20 40 00
 ----- CLR Header:
 Header size:                      0x00000048
 Major runtime version:            0x0002
 Minor runtime version:            0x0005
 0x0000239c [0x0000140c] address [size] of Metadata Directory:
 Flags:                            0x00000001
 Entry point token:                0x06000012
 0x000022e3 [0x000000b8] address [size] of Resources Directory:
 . . .
Metadata Header
    Storage Signature:
               0x424a5342 Signature
                  0x0001 Major Version
 . . .
     0x00000f0909a21557 MaskValid
     0x000016003301fa00 Sorted
Export Address Table Jumps:
// No data.
```

The MANIFEST line lists all the modules associated with the assembly as well as any external modules that the assembly references. You can see the assembly manifest in IL DASM by double-clicking on the MANIFEST line. The first thing you'll see is references to all the external assemblies that are required by the program. The Microsoft Core Library (mscorlib) assembly contains core managed types that must be included in every project. Microsoft.VisualBasic provides VB programmers with many constants and methods unique to VB, such as the UCase method, and constants such as vbCrLf. Finally, System includes many base classes for data types, event handlers, interfaces, and exceptions. The following shows a listing of this section:

```
// Metadata version: v2.0.50727
.assembly extern mscorlib
{
  .publickeytoken = (B7 7A 5C 56 19 34 E0 89 )                  // .z\V.4..
  .ver 2:0:0:0
}
.assembly extern Microsoft.VisualBasic
```

```
{
  .publickeytoken = (B0 3F 5F 7F 11 D5 0A 3A )              // .?_....:
  .ver 8:0:0:0
}
.assembly extern System
{
  .publickeytoken = (B7 7A 5C 56 19 34 E0 89 )              // .z\V.4..
  .ver 2:0:0:0
}
```

Assemblies also contain metadata. This metadata describes the contained types, such as classes, structures, and interfaces. It also contains information about methods and properties. The following is an abbreviated listing of the metadata for the Hello World! program. You can view the metadata in IL DASM by selecting View ➤ MetaInfo ➤ Show!

```
===============================================================
ScopeName : Hello World.exe
MVID      : {FD6E34EB-79C8-4645-A04C-2A6AC2B363DA}
===============================================================
Global functions
-------------------------------------------------------------


Global fields
-------------------------------------------------------------


Global MemberRefs
-------------------------------------------------------------


TypeDef #1 (02000002)
-------------------------------------------------------------
TypDefName: HelloWorld.My.MyApplication  (02000002)
Flags : [NotPublic] [AutoLayout] [Class] [AnsiClass]  (00000000)
Extends: 01000001 [TypeRef] . . . ApplicationServices.ConsoleApplicationBase
Method #1 (06000001)
-------------------------------------------------------------
MethodName: .ctor (06000001)
Flags: [Public] [ReuseSlot] [SpecialName] [RTSpecialName] [.ctor]  (00001806)
RVA: 0x00002108
ImplFlags: [IL] [Managed]  (00000000)
CallCnvntn: [DEFAULT]
hasThis
ReturnType: Void
No arguments.
CustomAttribute #1 (0c000001)
-------------------------------------------------------------
CustomAttribute Type: 0a000004
CustomAttributeName: . . . instance void .ctor()
```

```
Length: 4
Value : 01 00 00 00                                    >              <
ctor args: ()



CustomAttribute #1 (0c000011)
--------------------------------------------------------
    CustomAttribute Type: 0a000002
    CustomAttributeName: System.ComponentModel.EditorBrowsableAttribute . . .
. . .
CustomAttribute #2 (0c000012)
--------------------------------------------------------
    CustomAttribute Type: 0a000003
    CustomAttributeName: System.CodeDom.Compiler.GeneratedCodeAttribute . . .
    Length: 23
    Value : 01 00 0a 4d 79 54 65 6d  70 6c 61 74 65 07 38 2e >   MyTemplate 8.<
              : 30 2e 30 2e 30 00 00 >  0.0.0  <
    ctor args: ("MyTemplate_8.0.0.0", "8.0.0.0")
```

As discussed in Chapter 1, when you compile the Hello World! program, the result is an EXE file that is, in fact, an assembly. Managed assemblies are created using any managed language, and in most cases, managed assemblies can be consumed by any other managed language. Therefore, you can easily create complex systems developed with multiple languages. For example, when creating some low-level types, C++/CLI may be the most natural languages to get the job done. But it may make more sense to code the top-level user interface using VB.

Assembly Management

In the Hello World! example, the resultant assembly consists of only one file. However, assemblies can consist of multiple files. These files can include compiled modules, resources, and any other components listed in the assembly manifest. The assembly manifest is typically included in the main assembly module. It defines what pieces belong to the assembly and contains essential identification information, such as the producer's digital signature. By using this information, the assembly loader can determine, among other things, if an assembly is incomplete or has been tampered with.

Assemblies can be internally named in two ways, either strongly named or partially named. A strongly named assembly has a hash code built into its manifest that the loader can use to test the integrity of the assembly. Assembly names follow this convention:

- *Strongly (or fully) named*: An assembly that has a four-part name consisting of the short assembly name, a version number, a culture identifier in ISO format, and a hash token. If an assembly is named with all four parts, it is strongly named.

- *Partially named*: An assembly that contains only the short assembly name and a version number.

When a VB program launches, the CLR loads the assembly and starts executing the entry-point method. Of course, before it can do that, it must JIT-compile the entry-point method. At that stage, the CLR may have to resolve some external references to be able to JIT-compile the code. For example, if your entry-point method creates an instance of a class in an external assembly, the CLR must find and load the assembly that contains the referenced type before the JIT compiler can continue. However, since the CLR loads assemblies on demand, if you have a type that provides a method to print a document and it lives in a separate assembly from the main application assembly, then the separate assembly never gets loaded if the application never invokes the method. This keeps the working set of the application from growing unnecessarily large. When designing applications, it makes sense to segregate less commonly used features into separate assemblies so that they are only loaded when needed. Any time you can trim the working set of the application, you speed start-up time as well as shrink the memory footprint of the running application.

Private Assemblies

In the case of `HelloWorld.exe`, the assembly is deployed as a private assembly. Private assemblies must be located in its application directory or in a subdirectory of the application directory. In the assembly manifest, only the name and version are necessary for a private assembly. The following snippet shows the abbreviated manifest entry for the Hello World! assembly:

```
.assembly /*20000001*/ HelloWorld
{
. . .
  .hash algorithm 0x00008004
  .ver 1:0:0:0
}
```

Notice that, in comparison to the external assemblies (which are shared), there's no `publickeytoken` designation, and the version number is 1.0.0.0. These entries aren't needed because the assembly is private, and the CLR doesn't need to use the version number to resolve the location of the assembly; it assumes it's in the current application directory structure. To deploy a private assembly, all you need to do is copy all the files into a directory. This is referred to as XCopy deployment, and we recommend this approach for most of your applications.

Shared Assemblies and the Global Assembly Cache

A shared assembly contains the same elements as a private assembly with the difference that a single shared assembly can be used by other applications on that machine. For example, the Hello World! application needs an external assembly called `System`, which is contained in `System.dll`. It wouldn't make sense to have this file in every application directory that uses it, so shared assemblies are located in a single place. Shared assemblies are deployed to the global assembly cache (GAC).

The GAC, typically located in the `\windows\assembly` subdirectory, is a common area where .NET assemblies designed to be shared by multiple applications are stored. Assemblies installed in the GAC must be strongly named, and sharing assemblies allows multiple versions of the same assembly to be used. The GAC Explorer plug-in presents the GAC directory structure in your browser. If you navigate to the same directory by using a command prompt, you'll see the encoded directory names that the GAC uses to store the assemblies. Be sure not to tamper with this directory structure. Finally, installing an assembly into the GAC makes XCopy deployment unavailable, as you must move the assembly into the GAC when installing your application. Figure 5-2 shows the GAC listing. Notice that each assembly has a name, a version, a culture, and a public key token.

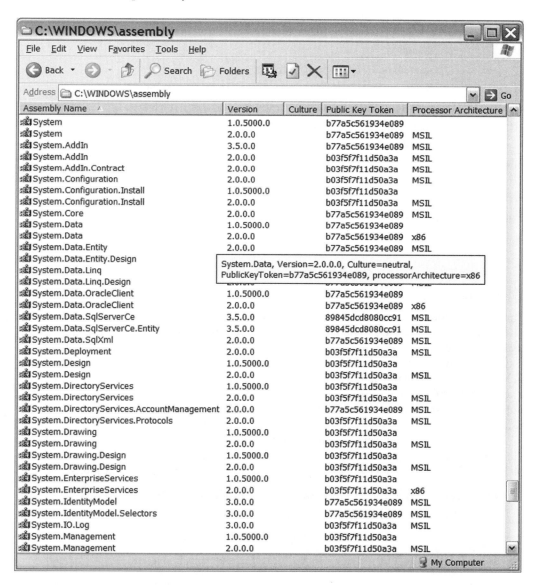

Figure 5-2. *Shared assemblies are located in the GAC.*

If the Culture column is blank for an assembly, it means that it's culture-neutral, which is common for assemblies that contain only code. If you develop applications that require localization, we recommend that you isolate all of the resources into a separate assembly that can be swapped out easily with a different culture without affecting the base code.

To deploy a shared assembly, use the command-line utility `gacutil.exe`. This utility is used to view, install, and uninstall assemblies in the GAC. Table 5-1 describes some of the available command-line switches that you can use with `gacutil.exe`.

Table 5-1. *gacutil.exe Command-Line Switches*

Switch	Meaning
/i	Install the assembly into the GAC.
/u	Remove the assembly from the GAC, if no other references to it exist.
/il	Use a text file containing assembly names to be installed.
/ul	Use a text file containing assembly names to be removed.
/l	Display a listing of installed assemblies.

■**Note** Using partially named assemblies with the /u or /ul switch may remove multiple assemblies.

Loading Assemblies

The assembly loader goes through a very detailed process, called *probing*, to load an assembly. The loader attempts to locate and load an assembly based on the exact version number in the manifest. However, you can direct the loader to load a different version of an assembly by specifying it in a config file, such as the application config file, the machine config file, or a publisher policy file (a file that directs an application to use a newer version of an assembly). The loader looks for partially named assemblies in the same directory as the running application or in a subdirectory. If an assembly is strongly named, then the loader will first search the GAC before probing local directories.

The assembly loader follows a certain process to locate the correct assembly during probing. This series of steps is quite detailed, and you can find more about how the runtime loads assemblies on Microsoft's developer website (see Appendix A), but here's the process in a nutshell:

1. The runtime first checks any config files for the correct version of the assembly that it's loading.

2. If the assembly has already been loaded, the runtime will use the loaded assembly.

3. The loader checks the GAC, and if it finds the assembly, it loads it.

4. The runtime then follows certain probing rules, first looking in the location specified by a <codebase> element in a config file or publisher policy. The loader attempts to locate the file based on the location, the assembly name, culture information, and version.

5. If the loader can't locate the assembly after probing for it, an error is thrown.

When architecting your application, keep in mind that there's overhead when locating and loading assemblies. This is something to consider when it comes to deciding on the number of assemblies you want to create. As you can see, versioning plays a key role at assembly load time, and all assemblies are versioned. Versioning is something that was built into the CLR loader from the beginning and removes the affliction, affectionately known as *DLL Hell*, which occurs when replacing a shared DLL with a newer version breaks applications that use the older version. In the CLR, multiple versions of the same assembly can exist simultaneously on the same machine without conflicting with each other. Moreover, applications can choose to default to using the most recent version of an assembly on the machine, or you can specify the exact version by applying a version policy in the relevant configuration files.

Cross-Language Compatibility

Because assemblies are self-describing and contain portable IL code, they are easily shared across multiple languages. Finally, there's a viable solution for creating complex systems in which components are coded using different languages. For example, in a complex system used for engineering analysis, you may have a group of VB developers coding the system infrastructure and a group of engineers developing the mathematical components. Many engineers still program in languages such as FORTRAN, and this works because there are FORTRAN compilers available that emit IL and create managed assemblies. Thus each development group can work in a language that's more natural to them and to their problem domains. Metadata is the key to cross-language compatibility. The metadata format is completely described in the CLI Ecma standards documents.

Metadata

All managed modules are self-describing through the use of *metadata*. Metadata is an extensible format for describing the contents of assemblies. In the managed world, just about every entity in a program with a type can have metadata attached to it, including classes, interfaces, methods, parameters, return values, assemblies, and so on.

You define custom attributes by deriving from the `System.Attribute` class. Then you can easily associate an instance of your custom attribute to just about any entity in your assembly. Your metadata is accessible at run time. For example, you can iterate over all the fields of an arbitrary class type without having to know its declaration ahead of time or at compile time.

In .NET, all assemblies follow the same metadata format; you never have to worry about consumers accessing your objects. Additionally, assembly structure and manifests mean no more issues related to registry entries and versioning that were prevalent previous to .NET.

Reflection

With metadata, you can programmatically access and examine type definitions and the attributes attached to them. Metadata can tell you if a particular object's class supports a given method before attempting to call it or if a given class is derived from another. The process of inspecting metadata is called *reflection*. Classes in the `System.Reflection` namespace are used to retrieve type information at run time. Typically, you start with a `System.Type` object when you reflect upon types in the assembly. Once you have a type object, you can find out if it's a class, an interface, a structure, and so on, what methods it has, and the number and types of fields it contains.

Summary

In this chapter, we covered the essentials of how a VB program is compiled, packaged, and executed. We looked at how your VB code gets compiled into IL and is then compiled on the fly by the JIT compiler. One of the requirements for JIT compilation is an expressive and extensible mechanism that the compiler can understand—thus we have assemblies.

By packaging IL into assemblies that are self-documenting, both the CLR and the JIT compiler have all the information they need to manage code execution. Private assemblies make it possible to run multiple versions of code without having to worry about registry entries, and shared assemblies provide the ability to access the functionality of a single assembly from multiple applications.

In the next chapter, we'll jump into the important topic of interface-based, or contract-based, programming.

■ ■ ■

Interfaces

An interface defines a *contract* between components. A contract, when applied to a type, imposes a set of requirements on that type. Typically, this means a set of methods and properties that any type implementing the interface is guaranteed to provide. Using interfaces, you can separate the definition of your objects from their implementation. Interfaces also make it easier for you to add functionality to your types, while minimizing compatibility issues with existing clients.

Contracts, however, are not the only thing interfaces provide. Since Visual Basic (VB) does not support inheritance from multiple types, but does allow types to implement multiple interfaces, interfaces become a foundation for polymorphic programming.

Interfaces Are Reference Types

An interface defines a reference type, but, unlike classes, interfaces cannot be instantiated. Classes and structures *implement* interfaces—that is, they define the methods and other members that form the contract defined by the interface. Variables declared as an interface type can hold a reference to any object that implements the interface.

Take a look at the following artificial but nonetheless typical pattern:

```
Public Interface IUIControl
    Sub Paint()
End Interface

Public Class Button
    Implements IUIControl

    Public Sub Paint() Implements IUIControl.Paint
        'Paint the Button
    End Sub
End Class

Public Class ListBox
    Implements IUIControl

    Public Sub Paint() Implements IUIControl.Paint
        'Paint the Listbox
    End Sub
End Class
```

This example declares an interface named IUIControl that simply exposes one method, Paint. This interface defines a contract, which states that any type that implements this interface must implement the Paint method.

Since the classes ListBox and Button implement the interface, you can treat them both as type IUIControl. You can store any instance of either Button or ListBox in a variable declared as IUIControl. The references to objects of these class types are implicitly convertible to the IUIControl type. However, to convert an IUIControl reference back into a ListBox or Button reference requires an explicit conversion, and that coercion will fail if the object pointed to by the IUIControl reference is not of the type specified by the conversion.

Finally, consider naming methods according to both the action they perform and where the action is directed. For example, suppose the IUIControl.Paint method takes a Graphics object as a parameter telling it where to paint itself. The code is more readable if the method is named IUIControl.PaintSelfTo(). This way, the method call reads like a spoken language in the sense that a method call that looks like control.PaintSelfTo(myGraphicsObject) is saying, "control, please paint yourself to myGraphicsObject."

Defining Interfaces

Interface declarations are similar to class declarations, but interfaces cannot declare fields, and they can only declare, but cannot implement, other members. For example, in the following code

```
Interface IUIControl
    Sub Paint()
End Interface
```

IUIControl has only one member, the method Paint, and it uses only a Sub statement to declare it, without providing a method body or an End Sub statement.

Interfaces, like classes, default to Friend accessibility in a namespace, but you can also declare them Public. Within classes, modules, interfaces, and structures, they default to Public, but they can also be Friend, Protected, or Private. Interface members are implicitly Public and may not have access modifiers.

■**Note** By convention, interface names start with I.

Let's code a trivial interface to get familiar with how you declare and use interfaces:

```
Interface ITrivial
End Interface

Class A
    Implements ITrivial
End Class
```

```
Class B
    Implements ITrivial
End Class

Public Class EntryPoint
    Shared Sub Main()
        Dim ca As ITrivial = New A
        Dim cb As ITrivial = New B
    End Sub
End Class
```

ITrivial is as trivial as an interface can get. Class A and Class B both implement it, but trivially, since it has no members to implement. However, by implementing ITrivial, you can store instances of both Class A and Class B in ITrivial variables. This is an example of how interfaces support polymorphism. Now let's code a less trivial interface and see how classes implement interface members:

```
Interface INonTrivial
    Sub SomeMethod()
End Interface

Class A
    Implements INonTrivial

    Public Sub SomeMethod() Implements INonTrivial.SomeMethod
        Console.WriteLine("Class A doing something.")
    End Sub
End Class

Class B
    Implements INonTrivial

    Public Sub SomeMethod() Implements INonTrivial.SomeMethod
        Console.WriteLine("Class B doing something.")
    End Sub
End Class

Public Class EntryPoint
    Shared Sub Main()
        Dim ca As INonTrivial = New A
        ca.SomeMethod()
        Dim cb As INonTrivial = New B
        cb.SomeMethod()
    End Sub
End Class
```

The following shows the output of this program:

```
Class A doing something.
Class B doing something.
```

In the example, each class implements INonTrivial's SomeMethod() to display a different string. Each class uses an Implements *statement*

```
Implements INonTrivial
```

to specify that it's implementing the INonTrivial interface; and it uses an Implements *clause*

```
Public Sub SomeMethod() Implements INonTrivial.SomeMethod
```

to specify the interface member being implemented. VB declarative mapping tests this interface contract via Implements INonTrivial.SomeMethod, and since the signatures match, you can use a method name of your choice.

Finally, while you can use interfaces without members, the best practice is to use attributes to indicate that types support a specific feature that doesn't actually require implementation. On the other hand, interfaces with only one method are common, and several important .NET Base Class Library (BCL) interfaces, including ICloneable, IComparable, IDisposable, and IFormattable, have only a single method as a member.

What Can Be in an Interface?

Interfaces may have methods, properties, events, and nested types (interfaces, classes, and structures) as members. Interfaces may inherit from one or more other interfaces. Here's an example of some things you can declare in an interface:

```
Public Interface IMyDatabase
    'Inherit from two other interfaces
    Inherits IDisposable, ICloneable

    'Method with no return type
    Sub Insert(ByVal element As Object)

    'Method with a return type
    Function Retrieve(ByVal element As Object) As Object

    'Property
    Property Count() As Integer

    'Event
    Event DBEvent()
End Interface
```

In this example, IMyDatabase declares two methods, a property and an event, all of which must be implemented by any type that implements the interface. It inherits IDisposable and ICloneable. So, any type that implements IMyDatabase must also implement the Dispose method of IDisposable and the Clone method of ICloneable.

Interface Inheritance

As mentioned previously, interfaces support inheritance from multiple interfaces in the syntactic sense, such as in the following code:

```
Public Interface IEditBox
    Sub Edit()
End Interface

Public Interface IDropList
    Sub DropDown()
End Interface

Public Interface IUIControl
    Inherits IEditBox, IDropList

    Sub Paint()
End Interface

Public Class ComboBox
    Implements IUIControl

    Sub Edit() Implements IUIControl.Edit
        'Edit
    End Sub

    Sub DropDown() Implements IUIControl.DropDown
        'Drop down
    End Sub

    Sub Paint() Implements IUIControl.Paint
        'Paint
    End Sub
End Class
```

In the previous example, IUIControl inherits from two interfaces, IEditBox and IDropList. The ComboBox class, though it explicitly declares that it implements only IUIControl, must also implement all the methods of the interfaces that IUIControl inherits.

Implementing Multiple Interfaces

Classes can also implement multiple interfaces, as in the following example:

```
Public Interface IUIControl
    Sub Paint()
End Interface

Public Interface IEditBox
    Inherits IUIControl
```

```
    Sub Edit()
End Interface

Public Interface IDropList
    Inherits IUIControl

    Sub DropDown()
End Interface

Public Class ComboBox
    Implements IEditBox, IDropList

    Sub Edit() Implements IEditBox.Edit
        'Edit implementation
    End Sub

    Sub DropDown() Implements IDropList.DropDown
        'Drop down implementation
    End Sub

    Public Sub Paint() Implements IDropList.Paint
        'Paint implementation
    End Sub
End Class
```

In this example, the ComboBox class implements both IEditBox and IDropList, and each inherits Paint() from IUIControl. Since ComboBox implements both of these interfaces, it must implement all the methods in them, plus the Paint method they inherit. Note that although both IEditBox and IDropList inherit Paint() from IUIControl, ComboBox only needs to implement it once. It also could have used either

```
Sub Paint() Implements IEditBox.Paint
```

or

```
Sub Paint() Implements IUIControl.Paint
```

and, as ComboBox has only one implementation of the Paint method, if you were to cast a ComboBox instance into either an IEditBox or IDropList variable, then calling Paint() on either variable would call the same implementation.

Hiding Interface Members

Sometimes—albeit rarely—you need to declare a method in an interface that hides a method in an inherited interface. You use the Overloads modifier to do so. For example, if IDropList needs its own version of Paint(), you'll have to change both IDropList and ComboBox as follows:

```
Public Interface IUIControl
    Sub Paint()
End Interface
```

```
Public Interface IEditBox
    Inherits IUIControl

    Sub Edit()
End Interface

Public Interface IDropList
    Inherits IUIControl

    Overloads Sub Paint()

    Sub DropDown()
End Interface

Public Class ComboBox
    Implements IEditBox, IDropList

    Sub Edit() Implements IEditBox.Edit
        'Edit implementation
    End Sub

    Sub DropDown() Implements IDropList.DropDown
        'Drop down implementation
    End Sub

    Public Sub Paint() Implements IEditBox.Paint
        'Paint implementation
    End Sub

    Public Sub DropPaint() Implements IDropList.Paint
        'Paint DropList
    End Sub
End Class
```

In this example, `Overloads Sub Paint()` has been added to `IDropList`, allowing it to hide the `Paint` method inherited from `IUIControl`. Next, the new `Paint()` is implemented via the `DropPaint` method in `ComboBox`. `IUIControl.Paint()` must still be implemented because it's part of `IEditBox`; either `IUIControl` or `IEditBox` could have been used as the qualifier.

Implementing Interfaces in Structures

While implementing interfaces in a class is most typical, it is possible to implement them in structures as well. Let's define two structures to represent integers and doubles and provide them with an interface that guarantees you can raise them to an integer power:

```
Public Interface IPowerable
    Function RaiseToN(ByVal n As Integer)
End Interface
```

```
Public Structure AnInteger
    Implements IPowerable

    Public i As Integer

    Public Sub New(ByVal value As Integer)
        Me.i = value
    End Sub

    Public Function RaiseToN(ByVal n As Integer) As Object _
        Implements IPowerable.RaiseToN

        Return i ^ n
    End Function
End Structure

Public Structure ADouble
    Implements IPowerable

    Public d As Double

    Public Sub New(ByVal value As Double)
        Me.d = value
    End Sub

    Public Function RaiseToN(ByVal n As Integer) As Object _
        Implements IPowerable.RaiseToN

        Return d ^ n
    End Function
End Structure

Public Class EntryPoint
    Shared Sub main()
        Dim i As AnInteger = New AnInteger(2)
        Dim d As ADouble = New ADouble(2.1)

        Console.WriteLine(i.i & " cubed is " & i.RaiseToN(3))
        Console.WriteLine(d.d & " squared is " & d.RaiseToN(2))
    End Sub
End Class
```

When run, the previous code displays the following results:

```
2 cubed is 8
2.1 squared is 4.41
```

In the example, both AnInteger and ADouble implement IPowerable. As IPowerable requires a RaiseToN() implementation, both classes oblige. Finally, main() features two calls to RaiseToN(), one for each object instance created.

Beware of Side Effects of Value Types Implementing Interfaces

As you've just seen, structures can implement interfaces. However, structures are value types, not reference types, so you'll incur a boxing penalty if you cast a value type to an interface type or vice versa. Also, if you modify the value via the interface reference, you're modifying the boxed copy and not the original.

To expand on the example, consider the primitive type Integer, which is really the value type System.Int32. It's one of the most basic types in the common language runtime (CLR). You may or may not have noticed that it implements several interfaces: IComparable, IFormattable, IConvertible, IComparable(Of Integer), and IEquatable(Of Integer). IConvertible has 17 methods; however, none of them are part of the public contract of System.Int32. If you want to call one of the IConvertible methods, you must first cast your Int32 value type to an IConvertible. Of course, since interface-typed variables are of reference type, this will box the Int32 value type.

Using Generics with Interfaces

We don't cover the topic of generics in detail until Chapter 12 because it's much easier to discuss it after you've learned more VB; but here are a couple of simple examples of using generics with interfaces to suggest some of their possibilities.

Using a Generic Interface

Interfaces can be generic—that is, they can provide one or more *type parameters* that are filled by *type arguments* when the interface is used. Take a look at this example:

```
Option Strict Off

Interface IGeneric(Of T)
    Sub SomeMethod(ByVal x As T)
End Interface

Class A
    Implements IGeneric(Of Integer)

    Public Sub SomeMethod(ByVal x As Integer) _
        Implements IGeneric(Of Integer).SomeMethod

        Console.WriteLine("A.SomeMethod received " + x.ToString())
    End Sub
End Class
```

```
Class B
    Implements IGeneric(Of Double)

    Public Sub SomeMethod(ByVal x As Double) _
        Implements IGeneric(Of Double).SomeMethod

        Console.WriteLine("B.SomeMethod received " + x.ToString())
    End Sub
End Class

Public Class EntryPoint
    Shared Sub Main()
        Dim ca As IGeneric(Of Integer) = New A()
        Dim cb As IGeneric(Of Double) = New B()

        ca.SomeMethod(123.456)
        cb.SomeMethod(123.456)
    End Sub
End Class
```

The previous code displays the following results when run:

```
A.SomeMethod received 123
B.SomeMethod received 123.456
```

In this example, the interface IGeneric(Of T) uses a type parameter, T, in both the interface and its method. Class A then implements IGeneric as Integer, and the SomeMethod parameter type becomes Integer. In Class B, these are implemented as Double. Option Strict Off permits 123.456 to be implicitly converted on the call to A.SomeMethod to allow a Double to be passed to the Integer method.

Using a Generic Method in an Interface

Interfaces don't have to be generic to have generic members. Take a look at this example:

```
Option Strict On

Interface INonGeneric
    Sub SomeMethod(Of T)(ByVal x As T)
End Interface

Class A
    Implements INonGeneric

    Public Sub SomeMethod(Of T)(ByVal x As T) _
        Implements INonGeneric.SomeMethod
```

```
            Console.WriteLine("A.SomeMethod received " + x.ToString())
        End Sub
End Class

Public Class EntryPoint
    Shared Sub Main()
        Dim ca As INonGeneric = New A()

        ca.SomeMethod(123.456)
        ca.SomeMethod("123 point 456")
    End Sub
End Class
```

This example, when run, displays the following results:

```
A.SomeMethod received 123.456
A.SomeMethod received 123 point 456
```

In the previous example, the interface INonGeneric is not generic, but the method SomeMethod(Of T) is, and unlike the earlier IGeneric.SomeMethod, it isn't limited to a specific type for a specific implementing class. This example uses Option Strict On to limit the possible implicit conversions and prove that disparate types are acceptable as arguments.

Contracts

You usually define a contract to facilitate communication between two types in your design. For example, suppose you have a virtual zoo, and in your zoo, you have animals. Now, an instance of your ZooKeeper needs a way to communicate to the collection of these ZooDweller objects that they should fly to a specific location. However, not all animals can fly, so clearly, not all of the types in the zoo can support this flying contract.

Implementing Contracts with Classes

Let's consider one way to manage the complexity of getting these creatures to fly from one location to the next. First, consider the assumptions that you can make here. Let's say that this Zoo can have only one ZooKeeper. Second, let's assume that you can model the locations within this Zoo by using a simple two-dimensional Point structure. It starts to look as though you can model this system by the following code:

```
Imports System.Collections.ObjectModel

Namespace CityOfShanoo.MyZoo
    Public Structure Point
        Public x As Double
        Public y As Double
    End Structure
```

```vbnet
Public MustInherit Class ZooDweller
    Sub EatSomeFood()
        EatTheFood()
    End Sub

    Protected MustOverride Sub EatTheFood()
End Class

Public NotInheritable Class ZooKeeper
    Public Sub SendFlyCommand(ByVal dest As Point)
        'Get creatures to fly
    End Sub
End Class

Public NotInheritable Class Zoo
    Private Shared instance As Zoo = New Zoo()
    Private keeper As ZooKeeper
    Private creatures As Collection(Of ZooDweller)

    Private Sub New()
        creatures = New Collection(Of ZooDweller)()
        keeper = New ZooKeeper()
    End Sub

    Public Shared ReadOnly Property TheZoo() As Zoo
        Get
            Return instance
        End Get
    End Property

    Public ReadOnly Property TheKeeper() As ZooKeeper
        Get
            Return keeper
        End Get
    End Property
End Class
End Namespace
```

Since only one zoo can exist in the CityOfShanoo, the Zoo is modeled as a Singleton object, and the only way to obtain the instance of the one and only Zoo is through the Zoo.TheZoo property. You can get a reference to the ZooKeeper via the Zoo.TheKeeper property.

■**Note** The Singleton design pattern is one of the most well-known and widely used design patterns. Essentially, the pattern allows only one instance of a type to exist at any one time. Many still argue about the best way to implement it, but in general, some `Private Shared` variable within the type itself is lazily initialized to the single instance at the point of first access. The `Zoo` class does that, since its constructor is `Private`, and the only instance that ever gets created is stored in the `instance` variable and initialized when the class is first loaded.

This initial design defines `ZooDweller` as a `MustInherit` class that implements a method, `EatSomeFood`, which calls a `MustOverride` method, `EatTheFood`. (This is an example of the Non-Virtual Interface (NVI) pattern, described in Chapter 14.)

The `ZooDweller` class does, in fact, define a contract even though it is not an interface. The contract, as written, states that any class that inherits from `ZooDweller` must implement `EatSomeFood()`. Any code that uses a `ZooDweller` instance can be guaranteed that this method is supported.

■**Note** An interface is not required in order to define a contract.

So far, this design is missing a key operation, and that is the one commanding creatures to fly to a destination within the zoo. Clearly, you cannot add a `Fly` method to the `ZooDweller` class because not all animals can fly. You must express this contract in a different way. One common way to model this in a class is to create a `Boolean` property, such as `CanFly`, to use as a flag that states the `ZooDweller`'s ability to fly.

Implementing Contracts with Interfaces

Interfaces provide an excellent mechanism for defining our flying contract. The following example implements an `IFly` interface:

```
Public Interface IFly
   Sub FlyTo(ByVal dest As Point)
End Interface

Public Class Bird
   Inherits ZooDweller
   Implements IFly

   Protected Overrides Sub EatTheFood()
     Console.WriteLine( "Eating some food." )
   End Sub
```

```
      Public Sub Fly(ByVal dest As Point) Implements IFly.FlyTo
         Console.WriteLine( _
            "Flying to ({0}. {1}).", dest)
      End Sub
   End Class
```

Now, using the interface IFly, Bird is defined such that it derives from ZooDweller and implements IFly.

Choosing Between Interfaces and Classes

You can implement a contract with classes or interfaces, and in the zoo example, it's pretty clear where you should use an interface rather than a class to define the contract. However, the choice is not always so clear, so let's consider some relevant issues.

When you implement a contract with an interface, you're defining a versioned contract. That means that the interface, once released, must never change, as if it were cast in stone. Sure, you could change it later, but you would not be very popular when all of your clients' code fails to compile with the modified interface. Consider the following example:

```
Public Interface IMyOperations
   Sub Operation1()
   Sub Operation2()
End Interface

Public Class ClientClass
   Implements IMyOperations

   Public Sub Operation1() Implements IMyOperations.Operation1
      'Do op 1
   End Sub

   Public Sub Operation2() Implements IMyOperations.Operation2
      'Do op 2
   End Sub
End Class
```

Now you've released this wonderful IMyOperations interface to the world, and thousands of clients have implemented it. Then, you start getting requests from your clients asking for Operation3() support in your library. It seems like it would be easy enough to simply add an Operation3 method to the IMyOperations interface, but that would be a mistake. If you add another operation to IMyOperations, then all of a sudden your clients' code won't compile until they implement the new operation. Also, code in another assembly that knows about the newer IMyOperations could attempt to cast a ClientClass instance into an IMyOperations reference and then call Operation3(), thus creating a runtime failure.

■**Caution** We strongly recommend that you do not modify a publicly published interface.

You could also address this problem by defining a completely new interface, say IMyOperations2. However, ClientClass would need to implement both interfaces in order to get the new behavior, as shown here:

```
Public Interface IMyOperations
    Sub Operation1()
    Sub Operation2()
End Interface

Public Interface IMyOperations2
    Sub Operation1()
    Sub Operation2()
    Sub Operation3()
End Interface

Public Class ClientClass
    Implements IMyOperations, IMyOperations2

    Public Sub Operation1() Implements IMyOperations.Operation1
        ' Do op 1
    End Sub

    Public Sub Operation2() Implements IMyOperations.Operation2
        ' Do op 2
    End Sub

    Public Sub Operation21() Implements IMyOperations2.Operation1
        ' Do op 2.1
    End Sub

    Public Sub Operation22() Implements IMyOperations2.Operation2
        ' Do op 2.2
    End Sub

    Public Sub Operation3() Implements IMyOperations2.Operation3
        ' Do op 2.3
    End Sub
End Class

Public Class AnotherClass
    Public Sub DoWork(ByVal ops As IMyOperations)
        ' Do ops
    End Sub
End Class
```

Modifying ClientClass to support the new operation from IMyOperations2 isn't terribly hard, but what about the code that already exists, such as the DoWork method in AnotherClass? The problem is that DoWork() accepts an argument of type IMyOperations. In order to make the new Operation3() available, the DoWork() parameter type must change, or the code within it must cast the argument to IMyOperations2, which could fail at run time. Since you want the compiler to be able to catch as many type bugs as possible, it would be better if you changed the DoWork() to accept a type of IMyOperations2.

■**Note** If you define your original IMyOperations interface within a fully versioned, strongly named assembly, then you can get away with creating a new interface with the same name in a new assembly, as long as the version of the new assembly is different. Although .NET supports this explicitly, it doesn't mean you should do it without careful consideration because introducing two IMyOperations interfaces that differ only by the version number of the containing assembly could be confusing to your clients.

That was a lot of work just to make a new operation available to clients. Let's examine the same situation, except this time using a MustInherit class:

```
Public MustInherit Class MyOperations
    Public MustOverride Sub Operation1()
    Public MustOverride Sub Operation2()
End Class

Public Class ClientClass
    Inherits MyOperations

    Public Overrides Sub Operation1()
        ' Do op 1
    End Sub

    Public Overrides Sub Operation2()
        ' Do op 2
    End Sub
End Class

Public Class AnotherClass
    Public Sub DoWork(ByVal ops As MyOperations)
        ' Do ops
    End Sub
End Class
```

MyOperations is the base class of ClientClass. One advantage is that MyOperations can contain default implementations if it wants to, though it doesn't do that here. Now, suppose you want to add a new Operation3 method to MyOperations, and you don't want to break existing clients. You can do this as long as the added operation is not MustOverride, such that it forces changes on derived types, as shown here:

```
Public MustInherit Class MyOperations
    Public MustOverride Sub Operation1()
    Public MustOverride Sub Operation2()

    Public Sub Operation3()
        'Do op 3
    End Sub
End Class

Public Class ClientClass
    Inherits MyOperations

    Public Overrides Sub Operation1()
        ' Do op 1
    End Sub

    Public Overrides Sub Operation2()
        ' Do op 2
    End Sub
End Class

Public Class AnotherClass
    Public Sub DoWork(ByVal ops As MyOperations)
        ops.Operation3()
    End Sub
End Class
```

Notice that the addition of Operation3() to MyOperations doesn't force any changes upon ClientClass, and AnotherClass.DoWork() can use Operation3() without making any changes to the parameter declaration. This technique doesn't come without its drawbacks, though. Since a class can have only one direct base class, ClientClass has to derive from MyOperations to get the functionality, so it uses up its only inheritance ticket. This may put complicated restrictions upon your client code. For example, what if one of your clients needs to create an object for use with .NET remoting? To do so, the class must derive from MarshalByRefObject, so it can't inherit from MyOperations.

Sometimes, it's tricky to find a happy medium when deciding between interfaces and classes. Use the following rules of thumb:

- *If modeling an* is-a *relationship, use a class*: If it makes sense to name your contract with a noun, then you should probably model it with a class.

- *If modeling an* IMPLEMENTS *relationship, use an interface*: If it makes sense to name your contract with an adjective, as if it were a quality, then you should probably model it as an interface.

- *Consider packaging your interface and* MustInherit *class declarations in a separate assembly*: Implementations in other assemblies can then reference this separate assembly.

- *If possible, prefer classes over interfaces*: This can be helpful for the sake of extensibility.

Polymorphism with Interfaces

Throughout this chapter, you've seen that different types that implement the same interface can be treated as the same type. Let's look more closely at how interfaces support polymorphism:

```
Public Interface IGeometricShape
    Sub Draw()
End Interface

Public Class Rectangle
    Implements IGeometricShape

    Public Sub Draw() Implements IGeometricShape.Draw
        'Draw a rectangle.
        Console.WriteLine("Rectangle drawn.")
    End Sub
End Class

Public Class Circle
    Implements IGeometricShape

    Public Sub Draw() Implements IGeometricShape.Draw
        'Draw a circle.
        Console.WriteLine("Circle drawn.")
    End Sub
End Class

Public Class EntryPoint
    Private Shared Sub DrawShape(ByVal shape As IGeometricShape)
        shape.Draw()
    End Sub

    Shared Sub Main()
        Dim aCircle As Circle = New Circle()
        Dim aRectangle As Rectangle = New Rectangle()

        DrawShape(aCircle)
        DrawShape(aRectangle)
    End Sub
End Class
```

Running the previous example returns the following results:

```
Circle drawn.
Rectangle drawn.
```

In this example, both the Rectangle and Circle classes implement IGeometricShape. Each of these classes contains a Draw method, which is required to fulfill their contract with IGeometricShape. In Main(), after you create aCircle and aRectangle, you call DrawShape(aCircle) and DrawShape(aRectangle). Notice that the DrawShape method receives ByVal shape As IGeometricShape as its parameter. Through the magic of polymorphism, DrawShape calls the appropriate Draw(), be it Circle or Square.

Summary

This chapter introduced interfaces and how you can define contracts using interfaces or classes. We then covered declaring interfaces and how to implement them in classes. Finally, we compared the use of interfaces vs. classes when defining contracts.

In the next chapter, we'll explain how to overload operators and why you may want to avoid overloading them when writing code to be used by other .NET languages.

CHAPTER 7

Operator Overloading

Overloaded operators were first introduced to VB programmers with VB 2005. Just as you can overload methods, VB allows you to overload operators such as +, -, and *. In addition to overloading arithmetic operators, you can also create custom conversion operators to convert from one type to another and allow objects to be used in Boolean test expressions.

Just Because You Can Doesn't Mean You Should

Overloading operators can make certain classes and structures more natural to use. You should carefully consider the semantics of a type's operators and not introduce something that is difficult to decipher or maintain. Aim for the most readable code, not only for the next fortunate soul who claps eyes on your code but also for yourself.

Another reason to take care when overloading operators is that not all .NET languages support overloaded operators, because overloading operators is not part of the Common Language Specification (CLS). For example, VB 2005 was the first version of VB to support operator overloading. It's important that your overloaded operators be syntactic shortcuts to functionality provided by secondary methods that perform the same operation and can be called by CLS-compliant languages.

Operators That Can Be Overloaded

Unary operators, binary operators, and conversion operators comprise the three general types of operators that you can overload in VB. Unary operators are those that have only one operand, such as the unary minus in the negative number –108, and the CType conversion operator. Binary operators have two operands, such as the addition operator in 2 + 2. Table 7-1 lists the operators that you can overload.

Table 7-1. *Operators That Can Be Overloaded*

Operator	Operator Type	Description
+	Binary	Addition
–	Binary	Subtraction
*	Binary	Multiplication
^	Binary	Exponentiation

Continued

Table 7-1. *Continued*

Operator	Operator Type	Description
/	Binary	Division
\	Binary	Integer division
Mod	Binary	Modulo division
<>	Binary	Not equal
>	Binary	Greater than
<	Binary	Less than
>=	Binary	Greater than or equal to
<=	Binary	Less than or equal to
=	Binary	Equal to
And	Binary	Logical and bitwise And
Or	Binary	Logical and bitwise inclusive Or
XOr	Binary	Bitwise exclusive Or
+	Unary	Positive
-	Unary	Negative
Not	Unary	Logical Not and one's complement
IsTrue	Unary	Is True testing
IsFalse	Unary	Is False testing
Like	Binary	String comparison
<<	Binary	Shift left
>>	Binary	Shift right
&	Binary	Concatenation
CType	Unary	Type conversion

Types and Formats of Overloaded Operators

You define all overloaded operators as Public Shared Operator methods on the classes they're meant to augment. Depending on the type of operator being overloaded, the method may accept either one or two parameters, and it always returns a value. For all operators except the CType conversion operator, one of the parameter types must be of the same type as the enclosing type for the method. A typical + operator for a class Complex could look like the following:

```
Public Shared Operator +(ByVal lhs As Complex, ByVal rhs As Complex) As Complex
```

where the lhs argument represents the left-hand side operator, and rhs represents the right-hand side.

Even though this method adds two instances of Complex together to produce a third instance of Complex, nothing says that one of the parameters cannot be that of type Double, thus adding a `Double` to a `Complex` instance. How you add a `Double` value to a `Complex` instance and produce another `Complex` instance is for you to decide. In general, operator overloading syntax follows the previous pattern, with the + replaced with the operator being overloaded.

The conversion operator (CType) defines a developer-crafted custom conversion and accepts only one parameter. The overload must have either the operand or the return value type declared the same as the containing class or structure type.

Operator overloads are marked with both `Shared` and `Public` and must have at least one parameter in their declaration that matches the *enclosing* type. Since these methods will be inherited by derived classes, it is impossible for the derived type's operator method to match the signature of the base class operator method exactly. For example, the `GreenApple` class in the following sample is not valid:

```
Public Class Apple
    Public Shared Operator +(ByVal rhs As Apple, ByVal lhs As Apple) As Apple
        'Method does nothing & exists only for example.
        Return rhs
    End Operator
End Class

Public Class GreenApple
    Inherits Apple

    'INVALID - This will not compile!
    Public Overloads Shared Operator +(ByVal rhs As Apple, ByVal lhs As Apple) _
        As Apple

        'Method does nothing & exists only for example.
        Return rhs
    End Operator
End Class
```

If you attempt to build the previous code, you'll get the following compiler error:

```
At least one parameter of this binary operator
must be of the containing type 'GreenApple'
```

Operators Shouldn't Mutate Their Operands

You already know that operator methods are `Shared`. Therefore, it is highly recommended that you do *not* mutate (or directly modify) the operands passed into the operator methods. Instead, you should create a new instance of the return value type and return the result of the operation. Structures and classes that are immutable, such as `System.String`, are perfect candidates for implementing custom operators. This behavior is natural for operators such as `Boolean`, which usually return a type different than the types passed into the operator.

Does Parameter Order Matter?

Let's create a structure to represent complex numbers. The first version looks like this:

```
Public Structure Complex
    Private Real As Double
    Private Imaginary As Double

    Public Sub New(ByVal real As Double, ByVal imaginary As Double)
        Me.Real = real
        Me.Imaginary = imaginary
    End Sub

    Public Shared Function Add(ByVal lhs As Complex, ByVal rhs As Complex) _
        As Complex

        Return New Complex(lhs.Real + rhs.Real, lhs.Imaginary + rhs.Imaginary)
    End Function

    Public Shared Operator +(ByVal lhs As Complex, ByVal rhs As Complex) As Complex
        Return Add(lhs, rhs)
    End Operator
End Structure
```

Suppose you need to add instances of Complex together, but would like to be able to add a plain-old Double variable to the Complex instance. Adding this functionality is no problem, since you can overload the Operator + method such that one parameter is a Complex and the other is a Double. That declaration could look like the following:

```
Public Shared Operator +(ByVal lhs As Complex, ByVal rhs As Double) As Complex
```

With this operator declared and defined on the Complex structure, you can now write code such as the following:

```
Dim cpx1 As New Complex(1.0, 2.0)
Dim cpx2 = cpx1 + 20.0
```

This saves you the time of having to create an extra Complex instance with just the Real member variable set to 20.0 in order to add it to cpx1. Here, the first operand is of type Complex, and the second operand is of type Double. However, suppose you want to be able to reverse the operands on the operator and do something like the following instead:

```
Dim cpx2 = 20.0 + cpx1
```

In this case, the first operand is of type Double, and the second operand is of type Complex. If you want to support different orderings of operands of different types, you must provide different overloads of the operator. If you overload a binary operator that uses different parameter types, you can create a *mirror* overload—that is, another operator method that reverses the parameters.

Overloading the Addition Operator

Let's add more operators to the Complex structure and build upon it throughout the chapter:

```
Imports System

Public Structure Complex
    Private Real As Double
    Private Imaginary As Double

    Public Sub New(ByVal real As Double, ByVal imaginary As Double)
        Me.Real = real
        Me.Imaginary = imaginary
    End Sub

    Public Shared Function Add _
        (ByVal lhs As Complex, ByVal rhs As Complex) As Complex

        Return New Complex(lhs.Real + rhs.Real, lhs.Imaginary + rhs.Imaginary)
    End Function

    Public Shared Function Add _
        (ByVal lhs As Complex, ByVal rhs As Double) As Complex

        Return New Complex(rhs + lhs.Real, lhs.Imaginary)
    End Function

    Public Overrides Function ToString() As String
        Return System.String.Format("({0}, {1})", Real, Imaginary)
    End Function

    Public Shared Operator +(ByVal lhs As Complex, ByVal rhs As Complex) As Complex
        Return Add(lhs, rhs)
    End Operator

    Public Shared Operator +(ByVal lhs As Double, ByVal rhs As Complex) As Complex
        Return Add(rhs, lhs)
    End Operator

    Public Shared Operator +(ByVal lhs As Complex, ByVal rhs As Double) As Complex
        Return Add(lhs, rhs)
    End Operator
End Structure
```

```vb
Public Class EntryPoint
    Shared Sub Main()
        Dim cpx1 As Complex = New Complex(1.0, 3.0)
        Dim cpx2 As Complex = New Complex(1.0, 2.0)

        Dim cpx3 As Complex = cpx1 + cpx2
        Dim cpx4 As Complex = 20.0 + cpx1
        Dim cpx5 As Complex = cpx1 + 25.0

        Console.WriteLine("cpx1 == {0}", cpx1)
        Console.WriteLine("cpx2 == {0}", cpx2)
        Console.WriteLine("cpx3 == {0}", cpx3)
        Console.WriteLine("cpx4 == {0}", cpx4)
        Console.WriteLine("cpx5 == {0}", cpx5)
    End Sub
End Class
```

Here are the results of running the previous code:

```
cpx1 == (1, 3)
cpx2 == (1, 2)
cpx3 == (2, 5)
cpx4 == (21, 3)
cpx5 == (26, 3)
```

Notice that, as recommended, the overloaded operator methods call Add methods that perform the same operation. Calling the Add methods in this way makes supporting both orderings of Operator + that add a Double to a Complex a snap.

However, if you're sure that your type will only be used in a VB 2005 / VB 2008 / C# environment, or in another language that supports overloaded operators, then you can forgo implementing the Add methods and simply stick with the overloaded operators.

Comparison Operators

The binary comparison operators = and <>, < and >, and >= and <= must be implemented as pairs. This makes perfect sense because there would probably never be a case where you'd want to allow users to use Operator IsTrue and not Operator IsFalse. Moreover, if your type allows ordering via implementation of the IComparable interface or its generic counterpart IComparable(Of T), then it makes sense to implement all comparison operators. Implementing these operators is trivial if you override Equals() and GetHashCode(), then implement IComparable (and optionally IComparable(Of T) and IEquatable(Of T)) appropriately. Given that, overloading the operators merely requires you to call those implementations. Let's look at a modified form of the Complex number that follows this pattern to implement all of the comparison operators:

```vb
Imports System

Public Structure Complex
    Implements IComparable
    Implements IEquatable(Of Complex)
    Implements IComparable(Of Complex)

    Private Real As Double
    Private Img As Double

    Public Sub New(ByVal real As Double, ByVal img As Double)
        Me.Real = real
        Me.Img = img
    End Sub

    'System.Object override
    Public Overrides Function Equals(ByVal other As Object) As Boolean
        Dim result As Boolean = False

        If TypeOf other Is Complex Then
            result = Equals(DirectCast(other, Complex))
        End If

        Return result
    End Function

    'Typesafe version
    Public Overloads Function Equals(ByVal that As Complex) As Boolean _
        Implements IEquatable(Of Complex).Equals

        Return (Me.Real = that.Real AndAlso Me.Img = that.Img)
    End Function

    'Must override if overriding Object.Equals()
    Public Overrides Function GetHashCode() As Integer
        Return CType(Me.Magnitude, Integer)
    End Function

    'Typesafe version
    Public Function CompareTo(ByVal that As Complex) As Integer _
        Implements IComparable(Of Complex).CompareTo

        Dim result As Integer
```

```vb
        If Equals(that) Then
            result = 0
        ElseIf Me.Magnitude > that.Magnitude Then
            result = 1
        Else
            result = -1
        End If

        Return result
    End Function

    'IComparable implementation
    Function CompareTo(ByVal other As Object) As Integer _
        Implements IComparable.CompareTo

        If Not (TypeOf other Is Complex) Then
            Throw New ArgumentException("Bad Comparison")
        End If

        Return CompareTo(DirectCast(other, Complex))
    End Function

    'System.Object override
    Public Overrides Function ToString() As String
        Return System.String.Format("({0}, {1})", Real, Img)
    End Function

    Public ReadOnly Property Magnitude() As Double
        Get
            Return Math.Sqrt(Math.Pow(Me.Real, 2) + Math.Pow(Me.Img, 2))
        End Get
    End Property

    'Overloaded operators
    Public Shared Operator =(ByVal lhs As Complex, ByVal rhs As Complex) As Boolean
        Return lhs.Equals(rhs)
    End Operator

    Public Shared Operator <>(ByVal lhs As Complex, ByVal rhs As Complex) _
        As Boolean

        Return Not lhs.Equals(rhs)
    End Operator

    Public Shared Operator <(ByVal lhs As Complex, ByVal rhs As Complex) As Boolean
        Return lhs.CompareTo(rhs) < 0
    End Operator
```

```vb
    Public Shared Operator >(ByVal lhs As Complex, ByVal rhs As Complex) As Boolean
        Return lhs.CompareTo(rhs) > 0
    End Operator

    Public Shared Operator <=(ByVal lhs As Complex, ByVal rhs As Complex) _
        As Boolean

        Return lhs.CompareTo(rhs) <= 0
    End Operator

    Public Shared Operator >=(ByVal lhs As Complex, ByVal rhs As Complex) _
        As Boolean

        Return lhs.CompareTo(rhs) >= 0
    End Operator

    'Other methods omitted for clarity.
End Structure

Public Class EntryPoint
    Shared Sub Main()
        Dim cpx1 As Complex = New Complex(1, 3)
        Dim cpx2 As Complex = New Complex(1, 2)

        Console.WriteLine("cpx1 = {0}, cpx1.Magnitude = {1}", cpx1, cpx1.Magnitude)
        Console.WriteLine("cpx2 = {0}, cpx2.Magnitude = {1}" _
            & Chr(10) & "", cpx2, cpx2.Magnitude)

        Console.WriteLine("cpx1 == cpx2 ? {0}", cpx1 = cpx2)
        Console.WriteLine("cpx1 != cpx2 ? {0}", cpx1 <> cpx2)
        Console.WriteLine("cpx1 <  cpx2 ? {0}", cpx1 < cpx2)
        Console.WriteLine("cpx1 >  cpx2 ? {0}", cpx1 > cpx2)
        Console.WriteLine("cpx1 <= cpx2 ? {0}", cpx1 <= cpx2)
        Console.WriteLine("cpx1 >= cpx2 ? {0}", cpx1 >= cpx2)
    End Sub
End Class
```

Here are the results from running the previous code:

```
cpx1 = (1, 3), cpx1.Magnitude = 3.16227766016838
cpx2 = (1, 2), cpx2.Magnitude = 2.23606797749979

cpx1 == cpx2 ? False
cpx1 != cpx2 ? True
cpx1 <  cpx2 ? False
cpx1 >  cpx2 ? True
cpx1 <= cpx2 ? False
cpx1 >= cpx2 ? True
```

Notice that the operator methods merely call the methods that implement `Equals()` and `CompareTo()`. We recommend you provide type-safe versions of the two methods by implementing `IComparable(Of Complex)` and `IEquatable(Of Complex)`. Since the `Complex` type is a value type, this will avoid boxing. Additionally, you implement the `IComparable.CompareTo` method explicitly to give the compiler a bigger type-safety hammer to wield by making it harder for users to inadvertently call the wrong one. Anytime you can, utilize the compiler's type system to sniff out errors at compile time rather than run time. Had you not implemented `IComparable.CompareTo()` explicitly, then the compiler would have happily compiled a statement where you attempt to compare an `Apple` instance to a `Complex` instance. Of course, you would expect an `InvalidCastException` at run time if you were to attempt this, but compile-time errors are preferred to runtime errors.

Boolean Comparisons

It makes sense for some types to participate in Boolean tests, such as within an `If . . . Then` block. In order for this to work, you have two alternatives. Let's consider the first alternative: you can implement two operators known as `Operator IsTrue` and `Operator IsFalse`. You must implement these two operators in pairs and allow the `Complex` number to participate in Boolean test expressions. Consider the following modification to the `Complex` type, where you now can use it in expressions where a value of (0, 0) means `IsFalse` and anything else means `IsTrue`:

```
Option Strict Off

Imports System

Public Structure Complex
    Private Real As Double
    Private Imaginary As Double

    Public Sub New(ByVal real As Double, ByVal imaginary As Double)
        Me.Real = real
        Me.Imaginary = imaginary
    End Sub

    'System.Object override
    Public Overrides Function ToString() As String
        Return System.String.Format("({0}, {1})", Real, Imaginary)
    End Function

    Public ReadOnly Property Magnitude() As Double
        Get
            Return Math.Sqrt(Math.Pow(Me.Real, 2) + Math.Pow(Me.Imaginary, 2))
        End Get
    End Property
```

```vb
    Public Shared Operator IsTrue(ByVal c As Complex) As Boolean
        Return (c.Real <> 0) OrElse (c.Imaginary <> 0)
    End Operator

    Public Shared Operator IsFalse(ByVal c As Complex) As Boolean
        Return (c.Real = 0) AndAlso (c.Imaginary = 0)
    End Operator

    Public Shared Widening Operator CType(ByVal d As Double) As Complex
        Return New Complex(d, 0)
    End Operator

    Public Shared Narrowing Operator CType(ByVal c As Complex) As Double
        Return c.Magnitude
    End Operator

    'Other methods omitted for clarity.
End Structure

Public Class EntryPoint
    Shared Sub Main()
        Dim cpx1 As Complex = New Complex(1.0, 3.0)

        If cpx1 Then
            Console.WriteLine("cpx1 is True")
        Else
            Console.WriteLine("cpx1 is False")
        End If

        Dim cpx2 As Complex = New Complex(0.0, 0.0)

        Console.WriteLine("cpx2 is {0}", IIf(cpx2, "True", "False"))
    End Sub
End Class
```

This code displays the following results:

```
cpx1 is True
cpx2 is False
```

You can see the two operators for applying the IsTrue and IsFalse tests to the Complex type. Notice that the declaration syntax looks almost the same as the conversion operators, except it includes the return type of Boolean. Also, you cannot mark these operators as Widening or Narrowing, because they're not conversion operators. Once you define these two operators on the type, you can use instances of Complex in Boolean test expressions, as shown in the Main method.

■**Note** In setting `Option Strict Off` in the previous example, you're forcing the narrowing conversion to `Boolean` to be accepted by the compiler. You should do this only if you're certain that a runtime error is not possible.

Alternatively, you can choose to implement a conversion to type `Boolean` to achieve the same result. Typically, you want to implement this operator implicitly for ease of use. Consider the modified form of the previous example using the widening Boolean conversion operator rather than `Operator IsTrue` and `Operator IsFalse`:

```
Imports System

Public Structure Complex
    Private Real As Double
    Private Imaginary As Double

    Public Sub New(ByVal real As Double, ByVal imaginary As Double)
        Me.Real = real
        Me.Imaginary = imaginary
    End Sub

    'System.Object override
    Public Overrides Function ToString() As String
        Return System.String.Format("({0}, {1})", Real, Imaginary)
    End Function

    Public ReadOnly Property Magnitude() As Double
        Get
            Return Math.Sqrt(Math.Pow(Me.Real, 2) + Math.Pow(Me.Imaginary, 2))
        End Get
    End Property

    Public Shared Widening Operator CType(ByVal c As Complex) As Boolean
        Return (c.Real <> 0) OrElse (c.Imaginary <> 0)
    End Operator

    Public Shared Widening Operator CType(ByVal d As Double) As Complex
        Return New Complex(d, 0)
    End Operator

    Public Shared Narrowing Operator CType(ByVal c As Complex) As Double
        Return c.Magnitude
    End Operator

    'Other methods omitted for clarity.
End Structure
```

```
Public Class EntryPoint
    Shared Sub Main()
        Dim cpx1 As Complex = New Complex(1.0, 3.0)

        If cpx1 Then
            Console.WriteLine("cpx1 is True")
        Else
            Console.WriteLine("cpx1 is False")
        End If

        Dim cpx2 As Complex = New Complex(0.0, 0.0)

        Console.WriteLine("cpx2 is {0}", IIf(cpx2, "True", "False"))
    End Sub
End Class
```

The end result is the same with this example. Now, you may be wondering why you would ever want to implement Operator IsTrue and Operator IsFalse rather than just use a widening Boolean conversion operator. The answer lies in the fact of whether it is valid for your type to be converted to a Boolean type or not. With the latter form, where you implement the widening conversion operator, the following statement would be valid:

```
cpx1 = f
```

This assignment would work because the compiler would find the widening conversion operator at compile time and apply it. The rule of thumb is to provide only enough of what is necessary to get the job done. If all you want is for your type—in this case, Complex—to participate in Boolean test expressions, only implement Operator IsTrue and Operator IsFalse. If you do have a need to implement the widening Boolean conversion operator, you don't need to implement Operator IsTrue and Operator IsFalse because they would be redundant. If you provide all three, the compiler will go with the widening conversion operator rather than Operator IsTrue and Operator IsFalse because invoking one is not more efficient than the other, assuming you code them the same.

Conversion Operators

Conversion operators are, as the name implies, operators that convert objects of one type into objects of another. Conversion operators can allow widening conversion as well as narrowing conversion. Widening conversion is done with a simple assignment, whereas narrowing conversion requires you to use CType() or one of the built-in casting methods, such as CDbl() or CStr().

An important restriction exists on widening conversion operators. Standards require that widening operators do not throw exceptions and that they're always guaranteed to succeed with no loss of information. If you cannot meet that requirement, then your conversion must be a narrowing one. For example, when converting from one type to another, there's always the possibility for loss of information if the target type is not as expressive as the original type. Consider the conversion from Long to Short. Clearly, it's possible that information could be lost if the value in the Long is greater than the highest value that can be held in a Short. Even though an exception is not thrown in this case if truncation occurs, in some cases it may make sense to throw an exception at run time. Such a conversion must be a narrowing one and requires the use of the casting method. Now, suppose you were going the other way and converting a Short into a Long. Such a conversion will always succeed, so therefore it can be widening.

Overloading the CType Operator

One conversion operator you should provide for Complex is from Double to Complex. Definitely, such a conversion should be a widening one because the Complex structure members are both of type Double. Another consideration is from Complex to Double. This case requires a narrowing conversion, and we chose to return the magnitude rather than just the real portion of the complex number when casting to a Double. Let's look at an example of implementing this conversion by overloading the CType operator:

```
Imports System

Public Structure Complex
    Private Real As Double
    Private Imaginary As Double

    Public Sub New(ByVal real As Double, ByVal imaginary As Double)
        Me.Real = real
        Me.Imaginary = imaginary
    End Sub

    'System.Object override
    Public Overrides Function ToString() As String
        Return System.String.Format("({0}, {1})", Real, Imaginary)
    End Function

    Public ReadOnly Property Magnitude() As Double
        Get
            Return Math.Sqrt(Math.Pow(Me.Real, 2) + Math.Pow(Me.Imaginary, 2))
        End Get
    End Property

    Public Shared Widening Operator CType(ByVal d As Double) As Complex
        Return New Complex(d, 0)
    End Operator

    Public Shared Narrowing Operator CType(ByVal c As Complex) As Double
        Return c.Magnitude
    End Operator

    'Other methods omitted for clarity.
End Structure
```

```
Public Class EntryPoint
    Shared Sub Main()
        Dim cpx1 As Complex = New Complex(1.0, 3.0)

        'Use Widening operator.
        Dim cpx2 As Complex = 2.0

        'Use Narrowing operator.
        Dim d As Double = cpx1

        Console.WriteLine("cpx1 = {0}", cpx1)
        Console.WriteLine("cpx2 = {0}", cpx2)
        Console.WriteLine("d = {0}", d)
    End Sub
End Class
```

Running this example produces the following output:

```
cpx1 = (1, 3)
cpx2 = (2, 0)
d = 3.16227766016838
```

The syntax in the Main method is natural when using our overloaded CType operator. However, be careful when implementing conversion operators to make sure that you don't open up users to any surprises, as inadvertent use of conversions can be a source of confusion. For example, the compiler could do a widening conversion when trying to coerce an argument on a method call. Even if the conversion does make semantic sense, they can still provide plenty of surprises, since the compiler will have the liberty of silently converting instances of one type to another when it feels it necessary.

Let's consider the case where Complex provides another narrowing conversion operator to convert to an instance of Fraction as well as to an instance of Double. This would give Complex two methods with the following signatures:

```
Public Shared Narrowing Operator CType(ByVal d As Complex) As Double
Public Shared Narrowing Operator CType(ByVal f As Complex) As Fraction
```

These two methods take the same type, Complex, and return another type. However, the overload rules clearly state that the return type doesn't participate in the method signature. Going by those rules, these two methods should be ambiguous and result in a compiler error. In fact, they are not ambiguous because a special rule exists to allow the return type of conversion operators to be considered in the signature. Incidentally, the Widening and Narrowing keywords don't participate in the signature of conversion operator methods. Therefore, it's impossible to have both widening and narrowing conversion operators with the same signature. Naturally, at least one of the types in the signature of a conversion operator must be the enclosing type. It is invalid for a type Complex to implement a conversion operator from type Apples to type Oranges.

Summary

This chapter covered some guidelines for overloading operators, including unary, binary, and conversion operators. Operator overloading is one of the features that makes VB 2008 such a powerful and expressive .NET language.

However, just because you can do something doesn't mean you should. Misuse of widening conversion operators and improperly defined semantics in other operator overloads can be the source of great user confusion, as well as unintended behavior. When it comes to overloading operators, provide only what is necessary and don't go counter to the general semantics of the various operators. Unless you're sure that your code will be consumed by .NET languages that support operator overloading, be sure to provide explicitly named methods that provide the same functionality.

In the next chapter, we'll cover the intricacies and tricks to creating exception-safe and exception-neutral code in the .NET Framework.

CHAPTER 8

■■■

Exception Handling

The common language runtime (CLR) contains strong support for exceptions. You can create and throw exceptions at a point where code execution cannot continue due to some exceptional condition (usually a method failure or invalid state). Once exceptions are thrown, the CLR begins the process of unwinding the call stack iteratively frame by frame.[1] As it does so, it cleans up any objects that are local to each stack frame. At some point, a frame on the stack could have an exception handler registered for the type of exception thrown. Once the CLR reaches that frame, it invokes the exception handler to remedy the situation. If the stack unwind finishes and a handler is not found for the exception thrown, then the unhandled exception event for the current application domain may be fired and the application could be aborted.

Writing exception-safe code is a difficult art to master. It would be a mistake to assume that the only tasks required when writing exception-safe code are simply throwing exceptions when an error occurs and catching them at some point. Instead, exception-safe coding techniques are those with which you can guarantee the integrity of the system in the face of exceptions. When an exception is thrown, the runtime will iteratively unwind the stack while cleaning up. Your job as an exception-safe programmer is to structure your code in such a way that the integrity of the state of your objects is not compromised as the stack unwinds. That is the true essence of exception-safe coding techniques.

Handling Exceptions

Where should you handle exceptions? You can find the answer by applying a variant of the Expert pattern, which states that work should be done by the entity that is the expert with respect to that work. That is a circuitous way of saying that you should catch the exception at the point where you can actually handle it with some degree of knowledge available to remedy the situation. Sometimes, the catching entity could be close to the point of the exception generation within the stack frame. The code could catch the exception, then take some corrective action, and then allow the program to continue to execute normally. Other times, the only reasonable place to catch an exception is at the entry-point `Main` method, at which point you

---

1. As each method is called throughout the execution of a program, a frame is built on the stack that contains the passed parameters and any local parameters to the method. The frame is deleted upon return from the method. As the method calls other methods, and so on, new frames are stacked on top of the current frame, thus implementing a "nested call-stack" structure.

could either abort the process after providing some useful data, or you could reset the process as if the application were just restarted. The bottom line is that you should figure out the best way to recover from exceptions and where it makes the most sense to do so.

Avoid Using Exceptions to Control Flow

It can be tempting to use exceptions to manage the flow of execution in complex methods. This is generally not a good idea. Exceptions are expensive to generate and handle. Therefore, if you were to use them to control execution flow within a method that is at the heart of your application, your performance will likely degrade. Secondly, it trivializes the nature of exceptions in the first place. The point is to indicate an exceptional condition in a way that you can handle or report it cleanly.

Programmers can be rather lazy when it comes to handling error conditions. You've probably seen code where the programmer didn't bother to check the return value of an API function or method call. Exceptions provide a syntactically succinct way to indicate and handle error conditions without littering your code with a plethora of If . . . Then blocks and other traditional (non-exception-based) error-handling constructs.

At the same time, the runtime supports exceptions, and it does a lot of work on your behalf when exceptions are thrown. Unwinding the stack is no trivial task in and of itself. Lastly, the point where an exception is thrown and the point where it's handled can be disjointed and have no connection to each other. Thus it can be difficult when reading code to determine where an exception will get caught and handled. These reasons alone are enough for you to stick to traditional techniques when managing normal execution flow.

Mechanics of Handling Exceptions in VB 2008

If you've ever used exceptions in other C-style languages such as C++, Java, or even C/C++ using the Microsoft structured exception-handling extensions (__try/__catch/__finally), then you're already familiar with the basic syntax of exceptions in Visual Basic (VB). In that case, you may find yourself skimming the next few sections or treating the material as a refresher.

Syntax Overview of the Try Statement

The code within a Try block is guarded against exceptions such that, if an exception is thrown, the runtime will search for a suitable Catch block to handle the exception. Whether a suitable Catch block exists or not, if a Finally block is provided, the Finally block will always execute, no matter how execution flow leaves the Try block. Let's look at an example of a Try statement:

```
Imports System
Imports System.Collections
Imports System.Runtime.CompilerServices

Public Class EntryPoint
    Shared Sub Main()
        Try
            Dim list As ArrayList = New ArrayList()
```

```
                list.Add(1)
                Console.WriteLine("Item 10 = {0}", list(10))
            Catch x As ArgumentOutOfRangeException
                Console.WriteLine("=== ArgumentOutOfRangeException Handler ===")
                Console.WriteLine(x)
                Console.WriteLine("=== ArgumentOutOfRangeException Handler ===")
            Catch x As Exception
                Console.WriteLine("=== Exception Handler ===")
                Console.WriteLine(x)
                Console.WriteLine("=== Exception Handler ===")
            Finally
                Console.WriteLine(vbCrLf & "Cleaning up . . .")
            End Try
        End Sub
    End Class
```

Running the preceding code displays the following output:

```
=== ArgumentOutOfRangeException Handler ===
System.ArgumentOutOfRangeException: Index was out of range. Must be non-negative
 and less than the size of the collection.
Parameter name: index
   at System.Collections.ArrayList.get_Item(Int32 index)
   at Exception_Handling1.EntryPoint.Main() in C:\Apress\AVB 2008\EH\EH.vb:line 11
=== ArgumentOutOfRangeException Handler ===

Cleaning up . . .
```

Once you see the code in the Try block, you know it is destined to throw an ArgumentOutOfRange exception, as we are trying to display the 10th element of a 1 element ArrayList to the console. Once the exception is thrown, the runtime begins searching for a suitable Catch clause that is part of this Try statement and matches the type of the exception as well as possible. As the first Catch clause is the one that fits best, the runtime will immediately begin executing the statements in this Catch block. We could have left off the declaration of the exception variable x in the Catch clause and only declared the type, but we wanted to demonstrate that exception objects produce a nice stack trace that can be useful during debugging.

The second Catch clause will catch exceptions of the general Exception type. Should the code in the Try block throw an exception derived from System.Exception other than ArgumentOutOfRangeException, then this Catch block would handle it. Multiple Catch clauses associated with a single Try block must be ordered such that more specific exception types are listed first. The compiler won't compile code where more general Catch clauses are listed before more specific Catch clauses. You can verify this by swapping the order of the first two Catch clauses in the previous example.

And finally (no pun intended), there is the Finally block. No matter how the Try block is exited, the Finally block will always execute. If there is a suitable Catch block in the same frame as the Finally block, it will execute before the Finally block.

Throwing Exceptions

The act of throwing an exception is actually quite easy. You simply execute a Throw statement where the parameter to the Throw statement is the exception you would like to throw. For example, suppose you've written a custom collection class that allows users to access items by index, and you'd like to notify users when an invalid index is passed as a parameter. You could throw an ArgumentOutOfRange exception, such as in the following code:

```
Public Class MyCollection
    Private Count As Integer

    Public Function GetItem(ByVal index As Integer) As Object
        If index < 0 OrElse index >= Count Then
            Throw New ArgumentOutOfRangeException()
        End If
    End Function
End Class
```

The runtime can also throw exceptions as a side effect to code execution. An example of a system-generated exception is NullReferenceException, which occurs if you attempt to access a field or call a method on an object when, in fact, the reference to the object doesn't exist.

Unhandled Exceptions in .NET 3.5

When an exception is thrown, the runtime begins to search up the stack for a matching Catch block for the exception. As it walks up the execution stack, it unwinds the stack at the same time, cleaning up each frame along the way.

If the search ends in the last frame for the thread, and it still finds no handler for the exception, the exception is considered unhandled at that point. In .NET 3.5, any unhandled exception, except for AppDomainUnloadException and ThreadAbortException, causes the thread to terminate. It sounds rude, but in reality, this is the behavior you should want from an unhandled exception. After all, it's an *unhandled* exception. Now that the thread terminates as expected, a big red flag is raised at the point of the exception that allows you to find the problem immediately and fix it. This is a good thing, as you want errors to present themselves as soon as possible and never let the system keep running as if everything were normal.

■**Note** You can install an unhandled exception filter by registering a delegate with AppDomain. UnhandledException. When an unhandled exception comes up through the stack, this delegate will get called, and it will receive an instance of UnhandledExceptionEventArgs. When creating Windows applications, you can manage unhandled exceptions via the My.Application.UnhandledException event.

Re-throwing Exceptions and Translating Exceptions

Within a particular stack frame, you may find it necessary to catch all exceptions, or a specific subset of exceptions, long enough to do some cleanup, and then re-throw the exceptions in order to let them continue to propagate up the stack. To do this, you use the Throw statement with no parameter, as follows:

```
Imports System
Imports System.Collections

Public Class EntryPoint
    Shared Sub Main()
        Try
            Try
                Dim list As ArrayList = New ArrayList()
                list.Add(1)

                Console.WriteLine("Item 10 = {0}", list(10))
            Catch ex As ArgumentOutOfRangeException
                Console.WriteLine("Do some useful work and then re-throw")

                'Re-throw caught exception.
                Throw
            Finally
                Console.WriteLine("Cleaning up . . .")
            End Try

        Catch
            Console.WriteLine("Done")
        End Try
    End Sub
End Class
```

Note that any Finally blocks associated with the exception frame that the Catch block is associated with will execute before any higher-level exception handlers are executed. You can see this in the output from the previous code:

```
Do some useful work and then re-throw
Cleaning up . . .
Done
```

The "Achieving Exception Neutrality" section later in this chapter introduces some techniques that can help you avoid having to catch an exception, do some cleanup, and then re-throw the exception. That sort of work flow is cumbersome, since you must be careful to re-throw the exception appropriately. If you accidentally forget to re-throw, things could get ugly, since you would not likely be remedying the exceptional situation. The techniques introduced will help you achieve the goal of only placing a Catch block where correctional action can occur.

Sometimes, you may find it necessary to "translate" an exception within an exception handler. In this case, you catch an exception of one type, but you throw an exception of a different, possibly more precise, type in the Catch block for the next level of exception handlers to deal with. Consider the following example:

```
Imports System
Imports System.Collections

Public Class MyException
    Inherits Exception

    Public Sub New(ByVal reason As String, ByVal inner As Exception)
        MyBase.New(reason, inner)
    End Sub
End Class

Public Class EntryPoint
    Shared Sub Main()
        Try
            Try
                Dim list As ArrayList = New ArrayList()
                list.Add(1)
                Console.WriteLine("Item 10 = {0}", list(10))

            Catch x As ArgumentOutOfRangeException
                Console.WriteLine("Do some useful work and then re-throw")
                Throw New MyException("I'd rather throw this", x)

            Finally
                Console.WriteLine("Cleaning up . . .")
            End Try

        Catch x As Exception
            Console.WriteLine(x)
            Console.WriteLine("Done")
        End Try
    End Sub
End Class
```

One special quality of the System.Exception type is its ability to contain an inner exception reference via the Exception.InnerException property. This way, when the new exception is thrown, you can preserve the chain of exceptions for the handlers that process them. We recommend you use this useful feature of the standard exception type of VB when you translate exceptions. The output from the previous code is as follows:

```
Do some useful work and then re-throw
Cleaning up . . .
Exceptions.MyException: I'd rather throw this --->
```

```
System.ArgumentOutOfRangeException: Index was out of range. Must be non-negative
and less than the size of the collection.
Parameter name: index
   at System.Collections.ArrayList.get_Item(Int32 index)
   at Exceptions.Entrypoint.Main() in C:\AVB9\Exceptions\Exception4.vb:line 18
   --- End of inner exception stack trace ---
   at Exceptions.Entrypoint.Main() in C:\AVB9\Exceptions\Exception4.vb:line 22
Done
```

Keep in mind that you should avoid translating exceptions if possible. The more you catch and then re-throw within a stack, the more you insulate the code handling the exception from the code throwing the exception. That is, it's harder to correlate the point of catch to the original point of throw. Yes, the Exception.InnerException property helps mitigate some of this disconnect, but it still can be tricky to find the root cause of a problem if there are exception translations along the way.

Exceptions Thrown in Finally Blocks

It is possible, but inadvisable, to throw exceptions within a Finally block. The following code shows an example:

```
Imports System
Imports System.Collections

Public Class EntryPoint
    Shared Sub Main()
        Try
            Try
                Dim list As ArrayList = New ArrayList()
                list.Add(1)
                Console.WriteLine("Item 10 = {0}", list(10))

            Finally
                Console.WriteLine("Cleaning up . . .")
                Throw New Exception("I like to throw")
            End Try

        Catch generatedExceptionName As ArgumentOutOfRangeException
            Console.WriteLine("Oops!  Argument out of range!")

        Catch
            Console.WriteLine("Done")
        End Try
    End Sub
End Class
```

The output from executing this code is as follows:

```
Cleaning up . . .
Done
```

The first exception is simply lost, and the new exception is propagated up the stack. Clearly, this is not desirable. You never want to lose track of exceptions because it becomes virtually impossible to determine what caused an exception in the first place.

Exceptions Thrown in Finalizers

Destructors in VB are not really deterministic destructors but, rather, CLR finalizers. Finalizers are run in the context of the finalizer thread, which is effectively an arbitrary thread context. If the finalizer were to throw an exception, the CLR may not know how to handle the situation and may simply shut down the thread (and the process). Consider the following code:

```
Imports System

Public Class Person
    Protected Overrides Sub Finalize()
        Try
            Console.WriteLine("Cleaning up Person . . .")
            Console.WriteLine("Done Cleaning up Person . . .")
        Finally
            MyBase.Finalize()
        End Try
    End Sub
End Class

Public Class Employee
    Inherits Person

    Protected Overrides Sub Finalize()
        Try
            Console.WriteLine("Cleaning up Employee . . .")

            Dim obj As Object = Nothing

            Console.WriteLine(obj.ToString())
            Console.WriteLine("Done cleaning up Employee . . .")
        Finally
            MyBase.Finalize()
        End Try
    End Sub
End Class
```

```
Public Class EntryPoint
    Shared Sub Main()
        Dim e As Employee = New Employee
    End Sub
End Class
```

The output from executing this code is as follows:

```
Cleaning up Employee . . .
```

Stepping through the preceding example will display the corresponding output, then the Exception Assistant will present you a "**NullReferenceException was unhandled** – Object reference not set to an instance of an object" dialog, which includes troubleshooting tips and actions. Finally, you should avoid knowingly throwing exceptions in finalizers, because you could abort the process.

Exceptions Thrown in Shared Constructors

If an exception is thrown and there is no handler in the stack and the search for the handler ends up in the shared constructor, the runtime handles this case specially. It translates the exception into a System.TypeInitializationException and throws that instead. Before throwing the new exception, it sets the InnerException property of the new exception to the original exception. That way, any handler for type-initialization exceptions can easily find out exactly why things failed.

Translating such an exception makes sense due to the fact that constructors cannot, by their very nature, have a return value to indicate success or failure. Exceptions are the only mechanism you have to indicate that a constructor has failed. More importantly, since the system calls shared constructors at system-defined times,[2] it makes sense for them to use the TypeInitializationException type in order to be more specific about when something went wrong. For example, suppose you have a shared constructor that can potentially throw an ArgumentOutOfRangeException. Now, imagine the frustration users would have if your exception propagated out to the enclosing thread at some seemingly random time due to the fact that the exact moment of a shared constructor call is system-defined. It could appear that the ArgumentOutOfRange exception materialized out of thin air. Wrapping your exception inside a TypeInitializationException takes a little of the mystery out of it and informs users and the developer that the problem happened during type initialization.

The following code shows an example of what a TypeInitializationException with an inner exception looks like:

```
Imports System
Imports System.IO

Class EventLogger
    Private Shared EventLog As StreamWriter
    Private Shared StrLogName As String
```

---

2. The system could call shared constructors at type load time or just prior to a shared member access, depending on how the CLR is configured for the current process.

```
    Shared Sub New()
        EventLog = File.CreateText("logfile.txt")
        StrLogName = DirectCast(StrLogName.Clone(), String)
    End Sub

    Public Shared Sub WriteLog(ByVal someText As String)
        EventLog.Write(someText)
    End Sub
End Class

Public Class EntryPoint
    Shared Sub Main()
        EventLogger.WriteLog("Log this!")
    End Sub
End Class
```

When you step through this example, the Exception Assistant presents you with a
"TypeInitializationException was unhandled – The type initializer for 'Exceptions.EventLogger'
threw an exception" dialog, which includes troubleshooting tips and actions. Click the "View
Detail . . ." link below "Actions:" to open the View Detail dialog, which shows an exception
snapshot listing System.TypeInitializationException as the outer exception and "Object
reference not set to an instance of an object" as the inner exception that started it all.

Figure 8-1 shows the Exception Assistant dialogs.

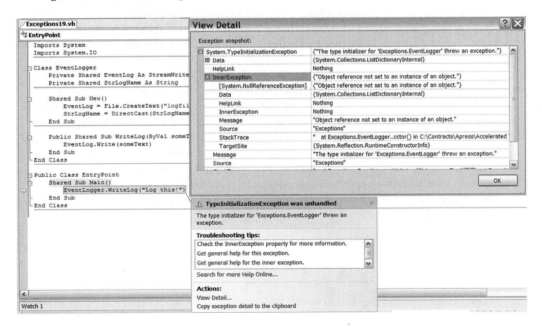

Figure 8-1. *The Exception Assistant in action*

Achieving Exception Neutrality

When exceptions were first added to C++, many developers were excited to be able to throw them, catch them, and handle them. A common misconception at the time was that exception handling simply consisted of strategically placing Try statements throughout the code and tossing in an occasional Throw when necessary. Over time, the developer community realized that dropping Try statements all over the place made their code difficult to read when, most of the time, the only thing they wanted to do was clean up gracefully when an exception was thrown and allow the exception to keep propagating up the stack. Even worse, it made the code hard to write and difficult to maintain. Code that doesn't handle exceptions but is expected to behave properly in the face of exceptions is generally called *exception-neutral* code.

Clearly, there had to be a better way to write exception-neutral code without having to rely on writing Try statements all over the place. In fact, the only place you need a Try statement is the point at which you perform any sort of system recovery or logging in response to an exception. Over time, developers started to realize that writing Try statements was the least significant part of writing exception-safe and exception-neutral code. Generally, the only code that should catch an exception is code that knows specifically how to remedy the situation. That code could even be in the main entry point and could merely reset the system to a known start state, effectively restarting the application.

Exception-neutral code is code that is in a position that doesn't really have the capability to specifically handle the exception but that must be able to handle exceptions gracefully. Usually, this code sits somewhere on the stack in between the code that throws the exception and the code that catches the exception, and it must not be adversely affected by the exception passing through on its way up the stack. At this point, some of you are probably starting to think about the Throw statement with no parameters that allows you to catch an exception, do some work, and then re-throw the exception. However, an arguably cleaner technique allows you to write exception-neutral code without using a single Try statement and also produces code that is easier to read and more robust.

Basic Structure of Exception-Neutral Code

The general idea behind writing exception-neutral code is similar to the idea behind creating commit/rollback code. You write such code with the guarantee that if it doesn't finish to completion, the entire operation is reverted with no change in state to the system. The changes in state are committed only if the code reaches the end of its execution path. You should code your methods like this in order for them to be exception-neutral. If an exception is thrown before the end of the method, the state of the system should remain unchanged. The following shows how you should structure your methods in order to achieve these goals:

```
Sub ExceptionNeutralMethod()
    ' All code that could possibly throw exceptions is in this
    ' first section. In this section, no changes in state are
    ' applied to any objects in the system including this.

    ' All changes are committed at this point using operations
    ' strictly guaranteed not to throw exceptions.
End Sub
```

As you can see, this technique doesn't work unless you have a set of operations that are guaranteed never to throw exceptions. Otherwise, it would be impossible to implement the commit/rollback behavior as illustrated. Thankfully, the .NET runtime does provide quite a few operations that the specification guarantees never to throw exceptions.

Let's start by building an example to describe what we mean. Suppose you have a system or application where you're managing employees. For the sake of argument, say that once an employee is created and represented by an `Employee` object, it must exist within one and only one collection in the system. Currently, the only two collections in the system are one to represent active employees and one to represent terminated employees. Additionally, the collections exist inside of an `EmployeeDatabase` object, as shown in the following example:

```
Imports System.Collections

Class EmployeeDatabase
    Private ActiveEmployees As ArrayList
    Private TerminatedEmployees As ArrayList
End Class
```

The example uses collections of the `ArrayList` type, which is contained in the `System.Collections` namespace. A real-world system would probably use something more useful, such as a database.

Now, let's see what happens when an employee quits. Naturally, you need to move that employee from the `ActiveEmployees` to the `TerminatedEmployees` collection. A first attempt at such a task could look like the following:

```
Imports System.Collections

Class Employee
End Class

Class EmployeeDatabase
    Private ActiveEmployees As ArrayList
    Private TerminatedEmployees As ArrayList

    Public Sub TerminateEmployee(ByVal index As Integer)
        Dim employee As Object = ActiveEmployees(index)

        ActiveEmployees.RemoveAt(index)
        TerminatedEmployees.Add(employee)
    End Sub
End Class
```

This code looks reasonable enough. The method that does the move assumes that the calling code somehow figured out the index for the current employee in the `ActiveEmployees` list prior to calling `TerminateEmployee()`. It copies a reference to the designated employee, removes that reference from `ActiveEmployees`, and adds it to the `TerminatedEmployees` collection. So what's so bad about this method?

Look at `TerminateEmployee()` closely, and see where exceptions could get generated. The fact is, an exception could be thrown upon execution of any of the methods called by this method. If the index is out of range, then you would expect to see ArgumentOutOfRange exceptions thrown from the first two lines. Of course, if the range exception is thrown from the first line, execution would never see the second line, but you get the idea. And, if memory is scarce, it's possible that the call to Add() could fail with an exception.

The danger comes from the possibility of the exception being thrown after the state of the system is modified. Suppose the index passed in is valid. The first two lines will likely succeed. However, if an exception is thrown while trying to add the employee to TerminatedEmployees, then the employee of interest will get lost in the system. So, what can you do to fix the glitch?

An initial attempt could use Try statements to avoid damage to the system state. Consider the following example:

```vb
Imports System.Collections

Class Employee
End Class

Class EmployeeDatabase
    Private ActiveEmployees As ArrayList
    Private TerminatedEmployees As ArrayList

    Public Sub TerminateEmployee(ByVal index As Integer)
        Dim employee As Object = Nothing

        Try
            employee = ActiveEmployees(index)
        Catch
        'Oops!  We must be out of range here.
        End Try

        If employee <> Nothing Then
            ActiveEmployees.RemoveAt(index)
            Try
                TerminatedEmployees.Add(employee)
            Catch
                'Allocation may have failed.
                ActiveEmployees.Add(employee)
            End Try
        End If
    End Sub
End Class
```

Look how quickly the code becomes hard to read and understand, thanks to the Try statements. You have to pull the Employee reference out of the Try statement and initialize it to Nothing. Once you attempt to get the reference to the employee, you have to check the reference for Nothing to make sure you actually got it. Once that succeeds, you can proceed to add the Employee to the TerminatedEmployees list. However, if that fails for some reason, you need to put the Employee back into the ActiveEmployees list.

You may have already spotted a multitude of problems with this approach. First of all, what happens if you have a failure to add the Employee back into the ActiveEmployees collection? Do you just fail at that point? That's unacceptable, since the state of the system has changed already. Second, you probably need to return an error code from this method to indicate why it may have failed to complete. Third, the code can quickly become difficult to follow and hard to read.

So what's the solution? Well, think of what you attempted to do with the Try statements. You want to do the actions that possibly throw exceptions, and if they fail, revert back to the previous state. You can actually perform a variation on this theme without Try statements that goes like this: attempt all of the actions in the method that could throw exceptions up front, and once you get past that point, commit those actions using operations that can't throw exceptions.

Let's see what this function would look like:

```
Imports System.Collections

Class Employee
End Class

Class EmployeeDatabase
    Private activeEmployees As ArrayList
    Private terminatedEmployees As ArrayList

    Public Sub TerminateEmployee(ByVal index As Integer)
        'Clone-sensitive objects.
        Dim tempActiveEmployees As ArrayList = _
        DirectCast(activeEmployees.Clone(), ArrayList)

        Dim tempTerminatedEmployees As ArrayList = _
        DirectCast(terminatedEmployees.Clone(), ArrayList)

        'Perform actions on our temp objects.
        Dim employee As Object = tempActiveEmployees(index)

        tempActiveEmployees.RemoveAt(index)
        tempTerminatedEmployees.Add(employee)

        'Now, commit the changes.
        Dim tempSpace As ArrayList = Nothing

        ListSwap(activeEmployees, tempActiveEmployees, tempSpace)
        ListSwap(terminatedEmployees, tempTerminatedEmployees, tempSpace)
    End Sub

    Sub ListSwap(ByRef first As ArrayList, ByRef second As ArrayList, _
        ByRef temp As ArrayList)
        temp = first
        first = second
        second = temp
        temp = Nothing
    End Sub
End Class
```

First, notice the absence of any Try statements. The nice thing about their absence is that the method doesn't need to return a result code. The caller can expect the method to either work as advertised or throw an exception. The only two lines in the method that affect the state of the system are the last two calls to ListSwap(). ListSwap() was introduced to allow you to swap the references of the ArrayList objects in the EmployeeDatabase with the references to the temporary modified copies that you made.

How is this technique so much better when it appears to be so much less efficient? There are two tricks here. The obvious one is that, no matter where in this method an exception is thrown, the state of the EmployeeDatabase will remain unaffected. But, what if an exception is thrown inside ListSwap()? Ah! Here you have the second trick: ListSwap() will never throw an exception. One of the most important features required in order to create exception-neutral code is that you have a small set of operations that are guaranteed not to fail under normal circumstances. No, we're not considering the case of a catastrophic earthquake or tornado at that point. Let's see why ListSwap() won't throw any exceptions.

In order to create exception-neutral code, it's imperative that you have a handful of operations, such as an assignment operation, that are guaranteed not to throw. Thankfully, the CLR provides such operations. The assignment of references, when no conversion is required, is one example. Every reference to an object is stored in a location, and that location has a type associated with it. However, once the locations exist, copying a reference from one to the other is a simple memory copy to already allocated locations, and that cannot fail. That's great for when you're copying references of one type to references of the same type.

But what happens when a conversion is necessary? Can that throw an exception? If your assignment invokes an implicit conversion, you're covered, assuming that any custom implicit conversion operators don't throw. You must take great care not to throw an exception in your custom implicit conversion operators. However, explicit conversions, in the form of casts, can throw. The bottom line is, a simple assignment from one reference to another, whether it requires implicit conversion or not, will not throw.

Simple assignment from one reference location to another is all that ListSwap() is doing. After you set up the temporary ArrayList objects with the desired state, and you've gotten to the point of even executing the ListSwap() calls, you've arrived at a point where you know that no more exceptions in the TerminateEmployee() method are possible. Now, you can make the switch safely. The ArrayList objects in the EmployeeDatabase object are swapped with the temporary ones. Once the method completes, the original ArrayList objects are free to be collected by the garbage collector (GC).

One more thing that you may have noticed regarding ListSwap() is that the temporary location to store an ArrayList instance during the swap is allocated outside of the ListSwap() method and passed in as a ByRef parameter. Doing this avoids a StackOverflowException inside ListSwap(). It's remotely possible that, when calling ListSwap(), the stack could be running on vapors, and the mere allocation of another stack slot could fail and generate an exception. So, you should perform that step outside of the confines of the ListSwap method. Once execution is inside ListSwap(), all the locations are allocated and ready for use.

This technique, when applied liberally in a system that requires rigid stability, will quickly point out methods that may be too complex and need to be broken up into smaller functional units. In essence, this idiom amplifies the complexity of a particular method it is applied to. Therefore, if you find that it becomes unwieldy and difficult to make the method bulletproof, you should analyze the method and make sure it's not trying to do too much work that you could break up into smaller units.

Incidentally, you may find it necessary to make swap operations, similar to ListSwap(), atomic in a multithreaded environment. You could modify ListSwap() to use some sort of exclusive lock object, such as a mutex or a System.Threading.Monitor object. However, you may find yourself inadvertently making ListSwap() capable of throwing exceptions, and that violates the requirements on ListSwap(). Thankfully, the System.Threading namespace offers the Interlocked class to perform these swap operations atomically, and best of all, the methods are guaranteed never to throw exceptions. The Interlocked class provides a generic overload of all of the useful methods, making them very efficient. The generic Interlocked methods come with a constraint that they only work with reference types.

The bottom line is, you should do everything that can possibly throw an exception before modifying the state of the object being operated on. Once you know you're past the point of possibly causing any exceptions, commit the changes using operations that are guaranteed not to throw exceptions. If you're tasked to create a robust, real-world system where many people rely on the integrity of the system, the importance of this idiom cannot be stressed enough.

Constrained Execution Regions

The example in the previous section demonstrates some of the level of paranoia you must endure in order to write bulletproof, exception-neutral code. We were so paranoid that a stack overflow would occur that we allocated the extra space needed by ListSwap() before we called the method. You would think that would take care of all of the issues. Unfortunately, you'd be wrong. In the CLR environment, other asynchronous exceptions could occur, such as ThreadAbortException, OutOfMemoryException, and StackOverflowException exceptions.

For example, what if during the commit phase of the TerminateEmployee method, the application domain is shut down, forcing a ThreadAbortException? Or what if during the first call to ListSwap(), the just-in-time (JIT) compiler fails to allocate enough memory to compile the method in the first place? Clearly, these bad situations are difficult to deal with. In .NET 3.5, you can use a *constrained execution region* (CER) or a *critical finalizer*.

A CER is a region of code that the CLR prepares prior to executing so that when the code is needed, everything is in place and the failure possibilities are mitigated. Moreover, the CLR postpones the delivery of any asynchronous exceptions, such as ThreadAbortException exceptions, if the code in the CER is executing. You can perform the magic of CERs using the RuntimeHelpers class in the System.Runtime.CompilerServices namespace. To create a CER, simply call RuntimeHelpers.PrepareConstrainedRegions() prior to a Try statement in your code. The CLR then examines the Catch and Finally blocks and prepares them by walking the call graph and making sure all methods in the execution path are JIT-compiled and sufficient stack space is available.[3] Even though you call PrepareConstrainedRegions() prior to a Try statement, the actual code within the Try block is not prepared. You can use the following to prepare these sections of code by wrapping the code in a Finally block within a CER:

---

3. Incidentally, overridable methods and delegates pose a problem because the call graph is not deducible at preparation time. However, if you know the target of the overridable method or delegate, you can prepare it explicitly by calling RuntimeHelpers.PrepareDelegate().

```vb
Imports System.Collections
Imports System.Runtime.CompilerServices
Imports System.Runtime.ConstrainedExecution

Class Employee
End Class

Class EmployeeDatabase
    Private ActiveEmployees As ArrayList
    Private TerminatedEmployees As ArrayList

    Public Sub TerminateEmployee(ByVal index As Integer)
        'Clone-sensitive objects
        Dim tempActiveEmployees As ArrayList = _
            DirectCast(ActiveEmployees.Clone(), ArrayList)
        Dim tempTerminatedEmployees As ArrayList = _
            DirectCast(TerminatedEmployees.Clone(), ArrayList)

        'Perform actions on temp objects.
        Dim employee As Object = tempActiveEmployees(index)
        tempActiveEmployees.RemoveAt(index)
        tempTerminatedEmployees.Add(employee)

        RuntimeHelpers.PrepareConstrainedRegions()

        Try

        Finally
            'Now commit the changes
            Dim tempSpace As ArrayList = Nothing

            ListSwap(ActiveEmployees, tempActiveEmployees, tempSpace)
            ListSwap(TerminatedEmployees, tempTerminatedEmployees, tempSpace)
        End Try
    End Sub

    <ReliabilityContract(Consistency.WillNotCorruptState, Cer.Success)> _
    Sub ListSwap(ByRef first As ArrayList, ByRef second As ArrayList, _
        ByRef temp As ArrayList)
        temp = first
        first = second
        second = temp
        temp = Nothing
    End Sub
End Class
```

Notice that the commit section of the TerminateEmployee method is wrapped inside a CER. At run time, prior to executing that code, the CLR prepares the code by also preparing the `ListSwap` method and ensuring that the stack can handle the work. Of course, this preparation operation may fail, and that's OK, because you're not yet into the code that commits the changes. Notice the addition of the `ReliabilityContractAttribute` to the `ListSwap` method. This informs the runtime of what sorts of guarantees the `ListSwap` method adheres to so that the CER can be formed properly. You could also attach a `ReliabilityContractAttribute` to the `TerminateEmployee` method, but it really is only useful for code executed inside of a CER. If you want to attach this attribute to the `TerminateEmployee` method so that you can use it in a CER created elsewhere, then you could add the following attribute:

`<ReliabilityContract(Consistency.WillNotCorruptState, Cer.MayFail)>`

This `ReliabilityContractAttribute` expresses the goal that you set out to achieve with `TerminateEmployee()` in the first place. That is, it may fail, but if it does, the state of the system won't be corrupted.

■Note Even though the CLR guarantees that asynchronous exceptions won't be injected into the thread while inside a CER, it doesn't provide any guarantee about suppressing all exceptions. It only suppresses the ones that are outside of your control. That means that if you create objects within a CER, you must be prepared to deal with `OutOfMemoryException` or any other such code-induced exception.

Critical Finalizers and SafeHandle

Critical finalizers are similar to CERs, in that the code within them is protected from asynchronous exceptions and other such dangers caused by running in a virtual execution system that are outside your control. To mark your object as having a critical finalizer, simply derive from `CriticalFinalizerObject`. By doing so, your object is guaranteed to have a finalizer that runs within the context of a CER, and therefore, must abide to all of the rules imposed by a CER. Additionally, the CLR will execute critical finalizers after it finishes dealing with all other non-critical finalizable objects.

In reality, it's rare that you'll ever need to create a critical finalizable object. Instead, you can usually get the behavior you need by deriving from `SafeHandle`. `SafeHandle` is a critical tool when creating native interop code through Platform Invoke (P/Invoke)[4] or COM interop, since it allows you to guarantee that you won't leak any unmanaged resources from within the CLR. Prior to .NET 2.0, this was not possible. By adding an extra level of indirection[5] in the form of a `SafeHandle`, you can mitigate these problems.

---

4. Platform Invoke (P/Invoke) allows your managed code to call the Win32 API, as well as other unmanaged code, such as third-party and legacy dynamic link libraries (DLLs). See Appendix A for resources.

5. Andrew Koenig of C++ fame likes to call this the Fundamental Theorem of Software Engineering—that is, that you can solve any software engineering problem by adding a level of indirection.

■**Caution** Before you jump to the conclusion that you need to create a SafeHandle derivative, be sure to check if one of the supplied SafeHandle derivatives in the .NET Framework will work for you. For example, if you're creating code to talk directly to a device driver by calling the Win32 DeviceIoControl() function via P/Invoke, then the SafeFileHandle type is sufficient for holding the handle that you open directly on the driver.

When creating your own SafeHandle derived class, you must follow a short list of steps. For the sake of example, let's create a SafeHandle derived class, SafeBluetoothRadioFindHandle, to enumerate through the Bluetooth radios on a system, assuming there are any. The pattern for enumerating Bluetooth radios in native code is quite simple and a common theme used throughout the Win32 API. You call the Win32 BluetoothFindFirstRadio() function, and if it succeeds, it returns the first radio handle through an out parameter and an enumeration handle through the return value. You can find any additional radios by calling the Win32 function BluetoothFindNextRadio(). When finished, you must be sure to call the Win32 function BluetoothFindRadioClose() on the enumeration handle. Consider the following code:

```
Imports System
Imports System.Runtime.InteropServices
Imports System.Runtime.ConstrainedExecution
Imports System.Security
Imports System.Security.Permissions
Imports System.Text
Imports Microsoft.Win32.SafeHandles

'Matches Win32 BLUETOOTH_FIND_RADIO_PARAMS
<StructLayout(LayoutKind.Sequential)> _
Class BluetoothFindRadioParams
    Public dwSize As UInteger

    Public Sub New()
        dwSize = 4
    End Sub
End Class

'Matches Win32 BLUETOOTH_RADIO_INFO
<StructLayout(LayoutKind.Sequential, CharSet:=CharSet.Unicode)> _
Structure BluetoothRadioInfo
    Public Const BLUETOOTH_MAX_NAME_SIZE As Integer = 248
    Public dwSize As UInteger
    Public address As ULong
```

```vb
    <MarshalAs(UnmanagedType.ByValTStr, SizeConst:=BLUETOOTH_MAX_NAME_SIZE)> _
    Public szName As String
    Public ulClassOfDevice As UInteger
    Public lmpSubversion As ULong
    Public manufacturer As UShort
End Structure

'Safe Bluetooth Enumeration handle
<SecurityPermission(SecurityAction.Demand, UnmanagedCode:=True)> _
Public NotInheritable Class SafeBluetoothRadioFindHandle
    Inherits SafeHandleZeroOrMinusOneIsInvalid

    Private Sub New()
        MyBase.New(True)
    End Sub

    Protected Overrides Function ReleaseHandle() As Boolean
        Return BluetoothFindRadioClose(handle)
    End Function

    <DllImport("Irprops.cpl")> _
    <ReliabilityContract(Consistency.WillNotCorruptState, Cer.Success)> _
    <SuppressUnmanagedCodeSecurity()> _
    Private Shared Function BluetoothFindRadioClose(ByVal hFind As IntPtr) _
        As Boolean
    End Function
End Class

Public Class EntryPoint
    Private Const ERROR_SUCCESS As Integer = 0

    Shared Sub Main()
        Dim PreexistingHandle As IntPtr
        Dim OwnsHandle As Boolean = True
        Dim RadioHandle As SafeFileHandle = _
        New SafeFileHandle(PreexistingHandle, OwnsHandle)

        Using radioFindHandle As SafeBluetoothRadioFindHandle = _
        BluetoothFindFirstRadio(New BluetoothFindRadioParams(), RadioHandle)
            If Not radioFindHandle.IsInvalid Then
                Dim radioInfo As BluetoothRadioInfo = New BluetoothRadioInfo()
                radioInfo.dwSize = 520
                Dim result As UInteger = BluetoothGetRadioInfo(RadioHandle, _
                    radioInfo)
```

```
                If result = ERROR_SUCCESS Then
                    'Let's send the contents of the radio info to the console.
                    Console.WriteLine("address = {0:X}", radioInfo.address)
                    Console.WriteLine("szName = {0}", radioInfo.szName)
                    Console.WriteLine("ulClassOfDevice = {0}", _
                        radioInfo.ulClassOfDevice)
                    Console.WriteLine("lmpSubversion = {0}", _
                        radioInfo.lmpSubversion)
                    Console.WriteLine("manufacturer = {0}", radioInfo.manufacturer)
                End If
                RadioHandle.Dispose()
            End If
        End Using
    End Sub

    <DllImport("Irprops.cpl")> _
    Private Shared Function _
        BluetoothFindFirstRadio(<MarshalAs(UnmanagedType.LPStruct)> _
        ByVal pbtfrp As BluetoothFindRadioParams, ByRef phRadio As SafeFileHandle) _
        As SafeBluetoothRadioFindHandle
    End Function

    <DllImport("Irprops.cpl")> _
    Private Shared Function BluetoothGetRadioInfo(ByVal hRadio As SafeFileHandle, _
    ByRef pRadioInfo As BluetoothRadioInfo) As UInteger
    End Function
End Class
```

The crux of this example is the SafeBluetoothRadioFindHandle. You could have derived it directly from SafeHandle, but the runtime provides two helper classes, SafeHandleZeroOrMinusOneIsInvalid and SafeHandleMinusOneIsInvalid, to derive from in order to make things easier.

■**Caution** Be careful when dealing with Win32 functions via P/Invoke, and always read the documentation carefully with regard to what constitutes an invalid handle value. The Win32 API is notorious for making this confusing. For example, the Win32 CreateFile() function returns -1 to represent a failure. The CreateEvent() function returns a NULL handle in the event of an error. In both cases, the return type is HANDLE.

Take several things into consideration when providing your own SafeHandle derivative:

- *Apply a code access security (CAS)[6] demand on the class requiring the ability to call unmanaged code*: You don't need to do this unless you really do call unmanaged code, but the odds of you ever creating a SafeHandle derivative and not calling unmanaged code are slim.

- *Provide a default constructor that initializes the* SafeHandle *derivative*: Notice that SafeBluetoothRadioFindHandle declares a private default constructor. The P/Invoke layer can create instances of the object even though the constructor is private. The private constructor keeps clients from creating instances without calling the Win32 functions that create the underlying resource.

- *Override the* IsInvalid *property*: In this case, that is not necessary since the base class SafeHandleZeroOrMinusOneIsInvalid handles that for you.

- *Override the* ReleaseHandle *method, which is used to clean up the resource*: Typically, this is where you'll make your call through P/Invoke to release the unmanaged resource. In the example, you make a call to BluetoothFindRadioClose(). Note that when declaring the method for P/Invoke, you apply a reliability contract, since the ReleaseHandle method is called within the context of a CER. Additionally, it's wise to apply the SuppressUnmanagedCodeSecurity attribute to the method.

Once you define your SafeHandle derivative, you're ready to use it in your P/Invoke declarations. In the preceding example, you declare the BluetoothFindFirstRadio method to be called through P/Invoke. If you look up this function in the Microsoft Developer Network (MSDN), you'll see that it returns a BLUETOOTH_RADIO_FIND type, which is a handle to an internal radio enumeration object that returns a SafeBluetoothRadioFindHandle type. The P/Invoke marshaling layer handles the rest. Now, the enumeration handle is safe from being leaked by the runtime in the event of some asynchronous event introduced by the virtual execution system.

■**Caution** When marshaling between a COM method or Win32 function that returns a handle in a structure, the interop layer doesn't provide support for dealing with SafeHandle derivatives. In these rare cases, you'll need to call SetHandle() on the SafeHandle derivative after getting the structure back from the function or COM method. However, if you have to do such a thing, you want to make sure that the operation that creates the handle and the subsequent SetHandle method call occurs within a CER so that nothing can interrupt the process of allocating the resource and assigning the handle to the SafeHandle object; otherwise, your application could leak resources.

---

6. CAS enhances role-based security by setting trust levels for code and programs. See Appendix A for resources.

Creating Custom Exception Classes

System.Exception has three public constructors and one protected constructor. The first is the default constructor, which doesn't really do much of anything. The second is a constructor that accepts a reference to a string object. This string is a general, programmer-defined message that you could consider a more user-friendly description of the exception. The third is a constructor that takes a message string, like the second constructor, but it also accepts a reference to another Exception. The reference to the other exception allows you to keep track of originating exceptions when one exception is translated into another exception within a Try block. It becomes the "inner" exception for the newly created exception.

A good example of that is when an exception is not handled and percolates up to the stack frame of a shared constructor. The runtime then throws a TypeInitializationException, but only after it sets the inner exception to that of the original exception so that the one who catches the TypeInitializationException will at least know why this exception occurred in the first place.

Finally, the protected constructor allows creation of an exception from a SerializationInfo object. You always want to create serializable exceptions so you can use them across context boundaries—for example, with .NET remoting. That means you also want to mark your custom exception classes with the SerializableAttribute as well.

The System.Exception class is useful with these three public constructors. However, it makes sense to create a new, more specific exception type that derives from System.Exception. That way, the type of the exception is much more expressive about the problem at hand. Even better than that is the fact that your derived exception class could contain data that is germane to the reason the exception was thrown in the first place. Note that all exceptions must derive from System.Exception. Let's see what it takes to effectively define custom exceptions.

Consider the previous EmployeeDatabase example. Suppose that in order to add an employee to the database, the employee's data must be validated. If an employee's data does not validate, the Add method will throw an exception of type EmployeeVerificationException. Notice that the new exception's type name ends with the word Exception. This is a recommended convention, since it makes it easy to spot exception types within your type system. Let's see what such an exception type could look like:

```
Imports System
Imports System.Collections
Imports System.Runtime.Serialization

Public Class Employee
    Private mEmployeeSSN As String
    Private mEmployeeBirthDate As Date

    Public Sub New()
        MyBase.New()
    End Sub
```

```vb
    Public Sub Add(ByVal anSSN As String, ByVal aBirthDate As Date)
        Me.EmployeeBirthDate = aBirthDate
        Me.EmployeeSSN = anSSN
    End Sub

    Public Property EmployeeSSN() As String
        Get
            Return mEmployeeSSN
        End Get
        Set(ByVal value As String)
            If value.Length = 9 Then
                mEmployeeSSN = value
            Else
                Throw New EmployeeVerificationException( _
                EmployeeVerificationException.Cause.InvalidSSN, _
                "Social Security Number must be 9 digits.")
            End If
        End Set
    End Property

    Public Property EmployeeBirthDate() As Date
        Get
            Return mEmployeeBirthDate
        End Get
        Set(ByVal value As Date)
            mEmployeeBirthDate = value
        End Set
    End Property
End Class

<Serializable()> _
Public Class EmployeeVerificationException
    Inherits Exception

    Private mReason As Cause

    Public Enum Cause
        InvalidSSN
        InvalidBirthDate
    End Enum

    Public Sub New(ByVal reason As Cause)
        MyBase.New()
        Me.mReason = reason
    End Sub
```

```
    Public Sub New(ByVal reason As Cause, ByVal msg As String)
        MyBase.New(msg)
        Me.mReason = reason
    End Sub

    Public Sub New(ByVal reason As Cause, ByVal msg As String, _
        ByVal inner As Exception)
        MyBase.New(msg, inner)
        Me.mReason = reason
    End Sub

    Protected Sub New(ByVal info As SerializationInfo, _
        ByVal context As StreamingContext)
        MyBase.New(info, context)
    End Sub

    Public ReadOnly Property Reason() As Cause
        Get
            Return mReason
        End Get
    End Property
End Class

Public Class EntryPoint
    Shared Sub Main()
        Dim anEmployeeSSN As String = New String("12345678")
        Dim anEmployeeBD As Date = New Date(1959, 3, 12)
        Dim anEmployee As Employee = New Employee()

        Try
            anEmployee.Add(anEmployeeSSN, anEmployeeBD)
        Catch e As EmployeeVerificationException
            Console.WriteLine(e.Message & vbCrLf & "Reason Code: " & _
                CStr(e.Reason))
        End Try
    End Sub
End Class
```

In the Employee.Add method, you can see a simple call to Me.EmployeeSSN, which validates the length of the Social Security number passed. This is a simplistic example, where you force the validation to fail by throwing an EmployeeVerificationException, but the main focus of the example is the creation of the new exception type. Many times, you'll find that just creating a new exception type is good enough to convey the extra information you need to convey. In this case, the exception type carries more information about the validation failure, so you create a Reason property whose backing field must be initialized in the constructor. Also, notice that EmployeeVerificationException derives from System.Exception. At one point, the school of thought was that all .NET Framework-defined exception types would derive from System.Exception, while all user-defined exceptions would derive from ApplicationException, thus making it easier to tell the two apart. This goal is lost partly due to the fact that some .NET Framework–defined exception types derive from `ApplicationException`. The `ApplicationException` class itself derives from `System.Exception`.

You may be wondering why we defined four exception constructors for this simple exception type. The traditional idiom when defining new exception types is to define the same four public constructors that `System.Exception` exposes. Had you decided not to carry the extra reason data, then the `EmployeeVerificationException` constructors would have matched the `System.Exception` constructors exactly in their form. If you follow this idiom when defining your own exception types, then users will be able to treat your new exception type in the same way as other system-defined exceptions. Plus, your derived exception can leverage the message and inner exception already encapsulated by `System.Exception`.

Working with Allocated Resources and Exceptions

One thing you may grapple with in the VB world is the lack of deterministic destruction. C++ developers have become accustomed to using constructors and destructors of stack-based objects to manage precious resources. This means that you can create objects on the C++ stack where some precious resource is allocated in the constructor of those objects, and if you put the de-allocation in the destructor, you can rely upon the destructor getting called at the proper time to clean up.

When the CLR was first introduced to developers during the beta program, many developers immediately became very vocal about this omission in the runtime. Whether you view it as an omission or not, it clearly was not addressed to its fullest extent until after the beta developer community applied a gentle nudge. The problem stems, in part, from the garbage-collected nature of objects in the CLR, coupled with the fact that the friendly destructor in the VB syntax was reused to implement object finalizers. Finalizers are very different than destructors, and using the destructor syntax for finalizers only added to the confusion of the matter.

The solution put on the table was the Disposable pattern, which you utilize by implementing the `IDisposable` interface. Essentially, if your object needs deterministic destruction, it obtains it by implementing the `IDisposable` interface. However, you have to call your `Dispose` method explicitly in order to clean up after the disposable object. If you forget to, and your object is coded properly, then the resource won't be lost—rather, it will just be cleaned up when the GC finally gets around to calling your finalizer.

Consider the following contrived example that illustrates the danger you can face:

```
Imports System
Imports System.IO
Imports System.Text

Public Class EntryPoint
    Public Shared Sub DoSomeStuff()
        Dim fs As FileStream = _
        File.Open("log.txt", FileMode.Append, FileAccess.Write, FileShare.None)

        Dim msg As Byte() = New UTF8Encoding(True).GetBytes("Doing Some" & "Stuff")
```

```
        fs.Write(msg, 0, msg.Length)
    End Sub

    Public Shared Sub DoSomeMoreStuff()
        Dim fs As FileStream = _
        File.Open("log.txt", FileMode.Append, FileAccess.Write, FileShare.None)

        Dim msg As Byte() = New UTF8Encoding(True).GetBytes("Doing Some" & _
            "More Stuff")

        fs.Write(msg, 0, msg.Length)
    End Sub

    Shared Sub Main()
        DoSomeStuff()
        DoSomeMoreStuff()
    End Sub
End Class
```

This code looks innocent enough. However, if you execute this code, you'll most likely encounter an IOException. The code in DoSomeStuff() creates a FileStream object with an exclusive lock on the file. Once the FileStream object goes out of scope at the end of the function, it is marked for collection, but you're at the mercy of the GC and when it decides to do the cleanup. Therefore, when you find yourself opening the file again in DoSomeMoreStuff(), you'll get the exception, since the precious resource is still locked by the unreachable FileStream object. Clearly, this is a horrible position to be in. You may consider making an explicit call to GC.Collect() in Main() before the call to DoSomeMoreStuff(), but fiddling with the GC algorithm by forcing it to collect at specific times is a recipe for poor performance. You cannot possibly help the GC do its job better, since you have no specific idea how it is implemented.

So what is one to do? One way or another, you must ensure that the file gets closed. However, here's the rub: no matter how you do it, you must remember to do it. One option would be to call the Close method on the FileStream at each of the methods that uses it. That works fine, but it's much less automatic and something you must always remember to do. However, even if you do, what happens if an exception is thrown before the Close() method is called? You find yourself back in the same boat as before, with a resource dangling out there that you can't get to in order to free it.

Those of you who are savvy with exception handling will notice that you can solve the problem using some Try/Finally blocks, as in the following example:

```
Imports System
Imports System.IO
Imports System.Text

Public Class EntryPoint
    Public Shared Sub DoSomeStuff()
        'Open a file.
        Dim fs As FileStream = Nothing
```

```vb
        Try
            fs = File.Open("log.txt", FileMode.Append, FileAccess.Write, _
                FileShare.None)
            Dim msg As Byte() = New UTF8Encoding(True).GetBytes("Doing Some" & _
                " Stuff")

            fs.Write(msg, 0, msg.Length)
        Finally
            If Not (fs Is Nothing) Then
                fs.Close()
            End If
        End Try
    End Sub

    Public Shared Sub DoSomeMoreStuff()
        'Open a file
        Dim fs As FileStream = Nothing

        Try
            fs = File.Open("log.txt", FileMode.Append, FileAccess.Write, _
                FileShare.None)
            Dim msg As Byte() = New UTF8Encoding(True).GetBytes("Doing Some" & _
                "More Stuff")

            fs.Write(msg, 0, msg.Length)
        Finally
            If Not (fs Is Nothing) Then
                fs.Close()
            End If
        End Try
    End Sub

    Shared Sub Main()
        DoSomeStuff()
        DoSomeMoreStuff()
    End Sub
End Class
```

The Try/Finally blocks solve the problem, but that was a lot of extra typing. Moreover, it makes the code difficult to read. As you'd expect, there is a better way. Many objects, such as FileStream, that have a Close method also implement the IDisposable pattern. Usually, calling Dispose() on these objects is the same as calling Close(). Of course, calling Close() over Dispose() or vice versa is arguing over apples and oranges, if you still have to explicitly call one or the other. Thankfully, there's a good reason why most classes that have a Close method implement Dispose()—so you can use them effectively with the Using keyword, which is typically used as part of the Disposable pattern. Therefore, you could change the code to the following:

```vb
Imports System
Imports System.IO
Imports System.Text

Public Class EntryPoint
    Public Shared Sub DoSomeStuff()
        'Open a file.
        Using fs As FileStream = _
        File.Open("log.txt", FileMode.Append, FileAccess.Write, FileShare.None)

            Dim msg As Byte() = New UTF8Encoding(True).GetBytes("Doing Some" & _
                " Stuff")

            fs.Write(msg, 0, msg.Length)
        End Using
    End Sub

    Public Shared Sub DoSomeMoreStuff()
        'Open a file.
        Using fs As FileStream = _
        File.Open("log.txt", FileMode.Append, FileAccess.Write, FileShare.None)

            Dim msg As Byte() = New UTF8Encoding(True).GetBytes("Doing Some" & _
                " More Stuff")

            fs.Write(msg, 0, msg.Length)
        End Using
    End Sub

    Shared Sub Main()
        DoSomeStuff()
        DoSomeMoreStuff()
    End Sub
End Class
```

As you can see, the code is much easier to follow, and the Using keyword takes care of having to type all those explicit Try/Finally blocks. You probably won't be surprised to know that if you look at the generated code in the Microsoft Intermediate Language (MSIL) Disassembler, the compiler has generated the Try/Finally blocks in place of the Using keyword. You can also nest the Using keywords within their compound blocks, just as you can nest Try/Finally blocks.

Even though the Using keyword solves the "ugly code" symptom and reduces the chances of typing in extra bugs, it still requires that you remember to use it in the first place. It's not as convenient as deterministic destruction of local objects, but it's better than littering your code with Try/Finally blocks all over the place. The end result is that VB does have a form of deterministic destruction via the Using keyword, but it's only deterministic if you remember to make it deterministic.

Providing Rollback Behavior

When producing exception-neutral methods, you'll often find it handy to employ a mechanism that can roll back any changes if an exception happens to be generated. You can solve this problem by using the classic technique of introducing one more level of indirection in the form of a helper class. For the sake of discussion, let's use an object that represents a database connection and has methods named Commit() and Rollback().

The helper class also has a method named Commit(). When called, it just passes through to the database object's method, but before doing so, it sets an internal flag. The trick is in the destructor. If the destructor executes before the flag is set, there are only a couple of ways that are possible. First, the user might have forgotten to call Commit(). Since that's a bug in the code, let's not consider that option. The second way to get into the destructor without the flag set is if the object is being cleaned up because the stack is unwinding as it looks for a handler for a thrown exception. Depending on the state of the flag in the destructor code, you can instantly tell if you got here via normal execution or via an exception. If you get here via an exception, all you have to do is call Rollback() on the database object, and you have the functionality you need.

To achieve this result, use the VB form of deterministic destruction, which is the marriage between IDisposable and the Using keyword. All you have to do is code the Dispose() method of the helper class. Let's take a look at what this helper class might look like:

```vb
Imports System
Imports System.Diagnostics

Public Class Database
    Public Sub Commit()
        Console.WriteLine("Changes Committed")
    End Sub

    Public Sub Rollback()
        Console.WriteLine("Changes Abandoned")
    End Sub
End Class

Public Class RollbackHelper
    Implements IDisposable

    Private DB As Database
    Private Disposed As Boolean = False
    Private Committed As Boolean = False

    Public Sub New(ByVal db As Database)
        Me.DB = db
    End Sub
```

```vb
    Protected Overrides Sub Finalize()
        Try
            Dispose(False)
        Finally
            MyBase.Finalize()
        End Try
    End Sub

    Public Sub Dispose() Implements System.IDisposable.Dispose
        Dispose(True)
    End Sub

    Public Sub Commit()
        DB.Commit()
        Committed = True
    End Sub

    Private Sub Dispose(ByVal disposing As Boolean)
        'Don't do anything if already disposed.
        'Remember, it is valid to call Dispose()
        'multiple times on a disposable object.
        If Not Disposed Then
            'We don't want to do anything to the db if
            'we got here from the finalizer because the database
            'field could already be finalized!  However, we do
            'want to free any unmanaged resources. But, in
            'this case, there are none.
            If disposing Then
                If Not Committed Then
                    DB.Rollback()
                End If
            Else
                Debug.Assert(False, "Failed to call Dispose()" & _
                    " on RollbackHelper")
            End If
            Me.Disposed = True
        End If
    End Sub
End Class

Public Class EntryPoint
    Private Shared db As Database
    Private Shared nullPtr As Object = Nothing
```

```
    Private Shared Sub DoSomeWork()
        Using guard As RollbackHelper = New RollbackHelper(db)
            'Here we do some work that could throw an exception.

            'Comment out the following line to cause an exception
            'nullPtr.GetType()

            guard.Commit()
        End Using
    End Sub

    Shared Sub Main()
        db = New Database()
        DoSomeWork()
    End Sub
End Class
```

Inside the DoSomeWork method is where you'll do some work that could fail with an exception. Should an exception occur, you'll want any changes that have gone into the Database object to be reverted. Inside the Using block, you've created a new RollbackHelper object that contains a reference to the Database object. If control flow gets to the point of calling Commit() on the guard reference, all is well, assuming the Commit method does not throw. Needless to say, you should code your Commit() in such a way that the Database remains in a valid state. However, if your code inside the guarded block throws an exception, the Dispose method in the RollbackHelper will diligently roll back your database.

No matter what happens, the Dispose method will be called on the RollbackHelper instance, thanks to the Using block. If you forget the Using block, the finalizer for the RollbackHelper will not be able to do anything for you, since finalization of objects goes in random order, and the Database referenced by the RollbackHelper could be finalized prior to the RollbackHelper instance. To help you find the places where you omitted Using, you can code an assertion into the helper object. Since the whole use of this pattern hinges on the Using block, for the sake of discussion, let's assume you didn't forget it.

Once execution is safely inside the Dispose method, and it got there via a call to Dispose() rather than through the finalizer, it simply checks the committed flag, and if it's not set, it calls Rollback() on the Database instance. That's all there is to it. If you'd like to see what happens in a case where an exception is thrown, simply uncomment the attempt to access the Nothing reference inside the DoSomeWork method.

You may have noticed that we haven't addressed what happens if Rollback() throws an exception. Clearly, for robust code, it's optimal to require that whatever operations RollbackHelper performs in the process of a rollback be guaranteed never to throw. This goes back to one of the most basic requirements for generating strong exception-safe and exception-neutral code: you must have a well-defined set of operations that are guaranteed not to throw in order for you to create robust exception-safe code.

A Using block is expanded into a Try/Finally block under the covers. And, when an exception is thrown within a Finally block that is executing as the result of a previous exception, that previous exception is simply lost and the new exception gets thrown. What's worse is that the Finally block that was executing never gets to finish.

As losing exception information makes it difficult to find problems, it is recommended that you never throw an exception inside a `Finally` block. We've mentioned this before in this chapter, but it's so important it deserves being echoed. The CLR won't abort your application, but your application will likely be in an undefined state if an exception is thrown during execution of a `Finally` block.

Summary

This chapter covered the basics of exception handling along with how you should apply the Expert pattern to determine the best place to handle a particular exception. The meat of this chapter described techniques for creating bulletproof exception-safe code that guarantees system stability in the face of unexpected exceptional events. We also described constrained execution regions that you can use to postpone asynchronous exceptions during thread termination. Creating bulletproof exception-safe and exception-neutral code is no easy task.

For many development efforts, exception safety is an afterthought. In reality, exception safety is a crucial issue that you should consider at software design time. Failure to do so will result in substandard systems that will do nothing but frustrate users and lose market share to those companies whose developers spent a little extra time getting exception safety right. Moreover, there's always the possibility, as computers integrate more and more into people's daily lives, that government regulations could force systems to undergo rigorous testing in order to prove they are worthy for society to rely upon. One might envision an environment where a government could force such rules on any commercially sold software.

In the next chapter, we'll cover the main facets of dealing with strings in VB and .NET. Additionally, we'll cover the all-important topic of globalization.

CHAPTER 9

∎∎∎

Working with Strings

Within the .NET Base Class Library (BCL), the System.String type is the model citizen. It offers an ideal example of how to create an immutable reference type that semantically acts like a value type.

String Overview

Instances of String are immutable in the sense that once you create them, you cannot change them. Although it may seem inefficient at first, this approach actually does make code more efficient. When you copy String instances liberally within the application, you create a new instance that points to the same raw string data as the source instance. Even if you call the ICloneable.Clone method on a string, you get an instance which points to the same string data as the source. This is entirely safe because the String public interface offers no way to modify the actual String data. If you require a string that is a deep copy of the original string, you may call the Copy method to do so.

Note Those of you who are familiar with common design patterns and idioms may recognize this usage pattern as the handle/body or envelope/letter idiom.

In environments such as C++ and C, the string is not a built-in type at all but, rather, a more primitive, raw construct, such as a pointer to the first character in an array of characters. Typically, string-manipulation routines are not part of the language but rather a part of a library used with the language. Although that is mostly true with Visual Basic (VB), the lines are somewhat blurred by the .NET runtime. The designers of the Common Language Infrastructure (CLI) specification could have chosen to represent all strings as simple arrays of System.Char types, but instead they chose to annex System.String into the collection of built-in types. In fact, System.String is an oddball in the built-in type collection, since it is a reference type, and most of the built-in types are value types. However, it's not always easy to see this difference because the String type behaves with value semantics.

You may already know that the System.String type represents a Unicode character string, and System.Char represents a 16-bit Unicode character. Of course, this makes portability and localization to other operating systems—especially systems with large character sets—easy. However, sometimes you might need to interface with external systems using encodings other than Unicode character strings. For times like these, you can employ the System.Text.Encoding class to convert to and from various encodings, including ASCII, UTF-7, UTF-8, and UTF-32. Incidentally, the Unicode format used internally by the runtime is UTF-16.[1]

String Literals

When you declare a string in your code, the compiler creates a System.String object for you that it then places into an internal table in the module called the *intern pool.* The idea is that each time you declare a new string literal within your code, the compiler first checks to see if you've declared the same string elsewhere, and if you have, then the code simply references the one already interned. Let's take a look at an example of ways to declare a string literal:

```
Imports System

Public Class EntryPoint
    Shared Sub Main(ByVal args As String())
        Dim lit1 As String = "c:\windows\system32"
        Dim lit2 As String = "c:\windows\system32"

        Dim lit3 As String = vbCrLf & "Jack and Jill" & vbCrLf & _
            "Went up the hill . . ." & vbCrLf

        Console.WriteLine(lit3)

        Console.WriteLine("Object.RefEq(lit1, lit2): {0}", _
            Object.ReferenceEquals(lit1, lit2))

        If args.Length > 0 Then
            Console.WriteLine("Parameter given: {0}", args(0))

            Dim strNew As String = String.Intern(args(0))

            Console.WriteLine("Object.RefEq(lit1, strNew): {0}", _
                Object.ReferenceEquals(lit1, strNew))
        End If
    End Sub
End Class
```

Here's the output from the previous example:

```
Jack and Jill
Went up the hill . . .
```

---

1. For more information regarding the Unicode standard, visit www.unicode.org.

```
Object.RefEq(lit1, lit2): True
Parameter given: This is an IP address: 123.124.125.126
Object.RefEq(lit1, strNew): False
```

■**Note** To run this example, you must create a command-line argument in your project properties. On the Debug tab, add "This is an IP address: 123.124.125.126" (including the double quotes) in the Start Options area.

First, notice the two declarations of the two literal strings lit1 and lit2. The declared type is String, which is the VB alias for System.String. Clearly, lit1 and lit2 contain strings of the same value. Based upon what you learned in the previous section, you would expect the two instances to reference the same string object. In fact, they do, and that is shown in the output from the program, where you test them using Object.ReferenceEquals().

Finally, this example demonstrates the use of the String.Intern() shared method. If you want to determine that a string you're declaring at run time is already in the intern pool, it may be more efficient to reference that string rather than create a new instance. The previous code accepts a string on the command line, and then creates a new instance from it using the String.Intern method. This method always returns a valid string reference, but it will either be a string instance referencing a string in the intern pool, or a new string copy based upon the passed-in value.

Format Specifiers and Globalization

You often need to format the data that an application displays to users in a specific way. For example, you may need to display a floating-point value representing some tangible metric in exponential form or in fixed-point form. If in fixed-point form, you may need to use a culture-specific character, such as the decimal mark. The .NET BCL offers powerful mechanisms for handling these two notions in a flexible and extensible manner. However, before we can get into the topic of format specifiers themselves, let's cover some preliminary topics.

■**Note** It's important to address any cultural concerns and globalization requirements your software may have early in the development cycle. The .NET designers put a lot of work into creating a rich library for handling globalization, though the richness and breadth of the globalization API indicates how difficult it can be.

Object.ToString(), IFormattable, and CultureInfo

Every object inherits a method from System.Object called ToString(), which is handy for getting a string representation of your object for output, even if only for debugging purposes. For your custom classes, the default implementation of ToString() merely returns the type name of the object itself, and you'll need to implement your own override to do anything useful. All of the built-in types do this, and if you call `ToString()` on a `System.Integer`, you'll get a string representation of the value within. But what if you want the string representation in hexadecimal format? For this case, you have another way to request the desired format, which involves implementing the `IFormattable` interface, which looks like the following:

```
Public Interface IFormattable
    Function ToString(ByVal Format As String, ByVal FormatProvider As _
        IFormatProvider) As String
End Interface
```

All built-in numeric types, as well as date-time types, implement this interface. Using this method, you can specify exactly how you want the value to be formatted by providing a format specifier string. Before we get into exactly what the format strings look like, you should understand a few more preliminary concepts, starting with the second parameter of the `IFormattable.ToString` method.

An object that implements the `IFormatProvider` interface is a format provider. A format provider's common task within the .NET Framework is to provide culture-specific formatting information, such as what character to use for monetary amounts, for decimal separators, and so on. When you pass `Nothing` for this parameter, the format provider that `IFormattable.ToString()` uses is typically the `CultureInfo` instance returned by `System.Globalization.CultureInfo.CurrentCulture` and `My.Application.Culture`. This instance of `CultureInfo` is the one that matches the culture that the current thread uses. However, you have the option of overriding it by passing a different `CultureInfo` instance, such as one obtained by creating a new instance of `CultureInfo` and passing into its constructor a string representing the desired locale. Finally, you can even provide a culture-neutral `CultureInfo` instance by passing the instance provided by `CultureInfo.InvariantCulture`.

Note Instances of `CultureInfo` are used as a convenient grouping mechanism for all formatting information relevant to a specific culture. For example, one `CultureInfo` instance could represent the cultural-specific qualities of English spoken in the United States, while another could contain properties specific to English spoken in the United Kingdom. Each `CultureInfo` instance contains specific instances of `DateTimeFormatInfo`, `NumberFormatInfo`, `TextInfo`, and `CompareInfo` that are germane to the language and region represented.

Once the `IFormattable.ToString()` implementation has a valid format provider— whether it was passed in or whether it was the one attached to the current thread—then it may query that format provider for a specific formatter by calling the `IFormatProvider.GetFormat` method. The formatters implemented by the .NET Framework are the `NumberFormatInfo` and `DateTimeFormatInfo` types. When you ask for one of these objects via `IFormatProvider.GetFormat()`, you ask for it by type. This mechanism is extremely extensible because you can provide your own formatter types, and other types you create that know how to consume them can ask a custom format provider for instances of them.

Suppose you want to convert a floating-point value into a string. The execution flow of the `IFormattable.ToString()` implementation on `System.Double` follows these general steps:

1. The implementation gets a reference to an `IFormatProvider` type, which is either the one passed in or the one attached to the current thread if the one passed in is `Nothing`.

2. It asks the format provider for an instance of the type `NumberFormatInfo` via a call to `IFormatProvider.GetFormat()`. The format provider initializes the `NumberFormatInfo` instance's properties based on the culture it represents.

3. It uses the `NumberFormatInfo` instance to format the number appropriately while creating a string representation of this based upon the specification of the format string.

Creating and Registering Custom CultureInfo Types

The globalization capabilities of the .NET Framework have been enhanced with the introduction of a new class named `CultureAndRegionInfoBuilder` in the `System.Globalization` namespace. Using `CultureAndRegionInfoBuilder`, you now have the capability to define and introduce new culture and region information into the system and register them for global usage. Similarly, you can modify preexisting culture and region information on the system and serialize the information into a Locale Data Markup Language (LDML) file, which is a standard-based XML format. Once you register your new culture and region with the system, your applications can create instances of `CultureInfo` and `RegionInfo` using the registered string-based name.

When naming your new cultures, you should adhere to the standard format for naming cultures. The format is generally `[prefix-]language[-region][-suffix[. . .]]`, where the language identifier is the only required part and the other pieces are optional. The prefix can be either of the following, in upper- or lowercase:

- `i-` for culture names registered with the Internet Assigned Numbers Authority (IANA)

- `x-` for all others

The language part is the lowercase two-letter code from the ISO 639-1 standard, while the region is a two-letter uppercase code from the ISO 3166 standard. For example, Russian spoken in Russia is `ru-RU`. The suffix component is used to further sub-identify the culture based on some other data. For example, Serbian spoken in Serbia could be either `sr-SP-Cyrl` or `sr-SP-Latn`—one for the Cyrillic alphabet and the other for the Latin alphabet. If you define a culture specific to your division within your company, you could create a culture using the name `x-en-US-MyCompany-WidgetDivision`.

Let's use `CultureAndRegionInfoBuilder` to create a fictitious culture based upon a preexisting culture. In the United States, the dominant measurement system is English units. Let's suppose that the United States decided to switch to the metric system at some point, and you now need to modify the culture information on some machines to match. Let's see what that code would look like:

```
Imports System
Imports System.Globalization
```

```
Public Class EntryPoint
    Shared Sub Main()
        Dim cib As CultureAndRegionInfoBuilder = Nothing

        cib = New CultureAndRegionInfoBuilder("x-en-US-metric", _
            CultureAndRegionModifiers.None)

        cib.LoadDataFromCultureInfo(New CultureInfo("en-US"))
        cib.LoadDataFromRegionInfo(New RegionInfo("US"))

        'Make the change.
        cib.IsMetric = True

        'Create the LDML file.
        cib.Save("x-en-US-metric.ldml")

        'Register with the system.
        cib.Register()
    End Sub
End Class
```

■**Note** In order to build the previous example, you'll need to add a reference to the `sysglobl.dll` assembly, located in the `Windows\Microsoft.NET\Framework\v2.0.xxxxx` directory.

You can see that the process is simple, since the `CultureAndRegionInfoBuilder` has a well-designed interface. For illustration purposes, we've sent the LDML to a file so you can see what it looks like, although it's too verbose to list in this text. One thing to consider is that you must have proper permissions in order to call the `Register` method. This typically requires that you be the administrator, although you can get around this by opening up the proper permissions to the %WINDIR%\Globalization directory and the `HKEY_LOCAL_MACHINE\SYSTEM\CurrentControlSet\ Control\Nls\CustomLocale` registry key. Once you register the culture with the system, you can reference it using the given name when specifying any culture information in the common language runtime (CLR). For example, to verify that the culture and information region is registered properly, you can build and execute the following code to test it out:

```
Imports System
Imports System.Globalization

Public Class EntryPoint
    Shared Sub Main()
        Dim ri As RegionInfo = New RegionInfo("x-en-US-metric")

        Console.WriteLine(ri.IsMetric)
    End Sub
End Class
```

Format Strings

You must consider what the format string looks like. The built-in numeric objects use the standard numeric format strings or the custom numeric format strings defined by the .NET Framework, which you can find in the Microsoft Developer Network (MSDN) documentation by searching for "standard numeric format strings." The standard format strings are typically in the form Axx, where A is the desired format requested and xx is an optional precision specifier. Examples of format specifiers for numbers are "C" for currency, "D" for decimal, "E" for scientific notation, "F" for fixed-point notation, and "X" for hexadecimal notation. Every type also supports "G" for general, which is the default format specifier and is also the format that you get when you call Object.ToString(), where you cannot specify a format string. If these format strings don't suit your needs, you can even use one of the custom format strings that allow you to describe what you'd like in a more-or-less picture format.

The point of this whole mechanism is that each type interprets and defines the format string specifically in the context of its own needs. In other words, System.Double is free to treat the "G" format specifier differently than the System.Integer type. Moreover, your own type—say, type Employee—is free to implement a format string in whatever way it likes. For example, a format string of "SSN" could create a string based on the Social Security number of the employee.

■Note It's even more useful to allow your own types to handle a format string of "DBG", thus creating a detailed string that represents the internal state to send to a debug output log.

Let's take a look at some example code that exercises these concepts:

```
Imports System
Imports System.Globalization
Imports System.Windows.Forms

Public Class EntryPoint
    Shared Sub Main()
        Dim current As CultureInfo = CultureInfo.CurrentCulture
        Dim germany As CultureInfo = New CultureInfo("de-DE")
        Dim russian As CultureInfo = New CultureInfo("ru-RU")

        Dim money As Double = 123.45

        Dim localMoney As String = money.ToString("C", current)
        MessageBox.Show(localMoney, "Local Money")

        localMoney = money.ToString("C", germany)
        MessageBox.Show(localMoney, "German Money")

        localMoney = money.ToString("C", russian)
        MessageBox.Show(localMoney, "Russian Money")
    End Sub
End Class
```

This code listing will display the three message boxes shown in Figure 9-1.

Figure 9-1. *Results displayed from running the previous code listing*

■**Note** In order to build the previous example, you'll need to add a reference to the `System.Windows.`
`Forms.dll` assembly, located in the `Windows\Microsoft.NET\Framework\v2.0.xxxxx` directory.

This example displays the strings using the `MessageBox` type defined in `Windows.Forms`, since the console isn't good at displaying Unicode characters. The format specifier that we've chosen is `"C"` to display the number in a currency format. For the first display, you use the `CultureInfo` instance attached to the current thread. For the following two, you create a `CultureInfo` for both Germany and Russia. Note that in forming the string, the `System.Double` type has used the `CurrencyDecimalSeparator`, `CurrencyDecimalDigits`, and `CurrencySymbol` properties of the `NumberFormatInfo` instance returned from the `CultureInfo.GetFormat` method. Had you displayed a `DateTime` instance, then the `DateTime` implementation of `IFormattable.ToString()` would have utilized an instance of `DateTimeFormatInfo` returned from the `CultureInfo.GetFormat()` in a similar way.

Console.WriteLine() and String.Format()

Throughout this book, you've seen `Console.WriteLine()` used in the examples. One of the forms of `WriteLine()` that is useful and identical to some overloads of `String.Format()` allows you to build a composite string by replacing format tags within a string with a variable number of parameters passed in. Let's look at a quick example of string format usage:

```
Imports System
Imports System.Globalization
Imports System.Windows.Forms

Public Class EntryPoint
    Shared Sub Main(ByVal args As String())
        If args.Length < 3 Then
            Console.WriteLine("Please provide 3 parameters")
            Return
        End If
```

```
        Dim composite As String = _
            String.Format("{0}, {1}, and {2}.", args(0), args(1), args(2))

        Console.WriteLine(composite)
    End Sub
End Class
```

Here are the results from the previous example:

```
Jack, Jill, and Spot.
```

▬**Note** To run this example, you must create a command-line argument in your project properties. On the Debug tab, add "Jack" "Jill" "Spot" (including the double quotes) in the Start Options area.

A placeholder is delimited by braces and the number within it is the zero-based index to the following parameter list. The `String.Format` method, as well as the `Console.WriteLine` method, has an overload that accepts a variable number of parameters to use as the replacement values. In this example, the `String.Format` method replaces each placeholder using the general formatting of the type that you can get via a call to the parameter-less version of `ToString()`. If the instance being placed in this spot supports `IFormattable`, the `IFormattable.ToString` method is called with a `Nothing` format specifier, which usually is the same if you had supplied the "G", or general, format specifier. Incidentally, within the source string, if you need to insert actual braces that will show in the output, you must double them by putting in either {{ or }}.

The exact format of the replacement item is {index[,alignment][:formatString]}, where the items within brackets are optional. The index value is a zero-based value used to reference one of the trailing parameters provided to the method. The alignment represents how wide the entry should be within the composite string. For example, if you set it to eight characters in width and the string is narrower than that, then the extra space is left-padded with spaces. Last, the `FormatString` portion of the replacement item allows you to denote precisely what formatting to use for the item. The format string is the same style of string that you would have used if you were to call `IFormattable.ToString()` on the instance itself. Unfortunately, you can't specify a particular `IFormatProvider` instance for each one of the replacement strings. If you need to create a composite string from items using multiple format providers or cultures, you must resort to using `IFormattable.ToString()` directly.

Examples of String Formatting in Custom Types

Let's take a look at another example using the venerable `Complex` type that we've used before. This time, let's implement `IFormattable` on it to make it a little more useful when generating a string version of the instance:

```vbnet
Imports System
Imports System.Text
Imports System.Globalization

Public Structure Complex
    Implements IFormattable

    Private real As Double
    Private imaginary As Double

    Public Sub New(ByVal real As Double, ByVal imaginary As Double)
        Me.real = real
        Me.imaginary = imaginary
    End Sub

    'IFormattable implementation
    Public Overloads Function ToString(ByVal format As String, _
        ByVal formatProvider As IFormatProvider) As String _
        Implements IFormattable.ToString

        Dim sb As StringBuilder = New StringBuilder()

        If format = "DBG" Then
            sb.Append(Me.[GetType]().ToString() & "" & vbCrLf & "")

            sb.AppendFormat("" & vbTab  & "real:" & vbTab & _
                "{0}" & vbCrLf & "", real)

            sb.AppendFormat("" & vbTab & "imaginary:" & vbTab & _
                "{0}" & vbCrLf & "", imaginary)
        Else
            sb.Append("( ")
            sb.Append(real.ToString(format, formatProvider))
            sb.Append(" : ")
            sb.Append(imaginary.ToString(format, formatProvider))
            sb.Append(" )")
        End If


        Return sb.ToString()
    End Function
End Structure

Public Class EntryPoint
    Shared Sub Main()
        Dim local As CultureInfo = CultureInfo.CurrentCulture
        Dim germany As CultureInfo = New CultureInfo("de-DE")
        Dim cpx As Complex = New Complex(12.3456, 1234.56)
        Dim strCpx As String = cpx.ToString("F", local)
```

```
            Console.WriteLine(strCpx)
            strCpx = cpx.ToString("F", germany)

            Console.WriteLine(strCpx)

            Console.WriteLine("" & vbCrLf & "Debugging output:" & vbCrLf & _
                "{0:DBG}", cpx)
        End Sub
End Class
```

This is the output from the previous example:

```
( 12.35 : 1234.56 )
( 12,35 : 1234,56 )

Debugging output:
Strings1.Complex
        real:    12.3456
        imaginary:      1234.56
```

The real meat of this example lies within the implementation of IFormattable.ToString(). You implement a "DBG" format string for this type that will create a string that shows the internal state of the object and may be useful for debug purposes. If the format string is not equal to "DBG", then you simply defer to the IFormattable implementation of System.Double. Notice the use of StringBuilder to create the string that is eventually returned. Also, we chose to use the Console.WriteLine method and its format item syntax to send the debugging output to the console just to show a little variety in usage.

ICustomFormatter

ICustomFormatter is an interface that allows you to replace or extend a built-in or already existing IFormattable interface for an object. Whenever you call String.Format() or StringBuilder.AppendFormat() to convert an object instance to a string, before the method calls through to the object's implementation of IFormattable.ToString(), it first checks to see if the passed-in IFormatProvider provides a custom formatter. It does this by calling IFormatProvider.GetFormat() while passing a type of ICustomFormatter. If the formatter returns an implementation of ICustomFormatter, then the method will use the custom formatter. Otherwise, it will use the object's implementation of IFormattable.ToString() or the object's implementation of Object.ToString() in cases where it doesn't implement IFormattable.

Consider the following example where we've reworked the previous Complex example but externalized the debugging output capabilities outside of the Complex structure:

```
Imports System
Imports System.Text
Imports System.Globalization
```

```vbnet
Public Class ComplexDbgFormatter
    Implements ICustomFormatter
    Implements IFormatProvider

    'IFormatProvider implementation
    Public Function GetFormat(ByVal formatType As Type) As Object _
        Implements System.IFormatProvider.GetFormat

        If formatType Is GetType(ICustomFormatter) Then
            Return Me
        Else
            Return CultureInfo.CurrentCulture.GetFormat(formatType)
        End If
    End Function

    'ICustomFormatter implementation
    Public Function Format(ByVal formatString As String, ByVal arg As Object, _
        ByVal formatProvider As IFormatProvider) As String _
        Implements System.ICustomFormatter.Format

        If TypeOf arg Is IFormattable AndAlso formatString = "DBG" Then
            Dim cpx As Complex = DirectCast(arg, Complex)

            'Generate debugging output for this object.
            Dim sb As StringBuilder = New StringBuilder()

            sb.Append(arg.[GetType]().ToString() & "" & vbLf & "")
            sb.AppendFormat("" & vbTab & "real:" & vbTab & "{0}" & _
                vbLf & "", cpx.Real)
            sb.AppendFormat("" & vbTab & "imaginary:" & vbTab & "{0}" & _
                vbLf & "", cpx.Img)

            Return sb.ToString()
        Else
            Dim formattable As IFormattable = TryCast(arg, IFormattable)

            If formattable Is Nothing Then
                Return formattable.ToString(formatString, formatProvider)
            Else
                Return arg.ToString()
            End If
        End If
    End Function
End Class

Public Structure Complex
    Implements IFormattable
```

```vbnet
        Private mReal As Double
        Private mImaginary As Double

        Public Sub New(ByVal real As Double, ByVal imaginary As Double)
            Me.mReal = real
            Me.mImaginary = imaginary
        End Sub

        Public ReadOnly Property Real() As Double
            Get
                Return mReal
            End Get
        End Property

        Public ReadOnly Property Img() As Double
            Get
                Return mImaginary
            End Get
        End Property

        'IFormattable implementation
        Public Overloads Function ToString(ByVal format As String, _
            ByVal formatProvider As IFormatProvider) As String _
            Implements IFormattable.ToString

            Dim sb As StringBuilder = New StringBuilder()

            sb.Append("( ")
            sb.Append(mReal.ToString(format, formatProvider))
            sb.Append(" : ")
            sb.Append(mImaginary.ToString(format, formatProvider))
            sb.Append(" )")

            Return sb.ToString()
        End Function
    End Structure

Public Class EntryPoint
    Shared Sub Main()
        Dim local As CultureInfo = CultureInfo.CurrentCulture
        Dim germany As CultureInfo = New CultureInfo("de-DE")
        Dim cpx As Complex = New Complex(12.3456, 1234.56)
        Dim strCpx As String = cpx.ToString("F", local)

        Console.WriteLine(strCpx)
        strCpx = cpx.ToString("F", germany)
```

```
        Console.WriteLine(strCpx)

        Dim dbgFormatter As ComplexDbgFormatter = New ComplexDbgFormatter()

        strCpx = [String].Format(dbgFormatter, "{0:DBG}", cpx)

        Console.WriteLine("" & vbCrLf & "Debugging output:" & _
            vbCrLf & "{0}", strCpx)
    End Sub
End Class
```

This example, whose output is identical to the last one, is a bit more complex (pun intended). But if you were not the original author of the Complex type, then this would be your only way to provide custom formatting for that type. Using this method, you can provide custom formatting to any of the other built-in types in the system.

Comparing Strings

When it comes to comparing strings, the .NET Framework provides quite a bit of flexibility. You can compare strings based on cultural information as well as without cultural consideration. You can also compare strings using case sensitivity or not, and the rules for how to do case-insensitive comparisons vary from culture to culture. There are several ways to compare strings offered within the Framework, some of which are exposed directly on the System.String type through the static String.Compare method. You can choose from a few overloads, and the most basic of them use the CultureInfo attached to the current thread to handle comparisons.

You often need to compare strings and don't want to carry the overhead of culture-specific comparisons. A perfect example is when you're comparing internal string data from a configuration file or when you're comparing file directories. The .NET Framework introduces a new enumeration, StringComparison, which allows you to choose a true non-culture-based comparison. The StringComparison enumeration looks like the following:

```
Public Enum StringComparison
    CurrentCulture
    CurrentCultureIgnoreCase
    InvariantCulture
    InvariantCultureIgnoreCase
    Ordinal
    OrdinalIgnoreCase
End Enum
```

The last two items in the enumeration are the items of interest. An ordinal-based comparison is the most basic string comparison that simply compares the character values of the two strings based on the numeric value of each character compared (it actually compares the raw binary values of each character). Doing comparisons this way removes all cultural bias from the comparisons and increases the efficiency of these comparisons tremendously.

The .NET Framework features a new class called StringComparer that implements the IComparer interface. Things such as sorted collections can use StringComparer to manage the sort. The System.StringComparer type follows the same pattern as the IFormattable locale support. You can use the StringComparer.CurrentCulture property to get a StringComparer instance specific to the culture of the current thread. Additionally, you can get the `StringComparer` instance from `StringComparer.CurrentCultureIgnoreCase` to do case-insensitive comparison, as well as culture-invariant instances using the `InvariantCulture` and `InvariantCultureIgnoreCase` properties. Lastly, you can use the `Ordinal` and `OrdinalIgnoreCase` properties to get instances that compare based on ordinal string comparison rules.

As you may expect, if the culture information attached to the current thread isn't what you need, you can create `StringComparer` instances based upon explicit locales simply by calling the `StringComparer.Create` method and passing the desired `CultureInfo` representing the locale you want, as well as a flag denoting whether you want a case-sensitive or case-insensitive comparer. The string used to specify which locale to use is the same as that for `CultureInfo`.

When choosing between the various comparison techniques, the general rule of thumb is to use the culture-specific or culture-invariant comparisons for any user-facing data—that is, data that will be presented to end users in some form or fashion—and ordinal comparisons otherwise. However, it's rare that you'd ever use `InvariantCulture` compared strings to display to users. Use the ordinal comparisons when dealing with data that is completely internal.

Working with Strings from Outside Sources

Within .NET, all strings are represented using Unicode UTF-16 character arrays. However, you may need to interface with the outside world using some other form of encoding, such as UTF-8. Sometimes, even when interfacing with other entities that use 16-bit Unicode strings, those entities may use big-endian Unicode strings,[2] whereas the Intel platform typically uses little-endian Unicode strings. This conversion work is easy with the `System.Text.Encoding` class.

This cursory example demonstrates how to convert to and from various encodings using the `Encoding` objects served up by the `System.Text.Encoding` class:

```
Imports System
Imports System.Text
Imports System.Windows.Forms

Public Class EntryPoint
    Shared Sub Main()
        Dim leUnicodeStr As String = " здорово!"
        Dim leUnicode As Encoding = Encoding.Unicode
        Dim beUnicode As Encoding = Encoding.BigEndianUnicode
        Dim utf8 As Encoding = Encoding.UTF8

        Dim leUnicodeBytes As Byte() = leUnicode.GetBytes(leUnicodeStr)
        Dim beUnicodeBytes As Byte() = _
            Encoding.Convert(leUnicode, beUnicode, leUnicodeBytes)
        Dim utf8Bytes As Byte() = Encoding.Convert(leUnicode, utf8, leUnicodeBytes)

        MessageBox.Show(leUnicodeStr, "Original String")
```

---

2. See the Unicode FAQs at `http://unicode.org/faq/utf_bom.html` for an introduction to UTF encoding.

```
        Dim sb As StringBuilder = New StringBuilder()
        For Each b As Byte In leUnicodeBytes
            sb.Append(b).Append(" : ")
        Next

        MessageBox.Show(sb.ToString(), "Little Endian Unicode Bytes")

        sb = New StringBuilder()
        For Each b As Byte In beUnicodeBytes
            sb.Append(b).Append(" : ")
        Next

        MessageBox.Show(sb.ToString(), "Big Endian Unicode Bytes")

        sb = New StringBuilder()
        For Each b As Byte In utf8Bytes
            sb.Append(b).Append(" : ")
        Next

        MessageBox.Show(sb.ToString(), "UTF Bytes")
    End Sub
End Class
```

The preceding example will display the four message boxes shown in Figure 9-2.

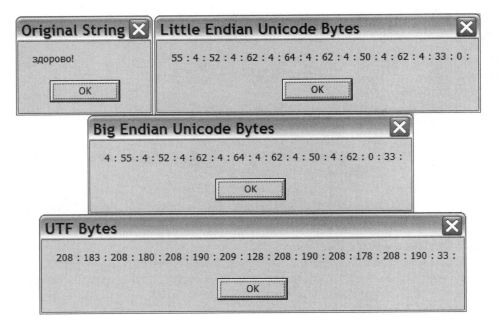

Figure 9-2. *Results displayed from running the previous code listing*

The example first starts by creating a System.String with some Russian text in it. As mentioned, the string contains a Unicode string, but is it a big-endian or little-endian Unicode string? The answer depends on what platform you're running on. On an Intel system, it is normally little-endian. However, since you're not supposed to access the underlying byte representation of the string because it is encapsulated from you, it doesn't matter. In order to get the bytes of the string, you should use one of the Encoding objects that you can get from System.Text.Encoding. In the example, you get local references to the Encoding objects for handling big-endian Unicode, little-endian Unicode, and UTF-8. Once you have those, you can use them to convert the string into any byte representation that you want. As you can see, you get three representations of the same string and send the byte sequence values to the console. Finally, you do not want to make any assumptions about the storage requirements for any of the encodings. If you need to know how much space is required to store the encoded string, call the Encoding.GetByteCount method to get that value.

■**Caution** Never make assumptions regarding the internal string representation format of the CLR. Nothing says that the internal representation cannot vary from one platform to the next. It would be unfortunate if your code made assumptions based upon an Intel platform and then failed to run on a Sun platform running the Mono CLR. Microsoft could even choose to run Windows on another platform one day, just as Apple has chosen to start using Intel processors.

As you work, you may need to go the opposite way with the conversion and convert an array of bytes from the outside world into a string that the system can then manipulate easily. For example, the Bluetooth protocol stack uses big-endian Unicode strings to transfer string data. To convert the bytes into a System.String, use the GetString method on the encoder that you're using. You must also use the encoder that matches the source encoding of your data.

This brings up an important note to keep in mind. When passing string data to and from other systems in raw byte format, you must always know the encoding scheme used by the protocol you're using. Most importantly, you must always use that encoding's matching Encoding object to convert the byte array into a System.String, even if you know that the encoding in the protocol is the same as that used internally with System.String on the platform you're building the application. Why? Suppose you're developing your application on an Intel platform and the protocol encoding is little-endian, which you know is the same as the platform encoding. If you take a shortcut and don't use the System.Text.Encoding.Unicode object to convert the bytes to the string, when you decide to run the application on a platform that happens to use big-endian strings internally, you'll be surprised when the application starts to crumble because you falsely assumed what encoding System.String uses internally. Efficiency is not a problem if you always use the encoder, because on platforms where the internal encoding is the same as the external encoding, the conversion will essentially boil down to nothing.

In the previous example, you saw the StringBuilder class used to send the array of bytes to the console. Let's now take a look at what the StringBuilder type is all about.

StringBuilder

Since System.String objects are immutable, sometimes they create efficiency bottlenecks when you're trying to build strings on the fly. You can create composite strings using the & operator as follows:

```
Dim compound As String = "Vote" & " for " & "Pedro"
```

However, this method isn't efficient because you have to create four strings to get the job done. Although this line of code is rather contrived, you can imagine that the efficiency of a complex system that does lots of string manipulation can quickly go downhill. Consider a case where you implement a custom base64 encoder that appends characters incrementally as it processes a binary file. The .NET library already offers this functionality in the System.Convert class, but let's ignore that for the sake of example. If you were to repeatedly use the & operator in a loop to create a large base64 string, your performance would quickly degrade as the source data increased in size. For these situations, you can use the System.Text.StringBuilder class, which implements a mutable string specifically for building composite strings efficiently.

StringBuilder internally maintains an array of characters that it manages dynamically. The workhorse methods of StringBuilder are Append(), Insert(), and AppendFormat(). These methods are richly overloaded in order to support appending and inserting string forms of the many common types. When you create a StringBuilder instance, you have various constructors to choose from. The default constructor creates a new StringBuilder instance with the system-defined default capacity. However, that capacity doesn't constrain the size of the string that it can create. Rather, it represents the amount of string data the StringBuilder can hold before it needs to grow the internal buffer and increase the capacity. If you know how big your string will likely end up being, you can give the StringBuilder that number in one of the constructor overloads, and it will initialize the buffer accordingly. This can help the StringBuilder instance from having to reallocate the buffer too often while you fill it.

You can also define the maximum-capacity property in the constructor overloads. By default, the maximum capacity is System.Int32.MaxValue, which is currently 2,147,483,647, but that exact value is subject to change as the system evolves. If you need to protect your StringBuilder buffer from growing over a certain size, you may provide an alternate maximum capacity in one of the constructor overloads. If either an append or insert operation forces the need for the buffer to grow greater than the maximum capacity, an ArgumentOutOfRangeException will be thrown.

For convenience, all the methods that append and insert data into an instance return a reference to the StringBuilder instance. Thus you can chain operations on a single string builder as shown:

```
Imports System
Imports System.Text

Public Class EntryPoint
    Shared Sub Main()
        Dim sb As StringBuilder = New StringBuilder()

        sb.Append("StringBuilder ").Append("is ").Append("very . . . ")
```

```
        Dim built1 As String = sb.ToString()

        sb.Append("cool")

        Dim built2 As String = sb.ToString()

        Console.WriteLine(built1)
        Console.WriteLine(built2)
    End Sub
End Class
```

Here are the results from running the previous code:

```
StringBuilder is very . . .
StringBuilder is very . . . cool
```

In the previous example, we converted the StringBuilder instance sb into a new System.String instance named built1 by calling sb.ToString(). For maximum efficiency, the StringBuilder simply hands off a reference to the character buffer to the string instance so that a copy is not necessary. If you think about it, part of the utility of StringBuilder would be compromised if it didn't do it this way. After all, if you create a huge string—say, some megabytes in size, such as a base64-encoded large image—you don't want that data to be copied in order to create a string from it. However, once you create the System.String, you now have the System.String and the StringBuilder holding references to the same array of characters. Since System.String is immutable, the StringBuilder's internal character array now becomes immutable as well. StringBuilder then switches to using a copy-on-write idiom with that buffer. Therefore, at the place where you append to the StringBuilder after having created the built1 string instance, the StringBuilder must make a new copy of the internal character array, thus handing off complete ownership of the old buffer to the built1 System.String instance. It's important to keep this behavior in mind if you're using StringBuilder to work with large string data.

Searching Strings with Regular Expressions

The System.String type offers some rudimentary searching methods, such as IndexOf(), IndexOfAny(), LastIndexOf(), LastIndexOfAny(), and StartsWith(). Using these methods, you can determine if a string contains certain substrings and where. The .NET Framework also contains classes that implement regular expressions (regexes).[3] This syntax is a language in and of itself, and full coverage of its capabilities is beyond the scope of this book. However, we'll describe the ways to use regular expressions that are specific to the .NET Framework.

There are really three main types of operations for which you employ regular expressions. The first is when searching a string just to verify that it contains a specific pattern, and if so, where. The search pattern can be extremely complex. The second is similar to the first, except,

---

3. See the Regular Expression page on Wikipedia at http://en.wikipedia.org/wiki/Regular_expression for an introduction.

in the process, you save off parts of the searched expression. For example, if you search a string for a date in a specific format, you may choose to break the three parts of the date into individual variables. And finally, regular expressions are often used for search-and-replace operations. This type of operation builds upon the capabilities of the previous two. Let's take a look at how to achieve these three goals using the .NET Framework's implementation of regular expressions.

Searching with Regular Expressions

As with the System.String class itself, most of the objects created from the regular expression classes are immutable. The workhorse class at the bottom of it all is the Regex class, which lives in the System.Text.RegularExpressions namespace. The general method of usage is to create a Regex instance to represent your regular expression by passing it a string of the pattern to search for. You then apply it to a string to find out if any matches exist. The results of the search will include whether a match was found, and if so, where. You can also find out where all subsequent instances of the match occur within the searched string. Let's go ahead and look at an example of what a basic Regex search looks like and then dig into more useful ways to use Regex:

```vb
Imports System
Imports System.Text.RegularExpressions

Public Class EntryPoint
    Shared Sub Main(ByVal args As String())
        If args.Length < 1 Then
            Console.WriteLine("You must provide a string.")
            Return
        End If

        'Create Regex to search for IP address pattern.
        Dim pattern As String = "\d\d?\d?\.\d\d?\d?.\d\d?\d?.\d\d?\d?"
        Dim regex As Regex = New Regex(pattern)
        Dim match As Match = regex.Match(args(0))

        While match.Success
            Console.WriteLine("IP Address found at {0} with value of {1}", _
                match.Index, match.Value)

            match = match.NextMatch()
        End While
    End Sub
End Class
```

The previous example searches a string provided as a command-line argument for an IP address. The search is simplistic, but we'll refine it a bit as we continue. Regular expressions can consist of literal characters to search for, as well as escaped characters that carry a special meaning. The familiar backslash is the method used to escape characters in a regular expression. In the previous example, \d means a numeric digit. The ones that are suffixed with a ? mean that there can be one or zero occurrences of the previous character or escaped expression. Notice that the period is escaped because the period by itself carries a special meaning: an un-escaped period matches any character in that position of the match. If you run the previous example and pass this quoted string as a command-line argument

```
"This is an IP address:123.123.1.123"
```

the output will look like the following:

```
IP Address found at 22 with value of 123.123.1.123
```

The previous example creates a new Regex instance named regex and then, using the Match method, applies the pattern to the given string. The results of the match are stored in the match variable. That match variable represents the first match within the searched string. You can use the Match.Success property to determine if the regex found anything at all. Next, you see the code using the Index and Value properties to find out more about the match. Lastly, you can go to the next match in the searched string by calling the Match.NextMatch method, and you can iterate through this chain until you find no more matches in the searched string.

Alternatively, instead of calling Match.NextMatch() in a loop, you can call the Regex.Matches method to retrieve a MatchCollection that gives you all of the matches at once rather than one at a time. Each of the examples using Regex in this chapter calls instance methods on a Regex instance. Many of the methods on Regex, such as Match() and Replace(), also offer shared versions where you don't have to create a Regex instance first, and you can just pass the regular expression pattern in the method call.

Searching and Grouping

From looking at the previous match, really all that is happening is that the pattern is looking for a series of four groups of digits separated by periods, where each group can be from one to three digits in length. This is a simplistic search because it will match an invalid IP address, such as 999.888.777.666. A better search for the IP address would look like the following:

```
Imports System
Imports System.Text.RegularExpressions

Public Class EntryPoint
    Shared Sub Main(ByVal args As String())
        If args.Length < 1 Then
            Console.WriteLine("You must provide a string.")
            Return
        End If

        'Create Regex to search for IP address pattern.
        Dim pattern As String = "([01]?\d\d?|2[0-4]\d|25[0-5])\." & _
            "([01]?\d\d?|2[0-4]\d|25[0-5])\." & _
            "([01]?\d\d?|2[0-4]\d|25[0-5])\." & _
            "([01]?\d\d?|2[0-4]\d|25[0-5])"
```

```
        Dim regex As Regex = New Regex(pattern)
        Dim match As Match = regex.Match(args(0))

        While match.Success
            Console.WriteLine("IP Address found at {0} with value of {1}", _
                match.Index, match.Value)

            match = match.NextMatch()
        End While
    End Sub
End Class
```

Essentially, four groupings of the same search pattern [01]?\d\d?|2[0-4]\d|25[0-5] are separated by periods, which, of course, are escaped in the preceding regular expression. Each one of these subexpressions matches a number between 0 and 255. This entire expression for searching for regular expressions is better, but still not perfect. However, you can see that it's getting closer, and with a little more fine-tuning, you can use it to validate the IP address given in a string. Thus you can use regular expressions to effectively validate input from users to make sure that it matches a certain form. For example, you may have a web server that expects U.S. telephone numbers to be entered in a pattern such as (xxx) xxx-xxxx. Regular expressions allow you to easily validate that the user has input the number correctly.

You may have noticed the addition of parentheses in the IP address search expression in the previous example. Parentheses are used to define groups that group subexpressions within regular expressions into discrete chunks. Groups can contain other groups as well. Therefore, the IP address regular-expression pattern in the previous example forms a group around each part of the IP address. In addition, you can access each individual group within the match. Consider the following modified version of the previous example:

```
Imports System
Imports System.Text.RegularExpressions

Public Class EntryPoint
    Shared Sub Main(ByVal args As String())
        If args.Length < 1 Then
            Console.WriteLine("You must provide a string.")
            Return
        End If

        'Create regex to search for IP address pattern.
        Dim pattern As String = "([01]?\d\d?|2[0-4]\d|25[0-5])\." & _
            "([01]?\d\d?|2[0-4]\d|25[0-5])\." & _
            "([01]?\d\d?|2[0-4]\d|25[0-5])\." & _
            "([01]?\d\d?|2[0-4]\d|25[0-5])"

        Dim regex As Regex = New Regex(pattern)
        Dim match As Match = regex.Match(args(0))
```

```
        While match.Success
            Console.WriteLine("IP Address found at {0} with value of {1}", _
                match.Index, match.Value)

            Console.WriteLine()
            Console.WriteLine("Groups are")

            For Each g As Group In match.Groups
                Console.WriteLine("" & Chr(9) & "{0} at {1}", g.Value, g.Index)
            Next

            match = match.NextMatch()
        End While
    End Sub
End Class
```

Within each match, you've added a loop that iterates through the individual groups within the match. As you'd expect, there will be at least four groups in the collection, one for each portion of the IP address. In fact, there is also a fifth item in the group that is the entire match. One of the groups within the groups collection returned from Match.Groups will always contain the entire match itself. Given the following input to the previous example

```
"This is an IP address:123.123.1.123"
```

the result will look like the following:

```
IP Address found at 22 with value of 123.123.1.123

Groups are
        123.123.1.123 at 22
        123 at 22
        123 at 26
        1 at 30
        123 at 32
```

Groups provide an excellent means of picking portions out of a given input string. For example, at the same time that you validate that a user has input a phone number of the required format, you could also capture the area code into a group for use later. Collecting substrings of a match into groups is handy. But even handier is being able to give those groups a name. Check out the following modified example:

```
Imports System
Imports System.Text.RegularExpressions
```

```vb
Public Class EntryPoint
    Shared Sub Main(ByVal args As String())
        If args.Length < 1 Then
            Console.WriteLine("You must provide a string.")
            Return
        End If

        Dim pattern As String = "(?<part1>[01]?\d\d?|2[0-4]\d|25[0-5])\." & _
            "(?<part2>[01]?\d\d?|2[0-4]\d|25[0-5])\." & _
            "(?<part3>[01]?\d\d?|2[0-4]\d|25[0-5])\." & _
            "(?<part4>[01]?\d\d?|2[0-4]\d|25[0-5])"

        Dim regex As Regex = New Regex(pattern)
        Dim match As Match = regex.Match(args(0))

        While match.Success
            Console.WriteLine("IP Address found at {0} with value of {1}" & _
                vbCrLf, match.Index, match.Value)

            Console.WriteLine("Groups are")
            Console.WriteLine("" & Chr(9) & "Part 1: {0}", match.Groups("part1"))
            Console.WriteLine("" & Chr(9) & "Part 2: {0}", match.Groups("part2"))
            Console.WriteLine("" & Chr(9) & "Part 3: {0}", match.Groups("part3"))
            Console.WriteLine("" & Chr(9) & "Part 4: {0}", match.Groups("part4"))

            match = match.NextMatch()
        End While
    End Sub
End Class
```

Here are the results from this version of the example:

```
IP Address found at 22 with value of 123.123.1.123

Groups are
        Part 1: 123
        Part 2: 123
        Part 3: 1
        Part 4: 123
```

In this variation, each part is captured into a group with a name, and when you send the result to the console, the group is accessed by name through an indexer on the GroupCollection returned by Match.Groups, which accepts a string argument.

With the ability to name groups comes the ability to back-reference groups within searches. For example, if you're looking for an exact repeat of a previous match, you can reference a previous group in what's called a back-reference by including a \k<*name*>, where *name* is the name of the group to back-reference. For example, consider the following example that looks for IP addresses where all four parts are the same:

```
Imports System
Imports System.Text.RegularExpressions

Public Class EntryPoint
    Shared Sub Main(ByVal args As String())
        If args.Length < 1 Then
            Console.WriteLine("You must provide a string.")
            Return
        End If

        Dim pattern As String = "(?<part1>[01]?\d\d?|2[0-4]\d|25[0-5])\." & _
            "\k<part1>\." & "\k<part1>\." & "\k<part1>"

        Dim regex As Regex = New Regex(pattern)
        Dim match As Match = regex.Match(args(0))

        While match.Success
            Console.WriteLine("IP Address found at {0} with value of {1}", _
                match.Index, match.Value)

            match = match.NextMatch()
        End While
    End Sub
End Class
```

The following output shows the results of running this code on the string "My IP address is 123.123.123.123":

```
IP Address found at 17 with value of 123.123.123.123
```

Replacing Text with Regex

The .NET Framework provides regular-expression text-substitution capabilities via overloads of the Regex.Replace method. Suppose that you want to process a string looking for an IP address that a user input, and you want to display the string. However, for security reasons, you want to replace the IP address with xxx.xxx.xxx.xxx. You can achieve this goal as follows:

```
Imports System
Imports System.Text.RegularExpressions

Public Class EntryPoint
    Shared Sub Main(ByVal args As String())
        If args.Length < 1 Then
            Console.WriteLine("You must provide a string.")
            Return
        End If
```

```
            Dim pattern As String = "([01]?\d\d?|2[0-4]\d|25[0-5])\." & _
                "([01]?\d\d?|2[0-4]\d|25[0-5])\." & _
                "([01]?\d\d?|2[0-4]\d|25[0-5])\." & _
                "([01]?\d\d?|2[0-4]\d|25[0-5])"

            Dim regex As Regex = New Regex(pattern)

            Console.WriteLine("Input given --> {0}", regex.Replace(args(0), _
                "xxx.xxx.xxx.xxx"))
        End Sub
End Class
```

Given this input

```
"My IP address is 123.123.123.123"
```

the output will look like the following:

```
Input given --> My IP address is xxx.xxx.xxx.xxx
```

Of course, when you find a match within a string, you may want to replace it with something that depends on what the match is. The previous example simply replaces each match with a static string. In order to replace based on the match instance, you can create an instance of the MatchEvaluator delegate and pass it to the Regex.Replace method. Then, whenever it finds a match, it calls through to the MatchEvaluator delegate instance given while passing it the match. Thus the delegate can create the replacement string based upon the actual match. The MatchEvaluator delegate has the following signature:

```
Public Delegate Function MatchEvaluator(ByVal match As Match) As String
```

Suppose you want to reverse the individual parts of an IP address. You can use a MatchEvaluator coupled with Regex.Replace() to get the job done, as in the following example:

```
Imports System
Imports System.Text
Imports System.Text.RegularExpressions

Public Class EntryPoint
    Shared Sub Main(ByVal args As String())
        If args.Length < 1 Then
            Console.WriteLine("You must provide a string.")
            Return
        End If

        Dim pattern As String = "(?<part1>[01]?\d\d?|2[0-4]\d|25[0-5])\." & _
            "(?<part2>[01]?\d\d?|2[0-4]\d|25[0-5])\." & _
            "(?<part3>[01]?\d\d?|2[0-4]\d|25[0-5])\." & _
            "(?<part4>[01]?\d\d?|2[0-4]\d|25[0-5])"
```

```
        Dim regex As Regex = New Regex(pattern)
        Dim match As Match = regex.Match(args(0))

        Dim eval As MatchEvaluator = _
            New MatchEvaluator(AddressOf EntryPoint.IPReverse)

        Console.WriteLine(regex.Replace(args(0), eval))
    End Sub

    Shared Function IPReverse(ByVal match As Match) As String
        Dim sb As StringBuilder = New StringBuilder()

        sb.Append(match.Groups("part4").ToString & ".")
        sb.Append(match.Groups("part3").ToString & ".")
        sb.Append(match.Groups("part2").ToString & ".")
        sb.Append(match.Groups("part1"))

        Return sb.ToString()
    End Function
End Class
```

Using "My IP address is 123.124.125.126" as your command-line argument outputs the following:

```
My IP address is 126.125.124.123
```

In the previous case, whenever a match is found, the delegate is called to determine what the replacement string should be. However, since all you're doing is changing the order, the job is not too complex for what are called *regular-expression substitutions*. If, in the example prior to this one, you had chosen to use the overload of Replace() that doesn't use a MatchEvaluator delegate, you could have achieved the same result, since the regex lets you reference the group variables in the replacement string. To reference one of the named groups, you can use the syntax shown in the following example:

```
Imports System
Imports System.Text
Imports System.Text.RegularExpressions

Public Class EntryPoint
    Shared Sub Main(ByVal args As String())
        If args.Length < 1 Then
            Console.WriteLine("You must provide a string.")
            Return
        End If
```

```
        Dim pattern As String = "(?<part1>[01]?\d\d?|2[0-4]\d|25[0-5])\." & _
            "(?<part2>[01]?\d\d?|2[0-4]\d|25[0-5])\." & _
            "(?<part3>[01]?\d\d?|2[0-4]\d|25[0-5])\." & _
            "(?<part4>[01]?\d\d?|2[0-4]\d|25[0-5])"

        Dim regex As Regex = New Regex(pattern)
        Dim match As Match = regex.Match(args(0))

        Dim replace As String = _
            "${part4}.${part3}.${part2}.${part1} (the reverse of $&)"

        Console.WriteLine(regex.Replace(args(0), replace))
    End Sub
End Class
```

Using the same command-line argument as the last example outputs the following:

```
My IP address is 126.125.124.123 (the reverse of 123.124.125.126)
```

Including one of the named groups requires the ${*name*} syntax, where *name* is the name of the group. You can also see that the code references the full text of the match using $&. Other substitution strings are available, such as $', which substitutes the part of the input string prior to and up to the match, and $', which substitutes all text after the match. Clearly, you can craft complex string-replacement capabilities using the regular-expression implementation within the .NET Framework.

Regex Creation Options

One of the constructor overloads of a Regex allows you to pass various options of type RegexOptions during the creation of a Regex instance. Likewise, the methods on Regex, such as Match() and Replace(), have a static overload, allowing you to pass RegexOptions flags. We'll discuss some of the more commonly used options in this section.

By default, regular expressions are interpreted at run time. Complex regular expressions can chew up quite a bit of processor time while the regex engine is processing them. For times like these, consider using the Compiled option. This option causes the regular expression to be represented internally by intermediate language (IL) code that is compiled by the just-in-time (JIT) compiler. This increases the latency for the first use of the regular expression, but if it's used often, it will pay off in the end. JIT-compiled code increases the working set of the application.

Many times, you'll find it useful to do case-insensitive searches. You could accommodate that in the regular-expression pattern, but it will make your pattern more difficult to read. It's easier to pass the IgnoreCase flag when creating the Regex instance. When you use this flag, the Regex engine will also take into account any culture-specific, case-sensitivity issues by referencing the CultureInfo attached to the current thread. If you want to do case-insensitive searches in a culture-invariant way, combine the IgnoreCase flag with the CultureInvariant flag.

The IgnorePatternWhitespace flag is also useful for complex regular expressions. This flag tells the regex engine to ignore any white space within the match expression and to ignore any comments on lines following the # character. This provides a nifty way to comment regular expressions that are really complex. For example, check out the IP address search from the previous example rewritten using IgnorePatternWhitespace:

```
Imports System
Imports System.Text.RegularExpressions

Public Class EntryPoint
    Shared Sub Main(ByVal args As String())
        If args.Length < 1 Then
            Console.WriteLine("You must provide a string.")
            Return
        End If

        Dim pattern As String = _
        "# First part match " & vbCrLf & _
        "([01]?\d\d?          # At least one digit," & vbCrLf & _
        "                     # possibly prepended by 0 or 1" & vbCrLf & _
        "                     # and possibly followed by another digit" & _
        vbCrLf & "# OR " & vbCrLf & _
        "|2[0-4]\d            # Starts with a 2, after a number from 0-4" & _
        vbCrLf & "            # and then any digit" & vbCrLf & _
        "# OR " & vbCrLf & _
        "|25[0-5])            # 25 followed by a number from 0-5" & vbCrLf & _
        "\.                   # The whole group is followed by a period." & _
        vbCrLf & "# REPEAT " & vbCrLf & "([01]?\d\d?|2[0-4]\d|25[0-5])\. " & _
        vbCrLf & "# REPEAT " & vbCrLf & "([01]?\d\d?|2[0-4]\d|25[0-5])\. " & _
        vbCrLf & "# REPEAT " & vbCrLf & "([01]?\d\d?|2[0-4]\d|25[0-5])"

        Dim regex As Regex = _
            New Regex(pattern, RegexOptions.IgnorePatternWhitespace)

        Dim match As Match = regex.Match(args(0))

        While match.Success
            Console.WriteLine("IP Address found at {0} with value of {1}", _
                match.Index, match.Value)

            match = match.NextMatch()
        End While
    End Sub
End Class
```

Continuing with the same command-line argument outputs the following:

```
IP Address found at 17 with value of 123.124.125.126
```

Notice how expressive you can be in the comments of your regular expression. And given how complex regular expressions can become, this is a good thing indeed.

Summary

In this chapter, we've touched the tip of the iceberg on the string-handling capabilities of .NET and VB. Since the string type is such a widely used type, rather than merely include it in the BCL, the CLR designers chose to annex it into the set of built-in types. This is good, considering how common string usage is. Furthermore, the library provides a thorough implementation of cultural-specific patterns, via `CultureInfo`, that you will typically need when creating global software that deals with strings.

We also demonstrated how to create your own cultures easily using the `CultureAndRegionInfoBuilder` class. Essentially, any software that interacts directly with the user and is meant to be used on a global basis needs to be prepared to service locale-specific needs. Finally, we gave a brief tour of the regular-expression capabilities of the .NET Framework. We think you'll agree that the string and text-handling facilities built into the CLR, .NET, and VB are well designed and easy to use.

In Chapter 10, we'll cover arrays and other, more versatile collection types. After arrays and collection types, our discussion will turn to the topic of iteration.

CHAPTER 10

Arrays and Collections

Collection types have been around in various forms since the beginning of computer programming, and the most basic type of collection is the array. This chapter provides an overview of arrays and explains the major generic collection interfaces. After arrays and collections, we will spend some time demonstrating enumerators and iteration using VB 2008.

Introduction to Arrays

A VB array is a built-in, implicit type to the runtime. When you declare a type—whether it's a class or structure—the runtime reserves the right to silently generate an array type based upon that new type. The array type that it generates is a reference type. The reference type that it generates is derived from `System.Array`, and ultimately from `System.Object`. Therefore, you can treat all arrays polymorphically through a reference to `System.Array`. That means that each array, no matter what concrete type of array it is, implements all of the methods and properties of `System.Array`.

You declare an array using parentheses following the array variable name. The following example shows three ways to create an array of integers and print them to the console:

```
Imports System

Public Class EntryPoint
    Shared Sub Main()
        Dim array1() As Integer = New Integer(5) {}
        Dim array2() As Integer = New Integer() {2, 4, 6, 8}
        Dim array3() As Integer = {1, 3, 5, 7}

        Dim i As Integer = 0

        For i = 0 To array1.Length - 1
            array1(i) = i * 2
        Next

        For Each item As Integer In array1
            Console.WriteLine("array1: " + item.ToString)
        Next
        Console.WriteLine(vbCrLf)
```

```
        For Each item As Integer In array2
            Console.WriteLine("array2: " + item.ToString)
        Next
        Console.WriteLine(vbCrLf)

        For Each item As Integer In array3
            Console.WriteLine("array3: " + item.ToString)
        Next
    End Sub
End Class
```

Executing the preceding code will display the following results:

```
array1: 0
array1: 2
array1: 4
array1: 6
array1: 8
array1: 10

array2: 2
array2: 4
array2: 6
array2: 8

array3: 1
array3: 3
array3: 5
array3: 7
```

The longhand way to create an array instance and fill it with initial values is shown where array1 is initialized. In VB, an array's lower bound is always 0 in order to meet the Common Language Specification (CLS) restriction that arrays have a 0 lower bound. The upper bound for array1 is 5, as stated in the code, making for an array with 6 elements. Notice the use of the New operator to allocate the array1 and array2 instances. The omission of New to allocate the array3 instance is a notational shortcut.

One convenience of .NET arrays is that they are range-checked. If you step off the end of one of them, going out of bounds, the runtime will throw an IndexOutOfRangeException.

You can iterate through the elements in the array using a For . . . Each statement. This works because System.Array implements IEnumerable. The section titled "How Iteration Works" describes IEnumerable and its cousin IEnumerator in more detail.

Type Convertibility

When you declare an array to contain instances of a certain type, the instances that you may place in that array can actually be instances of a more derived type. For example, if you create an array that contains instances of type Animal, then you can feasibly insert an instance of Dog or Cat if both of them derive from Animal.

You can also coerce array types in this other, even more interesting way:

```
Imports System

Public Class Animal
End Class

Public Class Dog
    Inherits Animal
End Class

Public Class Cat
    Inherits Animal
End Class

Public Class EntryPoint
    Shared Sub Main()
        Dim dogs() As Dog = New Dog(3) {}
        Dim cats() As Cat = New Cat(2) {}

        Dim animals() As Animal = dogs
        Dim moreAnimals() As Animal = cats
    End Sub
End Class
```

The assignment from dogs to animals and from cats to moreAnimals is something that you can do as long as their ranks match and the contained type is convertible from one to the other. Since both arrays in the previous example have a rank of 1, and Dog and Cat are type-convertible to Animal, the assignment works.

Note The full type information of an array comprises its rank (how many dimensions it has) and the type that it contains.

Array Covariance

An array element whose type is B may actually be of type A, provided that both A and B are reference types and that B is a base type of A or is implemented by A. This relationship is known as *array covariance*. Due to this covariance, all element assignments of reference type arrays are subject to a runtime type check to ensure that the value being assigned is an allowed type.

Sortability and Searchability

The System.Array interface includes several methods that deal with sorting the elements within an array. These methods are usable when the contained type implements IComparable, the standard interface through which items of a particular type are compared. You cannot sort a multidimensional array, as doing so will throw an exception of type RankException. Also, if you attempt to sort an array where one or more of the members do not support IComparable, you can expect to see an exception of type InvalidOperationException.

Using the shared methods Index() and LastIndexOf(), you can locate a specific value within an array. If the method fails to find the requested value, it returns –1. No particular search algorithm is involved with these methods other than the fact that the former starts searching from the beginning of the array and the latter starts at the end. To perform a faster search, you can use the BinarySearch shared method. However, before you can do so, you must sort your array, which requires that the elements within the array implement IComparable.

Synchronization

The System.Array type offers ICollection and IList to synchronize access to an array or a collection type that implements ICollection. One of the properties of ICollection is IsSynchronized, which always returns False for regular arrays. Regular arrays are not synchronized by default and enforcing such a rule would cause those who don't need synchronization to pay a penalty. Therefore, you must manage synchronization yourself.

The easiest way to manage synchronization is with the System.Monitor class, which you normally use with the SyncLock keyword. The class allows you to acquire the built-in synchronization lock on an object. However, instead of acquiring a lock on the array object itself, you should acquire a lock on the ICollection.SyncRoot object.

Many array and collection implementations are free to return a reference to the actual container here, but they may not for various reasons. ICollection.SyncRoot provides a common way for synchronizing access to both arrays and collections. The "Collection Synchronization" section covers synchronization in more detail.

Multidimensional Arrays

VB and the CLR contain direct support for multidimensional arrays. You can easily declare an array with multiple dimensions by simply introducing a comma into the curly brackets {} to separate the indices, as shown in the following example:

```
Imports System

Public Class EntryPoint
    Shared Sub Main()
        Dim twoDim1(,) As Integer = New Integer(5, 3) {}
        Dim twoDim2(,) As Integer = {{1, 2, 3}, {4, 5, 6}, {7, 8, 9}}
```

```
        For Each i As Integer In twoDim2
            Console.WriteLine(i)
        Next
    End Sub
End Class
```

Running the previous example will list each array element as follows:

```
1
2
3
4
5
6
7
8
9
```

The two declarations don't need the size of each dimension when declaring the type. That's because arrays are typed based on their containing type and the rank. However, once you create an instance of the array type, you must provide the size of the dimensions. The previous example does this in two different ways. In creating twoDim1, you explicitly say what the dimension sizes are, and in creating twoDim2, the compiler figures it out based upon the initialization expression.

The example lists all of the elements in the array using the For . . . Each loop, as shown. For . . . Each iterates over all elements in the array in a row-major fashion, meaning that elements in each array dimension are iterated over before moving on to the next dimension. You could achieve the same goal using two nested For loops. To iterate over the array elements in any other order, you would need two nested For loops. When doing so, keep in mind that the Array.Length property returns the total number of elements in the array. In order to get the count of each dimension, you must call the Array.GetLength method supplying the dimension that you're interested in. For example, you could iterate over the elements in the array using the following syntax, and the results would be the same:

```
Imports System

Public Class EntryPoint
    Shared Sub Main()
        Dim twoDim As Integer(,) = {{1, 2, 3}, {4, 5, 6}, {7, 8, 9}}

        For i As Integer = 0 To twoDim.GetLength(0) - 1
            For j As Integer = 0 To twoDim.GetLength(1) - 1
                Console.WriteLine(twoDim(i, j))
            Next
        Next

        Console.WriteLine(vbCrLf)
```

```
            For i As Integer = twoDim.GetLowerBound(0) To twoDim.GetUpperBound(0)
                For j As Integer = twoDim.GetLowerBound(1) To twoDim.GetUpperBound(1)
                    Console.WriteLine(twoDim(i, j))
                Next
            Next
        End Sub
    End Class
```

For good measure, we've shown how to iterate over the dimensions of the array using two methods. The first method assumes that the lower bound of each dimension is 0, and the second does not. In all of the calls to GetLength(), GetUpperBound(), and GetLowerBound(), you must supply a zero-based dimension of the Array that you're interested in.

When you access the elements of a multidimensional array, the compiler generates calls to Get and Set methods. These methods are overloaded to accept a variable list of integers to specify the ordinal of each dimension within the array.

When mapping multidimensional arrays to mathematical concepts, the multidimensional array is the most natural and preferred way to go. However, creating methods where an argument may be an array of varying rank is tricky because you must accept the argument as type System.Array and dynamically deal with the rank of the array. You access the rank of an array using the Array.Rank property.

Multidimensional Jagged Arrays

A jagged array is an array of arrays in which each element of the top-level array is an individual array instance, and each array instance in the top-level array can be any size. These differing array lengths give the array a "jagged" rather than rectangular appearance. The following example shows the syntactical pattern for declaring and allocating a jagged array in VB:

```
Imports System
Imports System.Text

Public Class EntryPoint
    Shared Sub Main()
        Dim jagged()() As Integer = New Integer(2)() {}
        jagged(0) = New Integer() {1, 2}
        jagged(1) = New Integer() {1, 2, 3, 4, 5}
        jagged(2) = New Integer() {6, 5, 4}

        For Each ar As Integer() In jagged
            Dim sb As StringBuilder = New StringBuilder()

            For Each n As Integer In ar
                sb.AppendFormat("{0} ", n)
            Next
            Console.WriteLine(sb.ToString())
        Next
        Console.WriteLine()
```

```
        For i As Integer = 0 To jagged.Length - 1
            Dim sb As StringBuilder = New StringBuilder

            For j As Integer = 0 To jagged(i).Length - 1
                sb.AppendFormat("{0} ", jagged(i)(j))
            Next
            Console.WriteLine(sb.ToString())
        Next
    End Sub
End Class
```

The preceding code will display the following when run:

```
1 2
1 2 3 4 5
6 5 4

1 2
1 2 3 4 5
6 5 4
```

The example shows two ways to iterate through the array just to show the syntax for accessing the individual elements within a jagged array. Notice how the output provides a jagged-looking output, since each subarray has a different size. As you can see, allocating and creating a jagged array is a bit more complex because you must handle all of the sub-array allocations individually.

The For . . . Each method of iterating through the array is more elegant, and as you'll see later on, using For . . . Each allows you to use the same code to iterate through collections that may not be an array.

Accessing elements within a jagged array requires more care, since you cannot assume that each subarray has the same number of elements in it.

Collection Types

A collection is any type that holds onto a set of objects and implements IEnumerable or IEnumerable(Of T). The objects in the set are typically related to each other in some way defined by the problem domain. The .NET Framework offers a host of collection types for managing everything from an expandable array via ArrayList, a Queue, a Stack, or even a dictionary via the HashTable class.

Comparing ICollection(Of T) with ICollection

Beginning with .NET 2.0, the System.Collections.Generic namespace defines ICollection(Of T). ICollection(Of T) is strongly typed, and when used to contain value types, it is quite efficient, since there is no gratuitous boxing. For more information on boxing, refer to Chapter 3. The root type of all the generic collection types is ICollection(Of T). This code includes the declaration for it:

```
Public Interface ICollection(Of T)
    Inherits IEnumerable(Of T)
    Inherits IEnumerable

    ReadOnly Property Count() As Integer
    ReadOnly Property IsReadOnly() As Boolean

    Sub Add(ByVal item As T)
    Sub Clear()

    Function Contains(ByVal item As T) As Boolean
    Sub CopyTo(ByVal array As T(), ByVal arrayIndex As Integer)
    Function Remove(ByVal item As T) As Boolean
End Interface
```

For the sake of comparison, this code includes the nongeneric ICollection interface definition as well:

```
Public Interface ICollection
    Inherits IEnumerable

    ReadOnly Property Count() As Integer
    ReadOnly Property IsSynchronized() As Boolean
    ReadOnly Property SyncRoot() As Object

    Sub CopyTo(ByVal array As Array, ByVal index As Integer)
End Interface
```

Now, let's take a look at the differences and what that means for your code. One thing that has been missing with the nongeneric collections is a uniform interface for managing the contents of the collection. For example, the nongeneric Stack and Queue types both have a Clear method to erase their contents. As expected, they both implement ICollection. However, since ICollection doesn't contain any modifying methods, you generally can't treat instances of these two types within code. Thus you would always have to cast an instance variable to type Stack in order to call Stack.Clear() and cast to type Queue in order to call Queue.Clear().

ICollection(Of T) solves this problem by declaring some methods for modifying the collection. As with most general-use solutions, it doesn't necessarily apply to all situations. For example, ICollection(Of T) also declares an IsReadOnly property because sometimes you need to introduce an immutable collection in your design. For those instances, you would expect calls to Add(), Clear(), and Remove() to throw an InvalidOperationException.

■**Note** For better performance, it's recommended that your code determine if such operations are forbidden by first checking the IsReadOnly property, thus avoiding the exception altogether.

Since a main purpose of ICollection(Of T) is to provide stronger type safety, ICollection(Of T) provides its own version of CopyTo() that is strongly typed. Whereas ICollection.CopyTo() knows that the first parameter is an array, ICollection(Of T).CopyTo() is given the array rank as well as the containing type. You can only pass a single-dimension array to ICollection(Of T).CopyTo(). The nongeneric ICollection.CopyTo() only accepts an array of single dimension as well, but since the compiler cannot determine the rank of a System.Array type at compile time, you get a runtime exception of the type ArgumentException if you pass an array with more than one dimension to a proper implementation of ICollection.CopyTo(). Not only is the caller of ICollection.CopyTo() supposed to know this rule, but so is the type implementing ICollection. The added type information in ICollection(Of T).CopyTo() not only protects both the caller and the implementer from making this mistake, but it also provides greater efficiency.

All of the generic collection types implement both ICollection(Of T) and ICollection. Both interfaces provide useful utility to the container type. Any methods in ICollection that overlap with ICollection(Of T) should be implemented explicitly.

Collection Synchronization

One capability present in ICollection that is missing in its generic counterpart is the provision for handling multithreaded synchronization generally across all collections. By default, most collection types are not synchronized. However, sometimes you'll require synchronization while accessing these collections from multiple threads. You can query the property IsSynchronized to determine whether the collection is synchronized. Most of the time, including the case with System.Array, the answer will be False.

There are a couple of ways to control synchronization to collections that return False from ICollection.IsSynchronized. The most basic way is to use the ICollection.SyncRoot property, which returns an object that you can subsequently use with the System.Monitor—usually via the VB SyncLock statement—to guard access to the collection. Handling it this way gives you much greater flexibility when accessing the collection because you control the granularity of exactly when the lock is acquired and released. However, the onus is on you to make sure that locking is handled appropriately, since the collection doesn't attempt to acquire the lock internally.

■**Note** Choosing how to implement synchronization is a classic engineering trade-off decision to make when designing new collections that implement ICollection. You can implement synchronization internally to the collection, but clients that don't need it pay a performance penalty. You also can externalize the synchronization by implementing ICollection.SyncRoot, but then you rely on the clients to manage the synchronization correctly. You should consider your application domain thoroughly when choosing between the two.

In some cases, collection types simply ireturn Me for ICollection.SyncRoot. Therefore, it's important that you never synchronize access to a collection by passing its reference to the System.Monitor. Instead, always use the object obtained through the SyncRoot property, even though it may actually return Me.

As an alternative to managing the SyncLock manually, most of the nongeneric collection types in the standard library implement a Synchronized method, which returns an object that wraps the collection and manages the synchronization lock for you. You may want to consider applying this same pattern when creating collection types of your own. By using the wrapper returned by the Synchronized method, client code that uses the collection doesn't have to change in order to work in a multithreaded environment. When implementing your own collections, allow clients to choose whether synchronization is used and never force it upon them. Threading and synchronization is discussed in great detail in Chapter 13.

Types That Produce Collections

If a collection's contents change while an enumerator is enumerating the collection, it could invalidate the enumerator. Although you can create an enumerator that locks access to the container while it is enumerating, it may not be the best thing to do from an efficiency standpoint. For example, what if it takes a long time to iterate over all of the elements in the collection? The For . . . Each loop could do some lengthy processing on each item within the loop, during which time anyone else could be blocked from modifying the collection.

In cases like these, it may make sense for the For . . . Each loop to iterate over a copy of the collection rather than the original collection itself. If you decide to do this, you need to make sure you understand what a copy of the collection means. If the collection contains value types, then the copy is a deep copy, as long as the value types within it don't hold onto reference types internally. If the collection contains reference types, you need to decide if the copy of the collection must clone each of the contained elements. Either way, it would be nice to have a design guideline to follow in order to know when to return a copy.

The current rule of thumb when returning collection types from within your types is to always return a copy of the collection from methods and return a reference to the actual collection if accessed through a property on your type. Although this rule is not set in stone, it does make some semantic sense. Methods tend to indicate that you're performing some sort of operation on the type, and you may expect results from that operation. On the other hand, property access tends to indicate that you need direct access to the state of the object itself.

Lists

One thing that is missing from ICollection(Of T) is an index operator that allows you to access the elements within the collection using the familiar array-access syntax. Not all concrete types that implement ICollection(Of T) need to have an index operator, and in some of those cases, it makes no sense. For example, an index operator for a list of integers would probably accept a parameter of type Integer, whereas a dictionary type would accept a parameter type that is the same as the key type in the dictionary. Therefore, it's impossible to define a general-use index operator to fit all collection types.

If you're defining a collection where it makes sense to index the items, then you want that collection to implement IList(Of T). Concrete generic list collection types typically implement the IList(Of T) and IList interfaces. IList(Of T) implements ICollection(Of T) and IList implements ICollection, so any type that is a list is also a collection. The IList(Of T) interface looks like the following:

```
Public Interface IList(Of T)
    Inherits ICollection(Of T)
    Inherits IEnumerable(Of T)
    Inherits IEnumerable

    Default Property Item(ByVal index As Integer) As T

    Function IndexOf(ByVal item As T) As Integer
        Sub Insert(ByVal index As Integer, ByVal item As T)
        Sub RemoveAt(ByVal index As Integer)
End Interface
```

The IList interface is a bit larger:

```
Public Interface IList
    Inherits ICollection
    Inherits IEnumerable

    ReadOnly Property IsFixedSize() As Boolean
    ReadOnly Property IsReadOnly() As Boolean

    Default ReadOnly Property Item(ByVal index As Integer) As Object

    Function Add(ByVal value As Object) As Integer
    Sub Clear()
    Function Contains(ByVal value As Object) As Boolean
    Function IndexOf(ByVal value As Object) As Integer
    Sub Insert(ByVal index As Integer, ByVal value As Object)
    Sub Remove(ByVal value As Object)
    Sub RemoveAt(ByVal index As Integer)
End Interface
```

Some overlap exists between IList(Of T) and IList, but there are plenty of useful properties and methods in IList that a generic container such as List(Of T), or any other generic list that you create, would want. As with ICollection(Of T) and ICollection, the typical pattern is to implement both interfaces. You should explicitly implement the methods of IList that overlap in functionality with those of IList(Of T) so that the only way to get to them is to convert the instance reference to the IList type first.

■**Note** Generally, when implementing your own list types, you should derive your implementation from Collection(Of T) in the System.Collections.ObjectModel namespace.

Dictionaries

The .NET Framework implements IDictionary(Of TKey, TValue) as a strongly typed counterpart to IDictionary. Concrete types that implement IDictionary(Of TKey, TValue) should implement IDictionary as well. There is overlap, and the generic interface declares more type-safe versions of some properties and methods declared in IDictionary. You can use TryGetValue(), a method available on IDictionary(Of TKey, TValue), to get a value based on the given key. The method returns the value through a ByRef parameter, and the actual return value from the method indicates whether the element was in the dictionary. Although you can do this same thing using the index operator and catching the KeyNotFoundException when the element is not in there, it is more efficient to avoid exceptions if you know the element is probably not there. Using exceptions for the purpose of control flow is a practice to avoid for two reasons. First, using exceptions for control flow is inefficient because exceptions are expensive. Second, it trivializes the exception by using it to handle an expected event.

■**Note** When implementing generic dictionaries, you have a couple of choices from which to derive implementations. First, you can use SortedDictionary(Of TKey, TValue), which provides $O(\log n)$ retrieval and implements IDictionary(Of TKey, TValue) as well as the collection interfaces. However, you can also choose to use KeyedCollection(Of TKey, TValue) in the System.Collections.ObjectModel namespace. Although it doesn't actually implement the dictionary interfaces, it does provide $O(1)$ retrieval most of the time.

System.Collections.ObjectModel

To define your own collection types, you'll find the types defined in the System.Collections.ObjectModel namespace most useful. This namespace contains only three types, and the main reason these types were broken out into their own namespace is that the VB environment already contains a Collection type that is implemented by a namespace it imports by default. The VB team was also concerned that VB users might be confused seeing two types with similar names and drastically different behaviors popping up in IntelliSense.

These types are extremely useful for those writing libraries or for code consumed by others, whether they are developers within your organization using corporate class libraries or external customers who have purchased your library for their own development use. One Microsoft guideline suggests that you should consider creating a subclass of these types when exposing collections, even if only to provide a richer type name describing the collection and an easily accessible extensibility point.

If you're defining collection types of your own, you can easily derive your type from Collection(Of T) in order to get default collection behavior, including implementation of ICollection(Of T), IList(Of T), and IEnumerable(Of T). Collection(Of T) also implements the nongeneric interfaces ICollection, IList, and IEnumerable. You may have to cast the type to one of these interfaces explicitly to access their properties and methods, since many of them are implemented explicitly. Moreover, the Collection(Of T) type uses the Non-Virtual Interface (NVI) pattern, described in Chapter 14, to provide the derived type with a set of protected overridable methods. We won't list the entire public interface to Collection(Of T); however, the protected overridable methods are shown here:

```
Public Class Collection(Of T)
    Implements ICollection(Of T)
    Implements IList(Of T)
    Implements IEnumerable(Of T)
    Implements ICollection
    Implements IList
    Implements IEnumerable

    Protected Overridable Sub ClearItems()
    End Sub

    Protected Overridable Sub InsertItem(ByVal index As Integer, ByVal item As T)
    End Sub

    Protected Overridable Sub RemoveItem(ByVal index As Integer)
    End Sub

    Protected Overridable Sub SetItem(ByVal index As Integer, ByVal item As T)
    End Sub
End Class
```

You cannot modify the storage location of the collection by overriding these methods. Collection(Of T) manages the storage of the elements, and the elements are held internally through a private field of type IList(Of T). However, you can override these methods to manage extra information triggered by these operations. Just be sure to call through to the base class versions in your overrides.

Finally, the Collection(Of T) type offers two constructors: one creates an empty instance and the other accepts an IList(Of T). The constructor copies the passed-in contents of the IList(Of T) instance into the new collection in the order that they are provided by the enumerator returned from IList(Of T).GetEnumerator(). The implementation of the source list's enumerator can do such things as reverse the order of the elements as they're put into the collection by providing a proper enumerator implementation.

To illustrate a more flexible way to fill a collection, the following example introduces extra constructors on Collection(Of T) that accept an interface of type IEnumerator(Of T) and IEnumerable(Of T):

```
Imports System
Imports System.Collections.Generic
Imports System.Collections.ObjectModel

Public Class MyCollection(Of T)
    Inherits Collection(Of T)
```

```vbnet
    Public Sub New()
        MyBase.New()
    End Sub

    Public Sub New(ByVal list As IList(Of T))
        MyBase.New(list)
    End Sub

    Public Sub New(ByVal enumerable As IEnumerable(Of T))
        MyBase.New()

        For Each item As T In enumerable
            Me.Add(item)
        Next
    End Sub

    Public Sub New(ByVal enumerator As IEnumerator(Of T))
        MyBase.New()

        While enumerator.MoveNext()
            Me.Add(enumerator.Current)
        End While
    End Sub
End Class

Public Class EntryPoint
    Shared Sub Main()
        Dim coll As MyCollection(Of Integer) = _
            New MyCollection(Of Integer)(GenerateNumbers())

        For Each n As Integer In coll
            Console.WriteLine(n)
        Next
    End Sub

    Shared Function GenerateNumbers() As IEnumerable(Of Integer)
        Dim SomeNumbers As New MyCollection(Of Integer)
        Dim i As Integer

        For i = 4 To 0 Step -1
            SomeNumbers.Add(i)
        Next

        Return SomeNumbers
    End Function
End Class
```

Running the previous example will display the following output:

```
4
3
2
1
0
```

In Main(), you can see the instance of MyCollection(Of Integer) created by passing in an IEnumerable(Of Integer) type returned from the GenerateNumbers method. You don't create constructors that accept the nongeneric IEnumerable and IEnumerator, simply because you want to favor stronger type safety.

You may have noticed the existence of List(Of T) in the System.Collections.Generic namespace. It would be tempting to use List(Of T) in your applications whenever you need to provide a generic list type to consumers. However, instead of using List(Of T), consider Collection(Of T). List(Of T) doesn't implement the protected overridable methods that Collection(Of T) implements. Therefore, if you derive your list type from List(Of T), your derived type has no way to respond when you make modifications to the list. On the other hand, List(Of T) serves as a great tool to use when you need to embed a raw list implementation within a custom collection, since it is devoid of overridable method calls, such as Collection(Of T), and is more efficient as a result.

Another useful type within the System.Collections.ObjectModel namespace is the ReadOnlyCollection(Of T) type, which is a wrapper you can use to implement read-only collections. The constructor for ReadOnlyCollection(Of T) accepts an IList(Of T) parameter type. Thus you can use a ReadOnlyCollection(Of T) to wrap any type that implements IList(Of T), including Collection(Of T). Naturally, if users access the ICollection(Of T).IsReadOnly property, the answer will be True. Any time users call a modifying method, such as ICollection(Of T).Clear(), an exception of type NotSupportedException will be thrown. Moreover, in order to call modifying methods, you must cast the ReadOnlyCollection(Of T) reference to the interface containing the method, since ReadOnlyCollection(Of T) implements all modifying methods explicitly. The biggest benefit of implementing these methods explicitly is to help you avoid their use at compile time.

How Iteration Works

You've seen how you can use the For . . . Each statement to conveniently iterate over a collection of objects, including a System.Array, ArrayList, List(Of T), and so on. How does this work? The answer is that each collection that expects to work with For . . . Each must implement the IEnumerable(Of T) or IEnumerable interface. For . . . Each then obtains an object that knows how to enumerate, or iterate over, the elements in the collection. The iterator object obtained from IEnumerable(Of T) must implement the IEnumerator(Of T) or IEnumerator interface. Generic collection types typically implement IEnumerable(Of T), and the enumerator object implements IEnumerator(Of T). IEnumerable(Of T) derives from IEnumerable, and IEnumerator(Of T) derives from IEnumerator. This allows you to use generic collections in places where nongeneric collections are used. Strictly speaking, your collection types are not required to implement enumerators, and users can iterate through the collection using a For loop if you provide an index operator by implementing IList(Of T), for example.

In the rest of this section, we'll quickly go over the salient points of creating enumerators in VB. The IEnumerable(Of T) interface exists so that clients have a well-defined way to obtain an enumerator on the collection. The following code defines the IEnumerable(Of T) and IEnumerable interfaces:

```
Public Interface IEnumerable(Of T)
    Inherits IEnumerable

    Overloads Function GetEnumerator() As IEnumerator(Of T)
End Interface

Public Interface IEnumerable
    Function GetEnumerator() As IEnumerator
End Interface
```

Since both interfaces implement GetEnumerator(), any collection that implements IEnumerable(Of T) needs to implement one of the GetEnumerator methods explicitly. It makes the most sense to implement the type-less IEnumerable.GetEnumerator method explicitly. The IEnumerator(Of T) and IEnumerator interfaces are shown here:

```
Public Interface IEnumerator(Of T)
    Inherits IEnumerator
    Inherits IDisposable

    Overloads ReadOnly Property Current() As T
End Interface

Public Interface IEnumerator
    ReadOnly Property Current() As Object

    Function MoveNext() As Boolean
    Sub Reset()
End Interface
```

Again, the two interfaces implement a member that has the same signature, which, in this case, is the Current property. When implementing IEnumerator(Of T), you should implement IEnumerator.Current explicitly. Finally, notice that IEnumerator(Of T) implements the IDisposable interface.

Let's look at an example of implementing IEnumerable(Of T) and IEnumerator(Of T) by introducing a home-grown collection of integers. We'll show how to implement the generic versions, since that implies that you must also implement the nongeneric versions as well. The code doesn't implement ICollection(Of T) so as not to clutter the example, since we're focusing on the enumeration interfaces:

```
Imports System
Imports System.Threading
Imports System.Collections
Imports System.Collections.Generic
```

```vb
Public Class MyColl(Of T)
    Implements IEnumerable(Of T)

    Private items As T()

    Public Sub New(ByVal items As T())
        Me.items = items
    End Sub

    Public Overloads Function GetEnumeratorOfT() As IEnumerator(Of T) _
        Implements IEnumerable(Of T).GetEnumerator
        Return New NestedEnumerator(Me)
    End Function

    Private Overloads Function GetEnumerator() As IEnumerator _
        Implements IEnumerable.GetEnumerator
        Return GetEnumerator()
    End Function

    'The enumerator definition.
    Private Class NestedEnumerator
        Implements IEnumerator(Of T)

        Private coll As MyColl(Of T)
        Private mCurrent As T
        Private index As Integer

        Public Sub New(ByVal coll As MyColl(Of T))
            Monitor.Enter(coll.items.SyncRoot)
            Me.index = -1
            Me.coll = coll
        End Sub

        Public ReadOnly Property CurrentOfT() As T _
            Implements IEnumerator(Of T).Current
            Get
                Return mCurrent
            End Get
        End Property

        Private ReadOnly Property Current() As Object Implements IEnumerator.Current
            Get
                Return mCurrent
            End Get
        End Property
```

```vb
        Public Function MoveNext() As Boolean Implements IEnumerator(Of T).MoveNext
            Me.index += 1

            If index >= coll.items.Length Then
                Return False
            Else
                mCurrent = coll.items(index)
                Return True
            End If
        End Function

        Public Sub Reset() Implements IEnumerator(Of T).Reset
            mCurrent = Nothing
            index = 0
        End Sub

        Public Sub Dispose() Implements IEnumerator(Of T).Dispose
            Try
                mCurrent = Nothing
                index = coll.items.Length
            Finally
                Monitor.Exit(coll.items.SyncRoot)
            End Try
        End Sub
    End Class
End Class

Public Class EntryPoint
    Shared Sub Main()
        Dim integers As MyColl(Of Integer) = _
            New MyColl(Of Integer)(New Integer() {1, 2, 3, 4})

        For Each n As Integer In integers
            Console.WriteLine(n)
        Next n
    End Sub
End Class
```

The preceding code will display the following integers when run:

```
1
2
3
4
```

This example initializes the internal array within `MyColl(Of T)` with a set of integers so that the enumerator will have some data to use. Usually, a container should implement `ICollection(Of T)` to allow you to populate the elements in the collection dynamically. The `For . . . Each` statement expands into code that obtains an enumerator by calling the `GetEnumeratorOfT()` method on the `IEnumerable(Of T)` interface. Once it gets the enumerator, it starts a loop, where it first calls `MoveNext()` and then initializes the variable n with the value returned from `CurrentOfT()`. If the loop contains no other exit paths, the loop will continue until `MoveNext()` returns `False`. At that point, the enumerator finishes enumerating the collection, and you must call `Reset()` on the enumerator in order to use it again.

Even though you could create and use an enumerator explicitly, we recommend that you use the `For . . . Each` construct instead. You have less code to write, which means fewer opportunities to introduce inadvertent bugs. If you have a reason to manipulate the enumerators directly, be sure to always do it inside a `Using` block, since `IEnumerator(Of T)` implements `IDisposable`.

There is no synchronization built into enumerators by default. Therefore, one thread could enumerate over a collection, while another thread modifies it. If the collection is modified while an enumerator is referencing it, the enumerator is semantically invalid and subsequent use could produce undefined behavior. If you must preserve integrity within such situations, then you may want your enumerator to lock the collection via the object provided by the `ICollection.SyncRoot` property. The obvious place to obtain the lock would be in the constructor for the enumerator. However, you must also release the lock at some point. In order to provide such deterministic cleanup, you must implement the `IDisposable` interface. That's one reason why `IEnumerator(Of T)` implements the `IDisposable` interface. Moreover, the code generated by a `For . . . Each` statement creates a `Try/Finally` block that calls `Dispose()` on the enumerator within the `Finally` block.

■Note In most real-world cases, you would derive your custom collection class from `Collection(Of T)` and get the `IEnumerable(Of T)` implementation for free.

Summary

This chapter provided an overview of how arrays work in the CLR and in VB. After turning our attention to the generic collection types defined in `System.Collections.Generic`, we covered efficiency and usage concerns and introduced you to the useful types defined in `System.Collections.ObjectModel`. Finally, we turned the spotlight on enumerators and demonstrated iteration in VB. Although this chapter didn't delve into the minute details of each of the collection types, we hope that after reading this chapter, you will be effectively armed with the information you need to make informed choices about which generic collection types to use and when.

In Chapter 11, we'll begin with a discussion of delegates, which provide a mechanism for defining and executing callbacks. This discussion will then lead into using events as a method for hooking up callbacks to the code that triggers them.

CHAPTER 11

∎ ∎ ∎

Delegates and Events

Delegates provide a built-in, language-supported mechanism for defining and executing callbacks. Their flexibility allows you to define the exact signature of the callback, and that information becomes part of the delegate type itself. Anonymous functions are forms of delegates that allow you to shortcut some of the delegate syntax that, in many cases, may be overkill. Building on top of delegates is the support for events in Visual Basic (VB) and the .NET platform. Events provide a uniform pattern for hooking up callback implementations, and possibly multiple instances thereof, to the code that triggers the callback.

Overview of Delegates

The common language runtime (CLR) provides a callback mechanism, or *delegates*, which are equivalent to function pointers in other languages. When you declare a delegate in your code, the VB compiler generates a class derived from `MulticastDelegate`, and the CLR implements all of the interesting methods of the delegate dynamically at run time. `MulticastDelegate` is a `NotInheritable` class that contains a linked list of delegates. This list is referred to as the *invocation list*.

Invoking a delegate is exactly the same syntactically as calling a regular function. Therefore, delegates are perfect for implementing callbacks, and they provide an excellent mechanism to decouple the method being called on an instance from the actual caller. In fact, the caller of the delegate has no idea, or necessity to know, if it is calling an instance method or a shared method or on what exact instance it is calling. To the caller, it is calling arbitrary code. The caller can obtain the delegate instance through any appropriate means, and it can be decoupled completely from the entity it actually calls.

Think for a moment about UI elements in a dialog, such as a Commit button, and how many external parties may be interested in knowing when that button is pressed. If the class that represents the button must call directly to the interested parties, it needs to have intimate knowledge of the layout of those parties, or objects, and it must know which method to call on each one of them. Clearly, this requirement adds too much coupling between the button class and the interested parties, and with coupling comes complexity. Delegates come to the rescue and break this link. Now interested parties need to only register a delegate with the button that is preconfigured to call whatever method they want. This decoupling mechanism describes events as supported by the CLR. The "Events" section of this chapter discusses CLR events in more detail. Let's go ahead and see how to create and use delegates.

Delegate Creation and Use

Delegate declarations look almost exactly like method declarations, except that they lack a method body and have one added keyword: the Delegate keyword. The following is a valid delegate declaration:

```
Public Delegate Function ProcessResults(ByVal x As Double, ByVal y As Double) _
    As Double
```

When the compiler encounters this line, it defines a type derived from MulticastDelegate, which also implements a method named Invoke that has the exact same signature of the method described in the delegate declaration. For all practical purposes, that class looks like the following:

```
NotInheritable Class ProcessResults
    Inherits System.MulticastDelegate

    Public Function Invoke(ByVal x As Double, ByVal y As Double) As Double
    End Function

    'Other stuff omitted for clarity.
End Class
```

Even though the compiler creates a type similar to that listed, the compiler also abstracts the use of delegates behind syntactical shortcuts. In fact, the compiler won't allow you to call the Invoke method on a delegate directly. Instead, you use a syntax that looks similar to a function call, which we'll show shortly.

When you use a delegate, you must wire it up to a method to call when it is invoked. The method that you wire it up to could be either a shared or instance method that has a signature compatible with that of the delegate. Thus the parameter types and the return type must either match the delegate declaration, or they must be implicitly convertible to the types in the delegate declaration.

Single Delegate

The following example shows the basic syntax of how to create a delegate:

```
Imports System

Public Delegate Function ProcessResults(ByVal x As Double, ByVal y As Double) _
    As Double

Public Class Processor
    Private factor As Double

    Public Sub New(ByVal factor As Double)
        Me.factor = factor
    End Sub
```

```vbnet
    Public Function Compute(ByVal x As Double, ByVal y As Double) As Double
        Dim result As Double = (x + y) * factor

        Console.WriteLine("InstanceResults: {0}", result)

        Return result
    End Function

    Public Shared Function StaticCompute(ByVal x As Double, ByVal y As Double) _
        As Double

        Dim result As Double = (x + y) * 0.5

        Console.WriteLine("StaticResult: {0}", result)

        Return result
    End Function
End Class

Public Class EntryPoint
    Shared Sub Main()
        Dim proc1 As Processor = New Processor(0.75)
        Dim proc2 As Processor = New Processor(0.83)

        Dim delegate1 As ProcessResults = _
            New ProcessResults(AddressOf proc1.Compute)
        Dim delegate2 As ProcessResults = _
            New ProcessResults(AddressOf proc2.Compute)
        Dim delegate3 As ProcessResults = _
            New ProcessResults(AddressOf Processor.StaticCompute)

        Dim combined As Double = _
            delegate1(4, 5) + delegate2(6, 2) + delegate3(5, 2)

        Console.WriteLine("Output: {0}", combined)
    End Sub
End Class
```

Running the previous code displays the following:

```
InstanceResults: 6.75
InstanceResults: 6.64
StaticResult: 3.5
Output: 16.89
```

This example creates three delegates. Two point to instance methods, and one points to a shared method. Notice that you create the delegates by creating instances of the ProcessResults type, which is the type created by the delegate declaration. When you create the delegate instances, you pass the address of the methods they must call in the constructor, using the AddressOf operator. AddressOf creates the function delegate that points to the method passed.

Take note of the format of the parameter. In the first two cases, you pass an instance method on the proc1 and proc2 instances. However, in the third case, you pass a method pointer on the type rather than an instance. This is the way you create a delegate that points to a shared method rather than an instance method. At the point where the delegates are called, the syntax is identical and independent of whether the delegate points to an instance method or a shared method.

In all of the cases in the previous code, a single action takes place when the delegate is called. It is also possible to chain delegates together so that multiple actions take place.

Delegate Chaining

Delegate chaining allows you to create a linked list of delegates such that when the delegate at the head of the list is called, all of the delegates in the chain are called. The System.Delegate class provides a few shared methods to manage lists of delegates. To create delegate lists, you rely on the following methods declared inside of the System.Delegate type:

```
Public Class Delegate
    Implements ICloneable
    Implements ISerializable

    Public Shared Function Combine(ByVal Delegates As Delegate()) _
        As Delegate
    End Function

    Public Shared Function Combine(ByVal First As Delegate, _
        ByVal Second As Delegate) As Delegate
    End Function
End Class
```

The Combine methods take the delegates to combine and return another Delegate. The Delegate returned is a new instance of a MulticastDelegate because Delegate instances are treated as immutable. For example, the caller of Combine() may wish to create a delegate list but leave the original delegate instances in the same state they were in. The only way to do that is to treat delegate instances as immutable when creating delegate chains.

Notice that the first version of Combine() listed in the preceding code takes an array of delegates to form the constituents of the new delegate list, and the second form takes just a pair of delegates. However, in both cases, any one of the Delegate instances could itself already be a delegate chain, allowing fairly complex nesting scenarios.

To remove delegates from a list, you rely upon the following two shared methods on System.Delegate:

```
Public Class Delegate
    Implements ICloneable
    Implements ISerializable
```

```
    Public Shared Function Remove(ByVal Source As Delegate, _
        ByVal Value As Delegate) As Delegate
    End Function

    Public Shared Function RemoveAll(ByVal Source As Delegate, _
        ByVal Value As Delegate) As Delegate
    End Function
End Class
```

As with the Combine methods, the Remove and RemoveAll methods return a new Delegate instance created from the previous two. The Remove method removes the last occurrence of Value in the source delegate list, whereas RemoveAll() removes all occurrences of the Value delegate from the source delegate list. The value parameter may represent a delegate list rather than just a single delegate.

Let's look at a modified form of the code example in the last section to see how you can combine the delegates:

```
Imports System

Public Delegate Function ProcessResults(ByVal x As Double, ByVal y As Double) _
    As Double

Public Class Processor
    Private factor As Double

    Public Sub New(ByVal factor As Double)
        Me.factor = factor
    End Sub

    Public Function Compute(ByVal x As Double, ByVal y As Double) As Double
        Dim Result As Double = (x + y) * factor

        Console.WriteLine("InstanceResults: {0}", Result)

        Return Result
    End Function

    Public Shared Function StaticCompute(ByVal x As Double, ByVal y As Double) _
        As Double

        Dim Result As Double = (x + y) * 0.5

        Console.WriteLine("StaticResult: {0}", Result)

        Return Result
    End Function
End Class
```

```
Public Class EntryPoint
    Shared Sub Main()
        Dim proc1 As Processor = New Processor(0.75)
        Dim proc2 As Processor = New Processor(0.83)

        Dim delegates As ProcessResults() = New ProcessResults() _
            {New ProcessResults(AddressOf proc1.Compute), _
            New ProcessResults(AddressOf proc2.Compute), _
            New ProcessResults(AddressOf Processor.StaticCompute)}

        Dim chained As ProcessResults = _
            CType(System.Delegate.Combine(delegates), ProcessResults)

        Dim combined As Double = chained(4, 5)

        Console.WriteLine("Output: {0}", combined)
    End Sub
End Class
```

Running this form of the code displays the following:

```
InstanceResults: 6.75
InstanceResults: 7.47
StaticResult: 4.5
Output: 4.5
```

Instead of calling all of the delegates, this example chains them together and then calls them by calling through the head of the chain. This example features some major differences from the previous example. First of all, the resultant Double that comes out of the chained invocation is the result of the last delegate called, which, in this case, is the delegate pointing to the shared method StaticCompute. The return values from the other delegates in the chain are simply lost. Also, if any of the delegates throws an exception, processing of the delegate chain will terminate, and the CLR will begin to search for the next exception-handling frame on the stack. If you declare delegates that take parameters by reference, each delegate that uses the reference parameter will see the changes made by the previous delegate in the chain. This could be a desired effect, or it could be a surprise, depending on what your intentions are. Finally, before invoking the delegate chain, you must cast the delegate back into the explicit delegate type. This is necessary for the compiler to know how to invoke the delegate. The type returned from the Combine and Remove methods is of type System.Delegate, which doesn't have enough type information for the compiler to figure out how to invoke it.

Iterating Through Delegate Chains

Sometimes you need to call a chain of delegates, but you need to harvest the return values from each invocation, or you may need to specify the ordering of the calls in the chain. For these times, the System.Delegate type offers the GetInvocationList method to acquire an array of delegates where each element in the array corresponds to a delegate in the invocation list. Once you obtain this array, you can call the delegates in any order you please, and you can process the return value from each delegate appropriately. You could also put an exception frame around each entry in the list so that an exception in one delegate invocation will not abort the remaining invocations. This modified version of the previous example shows how to call each delegate in the chain explicitly:

```
Imports System

Public Delegate Function ProcessResults(ByVal x As Double, ByVal y As Double) _
    As Double

Public Class Processor
    Private factor As Double

    Public Sub New(ByVal factor As Double)
        Me.factor = factor
    End Sub

    Public Function Compute(ByVal x As Double, ByVal y As Double) As Double
        Dim Result As Double = (x + y) * factor

        Console.WriteLine("InstanceResults: {0}", Result)

        Return Result
    End Function

    Public Shared Function StaticCompute(ByVal x As Double, ByVal y As Double) _
        As Double

        Dim Result As Double = (x + y) * 0.5

        Console.WriteLine("StaticResult: {0}", Result)

        Return Result
    End Function
End Class

Public Class EntryPoint
    Shared Sub Main()
        Dim proc1 As Processor = New Processor(0.75)
        Dim proc2 As Processor = New Processor(0.83)

        Dim delegates As ProcessResults() = New ProcessResults() _
            {New ProcessResults(AddressOf proc1.Compute), _
            New ProcessResults(AddressOf proc2.Compute), _
            New ProcessResults(AddressOf Processor.StaticCompute)}
```

```
        Dim chained As ProcessResults = _
            CType(System.Delegate.Combine(delegates), ProcessResults)
        Dim chain As System.Delegate() = chained.GetInvocationList()

        Dim accumulator As Double = 0

        For i As Integer = 0 To chain.Length - 1
            Dim current As ProcessResults = CType(chain(i), ProcessResults)

            accumulator += current(4, 5)
        Next i

        Console.WriteLine("Output: {0}", accumulator)
    End Sub
End Class
```

Calling each delegate in the chain explicitly displays the following:

```
InstanceResults: 6.75
InstanceResults: 7.47
StaticResult: 4.5
Output: 18.72
```

Open-Instance Delegates

All of the delegate examples so far show how to wire up a delegate to a shared method on a specific type or to an instance method on a specific instance. This abstraction provides excellent decoupling, but the delegate doesn't really imitate or represent a pointer to a method per se, since it is bound to a method on a specific instance. What if you want to have a delegate represent an instance method, and then you want to invoke that same delegate on a collection of instances?

For this task, you need to use an *open-instance delegate*. When you call a method on an instance, a hidden parameter at the beginning of the parameter list, known as Me, represents the current instance. When you wire up a closed-instance delegate to an instance method on an object instance, the delegate passes the object instance as the Me reference when it calls the instance method. With open-instance delegates, the delegate defers this action to the one that invokes the delegate. Thus you can provide the object instance to call on at delegate invocation time.

Let's look at an example of what this would look like. Imagine a collection of Employee types, and the company has decided to give everyone a 10% raise at the end of the year. All of the Employee objects are contained in a collection type, and now you need to iterate over each employee, applying the raise by calling the Employee.ApplyRaiseOf method:

```
Imports System
Imports System.Reflection
Imports System.Collections.Generic
```

```vb
Delegate Sub ApplyRaiseDelegate(ByVal emp As Employee, _
                                ByVal percent As Decimal)

Public Class Employee
    Private mSalary As Decimal

    Public Sub New(ByVal salary As Decimal)
        Me.mSalary = salary
    End Sub

    Public ReadOnly Property Salary() As Decimal
        Get
            Return mSalary
        End Get
    End Property

    Public Sub ApplyRaiseOf(ByVal percent As Decimal)
        mSalary *= 1 + percent
    End Sub
End Class

Public Class EntryPoint
    Shared Sub Main()
        Dim Employees As List(Of Employee) = New List(Of Employee)

        Employees.Add(New Employee(40000))
        Employees.Add(New Employee(65000))
        Employees.Add(New Employee(95000))

        'Create open-instance delegate
        Dim mi As MethodInfo = GetType(Employee).GetMethod("ApplyRaiseOf", _
            BindingFlags.Public Or BindingFlags.Instance)

        Dim applyRaise As ApplyRaiseDelegate = _
            CType(System.Delegate.CreateDelegate(GetType(ApplyRaiseDelegate), _
            mi), ApplyRaiseDelegate)

        'Apply raise.
        Dim e As Employee

        For Each e In Employees
            applyRaise(e, CType(0.1, Decimal))

            'Send new salary to console.
            Console.WriteLine("Employee's new salary = {0:C}", e.Salary)
        Next
    End Sub
End Class
```

Here are the employees' salaries after their raises:

```
Employee's new salary = $44,000.00
Employee's new salary = $71,500.00
Employee's new salary = $104,500.00
```

The declaration of the delegate has an Employee type declared at the beginning of the parameter list. This is how you expose the hidden instance pointer so that you can bind it later. Had you used this delegate to represent a closed-instance delegate, the Employee parameter would have been omitted. Unfortunately, VB doesn't have any special syntax for creating open-instance delegates. Therefore, you must use one of the more generalized Delegate.CreateDelegate() overloads to create the delegate instance as shown; but before you can do that, you must use reflection to obtain the MethodInfo instance representing the method to bind to.

Nowhere during the instantiation of the delegate do you provide a specific object instance. You won't provide that until the point of delegate invocation. The For Each loop shows how you invoke the delegate and provide the instance to call upon at the same time. Even though the ApplyRaiseOf method that the delegate is wired to takes only one parameter, the delegate invocation requires two parameters so that you can provide the instance on which to make the call.

The previous example shows how to create and invoke an open-instance delegate; however, the delegate could still be more general and more useful in a broad sense. In that example, you declared the delegate such that it knew it was going to be calling a method on a type of Employee. Thus at invocation time, you could have placed the call only on an instance of Employee or a type derived from Employee. You can use a generic delegate to declare the delegate such that the type on which it is called is unspecified at declaration time.[1] Such a delegate is potentially much more useful. It allows you to state the following: "I want to represent a method that matches this signature supported by an as-of-yet unspecified type." Only at the point of instantiation of the delegate are you required to provide the concrete type that will be called. Examine the following modifications (shown in bold) to the previous example:

```
Imports System
Imports System.Reflection
Imports System.Collections.Generic

Delegate Sub ApplyRaiseDelegate(Of T)(ByVal instance As T, _
                              ByVal percent As Decimal)

Public Class Employee
    Private mSalary As Decimal

    Public Sub New(ByVal salary As Decimal)
        Me.mSalary = salary
    End Sub
```

---

1. The next chapter covers generics in more detail.

```
    Public ReadOnly Property Salary() As Decimal
        Get
            Return mSalary
        End Get
    End Property

    Public Sub ApplyRaiseOf(ByVal percent As Decimal)
        mSalary *= 1 + percent
    End Sub
End Class

Public Class EntryPoint
    Shared Sub Main()
        Dim Employees As List(Of Employee) = New List(Of Employee)

        Employees.Add(New Employee(40000))
        Employees.Add(New Employee(65000))
        Employees.Add(New Employee(95000))

        'Create open-instance delegate
        Dim mi As MethodInfo = GetType(Employee).GetMethod("ApplyRaiseOf", _
                               BindingFlags.Public Or BindingFlags.Instance)

        Dim applyRaise As ApplyRaiseDelegate(Of Employee) = _
            CType([Delegate].CreateDelegate( _
            GetType(ApplyRaiseDelegate(Of Employee)), mi), _
            ApplyRaiseDelegate(Of Employee))

        'Apply raise.
        Dim e As Employee

        For Each e In Employees
            applyRaise(e, CType(0.1, Decimal))

            'Send new salary to console.
            Console.WriteLine("Employee's new salary = {0:C}", e.Salary)
        Next
    End Sub
End Class
```

Now, the delegate is much more generic. Consider an imaging program that supports applying filters to various objects on the canvas. Suppose you need a delegate to represent a generic filter type that, when applied, is provided a percentage value to indicate how much of an effect it should have on the object. Using generic open-instance delegates, you could represent such a notion.

Strategy Pattern

Delegates offer up a handy mechanism to implement the Strategy pattern. In a nutshell, the Strategy pattern allows you to dynamically swap computational algorithms based upon the runtime situation. For example, consider the common case of sorting a group of items. Let's suppose that you want the sort to occur as quickly as possible. However, due to system circumstances, more temporary memory is required in order to achieve this speed. This works great for collections of reasonably manageable size, but if the collection grows to be huge, it's possible that the amount of memory needed to perform the quick sort could exceed the system resource capacity. For those cases, you can provide a sort algorithm that is much slower but uses far fewer resources. The Strategy pattern allows you to swap out these algorithms at run time, depending on the conditions. This example illustrates the purpose of the Strategy pattern perfectly.

Typically, you implement the Strategy pattern using interfaces. You declare an interface that all implementations of the strategy implement. Then, the consumer of the algorithm doesn't care which concrete implementation of the strategy it is using. Figure 11-1 features a diagram that describes this typical usage.

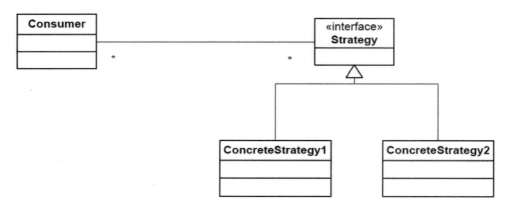

Figure 11-1. *Typical interface-based implementation of the Strategy pattern*

Delegates offer an alternative to interfaces to implement a simple strategy, as interfaces are merely a mechanism to implement a programming contract. Instead, imagine that your delegate declaration is used to implement the contract, and any method that matches the delegate signature is a potential concrete strategy. Now, instead of the consumer holding onto a reference to the abstract strategy interface, it holds onto a delegate instance. The following example illustrates this scenario:

```
Imports System
Imports System.Collections

Public Delegate Function SortStrategy(ByVal theCollection As ICollection) As Array

Public Class Consumer
    Private myCollection As ArrayList
    Private mStrategy As SortStrategy
```

```vb
    Public Sub New(ByVal defaultStrategy As SortStrategy)
        Me.mStrategy = defaultStrategy
    End Sub

    Public Property Strategy() As SortStrategy
        Get
            Return mStrategy
        End Get
        Set(ByVal value As SortStrategy)
            mStrategy = value
        End Set
    End Property

    Public Sub DoSomeWork()
        'Employ the strategy.
        Dim sorted As Array = mStrategy(myCollection)

        'Do something with the results.
    End Sub

End Class

Public Class SortAlgorithms
    Private Shared Function SortFast(ByVal theCollection As ICollection) As Array
        'Do the fast sort.
    End Function

    Private Shared Function SortSlow(ByVal theCollection As ICollection) As Array
        'Do the slow sort.
    End Function
End Class
```

When the Consumer object is instantiated, it is passed a default sort strategy, which is nothing more than a method that implements the SortStrategy delegate signature. If the conditions are right at run time, the sort strategy is swapped out, and the Consumer.DoSomeWork method automatically calls in the replacement strategy. You could argue that implementing a Strategy pattern this way is more flexible than using interfaces, since delegates can bind to both shared methods and instance methods. Therefore, you could create a concrete implementation of the strategy that also contains some state data that is needed for the operation, as long as the delegate points to an instance method on a class that contains that state data.

Events

In many cases, when you use delegates as a callback mechanism, you may want to notify someone that some event happened, such as a button press in a UI. Suppose that you're designing a media player application. Somewhere in the UI is a Play button. In a well-designed system, the UI and the control logic are separated by a well-defined abstraction. This abstraction will facilitate implementing an alternate UI later, or, since UI operations are normally platform-specific, it facilitates porting the application to another platform. This is known as the *Bridge pattern* and works well in situations where you want to decouple your control logic from the UI.

By using the Bridge pattern, you can facilitate the scenario where changes that occur in the core system don't force changes in the UI, and conversely, where changes in the UI don't force changes in the core system. One common way of implementing this pattern is by creating well-defined interfaces into the core system that the UI then uses to communicate with it, and vice versa. With a delegate, you can begin to say things as abstract as, "When the user wants to play, I want you to call registered methods passing any information germane to the action." The beauty here is that the core system doesn't care how the user indicates to the UI that he wants the player to start playing media. It could be a button press, a menu selection, or a brain-wave detection device that recognizes what the user is thinking. To the core system, it doesn't matter, and you can change and interchange both independently without breaking the other. Both sides adhere to the same agreed-upon interface contract, which in this case is a specifically formed delegate and a means to register that delegate with the event-generating entity.[2]

This pattern of usage, also known as *publish-subscribe*, is so common, even outside the realm of UI development, that the .NET runtime designers defined a formalized built-in event mechanism. When you declare an event within a class, the compiler implements some hidden methods that allow you to register and unregister delegates that get called when a specific event is raised. In essence, an event is a shortcut that saves you the time of having to write the register and unregister methods that manage a delegate chain. Let's take a look at a simple event sample based on the previous discussion:

```
Imports System

'Arguments passed from UI when play event occurs.
Public Class PlayEventArgs
    Inherits EventArgs

    Private mFilename As String

    Public Sub New(ByVal filename As String)
        Me.mFilename = filename
    End Sub

    Public ReadOnly Property Filename() As String
        Get
            Return mFilename
        End Get
    End Property
End Class

Public Class PlayerUI
    'Define event for play notifications.
    Public Event PlayEvent As EventHandler(Of PlayEventArgs)
```

---

2. Chapter 6 covers the topics of contracts and interfaces in detail.

```vb
    Public Sub UserPressedPlay()
        OnPlay()
    End Sub

    Protected Overridable Sub OnPlay()
        'Fire the event.
        Dim localHandler As EventHandler(Of PlayEventArgs) = PlayEventEvent

        If Not localHandler Is Nothing Then
            localHandler(Me, New PlayEventArgs("song.wav"))
        End If
    End Sub
End Class

Public Class CorePlayer
    Private ui As PlayerUI

    Public Sub New()
        ui = New PlayerUI()

        'Register our event handler.
        AddHandler ui.PlayEvent, AddressOf PlaySomething
    End Sub

    Private Sub PlaySomething(ByVal source As Object, ByVal args As PlayEventArgs)
        'Play the file.
    End Sub
End Class

Public Class EntryPoint
    Shared Sub Main()
        Dim player As CorePlayer = New CorePlayer()
    End Sub
End Class
```

Even though the syntax of this simple event may look complicated, the overall idea is that you're creating a well-defined interface through which to notify interested parties that the user wants to play a file. That well-defined interface is encapsulated inside the PlayEventArgs class. Events put certain rules upon how you use delegates. The delegate must not return anything, and it must accept two arguments. The first argument is an object reference representing the party generating the event. The second argument must be a type derived from System.EventArgs. Your EventArgs derived class is where you define any event-specific arguments.

In the same code, we declared the event using the generic EventHandler(Of T) class. The event is defined within the PlayerUI class using the Event keyword. The Event keyword is first followed by the name of the event, PlayEvent, and then followed by the defined event delegate. The PlayEvent identifier means two entirely different things, depending on what side of the decoupling fence you're on. From the perspective of the event generator—in this case,

PlayerUI—the PlayEvent event is used just like a delegate. You can see this usage inside the OnPlay method. Typically, a method such as OnPlay is called in response to a UI button press. It notifies all of the registered listeners by calling through the PlayEvent event (delegate).

■**Note** The popular idiom when raising events is to raise the event within a Protected Overridable method named On<event>, where <event> is replaced with the name of the event—in this case, OnPlay. This way, derived classes can easily modify the actions taken when the event needs to be raised. In VB, you must test the event for Nothing before calling it; otherwise, the result could be a NullReferenceException. The OnPlay() method makes a local copy of the event before testing it for Nothing. This avoids the race condition where the event is set to Nothing from another thread after the Nothing check passes and before the event is raised.

From the event consumer side of the fence, the PlayEvent identifier is used completely differently. As you can see in the CorePlayer constructor, the AddHandler statement is used to register the event listener.

That's the basic structure of events. As alluded to earlier, .NET events are a shortcut to creating delegates and the interfaces with which to register those delegates. As proof of this, you can examine the intermediate language (IL) generated from compiling the previous example to see that the compiler has generated two methods, add_PlayEvent() and remove_PlayEvent(), which get called when you use the AddHandler and RemoveHandler statements. These statements manage the addition and removal of delegates from the event delegate chain.

Custom Events

Beginning with VB 2005, you can use the keyword Custom as a modifier for the Event statement. Custom events allow you to specify actions when your code adds/removes an event handler or raises an event. You accomplish this by modifying the AddHandler, RemoveHandler, and RaiseEvent accessors. The following PlayerUI class is modified to show these operations:

```
Public Class PlayerUI
    'Define event for play notifications.
    Private PlayEventEvent As EventHandler(Of PlayEventArgs)

    Public Custom Event PlayEvent As EventHandler(Of PlayEventArgs)
        AddHandler(ByVal value As EventHandler(Of PlayEventArgs))
            PlayEventEvent = _
                CType(System.Delegate.Combine(PlayEventEvent, value), _
                EventHandler(Of PlayEventArgs))
        End AddHandler

        RemoveHandler(ByVal value As EventHandler(Of PlayEventArgs))
            PlayEventEvent = _
                CType(System.Delegate.Remove(PlayEventEvent, value), _
                EventHandler(Of PlayEventArgs))
        End RemoveHandler
```

```vb
        RaiseEvent(ByVal sender As Object, ByVal e As PlayEventArgs)
            If Not sender Is Nothing Then
                'Add event code here.
            End If
        End RaiseEvent
    End Event

    Public Sub UserPressedPlay()
        OnPlay()
    End Sub

    Protected Overridable Sub OnPlay()
        'Fire the event.
        Dim localHandler As EventHandler(Of PlayEventArgs) = PlayEventEvent

        If Not localHandler Is Nothing Then
            localHandler(Me, New PlayEventArgs("song.wav"))
        End If
    End Sub
End Class
```

Inside the AddHandler and RemoveHandler sections of the Event declaration, the delegate being added or removed is referenced through the value keyword, which is identical to the way property setters work. This example uses Delegate.Combine() and Delegate.Remove() to manage an internal delegate chain.

Events are ideal for implementing a publish-subscribe design pattern, where many listeners register for notification (publication) of an event. Similarly, you can use .NET events to implement a form of the Observer pattern, where various entities register to receive notifications that some other entity has changed.

Events and Relaxed Delegates

VB 2008 offers further enhancements to events and relaxed delegates. Where in VB 2005 you were allowed to pass subtypes of any parameters required, in VB 2008 you may omit these parameters entirely. The following code creates a dialog with three command buttons. These buttons are wired to each of the different ways you can create a button click event:

```vb
Imports System
Imports System.Drawing
Imports System.Windows.Forms

Public Class Form1
    Inherits Form

    Private Window1 As New Form
    Private Label1 As New Label
```

```vb
    Private Button1 As New Button
    Private Button2 As New Button
    Private Button3 As New Button

    Public Sub New()
        Me.Size = New Size(350, 150)
        Me.Text = "Event Handlers"

        Label1.Location = New Point(10, 15)
        Label1.Size = New Size(320, 50)
        Label1.TextAlign = ContentAlignment.MiddleCenter
        Label1.BorderStyle = BorderStyle.Fixed3D
        Label1.Text = "Press buttons below to fire each event handler."

        Button1.Location = New Point(15, 75)
        Button1.Size = New Size(110, 25)
        Button1.Text = "Object / EventArgs"
        Button2.Location = New Point(130, 75)
        Button2.Size = New Size(100, 25)
        Button2.Text = "Object / Object"
        Button3.Location = New Point(235, 75)
        Button3.Size = New Size(90, 25)
        Button3.Text = "No parameters"

        Me.Controls.Add(Label1)
        Me.Controls.Add(Button1)
        Me.Controls.Add(Button2)
        Me.Controls.Add(Button3)

        AddHandler Button1.Click, AddressOf Button1_Click
        AddHandler Button2.Click, AddressOf Button2_Click
        AddHandler Button3.Click, AddressOf Button3_Click
    End Sub

    Private Sub Button1_Click(ByVal sender As Object, ByVal e As EventArgs)
        Label1.Text = "The pre-VB 2005" + vbCrLf + _
            "(ByVal sender as Object, ByVal e As EventArgs) version."
    End Sub

    Private Sub Button2_Click(ByVal sender As Object, ByVal e As Object)
        Label1.Text = "The VB 2005 subtype" + vbCrLf + _
            "(ByVal sender as Object, ByVal e As Object) version."
    End Sub

    Private Sub Button3_Click()
        Label1.Text = "The parameterless, fully relaxed version in VB 2008."
    End Sub
End Class
```

```
Public Class EntryPoint
    Shared Sub Main()
        Dim SampleWin As Form1 = New Form1

        SampleWin.ShowDialog()
    End Sub
End Class
```

The preceding code creates a new form, and then adds one label and three command buttons to it. The form constructor positions, sizes, and adds text to each of the form's controls. After adding the controls to the form, we use the `AddHandler` statements to bind the delegates to the event procedures.

Running this code will perform the preceding steps and display a dialog with our form. Pressing each of the buttons on the form will change the message displayed in the form's label to let you know which event subroutine version you have called.

■**Note** In order to build the previous example, you'll need to add a reference to the `System.Windows.Forms.dll` and `System.Drawing.dll` assemblies, located in the `Windows\Microsoft.NET\Framework\v2.0.xxxxx` directory.

Summary

Delegates offer a first-class system-defined and system-implemented mechanism for uniformly representing callbacks. In this chapter, you saw various ways to declare and create delegates of different types, including single delegates, chained delegates, and open-instance delegates. Additionally, we showed how to use delegates as the building blocks of events. You can use delegates to implement a wide variety of design patterns, since delegates are a great means for defining a programming contract. And at the heart of just about all design patterns is a well-defined contract.

The next chapter will cover the details of generics, which is arguably one of the most exciting features in the VB language.

CHAPTER 12

■■■■

Generics

Generics have proven to be a welcome addition to VB, beginning with VB 2005. A generic class is defined by using data types as parameters, which can then be used throughout its implementation. Each generic class, when instantiated, becomes a unique type and will substitute the data types passed as parameters where used.

Generics allow you to enforce stronger typing in your classes, as the VB compiler will throw an exception when you make an error. Boxing is eliminated with generics because VB does not need to perform conversions with these types. Finally, generics can provide a great deal of code reuse. Using generics, you can often combine definitions for classes that are essentially the same but vary only by the data type used.

Introduction to Generics

Generics are defined through the use of *type parameters*. The Of keyword, followed by a type argument, specifies the type you should use when creating the generic type or executing the generic member at run time. To declare a generic type, you specify a list of type parameters in the declaration, as in the following example:

```
Public Class MyCollection(Of T)
    Private Storage As T()

    Public Sub New()
    End Sub
End Class
```

In this case, you declare a generic type, MyCollection(Of T), which treats the array within the class as an unspecified type. In this example, the type parameter list consists of only one type, and it is described with syntax where the generic type is listed between parentheses. The identifier T is really just a placeholder for any type. At some point, a consumer of MyCollection(Of T) specifies the concrete type that T is supposed to represent. For example, suppose you want to create a MyCollection(Of T) constructed type that contains members of type Integer. Then it would do so as shown in the following code:

```
Public Sub SomeMethod()
    Dim collectionOfNumbers As MyCollection(Of Integer) = _
        New MyCollection(Of Integer)()
End Sub
```

MyCollection(Of Integer) is now usable just as any other declared type, and it also follows all of the same rules that other nongeneric types follow. The only difference is that it was born from a generic type. At the point of instantiation, the intermediate language (IL) code behind the implementation of MyCollection(Of T) gets just-in-time (JIT)-compiled in a way that all of the usages of type T in the implementation of MyCollection(Of T) get replaced with type Integer.

All unique constructed types created from the same generic type are, in fact, completely different types that share no implicit conversion capabilities. For example, MyCollection(Of Long) is a completely different type than MyCollection(Of Integer), and you cannot do something like the following:

```
'THIS WILL NOT WORK!
Public Sub SomeMethod(ByVal intNumbers As MyCollection(Of Integer))
    Dim longNumbers As MyCollection(Of Long) = intNumbers ' ERROR!
End Sub
```

The array covariance rules, which allow a value of array A to reference an instance of array B if you can perform an implicit conversion from B to A, allow you to do the following:

```
Public Sub ProcessStrings(ByVal myStrings As String())
    Dim objs As Object() = myStrings

    For Each o As Object In objs
        Console.WriteLine(o)
    Next o
End Sub
```

You might be surprised to learn that you cannot accomplish the same idea using constructed generic types. The difference is that with array covariance, the source and the destination of the assignment are of the same type, System.Array. The array covariance rules simply allow you to assign one array from another, as long as the declared type of the elements in the array are implicitly convertible at compile time. However, in the case of two constructed generic types, they are completely separate types.

Efficiency and Type Safety of Generics

Efficiency is arguably one of the greatest gains from generics in VB. A regular array, based on System.Array, can contain a heterogeneous collection of instances created from many types. This does, however, come with its drawbacks. Take a look at the following usage:

```
Public Sub SomeMethod(ByVal col As ArrayList)
    For Each o As Object In col
        Dim iface As ISomeInterface = CType(o, ISomeInterface)

        iface.DoSomething()
    Next o
End Sub
```

Since everything in the common language runtime (CLR) is derived from System.Object, the ArrayList passed in via the col parameter could possibly contain a hodgepodge of things. Some of those things may not actually implement ISomeInterface. As you'd expect, an

InvalidCastException could erupt from this code. However, wouldn't it be nice to be able to utilize the compiler's type engine to help sniff out such things at compile time? That's exactly what generics allow you to do. Using generics, you can devise something like the following:

```
Public Sub SomeMethod(ByVal col As IList(Of ISomeInterface))
    For Each iface As ISomeInterface In col
        iface.DoSomething()
    Next iface
End Sub
```

In the previous example, the method accepts an interface IList(Of T). Since the type parameter to the constructed type is of type ISomeInterface, the only type of objects that the list may hold are those of type ISomeInterface. Now the compiler has everything it needs to enforce strong type safety.

■**Note** Added type safety at compile time is a good thing because it's better to capture bugs based on type mismatches at compile time rather than later at run time.

The previous example shows how to use generics for better type safety. However, you haven't gained much yet from an efficiency standpoint. The real efficiency gain comes into play when the type argument is a value type. Remember that a value type inserted into a collection in the System.Collections namespace, such as ArrayList, must first be boxed, since the ArrayList maintains a collection of System.Object types. An ArrayList meant to hold nothing but a bunch of integers suffers from severe efficiency problems because you must box and unbox the integers each time you insert and reference or extract them from the ArrayList, respectively. Also, an unboxing operation in VB is normally formed with an IL unbox operation paired with a copy operation on the value type's data. Generics comes to the rescue and stops the box/unbox cycle. As an example, compile the following code, and then load the assembly into the IL Disassembler (IL DASM) to compare the IL generated for each of the methods that accepts a stack:

```
Imports System
Imports System.Collections
Imports System.Collections.Generic

Public Class EntryPoint
    Shared Sub Main()
    End Sub

    Public Sub NonGeneric(ByVal stack As Stack)
        For Each o As Object In stack
            Dim number As Integer = CInt(Fix(o))

            Console.WriteLine(number)
        Next o
    End Sub
```

```
    Public Sub Generic(ByVal stack As Stack(Of Integer))
        For Each number As Integer In stack
            Console.WriteLine(number)
        Next number
    End Sub
End Class
```

You'll notice that the IL code generated by the NonGeneric method has more instructions than the generic version. Most of this is attributed to the type of coercing and unboxing that the NonGeneric method must do. Furthermore, the NonGeneric method could possibly throw an InvalidCastException if it encounters an object that you cannot explicitly cast and unbox into an integer at run time.

Clearly, generics offer the compiler greater latitude to help it do its job by not stripping away type information at compile time. However, you could argue that the efficiency gain is so high that the primary motivator for generics in the CLR is to avoid unnecessary boxing operations. Either way, both gains are significant and worth utilizing to the fullest extent.

Generic Type Placeholder Naming Conventions

Although there are no hard-and-fast rules for naming generic parameter placeholders, it is recommended that you at least provide a name that is somewhat descriptive for how the type is going to be used. Additionally, placeholder identifiers conventionally make the first letter a capital T to denote it as a type. Naming conventions like these, similar to the naming convention where interface names start with a capital I, provide for code that is generally easier to read. Generic type definitions commonly use type parameters such as T for type, K for keys, and V for values.

Generic Type Definitions and Constructed Types

As touched upon previously, a generic type is a compiled type that is unusable until a closed type is created from it. A nongeneric type is also known as a *closed* type, whereas a generic type is known as an *open* type. However, it is possible to define a new open type via a generic, as the following code shows:

```
Public Class A(Of T)
    Private innerObject As T
End Class

Public Class Consumer(Of T)
    Private obj As A(Of Stack(Of T))
End Class
```

In this case, a generic type, Consumer(Of T), is defined and also contains a field that is based on another generic type. When declaring the type of the Consumer(Of T).obj field, A(Stack(Of T)) remains open until someone declares a constructed type based on Consumer(Of T), thus creating a closed type for the contained field.

Generic Classes and Structures

So far, all of the examples have shown generic classes, but overall, the rules of generics map equally to structures. Any time a class declaration contains a type parameter list, it is, from that point on, a generic type. Likewise, any nested class declaration, whether it's generic or not, that is declared within the scope of a generic type is a generic type itself. That's because the enclosing type's fully qualified name requires a type argument in order to completely specify the nested type.

Generic types are overloaded based upon the number of arguments in their type argument lists. The following example illustrates this:

```
Public Class Container
End Class

Public Class Container(Of T)
End Class

Public Class Container(Of T, R)
End Class
```

Each of the previous declarations is valid within the same namespace. You can declare as many generic types based on the Container identifier as you want, as long as each one has a different count of type parameters. You cannot declare another type named Container(Of X, Y), even though the identifiers used in the type parameters list are different. The name overloading rules for generic declarations are based on the count of type parameters rather than the names given to their placeholders.

When you declare a generic type, you're declaring what is called an *open* type. It's called an open type because its fully specified type is not yet known. When you declare another type based upon the generic type definition, you're declaring what's called a *closed*, or *constructed* type, as shown here:

```
Public Class A(Of T)
    Private field1 As Container(Of Integer)
    Private field2 As Container(Of T)
End Class
```

Both fields in the previous declaration of A(Of T) are constructed types, since they declare a new type based upon the generic type Container(Of T). However, not every constructed type is a closed type. Only field1 is a closed type, whereas field2 is an open type, since its final type must still be determined at run time based on the type arguments from A(Of T).

In VB, all name declarations are declared and are valid within a specific scope. Within the confines of a method, for example, any local variable identifiers declared within the method are only available within that scope. Similar rules exist for type parameter identifiers within generics. In the previous example, the identifier T is only valid within the scope of the class declaration itself. Consider the following nested class example:

```
Public Class A(Of T)
    Public Class NestedClass(Of R)
    End Class
End Class
```

The identifier R is only valid within the scope of the nested class, and you may not use it within the outer scope of the declaration for A(Of T). However, you may use T in the nested class, since the nested class is defined within the scope in which T is valid. It is considered bad form to hide outer argument identifiers within nested scopes, just as it is with variable name identifiers within nested execution scopes.

Generic structures and classes, just like normal structures and classes, may contain shared types. However, each closed type based on the generic type contains its own instance of the shared type. When you consider that each closed type is a separate concrete type, this fact makes perfect sense. Therefore, if you need to share shared data between different closed types based on the same generic type, you must devise some other means to do so. One technique involves a separate, nongeneric type that contains shared data that is referenced by the generic types. You typically implement such a device with the Singleton pattern, which we discussed in Chapter 6.

■**Note** Generic types require their initialization code to be run each time the CLR creates a closed type based upon it. Complex type initializers, or shared constructors, can increase the working set of the application if too many closed types are created based upon such a generic type. For example, if you create a sizable per-type data structure in a generic type initializer, you could create a hidden source of memory consumption if many types are formed from it.

Generic Interfaces

Along with classes and structures, you can also create generic interface declarations. This concept is a natural progression from structure and class generics. A whole host of interfaces declared within the .NET standard library make excellent candidates to have generic versions fashioned after them. A perfect example is IEnumerable(Of T). Generic containers create much more efficient code than nongeneric containers when they contain value types, since they avoid any unnecessary boxing. Any enumerable container you implement yourself should also implement IEnumerable(Of T), or you could get it for free by deriving your custom containers from Collection(Of T).

■**Note** When creating your own custom collection types, you should derive them from Collection(Of T). Other types, such as List(Of T), are not meant to be derived from and are intended as a higher-level storage mechanism. Collection(Of T) implements Protected Friend methods that you can override to customize its behavior, whereas List(Of T) does not.

Generic Methods

Any method declaration that exists within a structure, class, or interface may be declared as a generic method, even if the type that contains the method is not generic. To declare a generic method, append a type argument list to the end of the method name (but before the parameter list) for the method. You can declare any of the types in the method parameter list, including the method return type, using one of the generic parameters. As with nested classes, it is bad form to hide outer type identifiers by reusing the same identifier in the nested scope, which, in this case, is the scope of the generic method. Let's consider an example of where a generic method may be useful. In the following example, you create a container to which you want to add the contents of another generic container:

```
Imports System
Imports System.Collections.ObjectModel

Public Class MyContainer(Of T)
    Inherits Collection(Of T)

    Private impl As List(Of T) = New List(Of T)()

    Public Overloads Sub Add(Of R)(ByVal otherContainer As MyContainer(Of R), _
        ByVal converter As Converter(Of R, T))

        For Each item As R In otherContainer
            MyBase.Add(converter(item))
        Next item
    End Sub
End Class

Public Class EntryPoint
    Shared Sub Main()
        Dim lContainer As MyContainer(Of Long) = New MyContainer(Of Long)()
        Dim iContainer As MyContainer(Of Integer) = New MyContainer(Of Integer)()

        'Add 2 items to long container
        lContainer.Add(1)
        lContainer.Add(2)

        'Add 2 items to integer container
        iContainer.Add(3)
        iContainer.Add(4)

        'Convert and append integer container to long container
        lContainer.Add(iContainer, AddressOf EntryPoint.IntToLongConverter)
```

```vbnet
        For Each i As Integer In iContainer
            Console.WriteLine("iContainer Item: {0}", i)
        Next i

        Console.WriteLine()

        For Each l As Long In lContainer
            Console.WriteLine("lContainer Item: {0}", l)
        Next l
    End Sub

    Private Shared Function IntToLongConverter(ByVal i As Integer) As Long
        Return i
    End Function
End Class
```

Here's the output from running the previous code:

```
iContainer Item: 3
iContainer Item: 4

lContainer Item: 1
lContainer Item: 2
lContainer Item: 3
lContainer Item: 4
```

Note the overload of Add() in MyContainer(Of T). This method uses the Converter(Of R, T) delegate, which we wire up to IntToLongConverter(). The IntToLongConverter method allows us to add an entire range of objects from another closed type formed from MyContainer(Of T). This works as long as the enclosed type of the source container is convertible to the enclosed type of the target. If you look at the Main method, you can see the intent here. You want to place the objects contained within an instance of MyContainer(Of Integer) into an instance of MyContainer(Of Long). Therefore, creating a generic method, Add(Of R), allows you to accept another container that contains any arbitrary type.

Logically, you want to add a collection of Integer to a collection of Long, and you know that an Integer is implicitly convertible to a Long. Although this is true, you have to take into consideration that generics are formed dynamically at run time and there is no guarantee as to what closed type formed from MyContainer(Of T) the Add(Of R) method will see. It could be MyContainer(Of Apples), and an Apple may not be implicitly convertible to a Long, assuming it was passed to MyContainer(Of Long).Add(Of Apples)(). The solution here is to provide a conversion delegate to get the job done.

The Base Class Library (BCL) provides the System.Converter(Of T, R) delegate specifically for this case. The syntax for this delegate may seem a bit foreign, but it's simply a generic delegate declaration, which the following "Generic Delegates" section covers in more detail. When Add(Of R)() is called, the caller must also provide an instance of the generic Converter(Of T, R) delegate pointing to a method that knows how to convert from the source type to the target type. This explains the need for the IntToLongConverter method in the previous example. The

Add(Of R) method then uses this delegate to do the actual conversion from one type to another. In this case, the conversion is an implicit one, but it still must be externalized this way, since, at compile time, the compiler must accommodate the fact that the Add(Of R) method can have any type thrown at it.

Generic Delegates

Quite often, generics are used in the context of container types, where a closed type's field or internal array is based on the type argument given. If you were to declare a delegate that takes two parameters, the first being a Long and the second being an Object, you would declare a delegate such as the following:

```
Public Delegate Sub MyDelegate(ByVal l As Long, ByVal o As Object)
```

In the previous section, you got a preview of a generic delegate when you saw how to use the generic converter delegate. The declaration for the generic converter delegate looks like this:

```
Public Delegate Function Converter(Of TInput, TOutput)(ByVal input As TInput) _
    As TOutput
```

It looks just like any other delegate, except it has the telltale form of a generic with a type parameter list immediately following the name of the delegate. Just as nongeneric delegates look similar to method declarations without a body, generic delegate declarations look almost identical to generic method declarations without a body. The type parameter list follows the name of the delegate, but it precedes the parameter list of the delegate.

The generic converter uses the placeholder identifiers TInput and TOutput within its type parameter list, and those types are used elsewhere in the declaration for the delegate. In generic delegate declarations, the types in the type parameter list are in scope for the entire declaration of the delegate, including the return type as shown in the previous declaration for the generic converter delegate.

Creating an instance of the Converter(TInput, TOutput) delegate is the same as creating an instance of any other delegate. When you create an instance of the generic delegate, you may use the New operator and explicitly provide the type list at compile time. Or, simply use the abbreviated syntax used in the MyContainer(Of T) example in the previous section, in which case the compiler deduces the type parameters. For convenience, we've reprinted the Main method of that example:

```
Shared Sub Main()
    Dim lContainer As MyContainer(Of Long) = New MyContainer(Of Long)()
    Dim iContainer As MyContainer(Of Integer) = New MyContainer(Of Integer)()

    'Add 2 items to long container
    lContainer.Add(1)
    lContainer.Add(2)

    'Add 2 items to integer container
    iContainer.Add(3)
    iContainer.Add(4)
```

```
            'Convert and append integer container to long container
            lContainer.Add(iContainer, AddressOf EntryPoint.IntToLongConverter)

            For Each i As Integer In iContainer
                Console.WriteLine("iContainer Item: {0}", i)
            Next i

            Console.WriteLine()

            For Each l As Long In lContainer
                Console.WriteLine("lContainer Item: {0}", l)
            Next l
        End Sub
```

The second parameter to the last Add method is simply a reference to the method rather than an explicit creation of the delegate itself. This works due to the method group conversion rules defined by the language. When the actual delegate is created from the method, the closed type of the generic is inferred using a complex pattern-matching algorithm from the parameter types of the IntToLongConverter method itself. As a matter of fact, the call to Add(Of T) is devoid of any explicit type parameter list at the point of invocation. The compiler is able to do the exact same type of pattern matching to infer the closed form of the Add(Of T) method called, which, in this case, is Add(Of Integer). You could have written the call as follows, where every type is provided explicitly:

```
        lContainer.Add(Of Integer)(iContainer, New Converter(Of Integer, Long) _
            (AddressOf EntryPoint.IntToLongConverter))
```

Here all types are given explicitly, and the compiler is not left with the task of inferring them at compile time. Either way, the generated IL code is the same. Most of the time, you can rely on the type inference engine of the compiler. However, depending on the complexity of your code, you may find yourself needing to provide an explicit type list.

Along with providing a way to externalize type conversion from a container type, as in the previous examples, generic delegates help solve a special problem described in the following code:

```
' THIS WON'T WORK AS EXPECTED!!!
Imports System
Imports System.Collections.Generic

Public Delegate Sub MyDelegate(ByVal i As Integer)

Public Class DelegateContainer(Of T)
    Private imp As List(Of T) = New List(Of T)()

    Public Sub Add(ByVal del As T)
        imp.Add(del)
    End Sub
```

```
    Public Sub CallDelegates(ByVal k As Integer)
        For Each del As T In imp
            'del(k)
        Next del
    End Sub

End Class

Public Class EntryPoint
    Shared Sub Main()
        Dim delegates As DelegateContainer(Of MyDelegate) = _
            New DelegateContainer(Of MyDelegate)()

        delegates.Add(AddressOf EntryPoint.PrintInt)
    End Sub

    Private Shared Sub PrintInt(ByVal i As Integer)
        Console.WriteLine(i)
    End Sub
End Class
```

As written, the previous code will compile. However, notice the commented line within the CallDelegates method. If you uncomment this line, you'll get the following error:

```
Error  1      Expression is not a method.
```

The problem is that the compiler has no way of knowing that the type represented by the placeholder T is a delegate. At run time, the delegate represented by del could take an arbitrary number of parameters. It rarely makes sense to create a closed type from a generic where one of the type arguments is a delegate type, since, after all, you cannot call through to it normally.

What you can do to help in this situation is apply a generic delegate to give the compiler a bit more information about what you want to do with this delegate. For example, using a generic delegate, you can effectively say, "I would like you to use delegates that only accept two parameters and return an arbitrary type." That's enough information to get the compiler past the block and allow it to generate code for the generic that makes sense. After all, if you give the compiler this amount of information, it at least knows how many parameters to push onto the stack before making the call through the delegate. The following code shows how you can remedy the previous situation:

```
Imports System
Imports System.Collections.Generic

Public Delegate Sub MyDelegate(Of T)(ByVal i As T)

Public Class DelegateContainer(Of T)
    Private imp As List(Of MyDelegate(Of T)) = New List(Of MyDelegate(Of T))()
```

```
    Public Sub Add(ByVal del As MyDelegate(Of T))
        imp.Add(del)
    End Sub

    Public Sub CallDelegates(ByVal k As T)
        For Each del As MyDelegate(Of T) In imp
            del(k)
        Next del
    End Sub
End Class

Public Class EntryPoint
    Shared Sub Main()
        Dim delegates As DelegateContainer(Of Integer) = _
            New DelegateContainer(Of Integer)()

        delegates.Add(AddressOf EntryPoint.PrintInt)
        delegates.CallDelegates(42)
    End Sub

    Private Shared Sub PrintInt(ByVal i As Integer)
        Console.WriteLine(i)
    End Sub
End Class
```

The previous example, as you might expect, returns the following:

```
42
```

Generic Type Conversion

As this chapter covered previously, there is no implicit type conversion for different constructed types formed from the same generic type. The same rules that apply when determining if an object of type X is implicitly convertible to an object of type Y apply equally when determining if an object of type List(Of Integer) is convertible to an object to type List(Of Object). When such conversion is desired, you must create a custom implicit conversion operator just as in the case of converting objects of type X to objects of type Y when they share no inheritance relationship. Otherwise, you need to create a conversion method to go from one type to another. For example, the following code is invalid:

```
' INVALID CODE!!!
Public Sub SomeMethod(ByVal theList As List(Of Integer))
    Dim theSameList As List(Of Object) = theList                ' Ooops!!!
End Sub
```

If you look at the documentation of List(Of T), you'll notice a generic method named ConvertAll(Of TOutput)(). Using this method, you can convert a generic list of type List(Of Integer) to List(Of Object). However, you must pass the method an instance of a generic conversion delegate as described in the previous section. This is the only way that the method will know how to convert each contained instance from the source type to the destination type. Even though you may call a method to convert List(Of Integer) to List(Of Object), you must still provide the explicit means by which it converts an Integer into an Object.

Those of you acquainted with the Strategy pattern, which we discussed in Chapter 11, may find this a familiar notion. In essence, you can provide the ConvertAll(Of TOutput) method at run time with a means of doing the conversion on the contained instances that, depending on the complexity of the conversion, may be tuned for the platform the program runs on. In other words, if you were converting List(Of Apples) to List(Of Oranges), you could provide a few different conversion methods to select from. One of them is highly tuned for an environment with lots of resources, so it runs faster. Another version may be optimized for minimal resource usage but is slower. At run time, the proper conversion delegate is built to bind to the conversion method that is logical for the job at hand.

Generic Nullable Types

In VB 2008, support for nullable types has been enhanced, making them easier to use and easier to read. Nullable types in VB have been expanded to support null propagation arithmetic, while automatically converting the result to nullable as needed. The .NET Framework provides the generic class System.Nullable(Of T), which may contain one extra value, Nothing, which represents an empty or undefined value. Here's an example using System.Nullable(Of T):

```
Imports System

Public Class Employee
    Public FirstName As String
    Public LastName As String
    Public StartDate As DateTime

    Public TerminationDate As Nullable(Of DateTime)
    Public SSN As Nullable(Of Long)

    Public Sub New(ByVal firstName As String, ByVal lastName As String, _
                ByVal startDate As DateTime)
        Me.FirstName = firstName
        Me.LastName = lastName
        Me.StartDate = startDate

        Me.TerminationDate = Nothing
        Me.SSN = Nothing
    End Sub

End Class
```

```
Public Class EntryPoint
    Shared Sub Main()
        Dim emp As Employee = New Employee("Jodi", "Fouche", "10/22/1988")
        Dim tempSSN As Long

        emp.SSN = 123456789

        Console.WriteLine("{0} {1} started on {2}", _
            emp.FirstName, emp.LastName, emp.StartDate.ToShortDateString)

        If emp.SSN.HasValue Then
            tempSSN = emp.SSN
        End If
        Console.WriteLine("SSN: {0}", tempSSN)

        If emp.TerminationDate.HasValue Then
            Console.WriteLine("Termination Date: {0}", _
                                emp.TerminationDate.HasValue)
        Else
            Console.WriteLine(emp.FirstName + " " + emp.LastName + _
                                " is still active.")
        End If
    End Sub
End Class
```

Running this code produces the following results:

```
Jodi Fouche started on 10/22/1988
SSN: 123456789
Jodi Fouche is still active.
```

The previous code demonstrates declaring a nullable type. The nullable fields within type Employee are declared using the System.Nullable(Of DateTime) and System.Nullable(Of Long) types. One of the properties of Nullable(Of T) is HasValue, which returns True when the nullable value is not Nothing and False otherwise.

Another thing to consider when using nullable types is how you assign to and from nullable types. In the constructor for Employee, you can see that you assign Nothing to the nullable types at first. The compiler uses an implicit conversion for the Nothing value. Finally, you must consider what it means to assign a nullable type to a non-nullable type. For example, in the Main method, you want to assign tempSSN based upon the value of emp.ssn. However, since emp.ssn is nullable, what should tempSSN be assigned to if emp.ssn happens to have no value? You can use the HasValue property to inspect emp.ssn and assign it to another value should it be Nothing.

Nullable types make it a snap to represent values within a system that may be semantically null, which is handy when you're using values to represent fields within a database field that is nullable.

Constructed Types Control Accessibility

When you build constructed types from generic types, you must consider the accessibility of both the generic type and the types provided as the type arguments, in order to determine the accessibility of the whole constructed type. For example, the following code is invalid and will not compile:

```
Public Class Outer
    Private Class Nested
    End Class

    Public Class GenericNested(Of T)
    End Class

    Private field1 As GenericNested(Of Nested)
    Public field2 As GenericNested(Of Nested) ' Ooops!
End Class
```

The problem is in regard to `field2`. The `Nested` type is private, so `GenericNested(Of Nested)` cannot be public. With constructed types, the accessibility is an intersection of the accessibility of the generic type and the types provided in the argument list.

Constraints

So far, the majority of the generics examples shown involve some sort of collection-style class that holds a bunch of objects or values of a specific type. But many times, you'll need to create generic types that not only contain instances of various types but also use those objects directly. For example, suppose you have a generic type that holds instances of arbitrary geometric shapes that all implement a property named Area. Also, suppose you need the generic type to implement a property, TotalArea, where all the areas of the contained shapes are accumulated. The guarantee here is that each geometric shape in the generic container will implement the Area property. You may be inclined to write code like the following:

```
Imports System
Imports System.Collections.Generic

Public Interface IShape
    ReadOnly Property Area() As Double
End Interface

Public Class Circle
    Implements IShape

    Private radius As Double
```

```vbnet
        Public Sub New(ByVal radius As Double)
            Me.radius = radius
        End Sub

        Public ReadOnly Property Area() As Double Implements IShape.Area
            Get
                Return 3.1415 * radius * radius
            End Get
        End Property
End Class

Public Class Rect
    Implements IShape

    Private width As Double
    Private height As Double

    Public Sub New(ByVal width As Double, ByVal height As Double)
        Me.width = width
        Me.height = height
    End Sub

    Public ReadOnly Property Area() As Double Implements IShape.Area
        Get
            Return width * height
        End Get
    End Property
End Class

Public Class Shapes(Of T)
    Private shapes As List(Of T) = New List(Of T)()

    Public ReadOnly Property TotalArea() As Double
        Get
            Dim acc As Double = 0
            For Each shape As T In shapes
                'THIS WON'T COMPILE!!!
                acc += shape.Area
            Next shape
            Return acc
        End Get
    End Property

    Public Sub Add(ByVal shape As T)
        shapes.Add(shape)
    End Sub
End Class
```

```
Public Class EntryPoint
    Shared Sub Main()
        Dim shapes As Shapes(Of IShape) = New Shapes(Of IShape)()

        shapes.Add(New Circle(2))
        shapes.Add(New Rect(3, 5))

        Console.WriteLine("Total Area: {0}", shapes.TotalArea)
    End Sub
End Class
```

There is one major problem, as the code won't compile. The offending line of code is inside the TotalArea property of Shapes(Of T). The compiler complains with the following error:

```
Error  1      'Area' is not a member of 'T'.
```

If this talk of requiring the contained type T to support the Area property sounds a lot like a contract, that's because it is. Generics are dynamic as opposed to static in nature, so you cannot achieve the same effect without some extra information. Whenever you hear the word *contract* within the VB world, you may start thinking about interfaces. Therefore, we've chosen to have both of the shapes implement the IShape interface. Thus the IShape interface defines the contract, and the shapes implement that contract. However, that still is not enough for the compiler to be able to compile the previous code.

Generics must have a way to enforce the rule that the type T supports a specific contract at run time, since constructed types are formed dynamically at run time. Another attempt to solve the problem could look like the following:

```
Public Class Shapes(Of T)
    Private shapes As List(Of T) = New List(Of T)()

    Public ReadOnly Property TotalArea() As Double
        Get
            Dim acc As Double = 0
            For Each shape As T In shapes
                'DON'T DO THIS!
                Dim theShape As IShape = CType(shape, IShape)
                acc += theShape.Area
            Next shape
            Return acc
        End Get
    End Property

    Public Sub Add(ByVal shape As T)
        shapes.Add(shape)
    End Sub
End Class
```

This modification to Shapes(Of T) indeed does compile and work most of the time. However, this generic has lost some value due to the type cast within the For Each loop. Just imagine if you attempted to create a constructed type Shapes(Of Integer). The compiler would happily oblige. But what would happen if you tried to get the TotalArea property from a Shapes(Of Integer) instance? As expected, you would receive a runtime exception as the TotalArea property accessor attempts to cast an Integer into an IShape. One of the primary benefits of using generics is for better type safety, but in this example, you toss type safety right out the window. So, what are you supposed to do? The answer lies in a concept called *generic constraints*. Check out the following implementation:

```
Public Class Shapes(Of T As IShape)
    Private shapes As List(Of T) = New List(Of T)()

    Public ReadOnly Property TotalArea() As Double
        Get
            Dim acc As Double = 0

            For Each shape As T In shapes
                acc += shape.Area
            Next shape

            Return acc
        End Get
    End Property

    Public Sub Add(ByVal shape As T)
        shapes.Add(shape)
    End Sub
End Class
```

Notice the extra clause in the first line of the class declaration using the As keyword. This says, "Define class Shapes(Of T) where T must implement IShape". Now the compiler has everything it needs to enforce type safety, and the JIT compiler has everything it needs to build working code at run time. The compiler has been given a hint to help it notify you, with a compile-time error, when you attempt to create constructed types where T does not implement IShape. Any number of interfaces, listed within curly brackets, may be listed following the type parameter in the As clause, but only one class at most. This restriction is intuitive, since a given type may only derive from one class but may implement an unlimited amount of interfaces.

Additionally, only one constraint can name a class type (since the CLR has no concept of multiple inheritance), so that constraint is known as the *primary constraint*. Instead of specifying a class name, the primary constraint may list the special words class or structure, which is used to indicate that the type parameter must be a class or a structure. The constraint clause can then include as many secondary constraints as needed, and they are usually a list of interfaces. Finally, you can list a constructor constraint that takes the form New. This constrains the parameterized type such that it is required to have a default, parameter-less constructor. Class types must have an explicitly defined default constructor, whereas the New constraint is automatic for value types, since they have a system-generated default constructor. Let's take a look at an example that shows two constraint clauses:

```
Imports System
Imports System.Collections.Generic

Public Interface IValue
    'IValue methods.
End Interface

Public Class MyDictionary(Of TKey As _
    {Structure, IComparable(Of TKey)}, TValue As {IValue, New})

    Private imp As Dictionary(Of TKey, TValue) = New Dictionary(Of TKey, TValue)()

    Public Sub Add(ByVal key As TKey, ByVal val As TValue)
        imp.Add(key, val)
    End Sub
End Class
```

You declare MyDictionary(Of TKey, Of TValue) in such a way that the key value is constrained to value types. You want those key values to be comparable, so you require the TKey type to implement IComparable(Of TKey). This example shows two constraint clauses, one for each type parameter. In this case, you allow the TValue type to be either a structure or a class, but you do require that it support the defined IValue interface as well as a default constructor.

As the language and the CLR evolve, the area of constraints will probably see some additions as more applications for generics are explored. Finally, the format for constraints on generic interfaces is identical to that of generic classes and structures.

Generic System Collections

It seems that the most natural use of generics within VB and the CLR is for collection types. Maybe that's because you can gain a huge amount of efficiency when using generic containers to hold value types when compared to the collection types within the System.Collections namespace. Of course, you cannot overlook the added type safety that comes with using the generic collections. Any time you get added type safety, you're guaranteed to reduce runtime type conversion exceptions, since the compiler can catch many of those at compile time.

We encourage you to look at the .NET Framework documentation for the System.Collections.Generic namespace. There you will find all of the generic collection classes made available by the Framework. Included in the namespace are Dictionary(Of TKey, TValue), LinkedList(Of T), List(Of T), Queue(Of T), SortedDictionary(Of TKey, TValue), SortedList(Of T), and Stack(Of T).

Based on their names, the uses of these types should feel familiar when compared to the nongeneric classes under System.Collections. Although the collections of containers within the System.Collections.Generic namespace may not seem complete for your needs, it opens up the possibility for you to create your own collections, especially given the extendable types in System.Collections.ObjectModel.

When creating your own collection types, you'll often want to compare the contained objects. While it may feel natural to use the built-in equality and inequality operators to perform the comparison, you should stay away from them because the support of operators by classes and structures, although possible, is not part of the Common Language Specification (CLS). Some languages don't have support for operators. Therefore, your container must be prepared for the case when it contains types that don't support operators for comparison. This is one of the reasons that interfaces such as IComparer and IComparable exist.

When you create an instance of the SortedList type within System.Collections, you have the opportunity to provide an instance of an object that supports IComparer. The SortedList then utilizes that object when it needs to compare two key instances that it contains. If you don't provide an object that supports IComparer, the SortedList looks for an IComparable interface on the contained key objects to do the comparison. Naturally, you'll need to provide an explicit comparer if the contained key objects don't support IComparable. The overloaded versions of the constructor that accept an IComparer type exist specifically for that case.

The generic version of the sorted list, SortedList(Of TKey, TValue), follows the same sort of pattern. When you create a SortedList(Of TKey, TValue), you have the option of providing an object that implements the IComparer(Of T) interface so it can compare two keys. If you don't provide one, the SortedList(Of TKey, TValue) defaults to using what's called the *generic comparer*. The generic comparer is simply an object that derives from the Comparer(Of T) class and can be obtained through the Comparer(Of T).Default property. Based upon the nongeneric SortedList, you might think that if the creator of SortedList(Of TKey, TValue) doesn't provide a comparer, it will just look for IComparable(Of T) on the contained key type. This approach would cause problems because the contained key type could either support IComparable(Of T) or the nongeneric IComparable. Therefore, the default comparer acts as an extra level of indirection. The default comparer checks to see if the type provided in the type parameter implements IComparable(Of T), and if it does not, it looks to see if it supports IComparable, using the first one that it finds. Using this extra level of indirection provides greater flexibility with regard to the contained types. Let's look at an example to illustrate this:

```
Imports System
Imports System.Collections.Generic

Public Class EntryPoint
    Shared Sub Main()
        Dim list1 As SortedList(Of Integer, String) = _
            New SortedList(Of Integer, String)()

        Dim list2 As SortedList(Of Integer, String) = _
            New SortedList(Of Integer, String)(Comparer(Of Integer).Default)

        list1.Add(1, "one")
        list1.Add(2, "two")
        list2.Add(3, "three")
        list2.Add(4, "four")
    End Sub
End Class
```

You declare two instances of SortedList(Of TKey, TValue). In the first instance, you use the default constructor, and in the second instance, you explicitly provide a comparer for integers. In both cases, the result is the same, because you provide the default generic comparer in the list2 constructor. Here you can see the syntax used to pass in the default generic comparer. You could have just as easily provided any other type in the type parameter list for Comparer as long as it supports either IComparable or IComparable(Of T).

Select Problems and Solutions

This section illustrates some examples of creating generic types that show some useful techniques when creating generic code. Learning how to use generics effectively will contain surprises from time to time and will sometimes require an unnatural or convoluted way of doing something that conceptually is natural.

Conversion and Operators Within Generic Types

Converting from one type to another or applying operators to parameterized types within generics can be tricky. To illustrate, let's develop a generic Complex structure that represents a complex number. Suppose you want to be able to designate what value type is used internally to represent the real and imaginary portions of a complex number. This example is a tad contrived, since you would normally represent the components of an imaginary number using something like System.Double. However, for the sake of example, let's imagine that you want to be able to represent the components using System.Int64. Throughout this discussion, in order to reduce clutter and focus on the issues regarding generics, we'll ignore all of the canonical constructs that the generic Complex structure should implement.

You could start out by defining the Complex number as follows:

```
Imports System

Public Structure Complex(Of T As Structure)
    Private mReal As T
    Private mImaginary As T

    Public Sub New(ByVal real As T, ByVal imaginary As T)
        Me.mReal = real
        Me.mImaginary = imaginary
    End Sub

    Public Property Real() As T
        Get
            Return mReal
        End Get
        Set(ByVal value As T)
            mReal = value
        End Set
    End Property

    Public Property Img() As T
        Get
            Return mImaginary
        End Get
```

```
            Set(ByVal value As T)
                mImaginary = value
            End Set
        End Property
End Structure

Public Class EntryPoint
    Shared Sub Main()
        Dim c As Complex(Of Int64) = New Complex(Of Int64)(4, 5)
    End Sub
End Class
```

While this is a good start, let's make this value type a little more useful. You could benefit from having a `Magnitude` property that returns the square root of the two components multiplied together. Let's attempt to create such a property:

```
Imports System

Public Structure Complex(Of T As Structure)
    Private mReal As T
    Private mImaginary As T

    Public Sub New(ByVal real As T, ByVal imaginary As T)
        Me.mReal = real
        Me.mImaginary = imaginary
    End Sub

    Public Property Real() As T
        Get
            Return mReal
        End Get
        Set(ByVal value As T)
            mReal = value
        End Set
    End Property

    Public Property Img() As T
        Get
            Return mImaginary
        End Get
        Set(ByVal value As T)
            mImaginary = value
        End Set
    End Property
```

```vbnet
        Public ReadOnly Property Magnitude() As T
            Get
                'This will not compile.
                Return Math.Sqrt(mReal * mReal + mImaginary * mImaginary)
            End Get
        End Property

End Structure

Public Class EntryPoint
    Shared Sub Main()
        Dim c As Complex(Of Int64) = New Complex(Of Int64)(4, 5)

        Console.WriteLine("Magnitude is {0}", c.Magnitude)
    End Sub
End Class
```

If you attempt to compile the previous code, you may be surprised to get the following compiler error:

```
Error  1      Operator '*' is not defined for types 'T' and 'T'.
```

This is a perfect example of the problem with using operators in generic code. The compilation problem stems from the fact that you must compile generic code in a generic way to accommodate the fact that constructed types formed at run time can be formed from a value type that may not support the operator. In this case, it's impossible for the compiler to know if the type given for T in a constructed type at some point in the future even supports the multiplication operator. What are you to do? A common technique is to externalize the operation from the Complex(Of T) definition itself and then require the user of the definition to provide the operation. A delegate is the perfect tool for this, as the following example shows:

```vbnet
Imports System

Public Structure Complex(Of T As {Structure, IConvertible})
    ' Delegate for doing multiplication.
    Public Delegate Function BinaryOp(ByVal val1 As T, ByVal val2 As T) As T

    Private mReal As T
    Private mImaginary As T
    Private mult As BinaryOp
    Private add As BinaryOp
    Private convToT As Converter(Of Double, T)

    Public Sub New(ByVal real As T, ByVal imaginary As T, ByVal mult As BinaryOp, _
        ByVal add As BinaryOp, ByVal convToT As Converter(Of Double, T))
```

```vbnet
            Me.mReal = real
            Me.mImaginary = imaginary
            Me.mult = mult
            Me.add = add
            Me.convToT = convToT
        End Sub

        Public Property Real() As T
            Get
                Return mReal
            End Get
            Set(ByVal value As T)
                mReal = value
            End Set
        End Property

        Public Property Img() As T
            Get
                Return mImaginary
            End Get
            Set(ByVal value As T)
                mImaginary = value
            End Set
        End Property

        Public ReadOnly Property Magnitude() As T
            Get
                Dim mMagnitude As Double = _
                    Math.Sqrt(Convert.ToDouble(add(mult(mReal, mReal), _
                    mult(mImaginary, mImaginary))))

                Return convToT(mMagnitude)
            End Get
        End Property
    End Structure

Public Class EntryPoint
    Shared Sub Main()
        Dim c As Complex(Of Int64) = New Complex(Of Int64)(4, 5, _
            AddressOf MultiplyInt64, AddressOf AddInt64, AddressOf DoubleToInt64)

        Console.WriteLine("Magnitude is {0}", c.Magnitude)
    End Sub
```

```
    Private Shared Function MultiplyInt64(ByVal val1 As Int64, _
        ByVal val2 As Int64) As Int64

        Return val1 * val2
    End Function

    Private Shared Function AddInt64(ByVal val1 As Int64, _
        ByVal val2 As Int64) As Int64

        Return val1 + val2
    End Function

    Private Shared Function DoubleToInt64(ByVal d As Double) As Int64
        Return Convert.ToInt64(d)
    End Function
End Class
```

The previous example returns the following value for `Magnitude`:

```
Magnitude is 6
```

You may be looking at the previous code and wondering why the complexity seems much higher when all you're trying to do is find the magnitude of a complex number. As mentioned previously, you have to provide a delegate to handle the multiplication external to the generic type. Thus you define the `Complex(Of T).Multiply` delegate. At construction time, the `Complex(Of T)` constructor must be passed a third parameter that references a method for the multiplication delegate to refer to. In this case, `EntryPoint.MultiplyInt64` handles the multiplication. So, when the `Magnitude` property needs to multiply the components, it must use the delegate rather than the multiplication operator. Naturally, when the delegate is called, it boils down to a call to the multiplication operator. However, the application of the operator is now effectively external to the generic type `Complex(Of T)`.

No doubt you noticed the extra complexities to the property accessor. First, `Math.Sqrt` accepts a type of `System.Double`. This explains the call to the `Convert.ToDouble` method. And to make sure things go smoothly, you add a constraint to `T` so that the type supplied supports `IConvertible`. But you're not done yet. `Math.Sqrt` returns a `System.Double`, and you have to convert that value type back into type `T`. In order to do so, you cannot rely on the `System.Convert` class because you don't know what type you're converting to at compile time. Yet again, you have to externalize an operation, which in this case is a conversion. This is one reason why the Framework defines the `Converter(Of TInput, TOuput)` delegate. In this case, `Complex(Of T)` needs a `Converter(Of Double, T)` conversion delegate. At construction time, you must pass a method for this delegate to call through to, which in this case is `EntryPoint.DoubleToInt64`. Now, after all of this, the `Complex(Of T).Magnitude` property works as expected.

Let's say you want instances of `Complex(Of T)` to be used as key values in a `SortedList(Of TKey, TValue)` generic type. In order for that to work, `Complex(Of T)` needs to implement `IComparable(Of T)`. Let's see what you need to do to make that a reality:

```vbnet
Imports System

Public Structure Complex(Of T As {Structure, IConvertible, IComparable})
    Implements IComparable(Of Complex(Of T))

    'Delegate for doing multiplication.
    Public Delegate Function BinaryOp(ByVal val1 As T, ByVal val2 As T) As T

    Private mReal As T
    Private mImaginary As T
    Private mult As BinaryOp
    Private add As BinaryOp
    Private convToT As Converter(Of Double, T)

    Public Sub New(ByVal real As T, ByVal imaginary As T, ByVal mult As BinaryOp, _
        ByVal add As BinaryOp, ByVal convToT As Converter(Of Double, T))

        Me.mReal = real
        Me.mImaginary = imaginary
        Me.mult = mult
        Me.add = add
        Me.convToT = convToT
    End Sub

    Public Property Real() As T
        Get
            Return mReal
        End Get
        Set(ByVal value As T)
            mReal = value
        End Set
    End Property

    Public Property Img() As T
        Get
            Return mImaginary
        End Get
        Set(ByVal value As T)
            mImaginary = value
        End Set
    End Property

    Public ReadOnly Property Magnitude() As T
        Get
            Dim mMagnitude As Double = _
                Math.Sqrt(Convert.ToDouble(add(mult(mReal, mReal), _
                mult(mImaginary, mImaginary))))
```

```vbnet
                Return convToT(mMagnitude)
            End Get
        End Property


        Public Function CompareTo(ByVal other As Complex(Of T)) As Integer _
            Implements IComparable(Of Complex(Of T)).CompareTo

            Return Magnitude.CompareTo(other.Magnitude)
        End Function
    End Structure

    Public Class EntryPoint
        Shared Sub Main()
            Dim c As Complex(Of Int64) = New Complex(Of Int64)(4, 5, _
                AddressOf MultiplyInt64, AddressOf AddInt64, AddressOf DoubleToInt64)

            Console.WriteLine("Magnitude is {0}", c.Magnitude)
        End Sub

        Private Shared Function MultiplyInt64(ByVal val1 As Int64, _
            ByVal val2 As Int64) As Int64

            Return val1 * val2
        End Function

        Private Shared Function AddInt64(ByVal val1 As Int64, _
            ByVal val2 As Int64) As Int64

            Return val1 + val2
        End Function

        Private Shared Function DoubleToInt64(ByVal d As Double) As Int64
            Return Convert.ToInt64(d)
        End Function
    End Class
```

This implementation of the IComparable(Complex(Of T)) interface considers two
Complex(Of T) types equivalent if they have the same magnitude. Therefore, most of the work
required to do the comparison is done already. However, instead of being able to rely upon the
inequality operator of the VB language, you need to use a mechanism that doesn't rely upon
operators. In this case, you use the CompareTo() method. Of course, this requires you to force
another constraint on type T: that it must support the nongeneric IComparable interface.

One thing worth noting is that the previous constraint on the nongeneric IComparable
interface makes it a bit difficult for Complex(Of T) to contain generic structures because
generic structures might implement IComparable(Of T) instead. In fact, given the current
definition, it is impossible to define a type of Complex(Of Complex(Of Integer)). It would be
nice if you could construct Complex(Of T) from types that may implement IComparable(Of T)
or IComparable, or even both. Let's see how you can do this:

```vbnet
Imports System
Imports System.Collections.Generic

Public Structure Complex(Of T As Structure)
    Implements IComparable(Of Complex(Of T))

    ' Delegate for doing multiplication.
    Public Delegate Function BinaryOp(ByVal val1 As T, ByVal val2 As T) As T

    Private mReal As T
    Private mImaginary As T
    Private mult As BinaryOp
    Private add As BinaryOp
    Private convToT As Converter(Of Double, T)

    Public Sub New(ByVal real As T, ByVal imaginary As T, ByVal mult As BinaryOp, _
        ByVal add As BinaryOp, ByVal convToT As Converter(Of Double, T))

        Me.mReal = real
        Me.mImaginary = imaginary
        Me.mult = mult
        Me.add = add
        Me.convToT = convToT
    End Sub

    Public Property Real() As T
        Get
            Return mReal
        End Get
        Set(ByVal value As T)
            mReal = value
        End Set
    End Property

    Public Property Img() As T
        Get
            Return mImaginary
        End Get
        Set(ByVal value As T)
            mImaginary = value
        End Set
    End Property
```

```vb
    Public ReadOnly Property Magnitude() As T
        Get
            Dim mMagnitude As Double = _
                Math.Sqrt(Convert.ToDouble(add(mult(mReal, mReal), _
                mult(mImaginary, mImaginary))))

            Return convToT(mMagnitude)
        End Get
    End Property

    Public Function CompareTo(ByVal other As Complex(Of T)) As Integer _
        Implements IComparable(Of Complex(Of T)).CompareTo

        Return Comparer(Of T).Default.Compare(Me.Magnitude, other.Magnitude)
    End Function
End Structure

Public Class EntryPoint
    Shared Sub Main()
        Dim c As Complex(Of Int64) = New Complex(Of Int64)(4, 5, _
            AddressOf MultiplyInt64, AddressOf AddInt64, AddressOf DoubleToInt64)

        Console.WriteLine("Magnitude is {0}", c.Magnitude)
    End Sub

    Private Shared Sub DummyMethod(ByVal c As Complex(Of Complex(Of Integer)))
    End Sub

    Private Shared Function MultiplyInt64(ByVal val1 As Int64, _
        ByVal val2 As Int64) As Int64

        Return val1 * val2
    End Function

    Private Shared Function AddInt64(ByVal val1 As Int64, _
        ByVal val2 As Int64) As Int64

        Return val1 + val2
    End Function

    Private Shared Function DoubleToInt64(ByVal d As Double) As Int64
        Return Convert.ToInt64(d)
    End Function
End Class
```

In this example, you have to remove the constraint on T requiring implementation of the IComparable interface. Instead, the CompareTo method relies upon the default generic comparer defined in the System.Collections.Generic namespace.

Note The generic comparer class Comparer(Of T) introduces one more level of indirection in the form of a class with regard to comparing two instances. In effect, it externalizes the comparability of the instances. If you need a custom implementation of IComparer, you should derive from Comparer(Of T).

Additionally, you have to remove the IConvertible constraint on T to get DummyMethod() to compile. That's because Complex(Of T) doesn't implement IConvertible, and when T is replaced with Complex(Of T) (thus forming Complex(Complex(Of T))), T doesn't implement IConvertible.

Tip When creating generic types, try not to be too restrictive by forcing too many constraints on the contained types. For example, don't force all the contained types to implement IConvertible. Many times, you can externalize such constraints by using a helper object coupled with a delegate.

Think about the removal of this constraint for a moment. In the Magnitude property, you rely on the Convert.ToDouble method. However, since you removed the constraint, the possibility of getting a runtime exception exists, for example, when the type represented by T doesn't implement IConvertible. Since generics are meant to provide better type safety and help you avoid runtime exceptions, there must be a better way. There is, and you can do better by giving Complex(Of T) yet another converter in the form of a Convert(Of T, Double) delegate in the constructor, as follows:

```
Imports System
Imports System.Collections.Generic

Public Structure Complex(Of T As Structure)
    Implements IComparable(Of Complex(Of T))

    'Delegate for doing multiplication.
    Public Delegate Function BinaryOp(ByVal val1 As T, ByVal val2 As T) As T

    Private mReal As T
    Private mImaginary As T
    Private mult As BinaryOp
    Private add As BinaryOp
    Private convToT As Converter(Of Double, T)
    Private convToDouble As Converter(Of T, Double)
```

```vb
    Public Sub New(ByVal real As T, ByVal imaginary As T, ByVal mult As BinaryOp, _
        ByVal add As BinaryOp, ByVal convToT As Converter(Of Double, T), _
        ByVal convToDouble As Converter(Of T, Double))

        Me.mReal = real
        Me.mImaginary = imaginary
        Me.mult = mult
        Me.add = add
        Me.convToT = convToT
        Me.convToDouble = convToDouble
    End Sub

    Public Property Real() As T
        Get
            Return mReal
        End Get
        Set(ByVal value As T)
            mReal = value
        End Set
    End Property

    Public Property Img() As T
        Get
            Return mImaginary
        End Get
        Set(ByVal value As T)
            mImaginary = value
        End Set
    End Property

    Public ReadOnly Property Magnitude() As T
        Get
            Dim mMagnitude As Double = _
                Math.Sqrt(convToDouble(add(mult(mReal, mReal), _
                mult(mImaginary, mImaginary))))

            Return convToT(mMagnitude)
        End Get
    End Property

    Public Function CompareTo(ByVal other As Complex(Of T)) As Integer _
        Implements IComparable(Of Complex(Of T)).CompareTo

        Return Comparer(Of T).Default.Compare(Me.Magnitude, other.Magnitude)
    End Function
End Structure
```

```
Public Class EntryPoint
    Shared Sub Main()
        Dim c As Complex(Of Int64) = New Complex(Of Int64)(4, 5, _
            AddressOf MultiplyInt64, AddressOf AddInt64, AddressOf DoubleToInt64, _
            AddressOf Int64ToDouble)

        Console.WriteLine("Magnitude is {0}", c.Magnitude)
    End Sub

    Private Shared Sub DummyMethod(ByVal c As Complex(Of Complex(Of Integer)))
    End Sub

    Private Shared Function MultiplyInt64(ByVal val1 As Int64, _
        ByVal val2 As Int64) As Int64

        Return val1 * val2
    End Function

    Private Shared Function AddInt64(ByVal val1 As Int64, _
        ByVal val2 As Int64) As Int64

        Return val1 + val2
    End Function

    Private Shared Function DoubleToInt64(ByVal d As Double) As Int64
        Return Convert.ToInt64(d)
    End Function

    Private Shared Function Int64ToDouble(ByVal i As Int64) As Double
        Return Convert.ToDouble(i)
    End Function
End Class
```

Now, the Complex(Of T) type can contain any kind of structure, whether it's generic or not. However, you must provide it with the necessary means to be able to convert to and from Double, as well as to multiply and add constituent types. This Complex(Of T) structure is by no means meant to be a reference for complex number representation. Rather, it is a contrived example meant to illustrate many of the concerns you must deal with in order to create effective generic types. You'll see some of these techniques in practice as you deal with the generic containers that exist in the Framework Class Library.

Creating Constructed Types Dynamically

Given the dynamic nature of the CLR and the fact that you can actually generate classes and code at run time, it is only natural to consider the possibility of constructing closed types from generics at run time. Until now, the examples in this book have dealt with creating closed types at compile time.

This functionality stems from a natural extension of the metadata specification to accommodate generics. The type System.Type is the cornerstone of functionality whenever you need to work with types dynamically within the CLR, and it has been extended to deal with generics as well. Some of the new methods on System.Type are self-explanatory by name and include GetGenericArguments(), GetGenericParameterConstraints(), and GetGenericTypeDefinition(). These methods are helpful when you already have a System.Type instance representing a closed type. However, the method that makes things interesting is MakeGenericType(), which allows you to pass an array of System.Type objects that represent the types that are to be used in the argument parameter list for the resultant constructed type. For example, creating a parsing engine for some sort of XML-based language that defines new types from generics is a snap. Let's take a look at an example of how you use the MakeGenericType method:

```
Imports System
Imports System.Collections.Generic

Public Class EntryPoint
    Shared Sub Main()
        Dim intList As IList(Of Integer) = _
            CType(CreateClosedType(Of Integer)(GetType(List(Of ))), _
            IList(Of Integer))

        Dim doubleList As IList(Of Double) = _
            CType(CreateClosedType(Of Double)(GetType(List(Of ))), _
            IList(Of Double))

        Console.WriteLine(intList)
        Console.WriteLine(doubleList)
    End Sub

    Private Shared Function CreateClosedType(Of T)(ByVal genericType As Type) _
        As Object

        Dim typeArguments As Type() = {GetType(T)}
        Dim closedType As Type = genericType.MakeGenericType(typeArguments)

        Return Activator.CreateInstance(closedType)
    End Function
End Class
```

Here's the output from the previous example:

```
System.Collections.Generic.List`1[System.Int32]
System.Collections.Generic.List`1[System.Double]
```

The meat of this code is inside the generic method CreateClosedType(Of T)(). You do all of the work through references to Type created from the available metadata. First, you need to get a reference to the generic, open type List(), which is passed in as a parameter. After that, you simply create an array of Type instances to pass to MakeGenericType() to obtain a reference to the closed type. Once that stage is complete, the only thing left to do is call CreateInstance() on the System.Activator class. System.Activator is the facility that you must use to create instances of types that are known only at run time. In this case, you're calling the default constructor for the closed type. However, Activator has overloads of CreateInstance() that allow you to call constructors that require parameters. When you run the previous example, you'll see that the closed types get streamed to the console showing their fully qualified type names, thus proving that you created the closed types properly.

The ability to create closed types at run time is yet another powerful tool in your toolbox for creating highly dynamic systems. Not only can you declare generic types within your code so that you can write flexible code, but you can also create closed types from those generic definitions at run time.

Summary

This chapter has shown you how to declare and use generics, including generic classes, structures, interfaces, methods, and delegates, with VB 2008. We also discussed generic constraints, which are necessary for the compiler to create code where certain functional assumptions are placed upon the type arguments provided for the generic type arguments at run time. Collection types achieve a real and measurable gain in efficiency and safety with generics.

Not only do generics allow you to generate more efficient code when using value types with containers, but it also gives the compiler more power when enforcing type safety. As a rule, you should always prefer compile-time type safety over runtime type safety. You can fix a compile-time failure before software is deployed, but a runtime failure usually results in an InvalidCastException being thrown. Finally, always provide the compiler with as much power as possible to enforce type safety.

The next chapter will tackle the topic of threading in VB and the .NET runtime. Along with threading comes the important topic of synchronization.

CHAPTER 13

■ ■ ■

Threading

Multithreading allows your program to run several unique paths of execution simultaneously. Each of these paths is called a *thread*. Using threads can make your application's user interface feel more responsive. They can also spread the burden of a lengthy calculation, or large data load, across multiple processors.

Every application has a *primary thread*, which is created at your application's entry point. During the life of your application, you may create, use, and destroy any number of threads, referred to as *worker threads*.

Multithreading, which we'll call *threading* from now on, is an area filled with challenges. Threading bugs can be some of the hardest bugs to find due to their asynchronous nature. In fact, some threading bugs don't even rear their ugly heads until you run your application on a multiprocessor machine, since that's the only way to get true concurrent multithreading. For this reason, anyone developing a multithreaded application should test it on a multiprocessor machine. Otherwise, you run the risk of sending your product out with lurking threading bugs.

Threading in VB 2008 and .NET 3.5

Even though threading environments have presented many challenges and hurdles, the common language runtime (CLR) and .NET Framework mitigate many of these risks and provide a clean model to build upon. It's still true that the greatest challenge of creating high-quality threaded code is that of synchronization. The .NET Framework makes it easier than ever to create new threads or utilize a system-managed pool of threads, and it provides intuitive objects that help you synchronize those threads with each other.

Managed threads are virtual threads in the sense that they don't map one to one to OS threads. Managed threads do actually run concurrently, but it would be erroneous to assume that the OS thread currently running a particular managed thread's code will only run managed code for that thread. In fact, an OS thread could run managed code for multiple managed threads in multiple application domains in the current implementation of the CLR. If you burrow down to the OS thread using the P/Invoke layer to make direct Win32 calls, be sure that you only use that information for debugging purposes and base no program logic on it. Otherwise, you'll end up with something that may break as soon as you run it on another CLR implementation.

Multithreaded programming is more than creating extra threads to do something that can take a long time to do. Sure, that's part of the puzzle. When you create a desktop application, you definitely want to use a threading technique to ensure that the UI stays responsive during a long computational operation, because we all know what impatient users tend to do when desktop applications become unresponsive: they kill them! But there is much more to the threading puzzle than creating an extra thread to run some busywork code. That task is actually quite easy, so let's take a look and see how easy it really is.

Starting Threads

As we said, creating a thread is simple. Take a look at the following example to see what we mean:

```
Imports System
Imports System.Threading

Public Class EntryPoint
    Private Shared Sub ThreadFunc()
        Console.WriteLine("Hello from new thread {0}!", _
            Thread.CurrentThread.GetHashCode())
    End Sub

    Shared Sub Main()
        'Create the new thread.
        Dim newThread As Thread = _
            New Thread(AddressOf EntryPoint.ThreadFunc)

        Console.WriteLine("Main Thread is {0}", _
            Thread.CurrentThread.GetHashCode())
        Console.WriteLine("Starting new thread . . . ")

        'Start the new thread.
        newThread.Start()

        'Wait for new thread to finish.
        newThread.Join()

        Console.WriteLine("New thread has finished")
    End Sub
End Class
```

The previous example displays the following when executed:

```
Main Thread is 1
Starting new thread . . .
Hello from new thread 3!
New thread has finished
```

All you have to do is create a new System.Thread object and pass an instance of the ThreadStart delegate as the parameter to the constructor. The ThreadStart delegate references a method that takes no parameters and returns no parameters. In the previous example, we chose to use the shared ThreadFunc method as the start of execution for the new thread. We could have just as easily chosen to use any other method visible to the code creating the thread that neither accepted nor returned parameters. Notice that the code also outputs the hash code from the thread, using GetHashCode(), to demonstrate how you identify threads in the managed world. As long as this thread is alive, it is guaranteed never to collide with any other thread in any other application domain of this process. The thread hash code is not globally unique on the entire system. Also, you can see how you can get a reference to the current thread by accessing the shared property Thread.CurrentThread. Finally, notice the call to the Join method on the newThread object. In this case, the code waits forever for the thread to finish. Thread.Join() also provides a few overloads that allow you to specify a time-out period on the wait.

In the managed environment, the System.Thread class encapsulates all of the operations that you may perform on a thread. If you have some sort of state data that you must transmit to the new thread so that it has that data available when it starts execution, you can simply create a helper object and initialize the ThreadStart delegate to point an instance method on that object. Yet again, you solve another problem by introducing another level of indirection in the form of a class. Suppose you have a system where you fill multiple queues with tasks, and then at some point, you want to create a new thread to process the items in a specific queue that you pass into it. The following code demonstrates one way you can achieve such a goal:

```vbnet
Imports System
Imports System.Threading
Imports System.Collections

Public Class QueueProcessor
    Private mQueue As Queue
    Private mThread As Thread

    Public Sub New(ByVal theQueue As Queue)
        Me.mQueue = theQueue
        mThread = New Thread(AddressOf Me.ThreadFunc)
    End Sub

    Public ReadOnly Property TheThread() As Thread
        Get
            Return mThread
        End Get
    End Property

    Public Sub BeginProcessData()
        mThread.Start()
    End Sub

    Public Sub EndProcessData()
        mThread.Join()
    End Sub
```

```
        Private Sub ThreadFunc()
            ' . . . drain theQueue here.
        End Sub
End Class

Public Class EntryPoint
    Shared Sub Main()
        Dim queue1 As Queue = New Queue()
        Dim queue2 As Queue = New Queue()

        ' . . . operations to fill the queues with data.

        'Process each queue in a separate thread.
        Dim proc1 As QueueProcessor = New QueueProcessor(queue1)
        proc1.BeginProcessData()

        Dim proc2 As QueueProcessor = New QueueProcessor(queue2)
        proc2.BeginProcessData()

        ' . . . do some other work in the meantime.

        'Wait for the work to finish.
        proc1.EndProcessData()
        proc2.EndProcessData()
    End Sub
End Class
```

There are some potential synchronization problems here if anyone were to access the queues after the new threads begin their work. However, we'll save synchronization issues until the "Synchronizing Threads" section later on in the chapter. The previous solution is a clean one and also loosely follows the typical pattern of asynchronous processing in the .NET Framework. The class adding the extra level of indirection is the QueueProcessor class. It cleanly encapsulates the worker thread and exposes a lightweight interface to get the work done. In this example, the main thread waits for the work to finish by calling EndProcessData(). That method merely calls Join() on the encapsulated thread. However, had you required some sort of status regarding the completion of the work, the EndProcessData method could have returned it to you.

When you create a separate thread, it is subject to the rules of the thread scheduler on the system, just like any other thread. However, sometimes you need to create threads that carry a different weight when the scheduler algorithm is deciding which thread to execute next. You control the priority of a managed thread via the Thread.Priority property, and you can adjust this value as necessary during execution of the thread. It's actually a rare occurrence that you'll need to adjust this value. All threads start out with the priority of Normal from the ThreadPriority enumeration.

States of a Thread

The states of a managed thread are well defined by the runtime. Although the state transitions may seem confusing at times, they aren't much more confusing than the state transitions of an OS thread. There are other considerations to address in the managed world, so the allowable states and state transitions are naturally more complex. Figure 13-1 shows a state diagram for managed threads.

The states in the state diagram are based upon the states defined by the CLR for managed threads, as defined in the ThreadState enumeration. Every managed thread starts life in the Unstarted state. As soon as you call Start() on the new thread, it enters the Running state. OS threads that enter the managed runtime start immediately in the Running state, thus bypassing the Unstarted state. Notice that there is no way to get back to the Unstarted state. The dominant state in the state diagram is the Running state. This is the state of the thread when it is executing code normally, including any exception handling and execution of any Finally blocks. If the main thread method, passed in via an instance of the ThreadStart delegate during thread creation, finishes normally, then the thread enters the Finished state, as shown in Figure 13-1. Once in this state, the thread is completely dead and will never wake up again. If all of the foreground threads in your process enter the Finished state, the process will exit normally.

The three states mentioned previously cover the basics of managed thread state transition, assuming you have a thread that simply executes some code and exits. Once you start to add synchronization constructs in the execution path or wish to control the state of the thread, whether from another thread or the current thread, things start to become more complicated.

For example, suppose you're writing code for a new thread and you want to put it to sleep for a while. You would call Thread.Sleep() and provide it a time-out, such as how many milliseconds to sleep. When you call Sleep(), the thread enters the WaitSleepJoin state, where its execution is suspended for the duration of the time-out. Once the sleep expires, the thread reenters the running state.

Synchronization operations can also put the thread into the WaitSleepJoin state. As may be obvious by the name of the state, calling Thread.Join() on another thread in order to wait for it to finish puts the calling thread into the WaitSleepJoin state. Calling Monitor.Wait() also enters the WaitSleepJoin state. You can use other synchronization methods with a thread, which the "Synchronizing Threads" section later in the chapter covers. As before, once the thread's wait requirements have been met, it reenters the Running state and continues execution normally.

Any time the thread is sitting in the WaitSleepJoin state, it can be forcefully pushed back into the Running state when another thread calls Thread.Interrupt() on the waiting thread. When a thread calls Thread.Interrupt() on another thread, the interrupted thread receives a thrown ThreadInterruptedException. So, even though the interrupted thread reenters the Running state, it won't stay there for long unless an appropriate exception-handling frame is in place. Otherwise, the thread will soon enter the Finished state once the exception boils its way up to the top of the thread's stack unhandled.

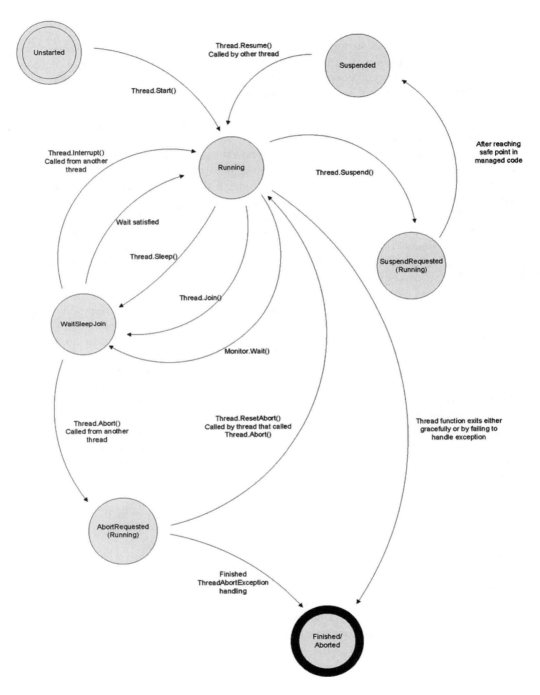

Figure 13-1. *State diagram of managed threads*

Another way that the thread state can transition out of the `WaitSleepJoin` state is when another thread calls `Thread.Abort()` on the current thread. Once `Thread.Abort()` is called, the thread enters the `AbortRequested` state. This state is actually a form of a running state, since the thread is thrown a `ThreadAbortException` and must handle the exception. However, as we explain later on, the managed thread treats this exception in a special way, such that the next state will be the final `Aborted` state, unless the thread that called `Thread.Abort()` manages to call `Thread.ResetAbort()` before that happens. Incidentally, there's nothing to stop the thread that is aborting from calling `Thread.ResetAbort()`. However, you must refrain from doing such a thing because it could create some ill behavior. For example, if you can never abort a foreground thread because it keeps resetting the abort, then the process will never exit.

■**Note** Beginning in .NET 2.0, the host now has the ability to forcefully kill threads during application domain shutdown by using what's called a *rude thread abort*. In such a situation, it is impossible for the thread to keep itself alive by using `Thread.ResetAbort()`.

Finally, a running thread enters the `SuspendRequested` state after calling `Thread.Suspend()` on itself or after another thread calls `Suspend()` on it. Very shortly after that, the thread automatically enters the `Suspended` state. Once a thread enters the `SuspendRequested` state, there is no way to keep it from eventually entering the `Suspended` state. Later on, in the section titled "Halting and Waking Threads," we discuss why this intermediate state is needed when a thread is suspended. But for now, it's important to realize that the `SuspendRequested` state is a form of a running state in the sense that it is still executing managed code.

That wraps up the big picture regarding managed-thread state transitions. Be sure to refer to Figure 13-1 throughout the rest of the chapter when reading about topics that affect the state of the thread.

Terminating Threads

When you call `Thread.Abort()`, the thread in question eventually receives a `ThreadAbortException`. So, naturally, in order to handle this situation gracefully, you must process the `ThreadAbortException` if there is anything specific you must do when the thread is being aborted. There is also an overload of `Abort()` that accepts an arbitrary object reference that is then encapsulated in the subsequent `ThreadAbortException`. This allows the code that is aborting the thread to pass some sort of context information to the `ThreadAbortException` handler, such as a reason why `Abort()` was called in the first place.

The CLR doesn't deliver a `ThreadAbortException` unless the thread is running within the managed context. If your thread has called out to a native function via the P/Invoke layer, and that function takes a long time to complete, then a thread abort on that thread is pended until execution returns to managed space.

■**Note** Beginning in .NET 2.0, if a `Finally` block is executing, delivery of a `ThreadAbortException` is pended until execution leaves the `Finally` block.

Calling Abort() on a thread doesn't forcefully terminate the thread, so if you need to wait until the thread is truly finished executing, you must call Join() on that thread to wait until all of the code in the ThreadAbortException exception handler is finished. During such a wait, it is wise to wait with a time-out so that you don't get stuck waiting forever on a thread to finish cleaning up after itself. Even though the code in the exception handler should follow exception-handler coding guidelines,[1] it's still possible for the handler to take a long time to complete its work. Let's take a look at a ThreadAbortException handler and see how this works:

```
Imports System
Imports System.Threading

Public Class EntryPoint
    Private Shared Sub ThreadFunc()
        Dim counter As ULong = 0

        Do While True
            Try
                Console.WriteLine("{0}", counter)

                counter += 1
            Catch e1 As ThreadAbortException
                'Attempt to swallow the exception and continue.
                Console.WriteLine("Abort!")
            End Try
        Loop
    End Sub

    Shared Sub Main()
        Dim newThread As Thread = _
            New Thread(AddressOf EntryPoint.ThreadFunc)

        newThread.Start()
        Thread.Sleep(2000)

        'Abort the thread.
        newThread.Abort()

        'Wait for thread to finish.
        newThread.Join()
    End Sub
End Class
```

From a cursory glance at the code, it would appear that the call to Join() on the newThread instance will block forever. However, that's not what happens. It would appear that since the ThreadAbortException is handled within the loop of the thread function, the exception will be

---

1. Chapter 8 discusses exception handlers in detail.

swallowed and the loop will continue no matter how many times the main thread attempts to abort the thread. As it turns out, the ThreadAbortException thrown via the Thread.Abort method is special. When your thread finishes processing the abort exception, the runtime implicitly re-throws it at the end of your exception handler. It's the same as if you had re-thrown the exception yourself. Therefore, any outer exception handlers or Finally blocks will still execute as normal. In the previous example, the call to Join() won't be waiting forever as initially expected.

Even though the runtime provides a cleaner mechanism for aborting threads, such that you can inform interested parties when the thread is aborting, you still have to implement a ThreadAbortException handler. Although you can keep the system from re-throwing the ThreadAbortException by calling the Thread.ResetAbort shared method, the general recommendation is that you only call ResetAbort() from the thread that called Abort().

Note The fact that ThreadAbortException instances can be thrown asynchronously into a random managed thread makes it tricky to create robust exception-safe code. Be sure to read the "Constrained Execution Regions" section in Chapter 8.

Halting and Waking Threads

There are mechanisms in place for putting a thread to sleep for a defined period of time or actually halting execution until it is explicitly released again. If a thread wants to suspend itself for a prescribed period of time, it may call the shared method Thread.Sleep(). The only parameter to the Sleep method is the number of milliseconds the thread should sleep. When called, this method causes the thread to relinquish the rest of its time slice with the processor and go to sleep. After the time has expired, the thread may be considered for scheduling again. Naturally, the time duration you pass to Sleep() is reasonably accurate, but not exact. That's because, at the end of the duration, the thread is not immediately given time on the processor. There could be other higher-priority threads in the queue before it. Therefore, using Sleep() to synchronize execution between two threads is strongly discouraged.

There is a special value, Timeout.Infinite, that you can pass to Sleep() to make the thread go to sleep forever. You can wake a sleeping thread by interrupting it via the Thread.Interrupt instance method. Interrupt() is similar to Abort() in that it wakes up the target thread and throws a ThreadInterruptedException. Therefore, if your thread function is not equipped to handle the exception, it will percolate all the way up the call stack until the runtime ends the thread's execution. To be safe, you should make your call to Sleep() within a Try block and catch the ThreadInterruptException. Unlike the ThreadAbortException, the ThreadInterruptException is not automatically re-thrown by the runtime at the end of the exception handler.

Note Another special parameter value for Thread.Sleep() is 0. If you pass 0, Thread.Sleep() will cause the thread to relinquish the rest of its time slice. The thread will then be allowed to run again once the system thread scheduler comes back around to it.

Another way to put a thread to sleep for an indefinite amount of time is via the `Thread.`
`Suspend` instance method. Calling `Suspend()` suspends execution of the thread until it is
explicitly resumed. You can resume the thread by calling the `Resume` instance method or
`Interrupt()`. However, the target thread will need an exception handler around the `Suspend()`
call; otherwise, the thread will exit. Technically, calling `Abort()` on the thread will resume the
thread, but only to send it a `ThreadAbortException` and cause the thread to exit. Keep in mind
that any thread with sufficient privileges can call `Suspend()` on a thread—even the current
thread can call `Suspend()`. If the current thread calls `Suspend()`, it blocks at that point, waiting
for the next `Resume()` call.

When you call `Suspend()` on a thread, the thread is not suspended immediately in its
tracks. Instead, the thread is allowed to execute to what's called a *safe point*. Once it reaches
the safe point, the thread is suspended. A safe point is a place in the managed code where
it is safe to allow garbage collection. For instance, if the CLR determines it is time to perform
garbage collection, it must suspend all threads temporarily while it performs the collection.
When the garbage collector (GC) suspends threads for collection, it must wait until they
all have reached a safe point where it is okay to move things around on the heap. The call
to `Suspend()` allows the thread to reach a safe point before actually suspending it. Never use
`Suspend()` and `Resume()` to orchestrate thread synchronization. The fact that the system allows
the thread to continue running until it reaches a safe point is a good enough reason not to rely
on this mechanism.

Waiting for a Thread to Exit

In this chapter's previous examples, we've used the `Join` method to wait for a specific thread to
exit. The name of the method is suggestive of the fact that you're joining the current thread's
execution path to that of the thread you're calling `Join()` on, and you cannot proceed until
your joined thread arrives.

Naturally, you'll want to avoid calling `Join()` on the current thread. The effect is similar to
calling `Suspend()` from the current thread. The thread is blocked until it is interrupted. Even
when a thread is blocked from calling `Join()`, you can awaken it by calling `Interrupt()` or
`Abort()`, as described in the previous section.

Sometimes, you'll want to call `Join()` to wait on another thread to complete, but you
won't want to get stuck waiting forever. `Join()` offers overloads that allow you to designate the
amount of time you're willing to wait. Those overloads return a `Boolean` value that returns `True`
to indicate that the thread actually terminated or returns `False` to indicate that the time-out
expired.

Foreground and Background Threads

When you create a thread in the .NET managed environment, it exists as a foreground thread
by default. This means that the managed execution environment, and thus the process, will
remain alive as long as the thread is alive. Consider the following code:

```
Imports System
Imports System.Threading
```

```
Public Class EntryPoint
    Private Shared Sub ThreadFunc1()
        Thread.Sleep(5000)
      Console.WriteLine("Exiting extra thread at " & Now() & ".")
    End Sub

    Shared Sub Main()
        Dim thread1 As Thread = _
            New Thread(AddressOf EntryPoint.ThreadFunc1)

        thread1.Start()

      Console.WriteLine("Exiting main thread at " & Now() & ".")
    End Sub
End Class
```

Running the previous code returns the following results:

```
Exiting main thread at 10/9/2007 3:56:50 AM.
Exiting extra thread at 10/9/2007 3:56:55 AM.
```

If you run the previous code, you'll see that Main() exits before the extra thread finishes, as expected. At times, you might want the process to terminate when the main thread finishes, even when extra threads exist in the background. You can accomplish this in the runtime by turning the extra thread into a background thread by setting the Thread.IsBackground property to True. You'll want to consider doing this for threads that perform background tasks, such as listening on a port for network connections. Keep in mind, though, that you always want to make sure that your threads get a proper chance to clean up if they need to before they are shut down. When a background thread is shut down as the process exits, it doesn't receive an exception of any type as it does when someone calls Interrupt() or Abort(). So, if the thread has persistent data in some sort of half-baked state, shutting down the process will not be good for that data. Therefore, when creating background threads, make sure you code them so that you can terminate them rudely at any point without any adverse effects. You could also implement a mechanism to notify the thread that the process is about to shut down. Creating such a mechanism will prove messy, since the main thread will need to wait after firing the notification for the extra thread to do its cleanup work. At that point, it almost becomes reasonable to turn the thread back into a foreground thread.

Thread-Local Storage

You can create thread-local storage in the managed environment. Depending on your application, it may be necessary for you to have a shared field of a class that is unique for each thread that the class is used in. If you have a shared field that must be thread-relative, simply adorn it with the ThreadStaticAttribute attribute. Once you do that, the field will be initialized for each thread that accesses it, and each thread will be given its own thread-relative location to save the value or reference. However, when using references to objects, be careful with your assumptions about object creation. The following code shows a pitfall to avoid:

```
Imports System
Imports System.Threading

Public Class TLSClass
    Public Sub New()
        Console.WriteLine("Creating TLSClass")
    End Sub
End Class

Public Class TLSFieldClass
    <ThreadStatic()> _
    Public Shared tlsdata As TLSClass = New TLSClass()
End Class

Public Class EntryPoint
    Private Shared Sub ThreadFunc()
        Console.WriteLine("Thread {0} starting . . . ", _
            Thread.CurrentThread.GetHashCode())

        Console.WriteLine("tlsdata for this thread is ""{0}""", _
            TLSFieldClass.tlsdata)

        Console.WriteLine("Thread {0} exiting", Thread.CurrentThread.GetHashCode())
    End Sub

    Shared Sub Main()
        Dim thread1 As Thread = _
            New Thread(AddressOf EntryPoint.ThreadFunc)
        Dim thread2 As Thread = _
            New Thread(AddressOf EntryPoint.ThreadFunc)

        thread1.Start()
        thread2.Start()
    End Sub
End Class
```

This code is creating two threads that access a thread-relative static member of TLSFieldClass. To illustrate the trap, we've made that thread-specific slot of type TLSClass, and the code attempts to initialize that slot with an initializer in the class definition that simply calls New on the default constructor of the class. Now, look how surprising the output is:

```
Thread 11 starting . . .
Creating TLSClass
tlsdata for this thread is "Threading.TLSClass"
```

```
Thread 11 exiting
Thread 12 starting . . .
tlsdata for this thread is ""
Thread 12 exiting
```

Caution Always remember that order of execution in multithreaded programs is never guaranteed unless you employ specific synchronization mechanisms. The previous output was generated on a single-processor system. If you run the same application on a multiprocessor system, you'll likely see that the output executes in a completely different order. Nevertheless, the purpose of the example does not change.

The constructor for TLSClass was only called once. The constructor was called for the first thread, but not for the second thread. For the second thread, the field is initialized to Nothing. Since tlsdata is shared, its initialization is actually done at the time the shared constructor for the TLSFieldClass is called. However, shared constructors can only be called once per class per application domain. For this reason, you want to avoid assigning thread-relative slots at the point of declaration. That way, they will always be assigned to their default values. For reference types, that means Nothing, and for value types, it means the equivalent of setting all of the bits in the value's underlying storage to 0. Then, upon first access to the thread-specific slot, you can test the value for Nothing and create an instance as appropriate. The cleanest way to achieve this is to access the thread-local slot via a shared property.

There is another way to use thread-local storage that doesn't involve decorating a shared property with an attribute. You can allocate thread-specific storage dynamically by using either of the Thread.AllocateDataSlot or Thread.AllocateNamedDataSlot methods. You'll want to use these methods if you don't know how many thread-specific slots you'll need to allocate until run time. Otherwise, it's generally much easier to use the shared field method. When you call AllocateDataSlot(), a new slot is allocated in all threads to hold a reference to an instance of type System.Object. The method returns a handle of sorts in the form of a LocalDataStoreSlot object instance. You can access this location using the GetData and SetData methods on the thread. Let's look at a modification of the previous example:

```
Imports System
Imports System.Threading

Public Class TLSClass
    Private Shared mSlot As LocalDataStoreSlot = Nothing

    Shared Sub New()
        mSlot = Thread.AllocateDataSlot()
    End Sub

    Public Sub New()
        Console.WriteLine("Creating TLSClass")
    End Sub
```

```
        Public Shared ReadOnly Property TlsSlot() As TLSClass
            Get
                Dim obj As Object = Thread.GetData(mSlot)
                If obj Is Nothing Then
                    obj = New TLSClass()
                    Thread.SetData(mSlot, obj)
                End If
                Return CType(obj, TLSClass)
            End Get
        End Property
End Class

Public Class EntryPoint
    Private Shared Sub ThreadFunc()
        Console.WriteLine("Thread {0} starting . . . ", _
            Thread.CurrentThread.GetHashCode())

        Console.WriteLine("tlsdata for this thread is ""{0}""", _
            TLSClass.TlsSlot)
        Console.WriteLine("Thread {0} exiting", _
            Thread.CurrentThread.GetHashCode())
    End Sub

    Shared Sub Main()
        Dim thread1 As Thread = _
            New Thread(AddressOf EntryPoint.ThreadFunc)
        Dim thread2 As Thread = _
            New Thread(AddressOf EntryPoint.ThreadFunc)

        thread1.Start()
        thread2.Start()
    End Sub
End Class
```

Executing the previous code returns the following results:

```
Thread 3 starting . . .
Thread 4 starting . . .
Creating TLSClass
tlsdata for this thread is "Threading.TLSClass"
Thread 3 exiting
Creating TLSClass
tlsdata for this thread is "Threading.TLSClass"
Thread 4 exiting
```

As you can see, using dynamic slots is a little more involved than using the shared field method. However, it does provide some extra flexibility. Notice that the slot is allocated in the type initializer, which is the shared constructor you see in the example. That way, the slot is allocated for all threads at the point where the runtime initializes the type for use. Notice that you're testing the slot for Nothing in the property accessor of the TLSClass. When you allocate the slot using AllocateDataSlot(), the slot is initialized to Nothing for each thread.

You may find it convenient to access your thread-specific storage via a string name rather than with a reference to a LocalDataStoreSlot instance. Consider naming your slot using a string representation of a Globally Unique Identifier (GUID) so that you can reasonably assume that nobody will attempt to create one with the same name. When you need to access the slot, you can call GetNamedDataSlot(), which will simply translate your string into a Local-DataStoreSlot instance. The Microsoft Developer Network (MSDN) documentation regarding named thread-local storage slots has more details.

Synchronizing Threads

Synchronization is arguably the most difficult part of creating multithreaded applications. You can create extra threads to do work all day long without having to worry about synchronization, as long as those threads consume some data at start-up that no other thread uses. Nobody needs to know when they finish or what the results of their operations are. Obviously, it's a rare case that you'll create such a thread. In most cases, you need to communicate with the running thread, wait for it to reach a defined state in the code, or possibly work on the same object or value instances that other threads are working on.

In all of those cases, you must rely upon synchronization techniques to synchronize the threads to avoid race conditions and deadlocks. With race conditions, two threads may need to access the same piece of memory, and only one can safely do so at a time. In these cases, you must use a synchronization mechanism that will only allow one thread at a time to access the data and lock out the other thread, making it wait until the first one is done. Multithreaded environments are stochastic in nature, and you never know when the scheduler will take away control from the thread. The classic example is where one thread gets halfway through changing a block of memory, loses control, and then the other thread is given control and starts reading the memory, assuming that it is in a valid state. An example of a deadlock is when two threads are waiting on each other to release a resource. Both threads end up waiting on each other, and since neither one of them can run until the wait is satisfied, they end up waiting forever.

In all synchronization tasks, you should use the lightest weight sync mechanism that you can get away with. For example, if you're trying to share a data block between two threads in the same process and you must gate access between the two, use something such as a Monitor lock rather than a Mutex. Why? Because a Mutex is meant to gate access to a shared resource between processes and, therefore, is a heavyweight OS object that slows down the process when acquiring and releasing the lock. If no interprocess locking is necessary, use the Monitor instead. Even lighter weight than the Monitor is a set of methods in the Interlocked class. These are ideal when you know that the likelihood of actually having to wait a good while when acquiring a lock is low.

■**Note** Any type of wait on a kernel object—such as waiting on a `Mutex`, `Semaphore`, `EventWaitHandle`, or any other wait that boils down to waiting on a Win32 kernel object—requires a transition to kernel mode. Transitions to kernel mode are expensive, and you should avoid them if at all possible. The lightest weight synchronization technique involves crafty use of the `Threading.Interlocked` class. Its methods are all implemented completely in user mode, thus allowing you to avoid the user-to-kernel mode transition.

When using synchronization objects in a multithreaded environment, you want to hold the lock for as little time as possible. For example, if you acquire a synchronization lock to read a shared structure instance, and code within the method that acquires the lock uses that instance of the structure for some purpose, it's best to make a local copy of the structure on the stack and then release the lock immediately, unless it is logically impossible. That way, you don't tie up other threads in the system that need to access the guarded variable.

When you need to synchronize thread execution, never rely upon methods such as `Thread.Suspend()` or `Thread.Resume()` to control thread synchronization. Remember, calling `Thread.Suspend()` doesn't actually suspend the thread immediately. Instead, it must get to a safe point within the managed code before it can suspend execution. And never use `Thread.Sleep()` to synchronize threads. `Thread.Sleep()` is appropriate when you're doing some sort of polling loop on an entity, such as device hardware that has just been reset and has no way of notifying anyone that it is back online. In that case, you don't want to check the state in a loop repeatedly. Instead, it's better to sleep a bit between polling, so as to allow the scheduler to let other threads run. If you find yourself solving a synchronization bug by introducing a call to `Thread.Sleep()` at some seemingly random point in your code, you're hiding, rather than solving the problem.

Lightweight Synchronization with the Interlocked Class

The `Interlocked` family of functions has been exposed to VB developers via shared methods on the `Interlocked` class in the `System.Threading` namespace. Sometimes, when running multiple threads, it's necessary to maintain a simple variable—typically a value, but possibly an object—between the multiple threads. For example, suppose you have some reason to track the amount of running threads in a shared integer somewhere. When a thread begins, it increments that value, and when it finishes, it decrements that value. Obviously, you must synchronize access to that value somehow, since the scheduler could take away control from one thread and give it to another when the first one is in the process of updating the value. Even worse, the exact same code could be executing concurrently on a multiprocessor machine. For this task, you can use `Interlocked.Increment()` and `Interlocked.Decrement()`. These methods are guaranteed to modify the value atomically across all processors in the system. Take a look at the following example:

```
Imports System
Imports System.Threading

Public Class EntryPoint
    Private Shared numberThreads As Integer = 0
    Private Shared rnd As Random = New Random()
```

```
    Private Shared Sub RndThreadFunc()
        'Manage thread count and wait for a random amount of time
        'between (1 and 12) seconds.
        Interlocked.Increment(numberThreads)

        Try
            Dim time As Integer = rnd.Next(1000, 12000)
            Thread.Sleep(time)
        Finally
            Interlocked.Decrement(numberThreads)
        End Try
    End Sub

    Private Shared Sub RptThreadFunc()
        Do While True
            Dim threadCount As Integer = 0
            threadCount = _
                Interlocked.Exchange(numberThreads, numberThreads)
            Console.WriteLine("{0} thread(s) alive", threadCount)
            Thread.Sleep(1000)
        Loop
    End Sub

    Shared Sub Main()
        'Start the reporting threads.
        Dim reporter As Thread = _
            New Thread(AddressOf EntryPoint.RptThreadFunc)

        reporter.IsBackground = True
        reporter.Start()

        'Start the threads that wait random time.
        Dim rndthreads As Thread() = New Thread(49) {}

        For i As UInteger = 0 To 49
            rndthreads(i) = _
                New Thread(AddressOf EntryPoint.RndThreadFunc)
            rndthreads(i).Start()
        Next i
    End Sub
End Class
```

This little program creates 50 foreground threads that do nothing but wait a random amount of time between 1 and 12 seconds. It also creates a background thread that reports how many threads are currently alive. If you look at the RndThreadFunc method, which is the thread function that the 50 threads use, you can see it increment and decrement the integer value using the Interlocked methods. Notice that you use a Finally block to ensure that the value gets decremented no matter how the thread exits. You could use the Using keyword by wrapping the increment and decrement in a separate class that implements IDisposable. That would get rid of the Finally block, but in this case, it wouldn't help you because you'd also have to create a reference type to contain the integer count variable.

You've already seen Interlocked.Increment() and Interlocked.Decrement() in action. But what about Interlocked.Exchange() that the reporter thread uses? Remember, since multiple threads are attempting to write to the threadCount variable, the reporter thread must read the value in a synchronized way as well. That's where Interlocked.Exchange() comes in. Interlocked.Exchange(), as its name implies, allows you to exchange the value of a variable with that of another in an atomic fashion, and it returns the value that was stored previously in that location. Since the Interlocked class doesn't provide a method to simply read an Integer value in an atomic operation, all you're doing is swapping the numberThreads variable's value with its own value, and, as a side effect, the Interlocked.Exchange method returns the value that was in the slot.

The last method to cover in the Interlocked class is CompareExchange(). This method is similar to Interlocked.Exchange() in that it allows you to exchange the value of a location or slot in an atomic fashion. However, it only does the exchange if the original value compares equal to a provided comparand. In any event, the method always returns the original value. One extremely handy use of the CompareExchange method is to use it to create a lightweight *spin lock*. A spin lock gets its name from the fact that if it cannot acquire the lock, it will spin in a tight loop until it can. Typically, when implementing a spin lock, you put your thread to sleep for a very small amount of time with each failed attempt to acquire the lock. That way, the thread scheduler can give processor time to another thread while you wait. If you don't want the thread to sleep but only to release its time slice, you can pass a value of 0 to Thread.Sleep(). Let's look at an example:

```
Imports System
Imports System.IO
Imports System.Threading

Public Class SpinLock
    Private theLock As Integer = 0
    Private spinWait As Integer

    Public Sub New(ByVal spinWait As Integer)
        Me.spinWait = spinWait
    End Sub

    Public Sub Enter()
        Do While Interlocked.CompareExchange(theLock, 1, 0) = 1
            'The lock is taken, spin.
            Thread.Sleep(spinWait)
        Loop
    End Sub
```

```vbnet
    Public Sub [Exit]()
        'Reset the lock.
        Interlocked.Exchange(theLock, 0)
    End Sub
End Class

Public Class SpinLockManager
    Implements IDisposable

    Private spinLock As SpinLock

    Public Sub New(ByVal spinLock As SpinLock)
        Me.spinLock = spinLock
        spinLock.Enter()
    End Sub

    Public Sub Dispose() Implements IDisposable.Dispose
        spinLock.Exit()
    End Sub
End Class

Public Class EntryPoint
    Private Shared rnd As Random = New Random()
    Private Shared logLock As SpinLock = New SpinLock(10)

    Private Shared fsLog As StreamWriter = _
        New StreamWriter(File.Open("log.txt", FileMode.Append, _
        FileAccess.Write, FileShare.None))

    Private Shared Sub RndThreadFunc()
        Using TempSpinLockManager As SpinLockManager = _
            New SpinLockManager(logLock)
            fsLog.WriteLine("Thread Starting")
            fsLog.Flush()
        End Using

        Dim time As Integer = rnd.Next(10, 200)
        Thread.Sleep(time)

        Using TempSpinLockManager As SpinLockManager = _
            New SpinLockManager(logLock)
            fsLog.WriteLine("Thread Exiting")
            fsLog.Flush()
        End Using
    End Sub
```

```
    Shared Sub Main()
        'Start the threads that wait random time.
        Dim rndthreads As Thread() = New Thread(49) {}

        For i As UInteger = 0 To 49
            rndthreads(i) = _
                New Thread(AddressOf EntryPoint.RndThreadFunc)
            rndthreads(i).Start()
        Next i
    End Sub
End Class
```

This example is similar to the previous one, in that it creates 50 threads that wait a random amount of time. However, instead of managing a thread count, it outputs a line to a log file. Since this writing is happening from multiple threads, and instance methods of StreamWriter are not thread-safe, you must do the writing in a safe manner within the context of a lock. That is where the SpinLock class comes in. Internally, it manages a lock variable in the form of an Integer, and it uses Interlocked.CompareExchange() to gate access to the lock. The call to Interlocked.CompareExchange() in SpinLock.Enter() is saying

1. If the lock value is equal to 0, replace the value with 1 to indicate the lock is taken; otherwise, do nothing.

2. If the value of the slot already contains 1, it's taken, and you must sleep and spin.

Both of those items occur in an atomic fashion via the Interlocked class, so there is no possible way that more than one thread can acquire the lock at a time. When the SpinLock.Exit method is called, all it needs to do is reset the lock. However, that must be done atomically as well—hence the call to Interlocked.Exchange().

This example illustrates the use of the disposable/using idiom, discussed in Chapter 3, to implement deterministic destruction, where you introduce another class—in this case, SpinLockManager—to implement the Resource Acquisition Is Initialization (RAII) idiom. This saves you from having to remember to write Finally blocks. Of course, you still have to remember to use the Using keyword, but if you follow the idiom closer than this example, you would implement a finalizer that would assert in the debug build if it ran and the object had not been disposed.

Spin locks implemented in this way are not reentrant. Any function that has acquired the lock cannot be called again until it has released the lock. While you can use spin locks with recursive programming techniques, you must release the lock before recursing or else suffer a deadlock.

■**Note** If you require a reentrant wait mechanism, you can use wait objects that are more structured, such as the Monitor class, which we cover next, or kernel-based wait objects.

Monitor Class

The previous section showed you how to implement a spin lock using the methods of the Interlocked class. A spin lock is not always the most efficient synchronization mechanism, especially if you use it in an environment where a wait is almost guaranteed. The thread scheduler has to continually wake up the thread and allow it to recheck the lock variable. As mentioned before, a spin lock is ideal when you need a lightweight, non-reentrant synchronization mechanism and the odds are low that a thread will have to wait in the first place. When you know the likelihood of waiting is high, you should use a synchronization mechanism that allows the scheduler to avoid waking the thread until the lock is available. .NET provides the System.Threading.Monitor class to allow synchronization between threads within the same process. You can use this class to guard access to certain variables or to gate access to code that should only be run on one thread at a time.

You cannot instantiate an instance of the Monitor class. The Monitor class, much like the Interlocked class, is merely a containing namespace for a collection of shared methods that do the work. Two such shared methods are Monitor.Enter() and Monitor.Exit(). These methods prevent multiple threads from entering the code section outlined by Enter() and Exit().

■**Note** Monitors provide a way to ensure synchronization such that only one method, or a block of protected code, executes at one time. A Mutex is typically used for the same task. However, the Monitor is much lighter and faster. Monitor is appropriate when you must guard access to code within a single process. Mutex is appropriate when you must guard access to a resource from multiple processes.

The CLR manages a sync block for every object instance in the process. Basically, it's a flag of sorts, similar to the integer used in the examples of the previous section describing the Interlocked class. When you obtain the lock on an object, this flag is set. When the lock is released, this flag is reset. The Monitor class is the gateway to accessing this flag. The versatility of this scheme is that every object instance in the CLR potentially contains one of these locks. We say *potentially* because the CLR allocates them in a lazy fashion, since not every object instance's lock will be utilized. Let's look at an example using the Monitor class by modifying the example from the previous section:

```
Imports System
Imports System.Threading

Public Class EntryPoint
    Private Shared theLock As Object = New Object()
    Private Shared numberThreads As Integer = 0
    Private Shared rnd As Random = New Random()

    Private Shared Sub RndThreadFunc()
        'Manage thread count and wait for a random amount of time
        'between(1 and 12) seconds.
```

```
        Try
            Monitor.Enter(theLock)
            numberThreads += 1
        Finally
            Monitor.Exit(theLock)
        End Try

        Dim time As Integer = rnd.Next(1000, 12000)

        Thread.Sleep(time)

        Try
            Monitor.Enter(theLock)
            numberThreads -= 1
        Finally
            Monitor.Exit(theLock)
        End Try
    End Sub

    Private Shared Sub RptThreadFunc()
        Do While True
            Dim threadCount As Integer = 0

            Try
                Monitor.Enter(theLock)
                threadCount = numberThreads
            Finally
                Monitor.Exit(theLock)
            End Try

            Console.WriteLine("{0} thread(s) alive", threadCount)

            Thread.Sleep(1000)
        Loop
    End Sub

    Shared Sub Main()
        'Start the reporting threads.
        Dim reporter As Thread = _
            New Thread(AddressOf EntryPoint.RptThreadFunc)

        reporter.IsBackground = True
        reporter.Start()

        'Start the threads that wait random time.
        Dim rndthreads As Thread() = New Thread(49) {}
```

```
        For i As UInteger = 0 To 49
            rndthreads(i) = _
                New Thread(AddressOf EntryPoint.RndThreadFunc)
            rndthreads(i).Start()
        Next i
    End Sub
End Class
```

Notice that you perform all access to the numberThreads variable in the form of an object lock. Before each access, the accessor must obtain the lock on the theLock object instance. The type of theLock field is of type Object simply because its actual type is inconsequential. The only thing that matters is that it is a reference type—that is, an instance of an Object rather than a value type. Since you only need the Object instance to utilize its internal sync block, you can just instantiate an object of type System.Object.

One thing you've probably also noticed is that the code is uglier than the version that used the Interlocked methods. Whenever you call Monitor.Enter(), you want to guarantee that the matching Monitor.Exit() executes no matter what. The examples mitigate this problem using the Interlocked class by wrapping the usage of the Interlocked class methods within a class named SpinLockManager. Can you imagine the chaos that could ensue if a Monitor.Exit() call was skipped because of an exception? Therefore, you always want to utilize a Try/Finally block in these situations. The VB language creators recognized that developers were going through a lot of effort to ensure that these Finally blocks were in place when all they were doing was calling Monitor.Exit(). So, they made our lives easier by introducing the SyncLock keyword. Consider the same example again, except this time using the SyncLock keyword:

```
Imports System
Imports System.Threading

Public Class EntryPoint
    Private Shared theLock As Object = New Object()
    Private Shared numberThreads As Integer = 0
    Private Shared rnd As Random = New Random()

    Private Shared Sub RndThreadFunc()
        'Manage thread count and wait for a random amount of time
        'between(1 and 12) seconds.
        SyncLock theLock
            numberThreads += 1
        End SyncLock

        Dim time As Integer = rnd.Next(1000, 12000)

        Thread.Sleep(time)

        SyncLock theLock
            numberThreads -= 1
        End SyncLock
    End Sub
```

```vbnet
        Private Shared Sub RptThreadFunc()
            Do While True
                Dim threadCount As Integer = 0

                SyncLock theLock
                    threadCount = numberThreads
                End SyncLock

                Console.WriteLine("{0} thread(s) alive", threadCount)

                Thread.Sleep(1000)
            Loop
        End Sub

        Shared Sub Main()
            'Start the reporting threads.
            Dim reporter As Thread = _
                New Thread(AddressOf EntryPoint.RptThreadFunc)

            reporter.IsBackground = True
            reporter.Start()

            'Start the threads that wait random time.
            Dim rndthreads As Thread() = New Thread(49) {}

            For i As UInteger = 0 To 49
                rndthreads(i) = _
                    New Thread(AddressOf EntryPoint.RndThreadFunc)
                rndthreads(i).Start()
            Next i
        End Sub
End Class
```

Notice that the code is much cleaner, and in fact, there are no explicit calls to any Monitor methods. The VB compiler expands the SyncLock keyword into the familiar Try/Finally block with calls to Monitor.Enter() and Monitor.Exit(). You can verify this by examining the generated intermediate language (IL) code using the IL Disassembler (IL DASM).

In many cases, synchronization implemented internally within a class is as simple as implementing it in the previous manner. But when only one lock object is needed across all methods within the class, you can simplify the model even more by eliminating the extra dummy instance of System.Object by using the Me keyword when acquiring the lock through the Monitor class. Although it saves you from having to instantiate an object of type System. Object—which is pretty lightweight—it does come with its own perils. For example, an external consumer of your object could actually attempt to utilize the sync block within your object by calling Monitor.Enter() before even calling one of your methods that will try to acquire the same lock. Technically, that's just fine, since the same thread can call Monitor.Enter() multiple times. In other words, Monitor locks are reentrant, unlike the spin locks of the previous section. However, when a lock is released, it must be released by calling Monitor.Exit() a matching number of times. So now you have to rely upon the consumers of your object to use either the SyncLock keyword or a Try/Finally block to ensure that their call to Monitor.Enter() is matched appropriately with Monitor.Exit().

We recommend against locking via the Me keyword and instead suggest using a private instance of System.Object as your lock. This will avoid relying on the consumer of your object to manage locking.

Beware of Boxing

When using the Monitor methods to implement locking, Monitor uses the sync block of object instances internally to manage the lock. Since every object instance can potentially have a sync block, you can use any reference to an object, even an object reference to a boxed value. Even though you can, you should never pass a value type instance to Monitor.Enter(), as in the following code example:

```
Imports System
Imports System.Threading

Public Class EntryPoint
    Private Shared counter As Integer = 0

    'NEVER DO THIS!!!
    Private Shared theLock As Integer = 0

    Private Shared Sub ThreadFunc()
        For i As Integer = 0 To 49
            Monitor.Enter(theLock)
            Try
                Console.WriteLine(counter)

                counter += 1
            Finally
                Monitor.Exit(theLock)
            End Try
        Next i
    End Sub

    Shared Sub Main()
        Dim thread1 As Thread = _
            New Thread(AddressOf EntryPoint.ThreadFunc)
        Dim thread2 As Thread = _
            New Thread(AddressOf EntryPoint.ThreadFunc)

        thread1.Start()
        thread2.Start()
    End Sub
End Class
```

If you try to execute this code, you will be presented with a SynchronizationLockException exception stating that an object synchronization method was called from an unsynchronized block of code. Why does this happen? Recall that implicit boxing occurs when you pass a value type to a method that accepts a reference type. Passing the same value type to the same method multiple times will result in a different boxing reference type each time. Therefore, the reference object used within the body of Monitor.Exit() is different from the one used inside the body of Monitor.Enter(). This is another example of how implicit boxing can cause you grief. You may have noticed that the example used the Try/Finally approach. That's because the designers of the VB language created the SyncLock statement such that it doesn't accept value types. If you use the SyncLock statement, you don't have to worry about inadvertently passing a boxed value type to the Monitor methods.

Pulse and Wait

In addition to the previously mentioned uses, you can use the Monitor methods to implement handshaking between threads, as well as to implement queued access to a shared resource.

When a thread has entered a locked region successfully, it can give up the lock and enter a waiting queue by calling Monitor.Wait(). The first parameter to Monitor.Wait() is the object reference whose sync block represents the lock being used. The second parameter is a time-out value. Monitor.Wait() returns a Boolean that indicates whether the wait succeeded or if the time-out was reached. If the wait succeeded, the result is True; otherwise, it is False. When a thread that calls Monitor.Wait() completes the wait successfully, it leaves the wait state as the owner of the lock again.

If threads can give up the lock and enter into a wait state, there must be some mechanism to tell the Monitor that it can give the lock back to one of the waiting threads as soon as possible. That mechanism is the Monitor.Pulse method. Only the thread that currently holds the lock is allowed to call Monitor.Pulse(). When called, the thread first in line in the waiting queue is moved to a ready queue. Once the thread that owns the lock releases the lock, either by calling Monitor.Exit() or by calling Monitor.Wait(), the first thread in the ready queue is allowed to run. The threads in the ready queue include those that are pulsed and those that have been blocked after a call to Monitor.Enter(). Additionally, the thread that owns the lock can move all waiting threads into the ready queue by calling Monitor.PulseAll().

There are many fancy synchronization tasks that you can accomplish using the Monitor.Pulse and Monitor.Wait methods. For example, consider the following example that implements a handshaking mechanism between two threads. The goal is to have both threads increment a counter in an alternating manner:

```
Imports System
Imports System.Threading

Public Class EntryPoint
    Private Shared counter As Integer = 0
    Private Shared theLock As Object = New Object()
```

```
    Private Shared Sub ThreadFunc1()
        SyncLock theLock
            For i As Integer = 0 To 5
                Monitor.Wait(theLock, Timeout.Infinite)

                Console.WriteLine("{0} from Thread {1}", counter, _
                    Thread.CurrentThread.GetHashCode())

                Monitor.Pulse(theLock)

                counter += 1
            Next i
        End SyncLock
    End Sub

    Private Shared Sub ThreadFunc2()
        SyncLock theLock
            For i As Integer = 0 To 5
                Monitor.Pulse(theLock)
                Monitor.Wait(theLock, Timeout.Infinite)

                Console.WriteLine("{0} from Thread {1}", counter, _
                    Thread.CurrentThread.GetHashCode())

                counter += 1
            Next i
        End SyncLock
    End Sub

    Shared Sub Main()
        Dim thread1 As Thread = _
            New Thread(AddressOf EntryPoint.ThreadFunc1)
        Dim thread2 As Thread = _
            New Thread(AddressOf EntryPoint.ThreadFunc2)

        thread1.Start()
        thread2.Start()
    End Sub
End Class
```

The results from the previous example show that the threads increment the counter in an alternating fashion:

```
0 from Thread 3
1 from Thread 4
2 from Thread 3
3 from Thread 4
4 from Thread 3
5 from Thread 4
6 from Thread 3
7 from Thread 4
8 from Thread 3
9 from Thread 4
10 from Thread 3
11 from Thread 4
```

As another example, you could implement a crude thread pool using `Monitor.Wait()` and `Monitor.Pulse()`. It may be unnecessary to actually do such a thing, since the .NET Framework offers the `ThreadPool` object, which is robust and likely uses optimized I/O completion ports of the underlying OS. For the sake of example, however, here's how you could implement a pool of worker threads that wait for work items to be queued:

```
Imports System
Imports System.Threading
Imports System.Collections

Public Class CrudeThreadPool
    Private workQueue As Queue
    Private workLock As Object
    Private threads As Thread()
    Private mStop As Integer

    Private Shared ReadOnly MAX_WORK_THREADS As Integer = 4
    Private Shared ReadOnly WAIT_TIMEOUT As Integer = 2000

    Public Delegate Sub WorkDelegate()

    Public Sub New()
        mStop = 0
        workLock = New Object()
        workQueue = New Queue()
        threads = New Thread(MAX_WORK_THREADS - 1) {}

        Dim i As Integer = 0
        Do While i < MAX_WORK_THREADS
            threads(i) = New Thread(AddressOf Me.ThreadFunc)
            threads(i).Start()

            i += 1
        Loop
    End Sub
```

```vb
    Private Sub ThreadFunc()
        SyncLock workLock
            Dim shouldStop As Integer = 0
            Do
                shouldStop = Interlocked.Exchange(mStop, mStop)
                If shouldStop = 0 Then
                    Dim workItem As WorkDelegate = Nothing

                    If Monitor.Wait(workLock, WAIT_TIMEOUT) Then
                        'Process the item on the front of the queue
                        SyncLock workQueue
                            workItem = CType(workQueue.Dequeue(), _
                                WorkDelegate)
                        End SyncLock
                        workItem()
                    End If
                End If
            Loop While shouldStop = 0
        End SyncLock
    End Sub

    Public Sub SubmitWorkItem(ByVal item As WorkDelegate)
        SyncLock workLock
            SyncLock workQueue
                workQueue.Enqueue(item)
            End SyncLock

            Monitor.Pulse(workLock)
        End SyncLock
    End Sub

    Public Sub Shutdown()
        Interlocked.Exchange(mStop, 1)
    End Sub
End Class

Public Class EntryPoint
    Private Shared Sub WorkFunction()
        Console.WriteLine("WorkFunction() called on Thread {0}", _
            Thread.CurrentThread.GetHashCode())
    End Sub

    Shared Sub Main()
        Dim pool As CrudeThreadPool = New CrudeThreadPool()
        For i As Integer = 0 To 11
            pool.SubmitWorkItem(New CrudeThreadPool.WorkDelegate _
                (AddressOf EntryPoint.WorkFunction))
        Next i
```

```
        pool.Shutdown()
    End Sub
End Class
```

The previous code returns results like the following:

```
WorkFunction() called on Thread 3
WorkFunction() called on Thread 4
WorkFunction() called on Thread 5
WorkFunction() called on Thread 6
WorkFunction() called on Thread 3
WorkFunction() called on Thread 4
WorkFunction() called on Thread 5
WorkFunction() called on Thread 6
```

In this case, the work item is represented by a delegate that neither accepts nor returns any values. When the `CrudeThreadPool` object is created, it creates a pool of threads and starts them running the main work item processing method. That method simply calls `Monitor.Wait()` to wait for an item to be queued. When `SubmitWorkItem()` is called, an item is pushed into the queue, and it calls `Monitor.Pulse()` to release one of the worker threads. Naturally, access to the queue must be synchronized. In this case, the reference type used to sync access is the queue itself. Additionally, the worker threads must not wait forever because they need to wake up periodically and check a flag to see if they should shut down gracefully. Optionally, you could simply turn the worker threads into background threads by setting the `IsBackground` property inside the `Shutdown` method. However, in that case, the worker threads may be shut down before they're finished processing their work. Depending on your situation, that may or may not be favorable. Notice that we chose to use the `Interlocked` methods to manage the stop flag used to indicate that the worker threads should exit.

▪**Note** Another useful technique is to create a special type of work item that tells a thread to shut down. The trick is that you need to make sure you push as many of these special work items onto the queue as there are threads in the pool.

Locking Objects

The .NET Framework offers several high-level locking objects that you can use to synchronize access to data from multiple threads. The previous section was dedicated entirely to one type of lock: the `Monitor`. However, the `Monitor` class doesn't implement a kernel lock object; rather, it provides access to the sync lock of every .NET object instance. Earlier in this chapter, we also covered the primitive `Interlocked` class methods that you can use to implement spin locks. One reason spin locks are so primitive is that they don't allow you to acquire the same lock multiple times. Other higher-level locking objects typically do allow that, as long as you match the amount of lock operations with release operations. In this section, we'll cover some useful locking objects that the .NET Framework provides.

No matter what type of locking object you use, you always want to strive to write code that keeps the lock for the smallest amount of time possible. For example, if you acquire a lock to access some data within a method that could take quite a bit of time to process that data, acquire the lock only long enough to make a copy of the data on the local stack, and then release the lock as soon as possible. By using this technique, you will ensure that other threads in your system don't block for inordinate amounts of time to access the same data.

ReaderWriterLock

When synchronizing access to shared data between threads, you'll often find yourself in a position where you have several threads reading, or consuming, the data, while only one thread writes, or produces, the data. Obviously, all threads must acquire a lock before they touch the data to prevent the race condition of when one thread writes to the data while another is in the middle of reading it, thus potentially producing garbage for the reader. However, it sure seems inefficient for multiple threads that are merely going to read the data rather than modify it to be locked out from each other. There is no reason why they should all not be able to read the data concurrently.

The ReaderWriterLock solves this inefficiency elegantly. In a nutshell, it allows multiple readers to access the data concurrently, but as soon as one thread needs to write the data, everyone except the writer must get their hands off. ReaderWriterLock manages this feat by using two internal queues. One queue is for waiting readers, and the other is for waiting writers. Figure 13-2 shows a high-level block diagram of what the inside of a ReaderWriterLock looks like. In this scenario, four threads are running in the system, and currently, none of the threads are attempting to access the data in the lock.

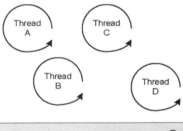

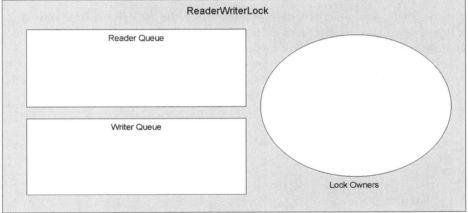

Figure 13-2. *Unutilized ReaderWriterLock*

To access the data, a reader calls AcquireReaderLock(). Given the state of the lock shown in Figure 13-2, the reader will be placed immediately into the Lock Owners category. Notice the use of plural here, since multiple read lock owners can exist. Things get interesting as soon as one of the threads attempts to acquire the write lock by calling AcquireWriterLock(). In this case, the writer is placed into the writer queue because readers currently own the lock, as shown in Figure 13-3.

As soon as all of the readers release their lock via a call to ReleaseReaderLock(), the writer—in this case, Thread B—is allowed to enter the Lock Owners region. But, what happens if Thread A releases its reader lock and then attempts to reacquire the reader lock before the writer has had a chance to acquire the lock? If Thread A were allowed to reacquire the lock, then any thread waiting in the writer queue could potentially be starved of any time with the lock. In order to avoid this, any thread that attempts to require the read lock while a writer is in the queue is placed into the reader queue, as shown in Figure 13-4.

Naturally, this scheme gives preference to the writer queue. That makes sense given the fact that you'd want readers to get the most up-to-date information. Of course, had the thread that needs the writer lock called AcquireWriterLock() while the ReaderWriterLock was in the state shown in Figure 13-2, it would have been placed immediately into the Lock Owners category without having to go through the writer queue.

The ReaderWriterLock is reentrant. Therefore, a thread can call any one of the lock-acquisition methods multiple times, as long as it calls the matching release method the same amount of times. Each time the lock is reacquired, an internal lock count is incremented. It should seem obvious that a single thread cannot own both the reader and the writer lock at the same time, nor can it wait in both queues in the ReaderWriterLock. It is possible, however, for a thread to upgrade or downgrade the type of lock it owns. For example, if a thread currently owns a reader lock and calls UpgradeToWriterLock(), its read lock is released no matter what the lock count is, and then it is placed into the writer queue. The UpgradeToWriterLock() returns an object of type LockCookie. You should hold onto this object and pass it to DowngradeFromWriterLock() when you're done with the write operation. The ReaderWriterLock uses the cookie to restore the reader lock count on the object. Even though you can increase the writer lock count once you've acquired it via UpgrateToWriterLock(), your call to DowngradeFromWriterLock() will release the writer lock no matter what the writer lock count is. Therefore, it's best that you avoid relying on the writer lock count within an upgraded writer lock.

As with just about every other synchronization object in the .NET Framework, you can provide a time-out with almost every lock acquisition method. This time-out is given in milliseconds. However, instead of the methods returning a Boolean to indicate whether the lock was acquired successfully, these methods throw an exception of type ApplicationException if the time-out expires. So if you pass in any time-out value other than Timeout.Infinite to one of these functions, be sure to wrap the call inside of a Try/Catch/Finally block to catch the potential exception.

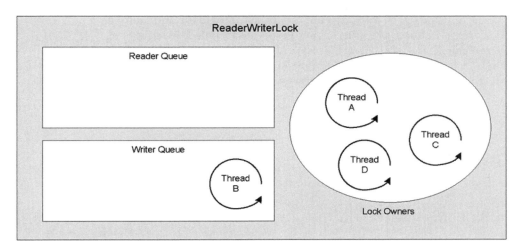

Figure 13-3. *The writer thread is waiting for ReaderWriterLock.*

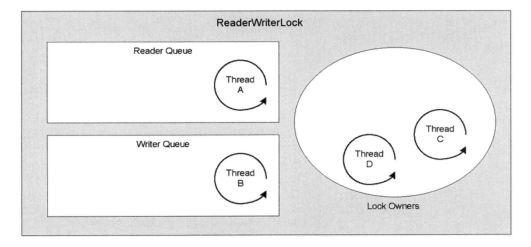

Figure 13-4. *Reader attempting to reacquire lock*

ReaderWriterLockSlim

New to VB and .NET is the System.Threading.ReaderWriterLockSlim class. This class performs 2 to 5 times faster, and will scale better on multi-processor and multi-core computers than the current ReaderWriterLock class. ReaderWriterLockSlim supports upgradeable read-lock support via the TryEnterUpgradeableReadLock method. Only one thread can be in UpgradeableRead mode at a time.

Recursion is disabled by default but may be activated at instantiation via
LockRecursionPolicy.SupportsRecursion. Properties include IsReadLockHeld,
IsUpgradeableReadLockHeld, IsWriteLockHeld, WaitingReadCount, WaitingWriteCount,
and WaitingUpgradeCount. The following example uses ReaderWriterLockSlim to create
two threads, which read and display threadData:

```vb
Imports System
Imports System.Threading

Public Class EntryPoint
    Private Shared threadData As Long = 1
    Private Shared rwl As New ReaderWriterLockSlim

    Shared Sub Main()
        Dim Thread1 As Thread
        Dim Thread2 As Thread

        Thread1 = New Thread(New ThreadStart(AddressOf Thread1Read))
        Thread2 = New Thread(New ThreadStart(AddressOf Thread2Read))
        Thread1.Start()
        Thread2.Start()
    End Sub

    Shared Sub Thread1Read()
        Dim iCounter As Integer

        For iCounter = 1 To 10
            rwl.EnterReadLock()
            Console.WriteLine("Thread 1 reads: " & threadData)
            Thread.Sleep(10)
            rwl.ExitReadLock()
        Next
    End Sub

    Shared Sub Thread2Read()
        Dim iCounter As Integer

        For iCounter = 1 To 10
            rwl.EnterReadLock()
            Console.WriteLine("Thread 2 reads: " & threadData)
            rwl.ExitReadLock()
        Next
    End Sub
End Class
```

Running the preceding code will produce results like the following:

```
Thread 1 reads: 1
Thread 1 reads: 1
Thread 2 reads: 1
Thread 2 reads: 1
Thread 2 reads: 1
Thread 2 reads: 1
Thread 2 reads: 1
Thread 1 reads: 1
Thread 1 reads: 1
Thread 1 reads: 1
```

Mutex

The Mutex object offered by the .NET Framework is one of the heaviest types of lock objects because it carries the most overhead when used to guard a protected resource from multiple threads. This is because you can use the Mutex object to synchronize thread execution across multiple processes.

As is true with other high-level synchronization objects, the Mutex is reentrant. When your thread needs to acquire the exclusive lock, you call the WaitOne method. As usual, you can pass in a time-out value expressed in milliseconds when waiting for the mutex object. The method returns a Boolean that will be True if the wait is successful or False if the time-out expired. A thread can call the WaitOne method as many times as it wants, as long as it matches the calls with the same amount of ReleaseMutex() calls.

Since you can use Mutex objects across multiple processes, each process needs a way to identify the Mutex. Therefore, you can supply an optional name when you create a Mutex instance. Providing a name is the easiest way for another process to identify and open the mutex. Since all Mutex names exist in the global namespace of the entire operating system, it is important to give the Mutex a sufficiently unique name so that it won't collide with Mutex names created by other applications. We recommend using a name that is based on the string form of a GUID generated by GUIDGEN.exe.

■**Note** We mentioned that the names of kernel objects are global to the entire machine. That statement is not entirely true if you consider Windows XP fast user switching and Terminal Services. In those cases, the namespace that contains the name of these kernel objects is instanced for each logged-in user. For times when you really do want your name to exist in the global namespace, you can prefix the name with the special string "\Global".

If everything about the Mutex object sounds familiar to those of you who are native Win32 developers, that's because the underlying mechanism is the Win32 Mutex object. In fact, you can get your hands on the actual OS handle via the SafeWaitHandle property inherited from the WaitHandle base class. The "Win32 Synchronization Objects and WaitHandle" section discusses the pros and cons of the WaitHandle class. Since you implement the Mutex using a kernel Mutex, you incur a transition to kernel mode any time you manipulate or wait upon the Mutex. Such transitions are extremely slow and should be minimized if you're running time-critical code.

■**Tip** Avoid using kernel mode objects for synchronization between threads in the same process if at all possible. Prefer lighter weight mechanisms, such as the Monitor class or the Interlocked class. When effectively synchronizing threads between multiple processes, you have no choice but to use kernel objects. On a current test machine, a simple test showed that using the Mutex took more than 44 times longer than the Interlocked class and 34 times longer than the Monitor class.

Events

In .NET, you can use two types to signal events: ManualResetEvent and AutoResetEvent. As with the Mutex object, these event objects map directly to Win32 event objects. Similar to Mutex objects, working with event objects incurs a slow transition to kernel mode. Both event types become signaled when someone calls the Set method on an event instance. At that point, a thread waiting on the event will be released. Threads wait for an event by calling the inherited WaitHandle.WaitOne method, which is the same method you call to wait on a Mutex to become signaled.

We were careful in stating that a waiting thread is released when the event becomes signaled. It's possible that multiple threads could be released when an event becomes signaled. That, in fact, is the difference between ManualResetEvent and AutoResetEvent. When a ManualResetEvent becomes signaled, all threads waiting on it are released. It stays signaled until someone calls its Reset method. If any thread calls WaitOne() while the ManualResetEvent is already signaled, then the wait is immediately completed successfully. On the other hand, AutoResetEvent objects only release one waiting thread and then immediately reset to the unsignaled set automatically. You can imagine that all threads waiting on the AutoResetEvent are waiting in a queue, where only the first thread in the queue is released when the event becomes signaled. However, even though it's useful to assume that the waiting threads are in a queue, you cannot make any assumptions about which waiting thread will be released first. AutoResetEvents are also known as *sync events* based on this behavior.

Using the AutoResetEvent type, you could implement a crude thread pool where several threads wait on an AutoResetEvent signal to be told that some piece of work is available. When a new piece of work is added to the work queue, the event is signaled to turn one of the waiting threads loose. Implementing a thread pool this way is not efficient and comes with its problems. For example, things become tricky to handle when all threads are busy and work items are pushed into the queue, especially if only one thread is allowed to complete one work item before going back to the waiting queue. If all threads are busy and, say, five work items are queued in the meantime, the event will be signaled but no threads will be waiting. The first thread back into the waiting queue will get released once it calls WaitOne(), but the others will not, even though four more work items exist in the queue. One solution to this problem is to not allow work items to be queued while all of the threads are busy. That's not really a solution because it defers some of the synchronization logic to the thread attempting to queue the work item by forcing it to do something appropriate in reaction to a failed attempt to queue a work item. In reality, creating an efficient thread pool is tricky business. Therefore, you should utilize the ThreadPool class before attempting such a feat. The "Using the Thread Pool" section covers the ThreadPool class in detail.

Since .NET event objects are based on Win32 event objects, you can use them to synchronize execution between multiple processes. Along with the Mutex, they are also more inefficient than an alternative, such as the Monitor class, because of the kernel mode transition involved. However, the creators of ManualResetEvent and AutoResetEvent did not expose the ability to name the event objects in their constructors, as they do for the Mutex object. Therefore, if you need to create a named event, you must call directly through to Win32 using the P/Invoke layer, and then you may create a WaitHandle object to manage the Win32 event object.

Win32 Synchronization Objects and WaitHandle

The previous two sections covered the Mutex, ManualResetEvent, and AutoResetEvent objects. Each one of these types is derived from WaitHandle. WaitHandle is a general mechanism that you can use in .NET to manage any type of Win32 synchronization object that you can wait upon. That includes more than just events and mutexes. No matter how you obtain the Win32 object handle, you can use a WaitHandle object to manage it. We prefer to use the word *manage* rather than *encapsulate* because the WaitHandle class doesn't do a great job of encapsulation, nor was it meant to. It's simply meant as a wrapper to help you avoid a lot of direct calls to Win32 via the P/Invoke layer when dealing with OS handles.

We've already discussed the WaitOne method used to wait for an object to become signaled. However, the WaitHandle class has two handy shared methods that you can use to wait on multiple objects. The first is WaitHandle.WaitAny(). You pass it an array of WaitHandle objects, and when any one of the objects becomes signaled, the WaitAny method returns an integer indexing into the array to the object that became signaled. The other method is WaitHandle.WaitAll, which won't return until all of the objects become signaled. Both of these methods have defined overloads that accept a time-out value. In the case of a call to WaitAny() that times out, the return value will be equal to the WaitHandle.WaitTimeout constant. In the case of a call to WaitAll(), a Boolean is returned, which is either True to indicate that all of the objects became signaled or False to indicate that the wait timed out.

In the previous section, we mentioned that you cannot create named AutoResetEvent or ManualResetEvent objects, even though you can name the underlying Win32 object types. However, you can achieve that exact goal using the P/Invoke layer, as the following example demonstrates:

```
Imports System
Imports System.Threading
Imports System.Runtime.InteropServices
Imports System.ComponentModel
Imports Microsoft.Win32.SafeHandles
```

```
Public Class NamedEventCreator
    <DllImport("KERNEL32.DLL", EntryPoint:="CreateEventW", SetLastError:=True)> _
    Private Shared Function CreateEvent(ByVal lpEventAttributes As IntPtr, _
        ByVal bManualReset As Boolean, ByVal bInitialState As Boolean, _
        ByVal lpName As String) As SafeWaitHandle
    End Function

    Public Const INVALID_HANDLE_VALUE As Integer = -1

    Public Shared Function CreateAutoResetEvent( _
        ByVal initialState As Boolean, _
        ByVal name As String) As AutoResetEvent

        'Create named event.
        Dim rawEvent As SafeWaitHandle = _
            CreateEvent(IntPtr.Zero, False, False, name)

        If rawEvent.IsInvalid Then
            Throw New Win32Exception(Marshal.GetLastWin32Error())
        End If

        'Create a managed event type based on this handle.
        Dim autoEvent As AutoResetEvent = New AutoResetEvent(False)

        'Must clean up handle currently in autoEvent
        'before swapping it with the named one.
        autoEvent.SafeWaitHandle = rawEvent

        Return autoEvent
    End Function
End Class
```

Here the P/Invoke layer calls down into the Win32 CreateEventW function to create a named event. Several things are worth noting in this example. For instance, we've avoided handle security, just as the rest of the .NET Framework standard library classes tend to do. Therefore, the first parameter to CreateEvent() is IntPtr.Zero, which is the best way to pass a Nothing pointer to the Win32 error. Notice that you detect the success or failure of the event creation by testing the IsInvalid property on the SafeWaitHandle. When you detect this value, you throw a Win32Exception type. You then create a new AutoResetEvent to wrap the raw handle just created. WaitHandle exposes a property named SafeWaitHandle, whereby you can modify the underlying Win32 handle of any WaitHandle derived type.

■Note You may have noticed the legacy `Handle` property in the documentation. You should avoid this property, since reassigning it with a new kernel handle won't close the previous handle, thus resulting in a resource leak unless you close it yourself. You should use `SafeHandle`-derived types instead. The `SafeHandle` type also uses constrained execution regions to guard against resource leaks in the event of an asynchronous exception, such as `ThreadAbortException`.

In the previous example, you can see that we declared the `CreateEvent` method to return a `SafeWaitHandle`. Although it's not obvious from the documentation of `SafeWaitHandle`, it has a private default constructor that the P/Invoke layer is capable of using to create and initialize an instance of this class.

Be sure to check out the rest of the `SafeHandle` derived types in the `Microsoft.Win32.SafeHandles` namespace. Specifically, the .NET 2.0 Framework provides `SafeHandleMinusOneIsInvalid` and `SafeHandleZeroOrMinusOneIsInvalid` for convenience when defining your own Win32-based `SafeWaitHandle` derivatives.

Be aware that the `WaitHandle` type implements the `IDisposable` interface. Therefore, you want to make judicious use of the `Using` keyword in your code whenever using `WaitHandle` instances or instances of any classes that derive from it, such as `Mutex`, `AutoResetEvent`, and `ManualResetEvent`.

When using `WaitHandle` objects and those objects that derive from them, you cannot abort or interrupt managed threads in a timely manner when they're blocked via a method to `WaitHandle`. Since the actual OS thread that is running under the managed thread is blocked inside the OS—thus outside of the managed execution environment—it can only be aborted or interrupted as soon as it reenters the managed environment. Therefore, if you call `Abort()` or `Interrupt()` on one of those threads, the operation will be pended until the thread completes the wait at the OS level. You want to be cognizant of this when you block using a `WaitHandle` object in managed threads.

Using the Thread Pool

A thread pool is ideal in a system where small units of work are performed regularly in an asynchronous manner. A good example is a web server listening for requests on a port. When a request comes in, a new thread is given the request and processes it. The server achieves a high level of concurrency and optimal utilization by servicing these requests in multiple threads. Typically, the slowest operation on a computer is an I/O operation. Storage devices, such as hard drives, are slow in comparison to the processor and its ability to access memory. Therefore, to make optimal use of the system, you want to begin other work items while it's waiting on an I/O operation to complete in another thread. The .NET environment exposes a prebuilt, ready-to-use thread pool via the `ThreadPool` class.

Use the shared methods of the ThreadPool class to manage the thread pool that each process gets by default in the CLR. You don't even have to worry about creating the thread pool; it gets created when it is first used. If you have used thread pools in the Win32 world, you'll notice that the .NET thread pool is the same, with a managed interface placed on top of it.

To queue an item to the thread pool, you simply call ThreadPool.QueueUserWorkItem(), passing it an instance of the WaitCallback delegate. The thread pool gets created the first time your process calls this function. The callback method that gets called through the WaitCallback delegate accepts a reference to System.Object. The object reference is an optional context object that the caller can supply to an overload of QueueUserWorkItem(). Once the work item is queued, a thread in the thread pool will execute the callback as soon as it becomes available. Once a work item is queued, it cannot be removed from the queue except by a thread that will complete the work item. So if you need to cancel a work item, you must craft a way to let your callback know that it should do nothing once it gets called.

The thread pool is tuned to keep the machine processing work items in the most efficient manner possible. It uses an algorithm based upon how many CPUs are available in the system to determine how many threads to create in the pool. However, even once it computes how many threads to create, the thread pool may, at times, contain more threads than originally calculated. For example, suppose the algorithm decides that the thread pool should contain four threads. Then, suppose the server receives four requests that access a backend database that takes some time. If a fifth request comes in during this time, no threads will be available to dispatch the work item. What's worse, the four busy threads are just sitting around waiting for the I/O to complete. In order to keep the system running at peak performance, the thread pool will actually create another thread when it knows all of the others are blocking. After the work items have all been completed and the system is at a steady state again, the thread pool will then kill off any extra threads created like this. Even though you cannot easily control how many threads are in a thread pool, you can easily control the minimum amount of threads that are idle in the pool waiting for work via calls to GetMinThreads() and SetMinThreads().

We urge you to read the details of the System.Threading.ThreadPool shared methods in the MSDN documentation if you plan on dealing directly with the thread pool. In reality, it's rare that you'll ever need to directly insert work items into the thread pool. There is another, more elegant entry point into the thread pool via delegates and asynchronous procedure calls, which the next sections cover.

The IOU Pattern

When we discuss asynchronous I/O and thread pools, you'll see that the BeginProcessData()/ EndProcessData() is a common pattern of asynchronous processing used throughout the .NET Framework. The BeginMethod()/EndMethod() pattern of asynchronous programming in the .NET Framework is similar to the "I owe you" (IOU) pattern. In that pattern, a function is called to start the asynchronous operation, and in return, the caller is given an IOU object. Later, the caller can use that object to retrieve the result of the asynchronous operation. The beauty of this pattern is that it completely decouples the caller wanting to get the asynchronous work done from the mechanism used to actually do the work. This pattern is used extensively in the .NET Framework, and we suggest that you employ it for asynchronous method calls, as it will give your clients a familiar look and feel.

Asynchronous Method Calls

Although you can manage the work items put into the thread pool directly via the ThreadPool class, a more popular way to employ the thread pool is via asynchronous delegate calls. When you declare a delegate, the CLR defines a class for you that derives from System.MulticastDelegate. One of the methods defined is the Invoke method, which takes the exact same function signature of the delegate definition. As you cannot explicitly call the Invoke method, VB offers a syntactical shortcut. The CLR defines two methods, BeginInvoke() and EndInvoke(), that are at the heart of the asynchronous processing pattern used throughout the CLR. This pattern is similar to the IOU pattern.

The basic idea is probably evident from the names of the methods. When you call the BeginInvoke method on the delegate, the operation is pended to be completed in another thread. When you call the EndInvoke method, the results of the operation are given back to you. If the operation has not completed at the time when you call EndInvoke(), the calling thread blocks until the operation is complete. Let's look at a short example that shows the general pattern in use. Suppose you have a method that computes your taxes for the year, and you want to call it asynchronously because it could take a reasonably long amount of time to do:

```vb
Imports System
Imports System.Threading

Public Class EntryPoint
    'Declare the delegate for the async call.
    Private Delegate Function ComputeTaxesDelegate( _
        ByVal year As Integer) _
        As Decimal

    'The method that computes the taxes.
    Private Shared Function ComputeTaxes(ByVal year As Integer) _
        As Decimal
        Console.WriteLine("Computing taxes in thread {0}", _
            Thread.CurrentThread.GetHashCode())

        'Here's where the long calculation happens.
        Thread.Sleep(6000)

        'Return the "Amount Owed"
        Return 4356.98D
    End Function

    Shared Sub Main()
        'Let's make the asynchronous call by creating the delegate and
        'calling it.
        Dim work As ComputeTaxesDelegate = _
            New ComputeTaxesDelegate( _
                AddressOf EntryPoint.ComputeTaxes)
```

```
      Dim pendingOp As IAsyncResult = _
          work.BeginInvoke(2004, Nothing, Nothing)

      'Do some other useful work.
      Thread.Sleep(3000)

      'Finish the async call.
      Console.WriteLine("Waiting for operation to complete.")
      Dim result As Decimal = work.EndInvoke(pendingOp)
      Console.WriteLine("Taxes owed: {0}", result)
    End Sub
End Class
```

This code displays results like the following:

```
Computing taxes in thread 3
Waiting for operation to complete.
Taxes owed: 4356.98
```

The first thing you'll notice with the pattern is that the BeginInvoke method's signature does not match that of the Invoke method. That's because you need some way to identify the particular work item that you just pended with the call to BeginInvoke(). Therefore, BeginInvoke() returns a reference to an object that implements the IAsyncResult interface. This object is like a cookie that you can hold on to so that you can identify the work item in progress. Through the methods on the IAsyncResult interface, you can check on the status of the operation, such as whether it is completed. We'll discuss this interface in more detail in a bit, along with the extra two parameters added onto the end of the BeginInvoke method declaration for which we're passing Nothing. When the thread that requested the operation is finally ready for the result, it calls EndInvoke() on the delegate. However, since the method must have a way to identify which asynchronous operation to get the results for, you must pass in the object that you got back from the BeginInvoke method. In the previous example, you'll notice the call to EndInvoke() blocking for some time as the operation completes.

■**Note** If an exception is generated while the delegate's target code is running asynchronously in the thread pool, the exception is re-thrown when the initiating thread makes a call to EndInvoke().

Part of the beauty of the IOU asynchronous pattern that delegates implement is that the called code doesn't even need to be aware of the fact that it's getting called asynchronously. Of course, it's rarely practical that a method may be able to be called asynchronously when it was never designed to be, if it touches data in the system that other methods touch without using any synchronization mechanisms. Nonetheless, the headache of creating an asynchronous calling infrastructure around the method has been mitigated by the delegate generated by the

CLR, along with the per-process thread pool. Moreover, the initiator of the asynchronous action doesn't even need to be aware of how the asynchronous behavior is implemented.

Now let's look a little closer at the IAsyncResult interface for the object returned from the BeginInvoke method. The interface declaration looks like the following:

```
Public Interface IAsyncResult
  ReadOnly Property AsyncState() As Object
  ReadOnly Property AsyncWaitHandle() As WaitHandle
  ReadOnly Property CompletedSynchronously() As Boolean
  ReadOnly Property IsCompleted() As Boolean
End Interface
```

In the previous example, you wait for the computation to finish by calling EndInvoke(). You also could have waited on the WaitHandle returned by the IAsyncResult.AsyncWaitHandle property before calling EndInvoke(). The end result would have been the same. However, the fact that the IAsyncResult interface exposes the WaitHandle allows multiple threads in the system to wait for this one action to complete if they need to.

Two other properties allow you to query whether the operation has completed. The IsCompleted property simply returns a Boolean representing the fact. You could construct a polling loop that checks this flag repeatedly. However, that would be much more inefficient than just waiting on the WaitHandle. Another Boolean property is the CompletedSynchronously property. The asynchronous processing pattern in the .NET Framework provides for the option that the call to BeginInvoke() could actually choose to process the work synchronously rather than asynchronously. The CompletedSynchronously property allows you to determine if this happened. As it is currently implemented, the CLR will never do such a thing when delegates are called asynchronously. However, since it is recommended that you apply this same asynchronous pattern whenever you design a type that can be called asynchronously, the capability was built into the pattern. For example, suppose you have a class where a method to process generalized operations synchronously is supported. If one of those operations simply returns the version number of the class, then you know that operation can be done quickly, and you may choose to perform it synchronously.

Finally, the AsyncState property of IAsyncResult allows you to attach any type of specific context data to an asynchronous call. This is the last of the extra two parameters added at the end of the BeginInvoke() signature. In the previous example, you passed in Nothing because you didn't need to use it. Although you chose to harvest the result of the operation via a call to EndInvoke(), you could have chosen to be notified via a callback. Consider the following modifications to the previous example:

```
Imports System
Imports System.Threading

Public Class EntryPoint
    'Declare the delegate for the async call.
    Private Delegate Function ComputeTaxesDelegate( _
        ByVal year As Integer) _
        As Decimal
```

```vbnet
'The method that computes the taxes.
Private Shared Function ComputeTaxes(ByVal year As Integer) _
    As Decimal
    Console.WriteLine("Computing taxes in thread {0}", _
        Thread.CurrentThread.GetHashCode())

    'Here's where the long calculation happens.
    Thread.Sleep(6000)

    'Return the "Amount Owed"
    Return 4356.98D
End Function

Private Shared Sub TaxesComputed(ByVal ar As IAsyncResult)
    'Let's get the results now.
    Dim work As ComputeTaxesDelegate = _
        CType(ar.AsyncState, ComputeTaxesDelegate)

    Dim result As Decimal = work.EndInvoke(ar)
    Console.WriteLine("Taxes owed: {0}", result)
End Sub

Shared Sub Main()
    'Let's make the asynchronous call by creating the delegate and
    'calling it.
    Dim work As ComputeTaxesDelegate = _
        New ComputeTaxesDelegate( _
            AddressOf EntryPoint.ComputeTaxes)

    work.BeginInvoke(2004, _
        New AsyncCallback(AddressOf EntryPoint.TaxesComputed), _
            work)

    'Do some other useful work.
    Thread.Sleep(3000)

    'Finish the async call.
    Console.WriteLine("Waiting for operation to complete.")
    Thread.Sleep(4000)
End Sub
End Class
```

Now, instead of calling EndInvoke() from the thread that called BeginInvoke(), you request that the thread pool call the TaxesComputed method via an instance of the AsyncCallback delegate that you passed in as the second-to-last parameter of BeginInvoke(). Using a callback to process the result completes the asynchronous processing pattern by allowing the thread that started the operation to continue to work without having to ever explicitly wait on the worker thread. Notice that the TaxesComputed callback method must still call EndInvoke() to harvest the results of the asynchronous call. In order to do that, though, it must have an instance of the delegate. That's where the `IAsyncResult.AsyncState` context object comes in handy. In the example, you initialize it to point to the delegate by passing the delegate as the last parameter to `BeginInvoke()`. The main thread that calls `BeginInvoke()` has no need for the object returned by the call because it never actively polls the state of the operation, nor does it wait explicitly for the operation to complete. The added `Sleep()` at the end of the `Main` method is there for the sake of the example. Remember, all threads in the thread pool run as background threads. Therefore, if you don't wait at this point, the process would exit long before the operation completes. If you need asynchronous work to occur in a foreground thread, it is best to create a new class that implements the asynchronous pattern of `BeginInvoke()`/`EndInvoke()` and use a foreground thread to do the work. If you try to change the background status of a thread in the thread pool via the `IsBackground` property on the current thread, you'll find that it has no effect.

■**Note** It's important to realize that when your asynchronous code is executing and when the callback is executing, you are running in an arbitrary thread context. You cannot make any assumptions about which thread is running your code.

Timers

Yet another entry point into the thread pool is via `Timer` objects in the `System.Threading` namespace. As the name implies, you can arrange for the thread pool to call a delegate at a specific time as well as at regular intervals. Let's look at an example of how to use the `Timer` object:

```vb
Imports Microsoft.VisualBasic
Imports System
Imports System.Threading

Public Class EntryPoint
    Private Shared Sub TimerProc(ByVal state As Object)
        Console.WriteLine("The current time is {0} on thread {1}", _
            DateTime.Now, Thread.CurrentThread.GetHashCode())

        Thread.Sleep(3000)
    End Sub

    Shared Sub Main()
        Console.WriteLine("Press <enter> when finished" & _
            Constants.vbCrLf)

        Dim myTimer As Timer = _
            New Timer(New TimerCallback( _
                AddressOf EntryPoint.TimerProc), _
                Nothing, 0, 2000)
```

```
        Console.ReadLine()
        myTimer.Dispose()
    End Sub
End Class
```

When the timer is created, you must give it a delegate to call at the required time. Therefore, you create a `TimerCallback` delegate that points back to the `Shared TimerProc` method. The second parameter to the `Timer` constructor is an arbitrary state object that you can pass in. When your timer callback gets called, this state object is passed to the timer callback. In the example, you have no need for a state object, so you simply pass `Nothing`. The last two parameters to the constructor define when the callback gets called. The second-to-last parameter indicates when the timer should fire for the first time. In the example, you pass 0, which indicates that it should fire immediately. The last parameter is the period at which the callback should be called: two seconds. If you don't want the timer to be called periodically, pass `Timeout.Infinite` as the last parameter. Finally, to shut down the timer, simply call its `Dispose` method.

Any code that executes as a result of your `TimerCallback` delegate must be thread-safe. In the example, the first thread in the thread pool to call `TimerProc()` sleeps longer than the next time-out, so the thread pool calls the `TimerProc` method two seconds later on another thread, as you can see in the generated output.

Summary

In this chapter, we covered the intricacies of managed threads in .NET. We covered the various mechanisms in place for managing synchronization between threads, including the `Interlocked`, `Monitor`, `AutoResetEvent`, `ManualResetEvent`, and `WaitHandle`-based objects. We then described the IOU pattern and how .NET uses it extensively to get work done asynchronously. That discussion centered on the CLR's usage of the `ThreadPool` based upon the Windows thread pool implementation.

Threading adds complexity to applications. However, when used properly, it can make applications more responsive to user commands and more efficient. Although multithreading development comes with its pitfalls, .NET and the CLR mitigate many of those risks and provide a model that shields you from the intricacies of the operating system—most of the time. Not only does .NET provide a nice buffer between your code and the Windows thread pool intricacies, but it also allows your code to run on other platforms that implement .NET. If you understand the details of the threading facilities provided by the CLR, and with the synchronization techniques covered in this chapter, then you're well on your way to producing effective multithreaded applications.

In the next chapter, we'll go in search of VB canonical forms for types and investigate the checklist of questions you should ask yourself when designing any type using VB.

CHAPTER 14

■ ■ ■

VB 2008 Best Practices

Many object-oriented languages—VB included—do not offer anything to force developers to create well-designed software. In much the same way that design patterns evolved, the development community has identified best practices useful for designing types to meet a specific purpose. We will present these practices as a set of checklists, or recipes, that you can use while designing new classes. Before a pilot can clear an airplane to back out of the gate, he must go through a strict checklist. The goal of this chapter is to identify such checklists for creating robust types in the VB world.

Overall, this chapter is sectioned into two partitions. The first partition covers reference types, while the latter covers value types. We cover the longer partition on reference types first, since some material applies to both reference types and value types. Finally, each partition concludes with a checklist to be used as a guide when designing new types.

Reference-Type Best Practices

When creating reference types, you should consider what behaviors will be required of the new type you're creating. You should ask yourself several questions before you create a new type. For example, will you allow your class to be derived from? Is your new type going to be cloneable? Does your object need a finalizer? What does it mean to compare two references of this object's type for equality? Does your new type support ordering if instances of it are placed in a collection?

Default to NotInheritable Classes

When you create a new class, automatically mark that class NotInheritable and only remove the NotInheritable keyword if your design requires the ability to derive from your class. Why not go the other way around and make the class inheritable by default and NotInheritable when you know someone should not derive from it? The main reason is because it's impossible to predict how your class will be used if you don't put in specific design measures to support inheritance. For example, classes that have no Overridable methods are not normally intended to be derived from. The lack of Overridable methods may indicate that the author didn't consider whether anyone would want to inherit from the type and probably should have marked the class NotInheritable. If your class is not NotInheritable, and you intend to allow others to inherit from it, be sure to include adequate documentation for the person deriving from your class.

Even classes that do have `Overridable` methods and are meant to be derived from can be problematic. For example, if you derive from a class that provides an `Overridable` method `DoSomething()`, and you'd like to extend that method by overriding it, do you call the base class version in your override? If so, do you call it before or after you get your derived work done? Does the ordering matter? Without good documentation for the class you're deriving from, it may be difficult to answer these questions. In fact, this is one reason why extension through containment is generally more flexible, and thus more powerful, at design time than extension through inheritance. Extension through containment is dynamic and performed at run time, whereas inheritance-based extension is more restrictive. Better yet, you can do containment-based extension even if the class you want to extend is marked `NotInheritable`.

Unless you can come up with a good reason why your class should serve as a base class, mark your class `NotInheritable`. Otherwise, be prepared to offer detailed documentation on how to best derive from your class. Since you can produce a different design to do the same job using interface inheritance together with containment, rather than implementation (class) inheritance, there's almost no reason why the classes you design should not be marked `NotInheritable`. Don't misunderstand: we're not saying that all inheritance is bad. On the contrary, it is useful when used properly. However, if you're implementing a deep hierarchy tree, as opposed to a shallow, flat one, this is a common sign that you should rethink the design.

Use the NVI Pattern

Many times, when you design a class specifically capable of acting as a base class in a hierarchy, you often declare methods that are `Overridable` so that deriving classes can modify the behavior. A first pass at such a base class may look something like the following:

```vb
Imports System

Public Class Base
    Public Overridable Sub DoWork()
        Console.WriteLine("Base.DoWork()")
    End Sub
End Class

Public Class Derived
    Inherits Base

    Public Overrides Sub DoWork()
        Console.WriteLine("Derived.DoWork()")
    End Sub
End Class

Public Class EntryPoint
    Shared Sub Main()
        Dim b As Base = New Derived()

        b.DoWork()
    End Sub
End Class
```

Not surprisingly, the output from the previous example looks like this:

```
Derived.DoWork()
```

However, the design could be subtly more robust. Imagine that you're the writer of Base and have deployed Base to many users. People are happily using Base all over the world when you decide that you should do some pre- and post-processing within DoWork(). For example, suppose you'd like to provide a debug version of Base that tracks how many times the DoWork method is called. As written previously, you cannot do such a thing without forcing breaking changes onto the many users who have used Base. For example, you could introduce two more methods, named PreDoWork() and PostDoWork(), and ask kindly that your users re-implement their overrides so that they call these methods at the correct time. Ouch! Now, let's consider a minor modification to the original design that doesn't change the public interface of Base:

```
Imports System

Public Class Base
    Public Sub DoWork()
        CoreDoWork()
    End Sub

    Protected Overridable Sub CoreDoWork()
        Console.WriteLine("Base.DoWork()")
    End Sub
End Class

Public Class Derived
    Inherits Base

    Protected Overrides Sub CoreDoWork()
        Console.WriteLine("Derived.DoWork()")
    End Sub
End Class

Public Class EntryPoint
    Shared Sub Main()
        Dim b As Base = New Derived()

        b.DoWork()
    End Sub
End Class
```

This example displays the following output, as expected:

```
Derived.DoWork()
```

This pattern is called the Non-Virtual Interface (NVI) pattern, and it does exactly that: it makes the public interface to the base class member non-overridable, but the overridable behavior is moved into another protected method named CoreDoWork(). The .NET Framework libraries use the NVI pattern widely, and it's circulated in library design guidelines at Microsoft for good reason. In order to add some metering to the DoWork method, you only need to modify Base and the assembly that contains it. Any other classes that derive from Base don't need to change.

Is the Object Cloneable?

Reference-type objects in VB and in the common language runtime (CLR) live on the heap and are accessed through references. You're not actually making a copy of the object when you assign one object variable to another, as in the following code:

```
Dim obj As Object = New Object()
Dim objCopy As Object = obj
```

After this code executes, objCopy doesn't refer to a copy of obj; rather, you now have two references to the same Object instance.

However, sometimes it makes sense to be able to make a copy of an object. For that purpose, the .NET standard library defines the ICloneable interface. When you implement ICloneable, your object supports the ability to have copies of it made. In other words, you can use it as a prototype to create new instances of objects. Objects of this type can participate in a prototype factory design pattern.

Let's have a quick look at the ICloneable interface:

```
Public Interface ICloneable
    Function Clone() As Object
End Interface
```

As you can see, the interface only defines one method, Clone, that returns an object reference. That object reference is intended to be a member-wise copy. All you have to do is return a copy of the object and you're done, right? Well, not so fast.

There's a not-so-subtle problem with the definition of this interface. The documentation for the interface doesn't indicate whether the copy returned should be a "deep copy" or a "shallow copy." In fact, the documentation leaves it open for the class designer to decide. The difference between a shallow copy and a deep copy is only relevant if the object contains references to other objects. A shallow copy of an object creates a copy of the object whose contained object references refer to the same objects as the prototype's references. A deep copy, on the other hand, creates a copy of the prototype where all of the contained objects are copied as well. In a deep copy, the object containment tree is traversed all the way down to the bottom, and copies of each of those objects are made. Therefore, the result of a deep copy shares no underlying objects with the prototype.

In order for an object to effectively implement a clone or deep copy of itself, all of its contained objects must implement a deep copy mechanism. The problem that comes with this requirement is that you cannot guarantee a deep copy if your object contains references to objects that cannot be deep-copied. This is precisely why the documentation for the ICloneable interface suffers from the lack of specification of copy semantics. More importantly, this lack of specification forces you to clearly document the ICloneable implementation on any object that implements it so that consumers will know if the object supports a shallow or deep copy.

Let's consider options for implementing the ICloneable interface on objects. If your object contains only value types, such as Integer, Long, or values based on structure definitions where the structures contain no reference types, then you can use a shortcut to implement the Clone method by using Object.MemberwiseClone(), as in the following code:

```
Imports System

Public NotInheritable Class Dimensions
    Implements ICloneable

    Private width As Long
    Private height As Long

    Public Sub New(ByVal width As Long, ByVal height As Long)
        Me.width = width
        Me.height = height
    End Sub

    'ICloneable implementation
    Public Function Clone() As Object Implements ICloneable.Clone
        Return Me.MemberwiseClone()
    End Function
End Class
```

MemberwiseClone() is a protected method implemented on System.Object that an object can use to create a shallow copy of itself. However, MemberwiseClone() creates a copy of the object without calling any constructors on the new object. It's an object-creation shortcut. If your object relies upon the constructor getting called during creation—for example, if you send debug traces to the console during object construction—then MemberwiseClone() is not for you. If you use MemberwiseClone(), and your object requires work to be done during the constructor call, then you must factor that work out into a separate method. You can call that method from the constructor, and in your Clone method you can call that worker method on the new object after calling MemberwiseClone() to create the new instance. Although doable, it's a tedious approach. An alternative way to implement the clone is to make use of a Private copy constructor, as in the following code:

```
Imports System

Public NotInheritable Class Dimensions
    Implements ICloneable

    Private width As Long
    Private height As Long

    Public Sub New(ByVal width As Long, ByVal height As Long)
        Console.WriteLine("Dimensions(long, long) called")
```

```vb
        Me.width = width
        Me.height = height
    End Sub

    'Private copy constructor used when making a copy of this object.
    Private Sub New(ByVal other As Dimensions)
        Console.WriteLine("Dimensions(Dimensions) called")

        Me.width = other.width
        Me.height = other.height
    End Sub

    'ICloneable implementation
    Public Function Clone() As Object Implements ICloneable.Clone
        Return New Dimensions(Me)
    End Function
End Class
```

This method of cloning an object is the safest in the sense that you have full control over how the copy is made. Any changes that need to be done regarding the way the object is copied can be made in the copy constructor. Any time you declare a constructor in a class, the compiler will no longer emit the default constructor that it normally does when you don't provide a constructor. If this private copy constructor listed previously was the only constructor defined in the class, users of the class would never be able to create instances of it. That's because the default constructor is now gone, and no other publicly accessible constructor would exist. In this case, you have nothing to worry about, since you also defined a public constructor that takes two parameters.

Now, let's also consider objects that, themselves, contain references to other objects. Suppose you have an employee database, and you represent each employee with an object of type Employee. This Employee type contains vital information, such as the employee's name, title, and ID number. The name and possibly the formatted ID number are represented by strings, which are themselves reference type objects. For the sake of example, let's implement the employee title as a separate class named Title. If you follow the guideline created previously where you always do a deep copy on a clone, then you would implement the following clone method:

```vb
Imports System

'Title class
Public NotInheritable Class Title
    Implements ICloneable

    Private mTitle As TitleNameEnum
    Private minPay As Double
    Private maxPay As Double

    Public Enum TitleNameEnum
        GreenHorn
        HotshotGuru
    End Enum
```

```vb
    Public Sub New(ByVal title As TitleNameEnum)
        Me.mTitle = title

        LookupPayScale()
    End Sub

    Private Sub New(ByVal other As Title)
        Me.mTitle = other.mTitle

        LookupPayScale()
    End Sub

    'ICloneable implementation
    Public Function Clone() As Object Implements ICloneable.Clone
        Return New Title(Me)
    End Function

    Private Sub LookupPayScale()
        'Looks up pay scale in a database. Payscale is based upon the title.
    End Sub
End Class

'Employee class
Public NotInheritable Class Employee
    Implements ICloneable

    Private name As String
    Private title As Title
    Private ssn As String

    Public Sub New(ByVal name As String, ByVal title As Title, ByVal ssn As String)
        Me.name = name
        Me.title = title
        Me.ssn = ssn
    End Sub

    Private Sub New(ByVal other As Employee)
        Me.name = String.Copy(other.name)
        Me.title = CType(other.title.Clone(), Title)
        Me.ssn = String.Copy(other.ssn)
    End Sub

    'ICloneable implementation
    Public Function Clone() As Object Implements ICloneable.Clone
        Return New Employee(Me)
    End Function
End Class
```

You cannot copy the Title object with MemberwiseClone() because a side effect of the constructor is to call LookupPayScale() on the new object to retrieve the pay scale for the title from the database. Let's assume it's possible that the pay scale for the position can change between the prototype's creation and the clone operation, so you always want to look that up in the database. Also, note that copies of the contained objects are made using their respective ICloneable methods. For the Title object, you merely call its implementation of Clone(). It turns out that System.String implements ICloneable. However, you cannot use the Clone method to create a deep copy of Employee. If you read the fine print on the String.Clone() implementation, you'll see that it just returns a reference to itself. This is a perfect example of the inconsistencies you'll see in Clone() implementations. Instead, you have to use the shared String.Copy method in order to get a real copy of the source string.

The fact that System.String returns a reference to itself when its ICloneable.Clone method is called is an optimization that its implementers introduced. Even though the implementation bars you from making a true deep clone of any object that contains string object references, the optimization is valid for two reasons. First, the documentation doesn't specify whether you need to implement a deep or shallow clone. Second, System.String is an immutable object. Immutability in objects is a powerful concept that we cover in the upcoming section, "Prefer Type Safety at All Times." The general idea is that once you create a string object, you can never change it for as long as it lives. Therefore, it becomes an efficiency burden to implement String.Clone() so that it always performs a deep copy. Clients of System.String() work the same way, whether String.Clone() performs a deep or shallow copy, because of its immutability.

In efforts to make the ICloneable implementation document itself, you can use a custom attribute to mark the Clone method. This way, consumers of your object can determine at design time or at run time whether your object supports a deep clone or a shallow clone. Consider the following custom attribute:

```
Imports System

Namespace CloneHelpers
    Public Enum CloneStyle
        Deep
        Shallow
    End Enum

    <AttributeUsageAttribute(AttributeTargets.Method)> _
    Public NotInheritable Class CloneStyleAttribute
        Inherits Attribute

        Private mClonestyle As CloneStyle

        Public Sub New(ByVal aClonestyle As CloneStyle)
            Me.mClonestyle = aClonestyle
        End Sub
```

```
    Public ReadOnly Property Style() As CloneStyle
        Get
            Return mClonestyle
        End Get
    End Property
    End Class
End Namespace
```

Using this attribute, you can tag your clone implementations such that they are explicit about what type of clone operation they perform. The attribute is only a marker and doesn't enforce anything at run time, but that's not to say you cannot create some other type that enforces a policy at run time based on attached custom attributes. Let's revisit the Dimensions class and apply this attribute:

■Note To compile this example, you may need to add a reference in your project to CloneHelpers.

```
Imports System

Namespace CloneHelpers
    Public Enum CloneStyle
        Deep
        Shallow
    End Enum

    <AttributeUsageAttribute(AttributeTargets.Method)> _
    Public NotInheritable Class CloneStyleAttribute
        Inherits Attribute

        Private mClonestyle As CloneStyle

        Public Sub New(ByVal aClonestyle As CloneStyle)
            Me.mClonestyle = aClonestyle
        End Sub

        Public ReadOnly Property Style() As CloneStyle
            Get
                Return mClonestyle
            End Get
        End Property
    End Class
End Namespace
```

```
Public NotInheritable Class Dimensions
    Implements ICloneable

    Private width As Long
    Private height As Long

    Public Sub New(ByVal width As Long, ByVal height As Long)
        Me.width = width
        Me.height = height
    End Sub

    'ICloneable implementation
    <CloneStyleAttribute(CloneStyle.Deep)> _
    Public Function Clone() As Object Implements ICloneable.Clone
        Return Me.MemberwiseClone()
    End Function
End Class
```

In the preceding example, there is no question as to how the Clone method is implemented, and consumers of this object will be well informed.

Is the Object Formattable?

When you create a new object, it inherits a method from System.Object called ToString(). This method accepts no parameters and simply returns a string representation of the object. In all cases, if it makes sense to call ToString() on your object, you'll need to override this method. The default implementation provided by System.Object merely returns a string representation of the object's type name, which of course is not useful for an object requiring a string representation based upon its internal state. You should consider overriding Object. ToString() for all of your types, even if only for the convenience of logging the object state to a debug output log.

Object.ToString() is useful for getting a quick string representation of an object; however, it's sometimes not useful enough. For example, consider the previous ComplexNumber example. Suppose you want to provide a ToString() override for that class. An obvious implementation would output the complex number as an ordered pair within a pair of parentheses, such as "(1, 2)" for example. However, the real and imaginary components of ComplexNumber are of type Double. Also, floating-point numbers don't always appear the same across all cultures. Americans use a period to separate the fractional element of a floating-point number, whereas most Europeans use a comma. This problem is solved easily if you utilize the default culture information attached to the thread. By accessing the My.Application.Culture property, you can get references to the default cultural information detailing how to represent numerical values, including monetary amounts, as well as information on how to represent time and date values.[1]

By default, the Culture property gives you access to System.Globalization. DateTimeFormatInfo and System.Globalization.NumberFormatInfo. Using the information provided by these objects, you can output the ComplexNumber in a form that is appropriate for

---

1. Chapter 9 covers globalization and cultural information in greater detail.

the default culture of the machine the application is running on. Check out Chapter 9 for an example of how this works.

That solution seems easy enough. However, there are times when using the default culture is not sufficient, and a user of your objects may need to specify which culture to use. Not only that, the user may want to specify the exact formatting of the output. For example, a user may prefer to say that the real and imaginary portions of a ComplexNumber instance should be displayed with only five significant digits while using the German cultural information. If you develop software for servers, you need this capability. A company that runs a financial services server in the United States and services requests from Japan will want to display Japanese currency in the format customary for the Japanese culture. You need to specify how to format an object when it is converted to a string via ToString() without having to change the CurrentCulture on the thread beforehand.

In fact, the standard library provides an interface for doing just that. When a class or structure needs the capability to respond to such requests, it implements the IFormattable interface. The following code shows the IFormattable interface, which looks simple but, depending on the complexity of your object, may be tricky to implement:

```
Public Interface IFormattable
    Function ToString(ByVal format As String, _
        ByVal formatProvider As IFormatProvider) As String
End Interface
```

Let's consider the second parameter first. If the client passes Nothing for formatProvider, you should default to using the culture information attached to the current thread as previously described. However, if formatProvider is not Nothing, you'll need to acquire the formatting information from the provider via the IFormatProvider.GetFormat method. IFormatProvider looks like this:

```
Public Interface IFormatProvider
    Function GetFormat(ByVal formatType As Type) As Object
End Interface
```

In an effort to be as generic as possible, GetFormat() is designed to accept an object of type System.Type. Thus it is extensible as to what types the object that implements IFormatProvider may support. This flexibility is handy if you intend to develop custom format providers that need to return as-of-yet-undefined formatting information.

The standard library provides a System.Globalization.CultureInfo type that will most likely suffice for all of your needs. The CultureInfo object implements the IFormatProvider interface, and you can pass instances of it as the second parameter to IFormattable. ToString(). Soon, you'll see an example of its usage when you make modifications to the ComplexNumber example, but first, let's look at the first parameter to ToString().

The format parameter of ToString() allows you to specify how to format a specific number. The format provider can describe how to display a date or how to display currency based upon cultural preferences, but you still need to know how to format the object in the first place. In a nutshell, the format string consists of a single letter specifying the format, and then an optional number between 0 and 99 that declares the precision. For example, you can specify that a double be output as a floating-point number of five significant digits with F5. Not all types are required to support all formats except for one—the G format—which stands for "general." In fact, the G format is what you get when you call the parameterless Object.ToString() on most objects in the standard library. Some types will ignore the format specification in special circumstances.

For example, a System.Double can contain special values that represent NaN (Not a Number), PositiveInfinity, or NegativeInfinity. In such cases, System.Double ignores the format specification and displays a symbol appropriate for the culture as provided by NumberFormatInfo.

The format specifier may also consist of a custom format string. Custom format strings allow the user to specify the exact layout of numbers as well as mixed-in string literals. The client can specify one format for negative numbers, another for positive numbers, and a third for zero values. Implementing IFormattable.ToString() can be quite a tedious experience, especially since your format string could be highly customized. However, in many cases—and the ComplexNumber example is one of those cases—you can rely upon the IFormattable implementations of standard types. Since ComplexNumber uses System.Double to represent its real and imaginary parts, you can defer most of your work to the implementation of IFormattable on System.Double. Assume that the ComplexNumber type will accept a format string exactly the same way that System.Double does, and that each component of the complex number will be output using this same format. Let's look at modifications to the ComplexNumber example to support IFormattable:

```vb
Imports System
Imports System.Globalization

Public NotInheritable Class ComplexNumber
    Implements IFormattable

    Private ReadOnly real As Double
    Private ReadOnly imaginary As Double

    'Other methods removed for clarity.

    Public Sub New(ByVal real As Double, ByVal imaginary As Double)
        Me.real = real
        Me.imaginary = imaginary
    End Sub

    Public Overrides Function ToString() As String
        Return ToString("G", Nothing)
    End Function

    'IFormattable implementation
    Public Overloads Function ToString(ByVal format As String, _
        ByVal formatProvider As IFormatProvider) As String _
        Implements IFormattable.ToString

        Dim result As String = "(" & real.ToString(format, formatProvider) & _
            " " & real.ToString(format, formatProvider) & ")"

        Return result
    End Function
End Class
```

```
Public NotInheritable Class EntryPoint
    Shared Sub Main()
        Dim num1 As ComplexNumber = New ComplexNumber(1.12345678, 2.12345678)

        Console.WriteLine("US format: {0}", num1.ToString("F5", _
            New CultureInfo("en-US")))
        Console.WriteLine("DE format: {0}", num1.ToString("F5", _
            New CultureInfo("de-DE")))
        Console.WriteLine("Object.ToString(): {0}", num1.ToString())
    End Sub
End Class
```

Here's the output from running the previous example:

```
US format: (1.12346 1.12346)
DE format: (1,12346 1,12346)
Object.ToString(): (1.12345678 1.12345678)
```

In `Main()`, notice the creation and use of two different `CultureInfo` instances. First, the `ComplexNumber` is output using American cultural formatting, and second, using German cultural formatting. In both cases, you output the string using only five significant digits, and `System.Double`'s implementation of `IFormattable.ToString()` even rounds the result as expected. Finally, the `Object.ToString()` override is implemented to defer to the `IFormattable.ToString` method using the G (general) format.

`IFormattable` provides the clients of your objects with powerful capabilities when they have specific formatting needs for your objects. However, that power comes at an implementation cost. Implementing `IFormattable.ToString()` can be a very detail-oriented task that takes a lot of time and attentiveness.

Is the Object Convertible?

VB provides support for converting instances of simple built-in value types, such as `Integer` and `Long`, from one type to another. But what do you do when you want to perform a nontrivial conversion that you cannot accomplish with casting? The .NET Framework provides several ways to get the job done. For these types of conversions, you should rely upon the `System.Convert` class. The list of functions `Convert` implements is quite long and can be found in the Microsoft Developer Network (MSDN) library. The `Convert` class contains methods to convert from just about any built-in type to another as long as it makes sense. So if you want to convert a `Double` to a `String`, you would simply call the `ToString` shared method, passing it the `Double` as follows:

```
Shared Sub Main()
    Dim d As Double = 12.1
    Dim str As String = Convert.ToString(d)
End Sub
```

In similar form to `IFormattable.ToString()`, `Convert.ToString()` has various overloads that also allow you to pass a `CultureInfo` object or any other object that supports `IFormatProvider`, in order to specify cultural information when doing the conversion. You can use other methods as well, such as ToBoolean() and ToUint32(). The general pattern of the method names is obviously ToXXX(), where XXX is the type you're converting to. System.Convert also has methods to convert byte arrays to and from base64-encoded strings. You'll find these methods handy if you store any binary data in XML text or other text-based medium.

Convert generally serves most of your conversion needs between built-in types. It's a one-stop shop for converting an object of one type to another. You can see this just by looking at the wealth of methods that it supports. However, what happens when your conversion involves a custom type that Convert doesn't know about? The answer lies in the Convert.ChangeType method.

ChangeType() is System.Convert's extensibility mechanism. It has several overloads, including some that take a format provider for cultural information. The general idea is that it takes an object reference and converts it to the type represented by the passed-in System.Type object. Consider the following code that uses the ComplexNumber from previous examples and tries to convert it into a string using System.Convert.ChangeType():

```
Imports System

Public NotInheritable Class ComplexNumber
    Public Sub New(ByVal real As Double, ByVal imaginary As Double)
        Me.real = real
        Me.imaginary = imaginary
    End Sub

    ' Other methods removed for clarity.

    Private ReadOnly real As Double
    Private ReadOnly imaginary As Double
End Class

Public NotInheritable Class EntryPoint
    Shared Sub Main()
        Dim num1 As ComplexNumber = New ComplexNumber(1.12345678, 2.12345678)

        Dim str As String = CStr(Convert.ChangeType(num1, GetType(String)))
    End Sub
End Class
```

You'll find that the code compiles just fine. However, you'll get a surprise at run time when it throws an InvalidCastException with the message, "Object must implement IConvertible." Even though ChangeType() is System.Convert's extensibility mechanism, extensibility doesn't come for free. You must expend some effort to make ChangeType() work with ComplexNumber. And, as you probably guessed, the work required is to implement the IConvertible interface. IConvertible has one method for converting to each of the built-in types, and it uses a catch-all method, IConvertible.ToType(), to convert one custom type to another custom type. Also, the IConvertible methods accept a format provider so that you can pass cultural information to the conversion method.

When you implement an interface, you're required to provide implementations for all of the interface's methods. However, if a particular conversion makes no sense for your object, then you can throw an `InvalidCastException`. Naturally, your implementation will most definitely throw an exception inside `IConvertible.ToType()` for any generic type that it doesn't support conversion to.

To sum up, it may appear that there are many ways to convert one type to another in VB, and in fact, there are. However, the general rule of thumb is to rely on `System.Convert` when casting won't do the trick. Moreover, your custom objects, such as the `ComplexNumber` class, should implement `IConvertible` so they can work in concert with the `System.Convert` class.

■**Note** VB offers conversion operators that allow you to do essentially the same thing you can do by implementing `IConvertible`. However, VB implicit and explicit conversion operators aren't Common Language Specification (CLS)–compliant. Therefore, not every language that consumes your VB code may call them to do the conversion. It is recommended that you not rely on them exclusively to handle conversion. Of course, if you code your project using .NET languages that do support conversion operators, then you can use them exclusively, but it's recommended that you also support `IConvertible`.

.NET offers yet another type of conversion mechanism, which works via the `System.ComponentModel.TypeConverter`. It is another converter that is external to the class of the object instance that needs to be converted. The advantage of using `TypeConverter` is that you can use it at design time within the Integrated Development Environment (IDE) as well as at run time. You create your own special `TypeConverter` for your class that derives from `TypeConverter`, then you associate your new type converter to your class via the `TypeConverterAttribute`. At design time, the IDE can examine the metadata for your type and, from the information gleaned from the metadata, create an instance of your type's converter. That way, it can convert your type to and from representations that it sees fit to use.[2]

Does the Object Support Ordering?

When you design a class for objects to be stored within a collection, and that collection needs to be sorted, you need a well-defined mechanism for comparing two objects. The pattern that the standard library designers provided hinges on implementing the `IComparable` interface:[3]

```
Public Interface IComparable
    Function CompareTo(ByVal obj As Object) As Integer
End Interface
```

`IComparable` contains one method, `CompareTo`. The `CompareTo` method is fairly straightforward. It returns a value that is either positive, negative, or zero. Table 14-1 lists the return value meanings.

---

2. Review the "Generalized Type Conversion" topic in MSDN for more on `TypeConverter`.

3. For value types, consider using the generic `IComparable(Of T)` interface as shown in Chapter 12.

Table 14-1. *Meaning of Return Values of* IComparable.CompareTo()

CompareTo() Return Value	Meaning
Positive	Me > obj
Zero	Me = obj
Negative	Me < obj

You should be aware of a few points when implementing IComparable.CompareTo(). First, the return value specification says nothing about the actual value of the returned integer; it only defines the sign of the return values. To indicate a situation where Me is less than obj, you can simply return -1. When your object represents a value that carries an integer meaning, an efficient way to compute the comparison value is by subtracting one from the other. While it may be tempting to treat the return value as an indication of the degree of inequality, we don't recommend it, since relying on such an implementation is outside the bounds of the IComparable specification, and not all objects can be expected to do that.

Second, CompareTo() provides no return value definition for two objects that cannot be compared. Since the parameter type to CompareTo() is System.Object, you could easily attempt to compare an Apple instance to an Orange instance. In such a case, there is no comparison, and you're forced to indicate such by throwing an ArgumentException object.

Finally, semantically, the IComparable interface is a superset of Object.Equals(). If you derive from an object that overrides Equals() and implements IComparable, then you're wise to override both Equals() and re-implement IComparable in your derived class, or do neither. You want to make certain that your implementation of Equals() and CompareTo() are aligned with each other.

Based upon all of this information, a compliant IComparable interface should adhere to the following rules:

- x.CompareTo(x) *must return* 0: This is the reflexive property.

- *If* x.CompareTo(y) = 0, *then* y.CompareTo(x) *must equal* 0: This is the symmetric property.

- *If* x.CompareTo(y) = 0, *and* y.CompareTo(z) = 0, *then* x.CompareTo(z) *must equal* 0: This is the transitive property.

- *If* x.CompareTo(y) *returns a value other than* 0, *then* y.CompareTo(x) *must return a non-*0 *value of the opposite sign*: In other terms, this statement says that if x < y, then y > x, or if x > y, then y < x.

- *If* x.CompareTo(y) *returns a value other than* 0, *and* y.CompareTo(z) *returns a value other than* 0 *with the same sign as the first, then* x.CompareTo(y) *is required to return a non-*0 *value of the same sign as the previous two*: In other terms, this statement says that if x < y and y < z, then x < z, or if x > y and y > z, then x > z.

The following code shows a modified form of the ComplexNumber class that implements IComparable and consolidates some code in private helper methods:

```vb
Imports System

Public NotInheritable Class ComplexNumber
    Implements IComparable

    Private ReadOnly real As Double
    Private ReadOnly imaginary As Double

    'Other methods removed for clarity.

    Public Sub New(ByVal real As Double, ByVal imaginary As Double)
        Me.real = real
        Me.imaginary = imaginary
    End Sub

    Public Overloads Overrides Function Equals(ByVal other As Object) As Boolean
        Dim result As Boolean = False
        Dim that As ComplexNumber = TryCast(other, ComplexNumber)

        If Not that Is Nothing Then
            result = InternalEquals(that)
        End If

        Return result
    End Function

    Public Overrides Function GetHashCode() As Integer
        Return Fix(Me.Magnitude)
    End Function

    Public Shared Operator =(ByVal num1 As ComplexNumber, _
        ByVal num2 As ComplexNumber) As Boolean

        Return Object.Equals(num1, num2)
    End Operator

    Public Shared Operator <>(ByVal num1 As ComplexNumber, _
        ByVal num2 As ComplexNumber) As Boolean

        Return Not Object.Equals(num1, num2)
    End Operator

    Public Function CompareTo(ByVal other As Object) As Integer _
        Implements IComparable.CompareTo
```

```
        Dim that As ComplexNumber = TryCast(other, ComplexNumber)
        If that Is Nothing Then
            Throw New ArgumentException("Bad Comparison!")
        End If

        Dim result As Integer
        If InternalEquals(that) Then
            result = 0
        ElseIf Me.Magnitude > that.Magnitude Then
            result = 1
        Else
            result = -1
        End If

        Return result
    End Function

    Private Function InternalEquals(ByVal that As ComplexNumber) As Boolean
        Return (Me.real = that.real) AndAlso (Me.imaginary = that.imaginary)
    End Function

    Public ReadOnly Property Magnitude() As Double
        Get
            Return Math.Sqrt(Math.Pow(Me.real, 2) + Math.Pow(Me.imaginary, 2))
        End Get
    End Property
End Class
```

Is the Object Disposable?

Let's cover some of the effects disposable objects can have on your design. First, you need to determine if your object should be disposable in the first place. Generally, if it manages some sort of unmanaged resource, such as a chunk of virtual memory, then the object needs to be disposable. If your object contains other objects that are themselves disposable, then your object should be disposable as well. For example, an object that holds a reference to a file opened with exclusive read/write privileges should be disposable so that the client of the object can control when the underlying resource is closed or cleaned up. An object is declared as disposable if it implements the IDisposable interface. Let's have a look at the interface itself:

```
Public Interface IDisposable
    Sub Dispose()
End Interface
```

It looks simple enough. Just implement the Dispose method so that it cleans up the resource, and you're done, right? Well, maybe.

If you create a disposable object that contains other objects that are disposable, then in your Dispose() implementation, you should call the Dispose method on the contained objects. Also, it's valid for clients to call Dispose() multiple times. So instead of throwing an exception on subsequent calls, which is invalid based upon the documentation for IDisposable, you should simply do nothing. Therefore, you'll need to maintain some sort of internal flag so that your code doesn't explode if Dispose() gets called multiple times. You can use this internal flag for another purpose, too. It is normally invalid to call a method on a disposed object, so in those cases, you can check the flag, and if it indicates that the object has been disposed previously, you can throw an ObjectDisposedException. You can already see that what appeared to be a simple interface is becoming difficult to implement properly. Let's look at an example of implementing IDisposable. The following code consists of a custom heap object that uses Win32 functions to manage a local heap:

```
Imports System
Imports System.Runtime.InteropServices

Public NotInheritable Class Win32Heap
    Implements IDisposable

    Private theHeap As IntPtr
    Private disposed As Boolean = False

    <DllImport("kernel32.dll")> _
    Shared Function HeapCreate(ByVal flOptions As UInteger, _
        ByVal dwInitialSize As UIntPtr, ByVal dwMaximumSize As UIntPtr) As IntPtr
    End Function

    <DllImport("kernel32.dll")> _
    Shared Function HeapDestroy(ByVal hHeap As IntPtr) As Boolean
    End Function

    Public Sub New()
        theHeap = HeapCreate(0, CType(4096, UIntPtr), UIntPtr.Zero)
    End Sub

    'IDisposable implementation
    Public Sub Dispose() Implements IDisposable.Dispose
        If (Not disposed) Then
            HeapDestroy(theHeap)
            theHeap = IntPtr.Zero
            disposed = True
        End If
    End Sub
End Class
```

This object doesn't contain any objects that implement IDisposable, so you don't need to iterate through the containment tree calling Dispose().

In the Disposable pattern,[4] the implementation of the contained objects shapes the container object by forcing it to implement IDisposable if the contained objects implement

---

4. Review the "Disposable Objects" section in Chapter 3 for more.

IDisposable. It's an inside-out relationship. Since the IDisposable pattern requires the user to call the Dispose method explicitly, the onus is thrown on the user to make sure that it is called, even in the face of exceptions. This makes the client code tedious to produce. For example, consider the following code that opens a file for write:

```
Imports System
Imports System.IO

Public NotInheritable Class WriteStuff
    Shared Sub Main()
        Dim sw As StreamWriter = New StreamWriter("Output.txt")

        Try
            sw.WriteLine("This is a test of the emergency dispose mechanism")
        Finally
            If Not sw Is Nothing Then
                CType(sw, IDisposable).Dispose()
            End If
        End Try
    End Sub
End Class
```

Writing code like this can become tedious, so the Using statement was introduced in VB 2005 to help us out. In a Using statement, you declare the disposable variables, and then when the scope leaves the code block, the objects are disposed of. The Using statement does essentially the same thing as the Try statement, and you can look at the generated intermediate language (IL) code to prove this. The Using statement definitely does help; however, the client of the object is still required to remember to use it in the first place. Let's modify the previous example with a Using statement:

```
Imports System
Imports System.IO

Public NotInheritable Class WriteStuff
    Shared Sub Main()
        Using sw As StreamWriter = New StreamWriter("Output.txt")
            sw.WriteLine("This is a test of the emergency dispose mechanism")
        End Using
    End Sub
End Class
```

Now, can you think of what happens if the client of your object forgets to call Dispose() or doesn't use a Using statement? Clearly, there is the chance that you will leak the resource. And that's why you need to also implement a finalizer, as the next section describes.

Does the Object Need a Finalizer?

A finalizer is a method you implement on your class that gets called prior to the garbage collector (GC) cleaning up your unused object from the heap. Let's get one important concept clear up front: finalizers are not destructors, nor should you view them as destructors.

Destructors are associated with deterministic destruction of objects, while finalizers are associated with nondeterministic destruction of objects.[5] You cannot overload `Object.Finalize()` explicitly in VB, but you never have to worry about calling the base class finalizer, as the compiler does that for you.

As an example, if you have an object that references a file in the file system, and your object needs some cleanup code, this cleanup will need to happen deterministically. In other words, it needs to happen explicitly when the user is finished with the object and not when the GC finally gets around to disposing of it. In these cases, you need to implement this functionality using the Disposable pattern by implementing the `IDisposable` interface.

■**Note** In reality, it's rare that you'll ever need to write a finalizer. Most of the time, you should implement the Disposable pattern to do any resource cleanup code in your object. However, finalizers can be useful for cleaning up unmanaged resources in a guaranteed way—that is, when the user has forgotten to call `IDisposable.Dispose()`.

In a perfect world, you could simply implement all of your typical destructor code in the `IDisposable.Dispose` method. However, there is one serious side effect of the VB language not supporting deterministic destruction. The VB compiler doesn't call `IDisposable.Dispose()` on your object automatically when it goes out of scope. VB, as we've mentioned in previous chapters, throws the onus on the user of the object to call `IDisposable.Dispose()`. The VB language does make it easier to guarantee this behavior in the face of exceptions through the `Using` keyword, but it still requires the client of your object to use the `Using` keyword in the first place.

In order to reliably clean up directly held resources, it's wise for any objects that implement the `IDisposable` interface to also implement a finalizer that merely defers to the `Dispose` method.[6] This way, you can catch those instances where users forget to use the Disposable pattern and don't dispose of the object properly. Of course, the cleanup of undisposed objects will now happen at the discretion of the GC,[7] but at least it will happen. Beware: the GC calls the finalizer for the objects being cleaned up from a separate thread, so you may have to worry about threading issues in your disposable objects. It's unlikely that threading issues will cause you trouble during finalization, since, in theory, the object being finalized is not being referenced anywhere. However, it could become a factor depending on what you do in your `Dispose` method. For example, if your `Dispose` method uses an external, possibly unmanaged, object to get work done that another

---

5. Chapter 3 also contains discussion of finalizers.

6. Objects that implement `IDisposable` only because they are forced to due to contained types that implement `IDisposable` should not have a finalizer. They don't directly manage resources, and the finalizer will impose undue stress on the finalizer thread of the GC.

7. See Chapters 2 and 3 for more discussion of garbage collection and the CLR.

entity may hold a reference to, then that object needs to be *thread-hot*—that is, it must work reliably in multithreaded environments. It's better to be safe than sorry and consider threading issues when you implement a finalizer.

When you call your Dispose method via the finalizer, you should not use reference objects contained in fields within this object. It may not sound intuitive at first, but there is no guaranteed ordering of how objects are finalized. The objects in the fields of your object could have been finalized before your finalizer runs. Therefore, it would elicit the dreaded undefined behavior if you were to use them and they just happened to be destroyed already. You'll likely agree that could be a tough bug to find, and that using finalizers comes with pitfalls.

■**Caution** Be wary of any object used during finalization, even if it's not a field of your object being finalized, because it too may already be marked for finalization and may or may not have been finalized already. In fact, many schools of thought recommend against using any external objects within a finalizer. But the fact is that any time an object that supports a finalizer is moved to the finalization queue in the GC, all objects in the object graph are moved, whether they are finalizable or not. So if your finalizable object contains a private, nonfinalizable object, then you can touch the private contained object in the finalizer because you know it's still alive, since it got promoted to the finalization queue with your object, and it cannot have been finalized before your object since it has no finalizer. However, see the next Note in the text!

Let's revisit the Win32Heap example from the previous section and modify it with a finalizer. Follow the recommended Disposable pattern, and see how it changes:

```
Imports System
Imports System.Runtime.InteropServices

Public Class Win32Heap
    Implements IDisposable

    Private theHeap As IntPtr
    Private disposed As Boolean = False

    <DllImport("kernel32.dll")> _
    Shared Function HeapCreate(ByVal flOptions As UInteger, _
        ByVal dwInitialSize As UIntPtr, ByVal dwMaximumSize As UIntPtr) As IntPtr
    End Function

    <DllImport("kernel32.dll")> _
    Shared Function HeapDestroy(ByVal hHeap As IntPtr) As Boolean
    End Function

    Public Sub New()
        theHeap = HeapCreate(0, CType(4096, UIntPtr), UIntPtr.Zero)
    End Sub
```

```
    'IDisposable implementation
    Protected Overridable Sub Dispose(ByVal disposing As Boolean)
        If (Not disposed) Then
            If disposing Then
                'It's OK to use any internal objects here.
                'This class happens not to have any.
            End If

            'If using objects that you know do still exist, such as objects
            'that implement the singleton pattern, it is important to make
            'sure those objects are thread-safe.

            HeapDestroy(theHeap)
            theHeap = IntPtr.Zero
            disposed = True
        End If
    End Sub

    Public Sub Dispose() Implements IDisposable.Dispose
        Dispose(True)
        GC.SuppressFinalize(Me)
    End Sub

    Protected Overrides Sub Finalize()
        Dispose(False)
    End Sub
End Class
```

Let's analyze the changes made to support a finalizer. You add a Finalize method and a second level of indirection in the Dispose implementation. This is so you know if your private Dispose method got called from a call to Dispose() or through the finalizer. Also, in this example, you implement the Dispose(Boolean) method as Overridable, so that any deriving type merely has to override this method to modify the dispose behavior. If the Win32Heap class were marked NotInheritable, you could change that method from Protected to Private and remove the Overridable keyword. Remember, you cannot reliably use subobjects if your Dispose method got called from the finalizer.

■**Note** Some people take the approach that all object references are off limits inside the Dispose method that is called by the finalizer. There's no reason you cannot use objects that you know to be alive and well. However, beware if the finalizer is called as a result of the application domain shutting down; objects that you assume to be alive may not actually be alive. In reality, it's almost impossible to determine if an object reference is still valid in 100% of the cases, and it's probably best to not reference any reference types within the finalization stage if you can avoid it.

The `Dispose` method features a performance boost via the call to `GC.SuppressFinalize()`. The finalizer of this object merely calls the private `Dispose` method, and you know that if your public `Dispose` method gets called, the finalizer doesn't need to do that any longer. So you can tell the GC not to put the object instance on the finalization queue when the `IDisposable.Dispose` method is called. This optimization is more than trivial once you consider the fact that objects that implement a finalizer live longer than those that don't. When the GC goes through the heap looking for dead objects to collect, it normally compacts the heap and reclaims their memory. However, if an object has a finalizer, instead of reclaiming the memory immediately, the GC moves the object over to a finalization list that the separate finalization thread handles. Once the finalization thread has completed its job on the object, the object is remarked for deletion, and the GC reclaims the space during a subsequent pass. That's why objects that implement a finalizer live longer than those that don't. If your objects eat up lots of heap memory, or your system creates lots of those objects, finalization starts to become a huge factor. Not only does it make the GC inefficient, but it also chews up processor time in the finalization thread.

■**Note** When an object has a finalizer, it is placed on an internal CLR queue to keep track of this fact, and, clearly, `GC.SuppressFinalize()` affects that status. During normal execution, you cannot guarantee that other object references are reachable. However, during application shutdown, the finalizer thread actually finalizes the objects right off of this internal finalizable queue, and therefore, those objects are reachable and can be referenced in finalizers. You can determine if this is the case by using `Environment.HasShutdownStarted` or `AppDomain.IsFinalizingForUnload`. However, give careful consideration before doing so, and don't be surprised if this behavior changes in future versions of the CLR.

Let's examine the finalizer performance impact on the GC a little closer. The CLR GC is implemented as a generational GC. This means that allocated objects that live in higher generations are assumed to live longer than those that live in lower generations and are collected less frequently than the generation below them. The fine details of the GC's collection algorithm are beyond the scope of this book, but it's beneficial to touch upon them at a high level. For example, the GC normally attempts to allocate any new objects in generation 0. Moreover, the GC assumes that objects in generation 0 will live a relatively short life span. So, when the GC attempts to allocate space for an object, and it sees that the heap must be compacted, it releases space due to dead generation 0 objects, and objects that are not dead get promoted to generation 1 during the compaction. Upon completion of this stage, if the GC is able to find enough space for the allocation, it will stop compacting the heap. It won't attempt to compact generation 1 unless it needs even more space or if it sees that the generation 1 heap is full and likely needs to be compacted. It will iterate through all the generations as necessary. However, during the entire pass of the garbage collector, an object can only be promoted one level. So, if an object is promoted from generation 0 to generation 1 during a collection and the GC must subsequently continue compacting generation 1 in the same collection pass, the object just promoted will stay in generation 1. Currently, the CLR heap only consists of three generations. So, naturally, if an object lives in generation 2, it cannot be promoted to a higher generation. The CLR also contains a special heap for large object allocation, which contains objects greater than 80 KB in size in the current release of the CLR. That number may change in future releases, though, so don't rely on it staying static.

Now, consider what happens when a generation 0 object gets promoted to generation 1 during a compaction. Even if all root references to an object in generation 1 are out of scope, the space may not be reclaimed for a while, since the GC will not compact generation 1 very often.

Objects that implement finalizers get put on the finalization queue. That reference on the queue counts as a root reference. Therefore, the object will be promoted to generation 1 if it currently lives in generation 0. But, you already know that the object is dying. In fact, once the finalization queue is drained, the object most likely will be dead, unless it is resurrected during the finalization process. So, this object with the finalizer is dying, but since it was put on the finalization queue and thus promoted to a higher generation, its shell will likely lay around in the GC until a higher generation compaction occurs.

For this reason, it's important that you not implement a finalizer unless you have to, and that should only be necessary when your object directly maintains resources that must be freed or cleaned up deterministically.

■**Note** Resources that must be cleaned up deterministically can be either managed or unmanaged resources. An example of an unmanaged resource is something like an instance of `System.IO.FileStream`, where `IDisposable.Dispose()` calls through to `FileStream.Close()`. `FileStream.Close()` releases the underlying unmanaged resources. It is likely undesirable for you to wait until the GC feels like calling the finalizer on the `FileStream` before the file is unlocked.

Suppose you create an object that allocates a nontrivial chunk of unmanaged system resources. Suppose also that the client of your object has created a website that takes many hits per minute, and with each hit, the client creates a new instance of your object. The client's system's performance will degrade significantly if the client forgets to dispose of these objects in a timely manner before all references to the object are gone. Of course, if you implement a finalizer as shown previously, the object will eventually get disposed of. However, disposal only happens when the GC feels it necessary, so resources will probably run dry and cripple the system. Moreover, failing to call `Dispose()` will likely result in more finalization, which will cripple the GC even more. Client code can force GC collection through the `GC.Collect` method, but it is strongly recommended that you never call it, since it interferes with the GC's algorithms.

It would be nice if you could inform the clients of your object when they forget to call `Dispose()` in their debug builds. Well, in fact, you can log an error whenever the finalizer for your object runs and it notices that the object has not been disposed of properly. You can even point them to the exact location of the object creation by storing off a stack trace at the point of creation. That way, they know which line of code created the offending instance. Let's modify the `Win32Heap` example with this approach:

```
Imports System
Imports System.Runtime.InteropServices
Imports System.Diagnostics
```

```vbnet
Public NotInheritable Class Win32Heap
    Implements IDisposable

    Private theHeap As IntPtr
    Private disposed As Boolean = False
    Private creationStackTrace As StackTrace

    <DllImport("kernel32.dll")> _
    Shared Function HeapCreate(ByVal flOptions As UInteger, _
        ByVal dwInitialSize As UIntPtr, ByVal dwMaximumSize As UIntPtr) As IntPtr
    End Function

    <DllImport("kernel32.dll")> _
    Shared Function HeapDestroy(ByVal hHeap As IntPtr) As Boolean
    End Function

    Public Sub New()
        creationStackTrace = New StackTrace(1, True)

        theHeap = HeapCreate(0, CType(4096, UIntPtr), UIntPtr.Zero)
    End Sub

    'IDisposable implementation
    Private Sub Dispose(ByVal disposing As Boolean)
        If (Not disposed) Then
            If disposing Then
                'It's OK to use any internal objects here.
                'This class happens to not have any.
            Else
                'OOPS!  We're finalizing this object, and it has not
                'been disposed.  Let's let the user know about it if
                'the app domain is not shutting down.
                Dim currentDomain As AppDomain =  AppDomain.CurrentDomain
                If (Not currentDomain.IsFinalizingForUnload()) AndAlso _
                    (Not Environment.HasShutdownStarted) Then

                    Console.WriteLine("Failed to dispose of object!!!")
                    Console.WriteLine("Object allocated at:")

                    Dim i As Integer = 0
                    Do While i < creationStackTrace.FrameCount
                        Dim frame As StackFrame = creationStackTrace.GetFrame(i)

                        Console.WriteLine("   {0}", frame.ToString())
                        i += 1
                    Loop
                End If
            End If
        End If
```

```vb
        'If using objects that you know do still exist, such
        'as objects that implement the singleton pattern, it
        'is important to make sure those objects are thread-safe.

        HeapDestroy(theHeap)
        theHeap = IntPtr.Zero
        disposed = True
      End If
    End Sub

    Public Sub Dispose() Implements IDisposable.Dispose
        Dispose(True)
        GC.SuppressFinalize(Me)
    End Sub

    Protected Overrides Sub Finalize()
        Dispose(False)
    End Sub
End Class

Public NotInheritable Class EntryPoint
    Shared Sub Main()
        Dim heap As Win32Heap = New Win32Heap()

        heap = Nothing
        GC.Collect()
        GC.WaitForPendingFinalizers()
    End Sub
End Class
```

This example returns the following results when run:

```
Failed to dispose of object!!!
Object allocated at:
    Main at offset 55 in file:line:column C:\Apress\AVB\Projects\Class3.vb:77:13
```

In the Main method, you allocate a new Win32Heap object, and then immediately force it to be finalized. Since the object was not disposed, this triggers the stack dumping code inside the private Dispose method. Since you probably don't care about objects being finalized as a result of the app domain getting unloaded, you wrap the stack-dumping code inside a block conditional on the result of AppDomain.IsFinalizingForUnload() AndAlso Environment.HasShutdownStarted. Had you called Dispose() prior to setting the reference to Nothing in Main(), then the stack trace would not be sent to the console. Clients of your library may thank you for pointing out undisposed objects.

Finalizers are potential resource sinks, since they make objects live longer, and yet they are hidden behind the innocuous syntax of destructors. One quality of finalizers is the ability to point out when objects are not disposed of properly, but we advise using that technique only in debug builds. Be aware of the efficiency implications you impose on your system when you implement a finalizer on an object. Finally, even though you can introduce dependencies between finalizable objects, the CLR team is actively considering moving finalization to the process thread pool rather than using a single finalization thread. That would mean those finalization techniques would need to be thread-safe. We recommend that you avoid writing a finalizer if at all possible.

What Does Equality Mean for This Object?

`Object.Equals()` is the overridable method that you call to determine, in the most general way, if two objects are equivalent. While overriding the `Object.Equals` method may seem trivial, it is yet another one of those simplistic looking things that can turn complex. The key to `Object.Equals()` is to understand that there are generally two semantic meanings of equivalence in the CLR. The default meaning of equivalence for reference types is identity equivalence. This means that two separate references are considered equal if they both reference the exact same object instance on the heap. With identity equality, even if you have two references each referencing different objects that just happen to have completely identical internal states, `Object.Equals()` will return `False` for those.

The other form of equivalence in the CLR is that of value equality. Value equality is the default equivalence for value types in VB. The default version of `Equals()`, which is provided by the override of `Equals()` inside the `ValueType` class that all value types derive from, uses reflection to iterate over the internal fields of two values comparing them for value equality. With two semantic meanings of `Equals()` in the CLR possible, some confusion can come from the fact that both value types and reference types have different default meanings for `Equals()`. In this section, we'll concentrate on implementing `Object.Equals()` for reference types. We'll save value types for the second major section of this chapter.

Reference Types and Identity Equality

What does it mean to say that a type is a reference type? Basically, it means that every variable of that type that you manipulate is actually a pointer to the actual object on the heap. When you make a copy of this reference, you get another reference pointing to the same object. Consider the following code:

```
Public Class EntryPoint
    Shared Sub Main()
        Dim referenceA As Object = New System.Object()
        Dim referenceB As Object = referenceA
    End Sub
End Class
```

In `Main()`, you create a new instance of type `System.Object`, and then you immediately make a copy of the reference. What you end up with is something that resembles the diagram in Figure 14-1.

In the CLR, the variables that represent the references are actually value types that embody a storage location (for the pointer to the object they represent) and an associated type. However, once a reference is copied, the actual object pointed to is not copied. Instead, you have two references that refer to the same object. Operations on the object performed through one reference will be visible to the client using the other reference.

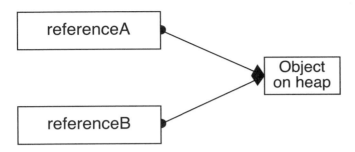

Figure 14-1. *Reference variables*

Now, let's consider what it means to compare these references. What does equality mean between two reference variables? The answer is, it depends on what your needs are and how you define equality. By default, equality of reference variables is meant to be an identity comparison. What that means is that two reference variables are equal if they refer to the same object, as in Figure 14-1. Again, this referential equality, or identity, is the default behavior of equality between two references to a heap-based object.

From the client code standpoint, you have to be careful about how you compare two object references for equality. Consider the following code:

```
Public Class EntryPoint
    Private Shared Function TestForEquality(ByVal obj1 As Object, _
        ByVal obj2 As Object) As Boolean

        Return obj1.Equals(obj2)
    End Function

    Shared Sub Main()
        Dim obj1 As Object = New System.Object()
        Dim obj2 As Object = Nothing

        System.Console.WriteLine("obj1 Equals obj2 is {0}", _
            TestForEquality(obj1, obj2))
    End Sub
End Class
```

The previous example outputs the following:

```
obj1 Equals obj2 is False
```

Here you create an instance of System.Object, and you want to find out if the variables obj1 and obj2 are equal. Since you're comparing references, the equality test determines if they're pointing to the same object instance. Looking at the code, you can see that the obvious result is False. This is expected. However, consider what would happen if you swapped the order of the parameters in the call to TestForEquality(). You would quickly find that your program crashes with an unhandled exception where TestForInequality() tries to call Equals() on a reference to Nothing. Therefore, you should modify the code to account for this:

```
Public Class EntryPoint
    Private Shared Function TestForEquality(ByVal obj1 As Object, _
        ByVal obj2 As Object) As Boolean

        If obj1 Is Nothing AndAlso obj2 Is Nothing Then
            Return True
        End If

        If obj1 Is Nothing Then
            Return False
        End If

        Return obj1.Equals(obj2)
    End Function

    Shared Sub Main()
        Dim obj1 As Object = New System.Object()
        Dim obj2 As Object = Nothing

        System.Console.WriteLine("obj1 Equals obj2 is {0}", _
            TestForEquality(obj2, obj1))
        System.Console.WriteLine("Nothing Equals Nothing is {0}", _
            TestForEquality(Nothing, Nothing))
    End Sub
End Class
```

This example produces the following output:

```
obj1 Equals obj2 is False
Nothing Equals Nothing is True
```

Now, the code can swap the order of the arguments in the call to TestForEquality(), and you get the expected result. You also put in a check to return the proper result if both arguments are Nothing. Now, TestForEquality() is complete. It sure seems like a lot of work to test two references for equality. Well, the designers of the .NET Framework recognized this problem and introduced the Shared version of Object.Equals() that does this exact comparison. As long as you call the Shared version of Object.Equals(), you don't have to worry about creating the code in TestForEquality() in the previous example.

You've seen how equality tests on references to objects test identity by default. However, there may be times when this type of equivalence test makes no sense. Consider an immutable object that represents a complex number:

```
Public Class ComplexNumber
    Public Sub New(ByVal real As Integer, ByVal imaginary As Integer)
        Me.real = real
        Me.imaginary = imaginary
    End Sub
```

```
        Private real As Integer
        Private imaginary As Integer
End Class

Public Class EntryPoint
    Shared Sub Main()
        Dim referenceA As ComplexNumber = New ComplexNumber(1, 2)
        Dim referenceB As ComplexNumber = New ComplexNumber(1, 2)

        System.Console.WriteLine("Result of Equality is {0}", _
            referenceA Is referenceB)
    End Sub
End Class
```

The output from the preceding code looks like this:

```
Result of Equality is False
```

Figure 14-2 shows the diagram representing the in-memory layout of the references.

Figure 14-2. *References to* ComplexNumber

This is the expected result based upon the default meaning of equality between references. However, this is hardly intuitive to the user of these ComplexNumber objects. It would make sense for the comparison of the two references in the diagram to return True, since the values of the two objects are the same. To achieve such a result, you need to provide a custom implementation of equality for these objects.

Overriding Object.Equals() for Reference Types

Many times, you may need to override the meaning of equivalence for an object. You may want equivalence for your reference type to be value equality as opposed to referential equality, or identity. Or, as you'll see in the "Override Equals() for Better Performance" section, you may have a custom value type where you want to override the default Equals method provided by System.ValueType in order to make the operation more efficient. No matter what your reason for overriding Equals(), you must follow several rules:

- x.Equals(x) = True: This is the reflexive property of equality.

- x.Equals(y) = y.Equals(x): This is the symmetric property of equality.

- x.Equals(y) AndAlso y.Equals(z) *implies* x.Equals(z) = True: This is the transitive property of equality.

- x.Equals(y) must return the same result as long as the internal state of x and y has not changed.

- x.Equals(Nothing) = False, for all x that are not Nothing.

- Equals() must not throw exceptions.

An Equals() implementation should adhere to these rules. The default version of Object. Equals() inherited by classes tests for referential equality. However, in cases like the example using ComplexNumber, such a test is not intuitive. It would be natural and expected that instances of such a type are compared on a field-by-field basis. It is for this very reason that you should override Object.Equals() for these types of classes that behave with value semantics.

Let's revisit the ComplexNumber example once again to see how you can do this:

```
Public Class ComplexNumber
    Private real As Double
    Private imaginary As Double

    Public Sub New(ByVal real As Integer, ByVal imaginary As Integer)
        Me.real = real
        Me.imaginary = imaginary
    End Sub

    Public Overrides Function Equals(ByVal obj As Object) As Boolean
        Dim other As ComplexNumber = TryCast(obj, ComplexNumber)

        If other Is Nothing Then
            Return False
        End If

        Return (Me.real = other.real) AndAlso (Me.imaginary = other.imaginary)
    End Function

    Public Overrides Function GetHashCode() As Integer
        'This function is discussed later in the chapter.
        Return Fix(real) Xor Fix(imaginary)
    End Function

    Public Shared Operator =(ByVal CN As ComplexNumber, _
        ByVal other As ComplexNumber) As Boolean

        Return Equals(CN, other)
    End Operator

    Public Shared Operator <>(ByVal CN As ComplexNumber, _
        ByVal other As ComplexNumber) As Boolean
```

```
            Return Not Equals(CN, other)
        End Operator
End Class

Public Class EntryPoint
    Shared Sub Main()
        Dim referenceA As ComplexNumber = New ComplexNumber(1, 2)
        Dim referenceB As ComplexNumber = New ComplexNumber(1, 2)

        System.Console.WriteLine("Result of Equality is {0}", _
            referenceA = referenceB)

        'If we really want referential equality.
        System.Console.WriteLine("Identity of references is {0}", _
            ReferenceEquals(referenceA, referenceB))
    End Sub
End Class
```

The previous code displays the following output when run:

```
Result of Equality is True
Identity of references is False
```

In this example, the implementation of Equals() is pretty straightforward, except you do have to test some conditions. Make sure that the object reference you're comparing to is not Nothing and does, in fact, reference an instance of ComplexNumber. Next, simply test the fields of the two references to make sure they're equal. In the majority of cases, you won't need to override Object.Equals() for your reference type objects. It is recommended that your objects treat equivalence using identity comparisons, which is what you get for free from Object.Equals(). However, there are times when it makes sense to override Equals() for an object. For example, if your object represents something that naturally feels like a value and is immutable, such as a complex number or the System.String class, then it could very well make sense to override Equals() in order to give that object's implementation of Equals() value equality semantics.

Sometimes, when you're dealing with reference types, you will want to test for referential equality. You cannot always rely on the Equals method for the object to determine the referential equality, so you must use other means because the method can be overridden as in the ComplexNumber example. Thankfully, you have a way to handle this job, and you can see it at the end of the Main method in the previous code sample. The System.Object supplies a Shared method named ReferenceEquals that takes two reference parameters and returns True if the identity test holds true.

If you do change the semantic meaning of Equals() for an object, it is best to clearly document this fact for the clients of your object. If you override Equals() for a class, we strongly recommend that you tag its semantic meaning with a custom attribute, similar to the technique introduced previously for Dispose() implementations. This way, people who derive from your class and want to change the semantic meaning of Equals() can quickly determine if they should call your implementation in the process. For maximum efficiency, the custom attribute should serve a documentation purpose. While it's possible to look for such an attribute at run time, doing so would be inefficient.

■**Note** You should never throw exceptions from an implementation of `Object.Equals()`. Instead of throwing an exception, return `False` as the result instead.

Throughout this entire discussion, we've purposely avoided talking about the equality operators because it is beneficial to consider them as an extra layer in addition to `Object.Equals()`. Support of operator overloading is not a requirement for languages to be compliant with the Common Language Specification (CLS). Therefore, not all languages that target the CLR support equality operators thoroughly. VB is one language that has taken a while to support operator overloading, and it now only supports equality operators fully starting with VB 2005. The best approach is to implement `Object.Equals()` as appropriate and base any `Operator =` or `Operator <>` implementations on `Equals()` while only providing them as a convenience for languages that support them.

■**Note** Consider implementing `IEquatable(Of T)` on your type to get a type-safe version of `Equals()`. This is especially important for value types, since type-specific versions of methods avoid unnecessary boxing.

If You Override Equals(), Override GetHashCode()

`GetHashCode()` is called when objects are used as keys of a hash table. When a hash table searches for an entry after given a key to look for, it asks the key for its hash code and then uses that to identify which hash bucket the key lives in. Once it finds the bucket, it can then see if that key is in the bucket. Theoretically, the search for the bucket should be quick, since the buckets should have very few keys in them. This occurs if your `GetHashCode` method returns a reasonably unique value for instances of your object that support value equivalence semantics.

From the previous discussion, you can see that it would be bad if your hash code algorithm could return a different value between two instances that contain values that are equivalent. In such a case, the hash table may fail to find the bucket your key is in. For this reason, it is imperative that you override `GetHashCode()` if you override `Equals()` for an object. In fact, if you override `Equals()` and not `GetHashCode()`, the VB compiler will let you know about it with a friendly warning.

`GetHashCode()` implementations should adhere to the following rules:

- If, for two instances, `x.Equals(y)` is `True`, then `x.GetHashCode() = y.GetHashCode()`.

- Hash codes generated by `GetHashCode()` need not be unique.

- `GetHashCode()` is not permitted to throw exceptions.

If two instances return the same hash code value, they must be further compared with `Equals()` to determine if they're equivalent. Incidentally, if your `GetHashCode` method is efficient, you can base the inequality code path of your `Operator <>` and `Operator =` implementations on it, since different hash codes for objects of the same type imply inequality. Implementing the operators this way can be more efficient in some cases, but it all depends on the efficiency of your GetHashCode() implementation and the complexity of your Equals method. In some cases, when using this technique, the calls to the operators could be less efficient than just calling Equals(), but in other cases, they could be remarkably more efficient. For example, consider an object that models a multidimensional point in space. Suppose the number of dimensions (rank) of this point could easily approach into the hundreds. Internally, you could represent the dimensions of the point by using an array of integers. Say you want to implement the GetHashCode method by computing a 32-bit cyclic redundancy check (CRC32) on the dimension points in the array. This also implies that this Point type is immutable. The GetHashCode() call could potentially be expensive if you compute the CRC32 each time it is called. Therefore, it may be wise to precompute the hash and store it in the object. In such a case, you could write the equality operators as shown in the following code:

```vb
Public NotInheritable Class Point
    Private coordinates As Single()
    Private precomputedHash As Integer

    'Other methods removed for clarity.

    Public Overrides Function Equals(ByVal other As Object) As Boolean
        Dim result As Boolean = False
        Dim that As Point = TryCast(other, Point)

        If Not that Is Nothing Then
            result = (Me.coordinates Is that.coordinates)
        End If

        Return result
    End Function

    Public Overrides Function GetHashCode() As Integer
        Return precomputedHash
    End Function

    Public Shared Operator = (ByVal pt1 As Point, ByVal pt2 As Point) As Boolean
        If pt1.GetHashCode() <> pt2.GetHashCode() Then
            Return False
        Else
            Return Object.Equals(pt1, pt2)
        End If
    End Operator

    Public Shared Operator <>(ByVal pt1 As Point, ByVal pt2 As Point) As Boolean
        If pt1.GetHashCode() <> pt2.GetHashCode() Then
            Return True
        Else
            Return Not Object.Equals(pt1, pt2)
        End If
    End Operator
End Class
```

In this example, as long as the precomputed hash is sufficiently unique, the overloaded operators will execute quickly in some cases. In the worst case, one more compare between two integers—the hash values—is executed along with the function calls to acquire them. If the call to Equals() is expensive, then this optimization will return some gains on a lot of the comparisons. If the call to Equals() is not expensive, then this technique could add overhead and make the code less efficient. It's best to apply optimizations after a profiler has pointed you in this direction and if you're sure it will help.

Object.GetHashCode() exists because the developers of the standard library felt it would be convenient to be able to use any object as a key to a hash table. The fact is, not all objects are good candidates for hash keys. Usually, it's best to use immutable types as hash keys. A good example of an immutable type is System.String. Once created, you cannot ever change it. Therefore, GetHashCode() on a string instance is guaranteed to always return the same value for the same string instance. It becomes more difficult to generate hash codes for objects that are mutable. In those cases, it's best to base your GetHashCode() implementation on calculations performed on immutable fields inside the mutable object.

For the sake of example, suppose you want to implement GetHashCode() for a ComplexNumber type. One solution is to compute the hash based on the magnitude of the complex number, as in the following example:

```
Imports System

Public NotInheritable Class ComplexNumber
    Private ReadOnly real As Double
    Private ReadOnly imaginary As Double

    'Other methods removed for clarity.

    Public Sub New(ByVal real As Double, ByVal imaginary As Double)
        Me.real = real
        Me.imaginary = imaginary
    End Sub

    Public Overrides Function Equals(ByVal other As Object) As Boolean
        Dim result As Boolean = False
        Dim that As ComplexNumber = TryCast(other, ComplexNumber)

        If Not that Is Nothing Then
            result = (Me.real = that.real) AndAlso (Me.imaginary = that.imaginary)
        End If

        Return result
    End Function

    Public Overrides Function GetHashCode() As Integer
        Return Fix(Math.Sqrt(Math.Pow(Me.real, 2) * Math.Pow(Me.imaginary, 2)))
    End Function
```

```
    Public Shared Operator =(ByVal num1 As ComplexNumber, _
        ByVal num2 As ComplexNumber) As Boolean

        Return Object.Equals(num1, num2)
    End Operator

    Public Shared Operator <>(ByVal num1 As ComplexNumber, _
        ByVal num2 As ComplexNumber) As Boolean

        Return Not Object.Equals(num1, num2)
    End Operator
End Class
```

The GetHashCode() algorithm is not meant as a highly efficient example. Also, due to the rounding, it could potentially cause many complex numbers to fall within the same bucket. In that case, the efficiency of the hash table would degrade. We'll leave a more efficient algorithm as an exercise to the reader. Notice that you don't use the GetHashCode method to implement Operator <> because of the efficiency concerns. But more importantly, you rely on the Shared Object.Equals method to compare them for equality. This handy method checks the references for Nothing before calling the instance Equals method, saving you from having to do that. Had you used GetHashCode() to implement Operator <>, then you would have had to check the references for Nothing before calling GetHashCode() on them. Both fields used to calculate the hash code are immutable. Thus this instance of this object will always return the same hash code value as long as it lives. In fact, you may consider caching the hash code value once you compute it the first time to gain greater efficiency.

Prefer Type Safety at All Times

Even though every object in the managed world derives from System.Object, it's a bad idea to treat every object generically via a System.Object reference. One reason is efficiency; for example, if you were to maintain a collection of Employee objects via references to System.Object, you would always have to cast instances of them to type Employee before you could call any Employee-specific method. Although this inefficiency is slight when reference types are used, the efficiency problem is amplified by magnitudes with value types, since unnecessary boxing operations are generated in the IL code. We'll cover the boxing inefficiencies in the following sections dealing with value types. A problem with all of this casting when using reference types is when the cast fails and an exception is thrown. By using strong types, you can catch these problems and deal with them at compile time.

Another prominent reason to prefer strong type usage is associated with catching errors. Consider the case when implementing interfaces such as ICloneable. That interface's Clone method returns an instance as type Object. Clearly, this is done so that the interface will work generically across all types. However, it can come at a price.

VB is a strongly typed language, and every variable is declared with a type. Along with this comes type safety, which the compiler supplies to help you avoid errors. For example, it keeps you from assigning an instance of class Apple from an instance of class MonkeyWrench. However, VB does allow you to work in a less type-safe way. You can reference every object through the type Object; however, doing so throws away the type safety, and the compiler will allow you to assign an instance of type Apple from an instance of type MonkeyWrench as long as both references are of type Object. Unfortunately, even though the code will compile, you run the risk of generating a runtime error once the CLR realizes what you're attempting to do. The more you utilize the type safety of the compiler, the more error detection it can do at compile time, and catching errors at compile time is *always* more desirable than catching errors at run time.

In some situations, the VB compiler will generate much more efficient code if you provide a type-safe implementation of a well-defined method. Consider this typical For . . . Each statement:

```
For Each emp As Employee In Employees
    'Do Something
Next emp
```

Quite simply, the code loops over all the items in Employees. Within the body of the For . . . Each statement, a variable emp of type Employee references the current item in the collection during iteration. One of the rules enforced by VB for the collection is that it must implement a public method named GetEnumerator, which returns a type used to enumerate the items in the collection. This method is implemented as a result of the collection type implementing the IEnumerable interface and typically returns a forward iterator on the collection of contained objects. One of the rules on the enumerator type is that it must implement a public property named Current, which allows access to the current element. This property is part of the IEnumerator interface; however, IEnumerator.Current is typed as System.Object. This leads to another rule with regard to the For . . . Each statement. It states that the object type of IEnumerator.Current, the real object type, must be explicitly castable to the type of the iterator in the For . . . Each statement, which in this example is type Employee. If your collection's enumerator types its Current property as System.Object, the compiler must always perform the cast to type Employee. However, you can see that the compiler can generate much more efficient code if your Current property on your enumerator is typed as Employee.

So, what can you do to remedy this situation? Basically, whenever you implement an interface that contains methods with essentially nontyped return values, consider hiding the method from the public interface of the class while implementing a more type-safe version as part of the public interface of the class. Let's look at an example using the IEnumerator interface:

```
Imports System
Imports System.Collections

Public Class Employee
    Public Sub Evaluate()
        Console.WriteLine("Evaluating Employee . . .")
    End Sub
End Class

Public Class WorkForceEnumerator
    Implements IEnumerator

    Private enumerator As IEnumerator

    Public Sub New(ByVal employees As ArrayList)
        Me.enumerator = employees.GetEnumerator()
    End Sub
```

```vb
    Public ReadOnly Property Current() As Employee
        Get
            Return CType(enumerator.Current, Employee)
        End Get
    End Property

    Private ReadOnly Property IEnumerator_Current() As Object _
        Implements IEnumerator.Current

        Get
            Return enumerator.Current
        End Get
    End Property

    Public Function MoveNext() As Boolean Implements IEnumerator.MoveNext
        Return enumerator.MoveNext()
    End Function

    Public Sub Reset() Implements IEnumerator.Reset
        enumerator.Reset()
    End Sub
End Class

Public Class WorkForce
    Implements IEnumerable

    Private employees As ArrayList

    Public Sub New()
        employees = New ArrayList()

        'Let's put an employee in here for demo purposes.
        employees.Add(New Employee())
    End Sub

    Public Overloads Function GetEnumerator() As WorkForceEnumerator
        Return New WorkForceEnumerator(employees)
    End Function

    Private Overloads Function IEnumerable_GetEnumerator() As IEnumerator _
        Implements IEnumerable.GetEnumerator

        Return New WorkForceEnumerator(employees)
    End Function
End Class
```

```
Public Class EntryPoint
    Shared Sub Main()
        Dim staff As WorkForce = New WorkForce()

        For Each emp As Employee In staff
            emp.Evaluate()
        Next emp
    End Sub
End Class
```

This example returns the following:

```
Evaluating Employee . . .
```

Look carefully at the example and notice how the type-less versions of the interface methods are implemented. Remember that in order to access those methods, you must first cast the instance to the interface type. However, the compiler doesn't do that when it generates the For . . . Each loop. Instead, it simply looks for methods that match the rules already mentioned. We encourage you to step through the code using a debugger to see it in action. Also, you can make this code more efficient by using generics, as covered in Chapter 12.

Let's take a closer look at the For . . . Each loop generated by the compiler to get a better idea of what sorts of efficiency gains you get. In the following code, you remove the strongly typed versions of the interface methods, and as expected, the example runs pretty much the same as before from an outside perspective:

```
Imports System
Imports System.Collections

Public Class Employee
    Public Sub Evaluate()
        Console.WriteLine("Evaluating Employee . . .")
    End Sub
End Class

Public Class WorkForceEnumerator
    Implements IEnumerator

    Private enumerator As IEnumerator

    Public Sub New(ByVal employees As ArrayList)
        Me.enumerator = employees.GetEnumerator()
    End Sub

    Public ReadOnly Property Current() As Object Implements IEnumerator.Current
        Get
            Return enumerator.Current
        End Get
    End Property
```

```
    Public Function MoveNext() As Boolean Implements IEnumerator.MoveNext
        Return enumerator.MoveNext()
    End Function

    Public Sub Reset() Implements IEnumerator.Reset
        enumerator.Reset()
    End Sub
End Class

Public Class WorkForce
    Implements IEnumerable

    Private employees As ArrayList

    Public Sub New()
        employees = New ArrayList()

        'Let's add an employee in here for demo purposes.
        employees.Add(New Employee())
    End Sub

    Public Function GetEnumerator() As IEnumerator _
        Implements IEnumerable.GetEnumerator

        Return New WorkForceEnumerator(employees)
    End Function
End Class

Public Class EntryPoint
    Shared Sub Main()
        Dim staff As WorkForce = New WorkForce()

        For Each emp As Employee In staff
            emp.Evaluate()
        Next emp
    End Sub
End Class
```

Likewise, this example returns the following:

```
Evaluating Employee . . .
```

Of course, the generated IL is not as efficient. To see the efficiency gains within the
For . . . Each loop, you must load the compiled versions of each example into the IL Disassembler (IL DASM) and open up the IL code for the Main method. You'll see that the weakly
typed example has extra castclass instructions in it that are not present in the strongly typed
example. On our development machine, we ran the For . . . Each loop 20,000,000 times in a
tight loop to create a crude benchmark. The typed version of the enumerator was 15% faster
than the untyped version.

Using Immutable Reference Types

When creating a well-designed contract or interface, you should always consider the mutability or immutability of types declared in the contract. For example, if you have a method that accepts a parameter, you should consider whether it is valid for the method to modify the parameter. Suppose you want to ensure that the method body cannot modify a parameter. If the parameter is a value type that is passed with the ByVal keyword, then the method receives a copy of the parameter, and you're guaranteed that the source value is not modified. However, for reference types, it's much more complicated, since only the reference is copied rather than the object the reference points to.

A great example of an immutable class within the standard library is System.String. Once you create a String object, you can never change it. The class is designed so that you can create copies, and those copies can be modified forms of the original, but you cannot change the original instance for as long as it lives without resorting to unsafe code. If you understand that, you get the gist of where we're going here: for a reference-based object to be passed into a method, such that the client can be guaranteed that it won't change during the method call, it must itself be immutable.

In the CLR, this notion of immutability becomes very important. Let's suppose that System.String is mutable, and let's suppose you could write the following fictitious method:

```vb
Public Sub PrintString(ByVal theString As String)
    'Assuming following line does not create a new
    'instance of String but modifies theString.
    theString &= ": there, I printed it!"
    Console.WriteLine(theString)
End Sub
```

Imagine the callers' dismay when they get farther along in the code that called this method, and now their string has this extra stuff appended onto the end of it. That's what could happen if System.String were mutable. You can see that String's immutability exists for a reason, and maybe you should consider adding the same capability to your designs.

As an example, let's revisit the previous ComplexNumber class. If implemented as an object rather than a value type, ComplexNumber would be a perfect candidate to be an immutable type, similar to String. In such cases, an operation such as ComplexNumber.Add() would need to produce a new instance of ComplexNumber rather than modify the object referenced by Me. But for the sake of argument, let's consider what you would want to do if ComplexNumber were allowed to be mutable. You could allow access to the real and imaginary fields via read/write properties. But how would you be able to pass the object to a method and be guaranteed that the method won't change it by accessing the setter of one of the properties? One answer, as in many other object-oriented designs, is the technique of introducing another class. Let's consider the following code:

```vb
Imports System

Public NotInheritable Class ComplexNumber
    Private mReal As Double
    Private mImaginary As Double
```

```vb
    Public Sub New(ByVal real As Double, ByVal imaginary As Double)
        Me.mReal = real
        Me.mImaginary = imaginary
    End Sub

    Public Property Real() As Double
        Get
            Return mReal
        End Get

        Set(ByVal value As Double)
            mReal = value
        End Set
    End Property

    Public Property Imaginary() As Double
        Get
            Return mImaginary
        End Get

        Set(ByVal value As Double)
            mImaginary = value
        End Set
    End Property

    'Other methods removed for clarity.
End Class

Public NotInheritable Class ConstComplexNumber
    Private ReadOnly pimpl As ComplexNumber

    Public Sub New(ByVal pimpl As ComplexNumber)
        Me.pimpl = pimpl
    End Sub

    Public ReadOnly Property Real() As Double
        Get
            Return pimpl.Real
        End Get
    End Property

    Public ReadOnly Property Imaginary() As Double
        Get
            Return pimpl.Imaginary
        End Get
    End Property
End Class
```

```
Public NotInheritable Class EntryPoint
    Shared Sub Main()
        Dim someNumber As ComplexNumber = New ComplexNumber(1, 2)

        SomeMethod(New ConstComplexNumber(someNumber))

        'We are guaranteed by the contract of ConstComplexNumber that
        'someNumber has not been changed at this point.
    End Sub

    Private Shared Sub SomeMethod(ByVal number As ConstComplexNumber)
        Console.WriteLine("( {0}, {1} )", number.Real, number.Imaginary)
    End Sub
End Class
```

This code displays the following results when executed:[8]

```
( 1, 2 )
```

In this example, we've introduced a *shim class* named ConstComplexNumber. Shim classes are often used as a template class between related classes or as a specialized wrapper to expose an interface.

When a method wants to accept a ComplexNumber object but guarantee that it won't change that parameter, then it accepts a ConstComplexNumber rather than a ComplexNumber. Of course, for the case of ComplexNumber, the best solution would have been to implement it as an immutable type in the first place.[9] But, you can easily imagine a class much more complex than ComplexNumber (no pun intended . . . really!) that may require a technique similar to this to guarantee that a method won't modify an instance of it.

As with many problems in software design, you can achieve the same goal in many ways. This shim technique isn't the only way to solve this problem. You could also achieve the same goal with interfaces. You could define one interface that declares all of the methods that modify the object—say, IModifyableComplexNumber—and another interface that declares methods that don't modify the object—say, IConstantComplexNumber. Then, you could create a third interface, IComplexNumber, which derives from both of these, and, finally, ComplexNumber would then implement the IComplexNumber interface. For methods that must take the parameter as immutable, you can simply pass the instance as the IConstantComplexNumber type.

Before you write these techniques off as academic exercises, please take time to consider and understand the power of immutability in robust software designs, and why you might apply these same techniques to your VB designs.

---

8. To find out more about the curious name of the pimpl field, read about the Pimpl Idiom in Herb Sutter's *Exceptional C++: 47 Engineering Puzzles, Programming Problems, and Solutions* (Addison-Wesley Professional, 1999).

9. To avoid this complex ball of yarn, many of the value types defined by the .NET Framework are immutable.

CHECKLIST FOR REFERENCE TYPES

When you design a new class or structure, it is good design practice to go through this checklist for each type, just as a pilot does before the plane leaves the gate. If you take this approach, you can always feel confident about your designs. This checklist has been a work in progress for some time and is not meant to be complete. You will find the need to augment it and create new entries for new scenarios. This checklist is meant to address the most common scenarios that you're likely to encounter in the VB design process.

- *Should the class be unsealed?* Classes should be declared `NotInheritable` by default unless they're clearly intended to be used as a base class. Even then, you should document well how to use them as a base class. Choose sealed classes over unsealed classes.

- *Is an object cloneable?*

  - *Implement* `ICloneable`, *while defaulting to a deep copy.* If an object is mutable, default to a deep copy. Otherwise, if immutable, consider a shallow copy as an optimization.

  - *Avoid use of* `MemberwiseClone()`: Calling `MemberwiseClone()` creates a new object without calling any constructors. This practice can be dangerous.

- *Is an object disposable?*

  - *Implement* `IDisposable`: If you find the need to implement a conventional destructor, use the `IDispose` pattern instead.

  - *Implement a finalizer.* Disposable objects should implement a finalizer to either catch objects that clients forgot to dispose of or to warn clients that they forgot to do so. Don't do deterministic destruction work in the VB destructor, which is the finalizer. Only do that kind of work in the `Dispose` method.

  - *Suppress finalization during a call to* `Dispose()`: This will make the GC perform much more efficiently. Otherwise, objects live on the heap longer than they need to.

- *Should object equivalence checks carry value semantics?*

  - *Override* `Object.Equals()`: Before changing the semantic meaning of `Equals()`, come up with a solid argument to do so; otherwise, leave the default identity equivalence in place for objects. It is an error to throw exceptions from within your `Equals()` override.

  - *Know when to call the base class* `Equals()` *implementation.* If your object derives from a type whose version of `Equals()` differs in semantic meaning from your implementation, don't call the base class version in the override. Otherwise, be sure to do so and include its result with yours.

  - *Override* `GetHashCode()` *too.* This is a necessary step to ensure that you can use objects of this type as a hash code key. If you override `Equals()`, always override `GetHashCode()`, too.

- *Are objects of this type comparable?*

  - *Implement* `IComparable` *and override* `Equals()` *and* `GetHashCode()`: You'll want to override these as a group, since they have intertwined implementations.

continued

CHECKLIST FOR REFERENCE TYPES

- *Is an object convertible to* System.String() *or vice versa?*

    - *Override* Object.ToString(): The implementation inherited from Object.ToString() merely returns a string name of the object's type.

    - *Implement* IFormattable *if users need finer control over string formatting*: Implement the Object.ToString() override by calling IFormattable.ToString() with a format string of G and a Nothing format provider.

- *Is an object convertible?*

    - *Override* IConvertible *so the class will work with* System.Convert: In VB, you must implement all methods of the interface. However, for conversion methods that don't make sense for your class, simply throw an InvalidCastException object.

- *Should an object be immutable?*

    - *Consider making fields read-only and provide only read-only properties*: Objects that fundamentally represent a simple value, such as a string or a complex number, are excellent candidates to be immutable objects.

- *Do you need to pass an object as a constant immutable method parameter?*

    - *Consider implementing an immutable shim class that contains a reference to a mutable object, which can be passed a method parameter*: First, see if it makes sense for your class to be immutable. If so, then there's no need for this action. If you do need to be able to pass your mutable objects to methods as immutable objects, you can achieve the same effect by using interfaces.

Value-Type Best Practices

While investigating the notions of canonical forms for value types, you'll find that some of the concepts that apply to reference types may be applied here as well. However, there are notable differences. For example, it makes no sense to implement ICloneable on a value type. Technically, you could, but since ICloneable returns an instance of type Object, your value type's implementation of ICloneable.Clone() would most likely just be returning a boxed copy of itself. You can get the exact same behavior by simply casting a value type instance into a reference to System.Object, as long as your value type doesn't contain any reference types. In fact, you could argue that value types that contain mutable reference types are bordering on poor design. Value types are best used for immutable, lightweight data chunks. As long as the reference types your value type contains are immutable—similar to System.String, for example—you don't have to worry about implementing ICloneable on your value type. If you find yourself being forced to implement ICloneable on your value type, take a closer look at the design. It's possible that your value type should be a reference type.

Value types don't need a finalizer, and, in fact, VB won't let you create a finalizer on a structure. Similarly, value types have no need to implement the IDisposable interface, unless they contain objects by reference, which implement IDisposable, or if they hold onto scarce system resources. In those cases, it's important that value types implement IDisposable. You can use the Using statement with value types that implement IDisposable.

■**Tip** Since value types cannot implement finalizers, they cannot guarantee that the cleanup code in `Dispose()` executes, even if the user forgets to call it explicitly. Therefore, declaring fields of reference type within value types should be discouraged. If a field is a value type that requires disposal, you cannot guarantee that disposal happens.

Value types and reference types do share many implementation idioms. For example, it makes sense for both to consider implementing `IComparable`, `IFormattable`, and possibly `IConvertible`.

In the rest of this section, we'll cover the different canonical concepts that you should apply while designing value types. Specifically, you'll want to override `Equals()` for greater runtime efficiency, and you'll want to be cognizant of what it means for a value type to implement an interface.

Override Equals() for Better Performance

You've already seen the main differences between the two types of equivalence in the CLR and in VB. For example, you now know that reference types (class instances) define equality as an identity test by default, and value types (structure instances) use value equality as an equivalence test. Reference types get their default implementation from `Object.Equals()`, whereas value types get their default implementation from `System.ValueType`'s override of `Equals()`. All structure types implicitly derive from `System.ValueType`.

You should implement your own override of `Equals()` for structures that you define. You can compare the fields of your object more efficiently; since you know their types and what they are at compile time. Let's update the `ComplexNumber` example from previous sections, converting it to a structure and implementing a custom `Equals()` override:

```
Imports System

Public Structure ComplexNumber
    Implements IComparable

    Private ReadOnly real As Double
    Private ReadOnly imaginary As Double

    Public Sub New(ByVal real As Double, ByVal imaginary As Double)
        Me.real = real
        Me.imaginary = imaginary
    End Sub

    Public Overloads Overrides Function Equals(ByVal other As Object) As Boolean
        Dim result As Boolean = False

        If TypeOf other Is ComplexNumber Then
            Dim that As ComplexNumber = CType(other, ComplexNumber)

            result = InternalEquals(that)
        End If
```

```vb
        Return result
    End Function

    Public Overrides Function GetHashCode() As Integer
        Return CInt(Fix(Me.Magnitude))
    End Function

    Public Shared Operator =(ByVal num1 As ComplexNumber, _
        ByVal num2 As ComplexNumber) As Boolean

        Return num1.Equals(num2)
    End Operator

    Public Shared Operator <>(ByVal num1 As ComplexNumber, _
        ByVal num2 As ComplexNumber) As Boolean

        Return Not num1.Equals(num2)
    End Operator

    Public Function CompareTo(ByVal other As Object) As Integer _
        Implements IComparable.CompareTo

        If Not (TypeOf other Is ComplexNumber) Then
            Throw New ArgumentException("Bad Comparison!")
        End If

        Dim that As ComplexNumber = CType(other, ComplexNumber)

        Dim result As Integer
        If InternalEquals(that) Then
            result = 0
        ElseIf Me.Magnitude > that.Magnitude Then
            result = 1
        Else
            result = -1
        End If

        Return result
    End Function

    Private Function InternalEquals(ByVal that As ComplexNumber) As Boolean
        Return (Me.real = that.real) AndAlso (Me.imaginary = that.imaginary)
    End Function

    Public ReadOnly Property Magnitude() As Double
        Get
            Return Math.Sqrt(Math.Pow(Me.real, 2) + Math.Pow(Me.imaginary, 2))
        End Get
    End Property
```

```
        'Other methods removed for clarity.
End Structure

Public NotInheritable Class EntryPoint
    Shared Sub Main()
        Dim num1 As ComplexNumber = New ComplexNumber(1, 2)
        Dim num2 As ComplexNumber = New ComplexNumber(1, 2)

        Dim result As Boolean = num1.Equals(num2)
    End Sub
End Class
```

From looking at the example code, you can see that it has only minimal changes compared to the reference type version. The type is now declared as a structure rather than a class, and notice that it also still supports IComparable. You may notice that the efficiency still stands to improve by a fair amount. The trick lies in the concept of boxing and unboxing. Remember, any time a value type instance is passed as an object in a method parameter list, it must be implicitly boxed if it is not boxed already. This means that when the Main method calls the Equals method, it must first box the num2 value. What's worse is that the method will typically unbox the value in order to use it. Thus in the process of comparing two values for equality, you've made two more copies of one of them.

To solve this problem, you can define two overloads of Equals(). You want a type-safe version that takes a ComplexNumber as its parameter type, and you still need to override the Object.Equals method as before.

■**Note** .NET 2.0 formalized this concept with the generic interface IEquatable(Of T), which declares one method that is the type-safe version of Equals().

Let's take a look at how the code changes:

```
Imports System

Public Structure ComplexNumber
    Implements IComparable
    Implements IComparable(Of ComplexNumber)
    Implements IEquatable(Of ComplexNumber)

    Private ReadOnly real As Double
    Private ReadOnly imaginary As Double

    Public Sub New(ByVal real As Double, ByVal imaginary As Double)
        Me.real = real
        Me.imaginary = imaginary
    End Sub
```

```vb
Public Overloads Function Equals(ByVal other As ComplexNumber) As Boolean
    Return (Me.real = other.real) AndAlso (Me.imaginary = other.imaginary)
End Function

Public Overloads Overrides Function Equals(ByVal other As Object) As Boolean
    Dim result As Boolean = False

    If TypeOf other Is ComplexNumber Then
        Dim that As ComplexNumber = CType(other, ComplexNumber)

        result = Equals(that)
    End If

    Return result
End Function

Public Function IEquatableOfT_Equals(ByVal other As ComplexNumber) _
    As Boolean Implements System.IEquatable(Of ComplexNumber).Equals
End Function

Public Overrides Function GetHashCode() As Integer
    Return CInt(Fix(Me.Magnitude))
End Function

Public Shared Operator =(ByVal num1 As ComplexNumber, _
    ByVal num2 As ComplexNumber) As Boolean

    Return num1.Equals(num2)
End Operator

Public Shared Operator <>(ByVal num1 As ComplexNumber, _
    ByVal num2 As ComplexNumber) As Boolean

    Return Not num1.Equals(num2)
End Operator

Public Function CompareTo(ByVal other As Object) As Integer _
    Implements IComparable.CompareTo

    If Not (TypeOf other Is ComplexNumber) Then
        Throw New ArgumentException("Bad Comparison!")
    End If

    Return CompareTo(CType(other, ComplexNumber))
End Function

Public Function CompareTo(ByVal that As ComplexNumber) As Integer
    Dim result As Integer
```

```vb
        If Equals(that) Then
            result = 0
        ElseIf Me.Magnitude > that.Magnitude Then
            result = 1
        Else
            result = -1
        End If

        Return result
    End Function

    Public Function IComparableOfT_CompareTo(ByVal other As ComplexNumber) _
        As Integer Implements System.IComparable(Of ComplexNumber).CompareTo
    End Function

    Public ReadOnly Property Magnitude() As Double
        Get
            Return Math.Sqrt(Math.Pow(Me.real, 2) + Math.Pow(Me.imaginary, 2))
        End Get
    End Property

    'Other methods removed for clarity.
End Structure

Public NotInheritable Class EntryPoint
    Shared Sub Main()
        Dim num1 As ComplexNumber = New ComplexNumber(1, 2)
        Dim num2 As ComplexNumber = New ComplexNumber(1, 2)

        Dim result As Boolean = num1.Equals(num2)
    End Sub
End Class
```

Now, the comparison inside Main() is much more efficient, since the value doesn't need to be boxed. The compiler chooses the closest match of the two overloads, which is the strongly typed overload of Equals() that accepts a ComplexNumber rather than a generic object type. Internally, the Object.Equals() override delegates to the type-safe version of Equals() after it checks the type of the object and unboxes it. The Object.Equals() override first checks the type to see if it is a ComplexNumber, or more specifically a boxed ComplexNumber, before it unboxes it so as to avoid throwing an exception. The standard library documentation for Object.Equals() clearly states that overrides of Object.Equals() must not throw exceptions. Finally, notice that the same rule of thumb for GetHashCode() exists for structures as well as classes. If you override Object.Equals(), you should also override Object.GetHashCode(), or vice versa.

Note that you also implement IComparable(Of ComplexNumber), which uses the same technique as IEquatable(Of ComplexNumber) to provide a type-safe version of IComparable. You should consider implementing these generic interfaces so the compiler has greater latitude when enforcing type safety.

Implement Type-Safe Forms of Interface Members and Derived Methods

We covered this topic with respect to reference types in the "Prefer Type Safety at All Times" section. Most of those same points are applicable to value types, along with some added efficiency considerations. These efficiency problems stem from explicit conversion operations from value types to reference types, and vice versa. These conversions also produce hidden boxing and unboxing operations in the generated IL code. Boxing operations can easily kill your efficiency in many situations. The points made previously about how type-safe versions of the enumeration methods help the VB compiler create much more efficient code in a For . . . Each loop apply tenfold to value types. That is because boxing operations from conversions to and from value types take much more processor time when compared to a typecast of a reference type, which is relatively quick.

You've seen how the ComplexNumber value type implements an interface—in this case, IComparable. That is because you still want value types to be sortable if they're stored within a container. You'll notice that core types within the CLR, such as System.Int32, also support interfaces such as IComparable. However, from an efficiency standpoint, you don't want to box a value type each time you want to compare it to another. In fact, as it is currently written, the following code boxes both values:

```
Public Sub Main()
    Dim num1 As ComplexNumber = New ComplexNumber(1, 3)
    Dim num2 As ComplexNumber = New ComplexNumber(1, 2)

    Dim result As Integer = (CType(num1, IComparable)).CompareTo(num2)
End Sub
```

Can you see both of the boxing operations? The num1 instance must be boxed in order to acquire a reference to the IComparable interface on it. Secondly, since CompareTo() accepts a reference of type System.Object, the num2 instance must be boxed. This is terrible for efficiency. Technically, you don't have to box num1 in order to call through IComparable. However, if the previous ComplexNumber example had implemented the IComparable interface explicitly, you would have had no choice.

To solve this problem, you want to implement a type-safe version of the CompareTo method, while at the same time implementing the IComparable.CompareTo method. Using this technique, the comparison call in the previous code will incur absolutely no boxing operations. Let's look at how to modify the ComplexNumber structure to do this:

```
Imports System

Public Structure ComplexNumber
    Implements IComparable
    Implements IComparable(Of ComplexNumber)
    Implements IEquatable(Of ComplexNumber)

    Private ReadOnly real As Double
    Private ReadOnly imaginary As Double
```

```vb
Public Sub New(ByVal real As Double, ByVal imaginary As Double)
    Me.real = real
    Me.imaginary = imaginary
End Sub

Public Overloads Function Equals(ByVal other As ComplexNumber) As Boolean
    Return (Me.real = other.real) AndAlso (Me.imaginary = other.imaginary)
End Function

Public Overloads Overrides Function Equals(ByVal other As Object) As Boolean
    Dim result As Boolean = False

    If TypeOf other Is ComplexNumber Then
        Dim that As ComplexNumber = CType(other, ComplexNumber)

        result = Equals(that)
    End If

    Return result
End Function

Public Function IEquatableOfT_Equals(ByVal other As ComplexNumber) As Boolean _
    Implements System.IEquatable(Of ComplexNumber).Equals
End Function

Public Overrides Function GetHashCode() As Integer
    Return CInt(Fix(Me.Magnitude))
End Function

Public Shared Operator =(ByVal num1 As ComplexNumber, _
    ByVal num2 As ComplexNumber) As Boolean

    Return num1.Equals(num2)
End Operator

Public Shared Operator <>(ByVal num1 As ComplexNumber, _
    ByVal num2 As ComplexNumber) As Boolean

    Return Not num1.Equals(num2)
End Operator

Public Function CompareTo(ByVal that As ComplexNumber) As Integer
    Dim result As Integer
```

```vb
            If Equals(that) Then
                result = 0
            ElseIf Me.Magnitude > that.Magnitude Then
                result = 1
            Else
                result = -1
            End If


            Return result
        End Function

        Private Function CompareTo(ByVal other As Object) As Integer _
            Implements IComparable.CompareTo

            If Not (TypeOf other Is ComplexNumber) Then
                Throw New ArgumentException("Bad Comparison!")
            End If

            Return CompareTo(CType(other, ComplexNumber))
        End Function

        Public Function IComparableOfT_CompareTo(ByVal other As ComplexNumber) _
            As Integer Implements System.IComparable(Of ComplexNumber).CompareTo
        End Function

        Public ReadOnly Property Magnitude() As Double
            Get
                Return Math.Sqrt(Math.Pow(Me.real, 2) + Math.Pow(Me.imaginary, 2))
            End Get
        End Property

        'Other methods removed for clarity.
    End Structure

Public NotInheritable Class EntryPoint
    Shared Sub Main()
        Dim num1 As ComplexNumber = New ComplexNumber(1, 3)
        Dim num2 As ComplexNumber = New ComplexNumber(1, 2)

        Dim result As Integer = num1.CompareTo(num2)

        'Now, try the type-generic version
        result = (CType(num1, IComparable)).CompareTo(num2)
    End Sub
End Class
```

After the modifications, the first call to `CompareTo()` in `Main()` will incur no boxing opera-tions. You'll notice that we went one step further and implemented the `IComparable.CompareTo` method explicitly in order to make it harder to call the type-less version of `CompareTo()` inad-vertently without first explicitly casting the value instance to a reference of type `IComparable`. The `Main` method also demonstrates how to call the type-less version of `CompareTo()`. Now, the idea is that clients who use the `ComplexNumber` value can write code in a natural-looking way and get the benefits of better performance. Clients who require going through the interface, such as some container types, can use the `IComparable` interface, albeit with some boxing. If you're curious, go ahead and open up the compiled executable with the previous example code inside the IL Disassembler and examine the `Main` method. You'll see that the first call to `CompareTo()` results in no boxing, whereas the second call to `CompareTo()` does, in fact, result in two boxing operations as expected.

As a general rule of thumb, you can apply this idiom to just about any value type's methods that accept or return a boxed instance of the value type. So far, you've seen two such examples of the idiom in use. The first was while implementing `Equals()` for the `ComplexNumber` type, and the second was while implementing `IComparable.CompareTo()`.

CHECKLIST FOR VALUE TYPES

This checklist, similar to the preceding one we presented for reference types, is meant to aid you when creating value types in VB. As you gain experience creating value types in VB, you will find the need to augment this list and create new entries.

- *Do you desire greater efficiency for your value types?*

  - *Override* `Equals()` *and* `GetHashCode()`: The generic version of `ValueType.Equals()` is not efficient because it relies upon reflection. Generally, it's best to provide a type-safe version of `Equals()` by implementing `IEquatable(Of T)` and then have the type-less version call it. Don't forget to override `GetHashCode()` too.

  - *Provide type-safe overloads of inherited type-less methods and interface methods*: For any method that accepts or returns a parameter of type `System.Object`, provide an overload that uses the concrete value type in its place. That way, clients of the value type can avoid unnecessary boxing. For interfaces, consider hiding the type-less implementation behind explicit interface implementation, if desired.

- *Do you need to modify boxed instances of value?*

  - *Implement an interface to do so*: Calling through an interface member implemented by a value type is the only way to change a value type within a boxed instance.

- *Are values of this type comparable?*

  - *Implement* `IComparable` *and override* `Equals()` *and* `GetHashCode()`: You'll want to override these as a triplet, since they have intertwined implementations. If you override `Equals()`, take the previous advice and create a type-safe version as well.

continued

CHECKLIST FOR VALUE TYPES

- *Is the value convertible to* System.String() *or vice versa?*

  - *Override* ValueType.ToString(): The implementation inherited from ValueType merely returns a string name of the value's type.

  - *Implement* IFormattable *if users need finer control over string formatting:* Implement a ValueType.ToString() override that calls IFormattable.ToString() with a format string of G and a Nothing format provider.

- *Is the value convertible?*

  - *Override* IConvertible *so structures will work with* System.Convert: In VB, all methods of the interface must be implemented. However, for conversion methods that don't make sense for your structure, simply throw an InvalidCastException object.

- *Should this structure be immutable?*

  - *Consider making fields read-only, and provide only read-only properties:* Values are excellent candidates to be immutable types.

Summary

This chapter introduced and discussed a variety of best practices for developing new types in VB. We also offered two checklists that you can use as a guide when you develop your types.

In the next chapter, we will explore the new LINQ technologies and how they can be used to standardize your data manipulation needs across different data sources.

CHAPTER 15

■■■

LINQ with VB 2008

Language-Integrated Query (LINQ) is a set of new technologies built into the .NET 3.5 Framework. If you currently use ADO.NET to consume data from Microsoft Access/SQL Server, XMLTextReader for XML, or FileSystemObject for other files, LINQ will change the way you work. LINQ eases your use of disparate data sources by providing a common object model and syntax to consume data within your VB 2008 applications.

In this chapter, we will discuss LINQ to Objects, LINQ to XML, and LINQ to SQL. LINQ to Objects allows you to perform queries against any object that implements the IEnumerable(Of T) interface, while with LINQ to XML you can query XML sources. LINQ to SQL enables querying of many relational database management systems (RDBMS), as well as any data source that implements the IQueryable(Of T) interface.

LINQ queries are similar in look and feel to standard SQL statements. In addition, we will cover several technologies that support LINQ, including type inference, anonymous types, extension methods, and Lambda expressions.

LINQ Overview

LINQ allows you to create data queries directly in your VB code and provides a common syntax regardless of the source of your data. Using LINQ, you will become more productive when working with data, as you can apply a single syntactical model to your data manipulation requirements. For example, the LINQ syntax allows you to query XML, in-memory objects, and even the file system.

Using SQL-like expressions, you can retrieve, filter, sort, group, and aggregate data sets. LINQ operators, such as Min, Max, and Count, can greatly reduce the amount of looping code usually required to perform these types of functions.

Using LINQ, query syntax and schema checking is accomplished at compile time, saving you from associated runtime errors. Finally, VB shortens your learning curve by giving you IntelliSense for your LINQ queries.

Query Comprehensions

Query comprehensions form the basis of LINQ queries and are comprised of the familiar Select, From, and Where clauses, named *query operators*. You combine query operator clauses to form *query expressions*. These expressions can then be used to return a data set from various sources, such as XML and collections. An example statement would look like this:

```
Dim SmallCapStocks = From Stock In AllStocks _
    Where Stock.Price < 10.0 _
    Select Stock.Ticker, Stock.Price
```

This code snippet will create `SmallCapStocks` and populate it with stocks priced less than $10.00 from `AllStocks`. `SmallCapStocks` is an example of an *anonymous type*, which is discussed in more detail in the upcoming "Anonymous Types and Type Inference" section.

LINQ Syntax

The ordering of the previous statement may seem a bit odd to those of you familiar with SQL statements. Standard SQL syntax defines a query using the `Select/From/Where/Order By` clauses, as in the following code snippet:

```
Select Stock From AllStocks Where Price < 10 Order By Price
```

In comparison, LINQ syntax defines queries as `From/Where/Order By/Select`. This change of clause order is what enables IntelliSense to present you with a list of possible choices to complete your statement.

From

Every LINQ query begins with a required `From` operator. The `From` clause specifies the data source that you want to query. The following `From` clause sets up a query against an `Employees` data source and uses `E` to represent each item. The following code snippet demonstrates:

```
From E in Employees
```

Select

Using a `Select` clause works the same way it does in SQL. Using `Select`, you can retrieve only the employees' first and last names with the following code snippet:

```
From E In Employees
Select E.FirstName, E.LastName
```

Unlike standard SQL, the `Select` clause is optional in LINQ. Omitting `Select` will return all data points, or fields, in your data set. This is equivalent to using `Select *` in SQL.

Distinct

`Distinct` eliminates duplicates from your result set, returning only unique items. For example, to query for departments that actually have employees working in them, you can execute the following:

```
From E In Employees
Select E.Department
Distinct
```

Where

The `Where` clause allows you to filter your result set to meet a specific criterion. For example, if you only want to retrieve employees who work in the warehouse, you can use the following query:

```
From E In Employees
Where E.Department = "Warehouse"
Select E.FirstName, E.LastName
```

Order By

Using an `Order By` clause, you can sort your data set by the specified criterion. `Order By` supports ascending as well as descending orders. Using `Order By`, you can further refine your query to return your warehouse employees in the order hired, returning the newest employees first. Here's an example:

```
From E In Employees
Where E.Department = "Warehouse"
Order By E.HireDate Descending
Select E.FirstName, E.LastName
```

Join

The `Join` clause is used to create a single result set from two or more data sets that are related by a key. Using `Join`, you can query a combined employees/warehouses result set and return each warehouse employees' location. This query can be written as follows:

```
From E In Employees
Join L In Locations On E.LocationID Equals L.ID
Where L.DepartmentType = "Warehouse"
Select E.FirstName, E.LastName, L.City, L.State
```

Anonymous Types and Type Inference

Type inference, which helps the VB compiler implicitly infer a type at the point of declaration, has been updated in VB 2008 to support LINQ. Earlier versions of VB defaulted to a type of `Object` when a member was created in code with no declared type. Now your member is inferred by evaluating the right-hand side of your declaration statement. Any types that you define in this manner are referred to as *anonymous types*.

For example, in VB 2008, you can write the following code, which will create three variables of type `Int32`, `DateTime`, and `String`, respectively:

```
Public Class EntryPoint
    Shared Sub Main()
        Dim x = 300
        Dim CurrentTime = DateTime.Now
        Dim Publisher = "Apress"
```

```
      Console.WriteLine(x.GetType)
      Console.WriteLine(CurrentTime.GetType)
      Console.WriteLine(Publisher.GetType)
   End Sub
End Class
```

The preceding example will output the following to the console:

```
System.Int32
System.DateTime
System.String
```

In this example, three variables, x, CurrentTime, and Publisher, are created. These are declared and initialized without using As or New(). Finally, their types are displayed to the console by using the GetType method.

Type inference saves you from having to declare types for LINQ queries. For example, in the following statement, WarehouseEmployees is inferred to be IEnumerable(Of <anonymous type>), while Department, FirstName, and LastName are inferred as String:

```
Dim WarehouseEmployees =
From E In Employees
Where E.Department = "Warehouse"
Select E.FirstName, E.LastName
```

Extension Methods

Extension methods allow you to add methods to an existing CLR type. This enables you to expand the functionality of a type without needing to create a subclass. The following example shows the syntax for an extension method on String:

```
   <Extension()> _
   Public Function IsTickerValid(ByVal aTicker As String) As Boolean
      Dim ValidTicker As Boolean = True

      If aTicker.Length > 4 Then
         ValidTicker = False
      End If

      Return ValidTicker
   End Function
```

Extension methods avoid the need to create a separate class with a shared method to validate the ticker symbol. LINQ uses extension methods throughout the .NET Framework. The query operators, including From, Where, and Select, are implemented using extension methods.

Let's create and use an extension method on the Integer type. The IsPrime method's first parameter will accept an Integer, which also indicates the type being extended. IsPrime returns a Boolean to indicate whether the passed integer is indeed a prime number. Here's an example:

```
Imports System.Runtime.CompilerServices

Public Module Extensions
    <Extension()> _
    Public Function IsPrime(ByVal i As Integer) As Boolean
        Dim PrimeNumbers As Integer() = {2, 3, 5, 7}

        For Each item In PrimeNumbers
            If i Mod item = 0 Then
                Return False
            End If
        Next

        Return True
    End Function
End Module

Public Class EntryPoint
    Shared Sub Main()
        Dim x As Integer = 11
        Dim y As Integer = 6

        If x.IsPrime Then
            Console.WriteLine("x is a prime number.")
        Else
            Console.WriteLine("x is not a prime number.")
        End If

        If y.IsPrime Then
            Console.WriteLine("y is a prime number.")
        Else
            Console.WriteLine("y is not a prime number.")
        End If
    End Sub
End Class
```

The preceding example returns the following to the console:

```
x is a prime number.
y is not a prime number.
```

To create an extension method, it is required to import System.Runtime.CompilerServices. Extension methods must be defined in a Module and are decorated with <Extension()>. In Main(), we declare two Integers, x and y, and assign them values of 11 and 6, respectively. The following If . . . Then illustrates that you can indeed call IsPrime() in the same manner as any other method belonging to Integer. In fact, IsPrime() will be available in IntelliSense, making it easy to find as you develop.

Lambda Expressions

New in VB 2008, Lambda expressions have been added to support LINQ queries. Where clauses, for example, are compiled as Lambda expressions and called on the applicable items in your data set. Lambda expressions are a form of delegate that can be passed to, or returned from, another function.

Func Type

The Func delegate type, defined in the System namespace, can be passed up to four parameters and one return type. Func(Of T, TResult) is a delegate that accepts an Integer parameter and returns a Boolean. Here's an example of Func usage:

```
Public Class EntryPoint
   Shared Sub Main()
      Dim IsEven As Func(Of Integer, Boolean) = _
         Function(n) n Mod 2 = 0

      Console.WriteLine(IsEven(20))
   End Sub
End Class
```

Running the preceding example returns the following to the console:

```
True
```

The delegate, defined in the Dim IsEven As Func line of code, is designed to return a Boolean, indicating whether the passed Integer is even. The next line of code shows IsEven() usage by passing a value of 20 into it and writing True to the console.

Inline Function

Lambda expressions can also be used directly in a statement as an inline function. VB 2008 can infer the type of each variable, which allows you to simplify many code statements. Here's an example inline function:

```
Public Class EntryPoint
   Shared Sub Main()
      Dim Cube = Function(x) x ^ 3

      Console.WriteLine(Cube(5))
   End Sub
End Class
```

This example returns the following to the console:

Here a new variable, Cube, is created and assigned an inline function. The function, defined by Function(x) x ^ 3, will be executed when passing a value to Cube. In this example, a value of 5 is passed to Cube, which writes 125 to the console.

LINQ to Objects

LINQ to Objects allows you to create and execute SQL-like queries over your arrays and collections. LINQ to Objects reduces the need to loop through an array, collection, or other type that implements IEnumerable(Of T) to find the items you want to work with. By executing a LINQ to Objects query, you are able to filter your collection for more specific processing with a single statement.

LINQ to Objects Queries

Let's try our hand at some LINQ to Objects queries by using query clauses described earlier in the "LINQ Syntax" section. These include From, Where, and Order By. Next we will look at the Min, Max, and Count operators. In addition, we will create an example with the Contains extension method, new to VB 2008.

From

This example demonstrates the simplest of LINQ queries. It simply specifies a From clause to return all Numbers.

```
Imports System
Imports System.Linq

Public Class EntryPoint
    Shared Sub Main()
        Dim Numbers() = {1, 2, 3, 4, 5, 6, 7, 8, 9, 10, 11, 12, 13, 14, _
            15, 16, 17, 18, 19, 20, 21, 22, 23, 24, 25, 26, 27, 28, 29, 30, 31, 32, _
            33, 34, 35, 36, 37, 38, 39, 40, 41, 42, 43, 44, 45, 46, 47, 48, 49, 50}

        Dim Query = From x In Numbers

        For Each Item In Query
            Console.WriteLine(Item.ToString)
        Next
    End Sub
End Class
```

The preceding example will output integers from 1 to 50 to the console. Imports System.Linq is a required import to enable LINQ functionality. The Dim Numbers() = line of code takes advantage of VB's new implicitly typed local variables feature. VB infers the data type of Numbers() to be an integer based on the values assigned to it. Finally, From x In Numbers simply loads all Numbers into Query.

Where

This example demonstrates Where usage in LINQ. You will use the same Numbers array and return only Numbers whose first digit is 3.

```vb
Imports System
Imports System.Linq

Public Class EntryPoint
    Shared Sub Main()
        Dim Numbers() = {1, 2, 3, 4, 5, 6, 7, 8, 9, 10, 11, 12, 13, 14, _
            15, 16, 17, 18, 19, 20, 21, 22, 23, 24, 25, 26, 27, 28, 29, 30, 31, 32, _
            33, 34, 35, 36, 37, 38, 39, 40, 41, 42, 43, 44, 45, 46, 47, 48, 49, 50}

        Dim Query = From x In Numbers _
                    Where x.ToString.Chars(0) = "3" _
                    Select x

        For Each Item In Query
            Console.WriteLine(Item.ToString)
        Next
    End Sub
End Class
```

The preceding example will output the following to the console:

```
3
30
31
32
33
34
35
36
37
38
39
```

In this code example, the Where x.ToString.Chars(0) = "3" line of code filters the Numbers array. After filtering Numbers, each qualifying item is written to the console.

Order By

Using Order By in LINQ orders the data in either ascending or descending order. Using the Numbers array, let's return numbers evenly divisible by 5 in descending order.

```vb
Imports System
Imports System.Linq
```

```
Public Class EntryPoint
    Shared Sub Main()
        Dim Numbers() = {1, 2, 3, 4, 5, 6, 7, 8, 9, 10, 11, 12, 13, 14, _
            15, 16, 17, 18, 19, 20, 21, 22, 23, 24, 25, 26, 27, 28, 29, 30, 31, 32, _
            33, 34, 35, 36, 37, 38, 39, 40, 41, 42, 43, 44, 45, 46, 47, 48, 49, 50}

        Dim Query = From x In Numbers _
                    Where x Mod 5 = 0 _
                    Order By x Descending _
                    Select x

        For Each Item In Query
            Console.WriteLine(Item.ToString)
        Next
    End Sub
End Class
```

The preceding code will output the following to the console:

```
50
45
40
35
30
25
20
15
10
5
```

In this example, the Where x Mod 5 = 0 code line filters the Numbers array. Then the Order By x Descending line orders the result set. Finally, the results are written to the console.

Min, Max, and Count

The Min, Max, and Count extension methods return the smallest value, the largest value, and the number of values in a data set, respectively. Using the Numbers array, let's get its Min, Max, and Count.

```
Imports System
Imports System.Linq

Public Class EntryPoint
    Shared Sub Main()
        Dim Numbers() = {1, 2, 3, 4, 5, 6, 7, 8, 9, 10, 11, 12, 13, 14, _
            15, 16, 17, 18, 19, 20, 21, 22, 23, 24, 25, 26, 27, 28, 29, 30, 31, 32, _
            33, 34, 35, 36, 37, 38, 39, 40, 41, 42, 43, 44, 45, 46, 47, 48, 49, 50}
```

```
        Dim Query = From x In Numbers _
                    Select x

    Console.WriteLine(Query.Min())
    Console.WriteLine(Query.Max())
    Console.WriteLine(Query.Count())
  End Sub
End Class
```

The preceding code will output the following to the console:

```
1
50
50
```

In this example, Query.Min() returns 1, while Query.Max() and Query.Count() each return 50 to the console.

Count Using a Lambda Expression

In this example, Count is passed a Lambda expression, which defines the items in Numbers that you want to count. Using the Numbers array, let's find the Numbers that are evenly divisible by 10.

```
Imports System
Imports System.Linq

Public Class EntryPoint
    Shared Sub Main()
        Dim Numbers() = {1, 2, 3, 4, 5, 6, 7, 8, 9, 10, 11, 12, 13, 14, _
            15, 16, 17, 18, 19, 20, 21, 22, 23, 24, 25, 26, 27, 28, 29, 30, 31, 32, _
            33, 34, 35, 36, 37, 38, 39, 40, 41, 42, 43, 44, 45, 46, 47, 48, 49, 50}

        Dim DivisibleBy10 = Numbers.Count(Function(n) n Mod 10 = 0)

        Console.WriteLine(DivisibleBy10)
    End Sub
End Class
```

The preceding code outputs the following to the console:

```
5
```

In this example, Numbers.Count(Function(n) n Mod 10 = 0) returns 5, which represents Numbers evenly divisible by 10.

Let

Using Let in a LINQ query creates a variable within your query that you can assign to. These variables can evaluate to such things as text expressions and calculations. Let acts in the same way as Select @LocalVariable = or Set @LocalVariable = does in SQL. Using the Numbers array, let's create some code that uses Let:

```
Imports System
Imports System.Linq

Public Class EntryPoint
    Shared Sub Main()
        Dim Numbers() = {1, 2, 3, 4, 5, 6, 7, 8, 9, 10, 11, 12, 13, 14, _
            15, 16, 17, 18, 19, 20, 21, 22, 23, 24, 25, 26, 27, 28, 29, 30, 31, 32, _
            33, 34, 35, 36, 37, 38, 39, 40, 41, 42, 43, 44, 45, 46, 47, 48, 49, 50}

        Dim Query = From n In Numbers _
                    Let MultipliedBy10 = n ^ 2 _
                    Let ConstantString = "Squared" _
                    Where n >= 25 And n <= 35 _
                    Select n, ConstantString, MultipliedBy10

        For Each Item In Query
            Console.WriteLine(Item.n.ToString & " " & Item.ConstantString & _
                            " Equals " & Item.MultipliedBy10 & ".")
        Next
    End Sub
End Class
```

Running this code outputs the following to the console:

```
25 Squared Equals 625.
26 Squared Equals 676.
27 Squared Equals 729.
28 Squared Equals 784.
29 Squared Equals 841.
30 Squared Equals 900.
31 Squared Equals 961.
32 Squared Equals 1024.
33 Squared Equals 1089.
34 Squared Equals 1156.
35 Squared Equals 1225.
```

In this example, Let MultipliedBy10 = holds the results of the $n \wedge 2$ calculation, while Let ConstantString = holds "Squared". In the Where clause, you filter the return set to Numbers between 25 and 35, inclusive. In the Select clause, notice that the variables created via Let are available. Finally, IntelliSense offers the newly created variables as a choice for Console. WriteLine(Item. in the For . . . Each.

Contains

In this LINQ to Objects example, we use the new `Contains` extension method introduced with VB 2008:

```
Imports System
Imports System.Linq

Public Class EntryPoint
    Shared Sub Main()
        Dim Numbers() = {1, 2, 3, 4, 5, 6, 7, 8, 9, 10, 11, 12, 13, 14, _
            15, 16, 17, 18, 19, 20, 21, 22, 23, 24, 25, 26, 27, 28, 29, 30, 31, 32, _
            33, 34, 35, 36, 37, 38, 39, 40, 41, 42, 43, 44, 45, 46, 47, 48, 49, 50}

        Dim Subset() = {3, 11, 42}

        Dim Query = From x In Numbers _
                    Where Subset.Contains(x) _
                    Select x

        For Each Item In Query
            Console.WriteLine(Item.ToString)
        Next
    End Sub
End Class
```

This code will output the following to the console:

```
3
11
42
```

In this example, two integer arrays, Numbers and Subset, are created. `Subset.Contains(x)` is used to return 3, 11, and 42 to the `Where` clause for filtering. This works in the same manner that SQL uses `In`.

A LINQ Subquery

Subqueries are query expressions contained within other queries, or, basically, a nested query. In SQL, a subquery can be used for such things as filtering your data set or to return a single value from a lookup table. Let's create a LINQ query that uses a subquery to filter a data set:

```
Imports System
Imports System.Linq

Public Class EntryPoint
    Shared Sub Main()
        Dim Names() = {"Jodi", "Charlotte", "James", "Kay"}
```

```vbnet
        Dim Query = From n In Names _
                      Let FirstName = _
                         (From a In Names _
                          Where (Left(a, 1) = "J") _
                          Select a) _
                      Where FirstName.Contains(n) _
                      Select n

        For Each Item In Query
            Console.WriteLine(Item)
        Next
    End Sub
End Class
```

Running the preceding code will output the following to the console:

```
Jodi
James
```

In this example, you query the Names array to return only the Names that begin with "J". A LINQ query that acts as the subquery returns the qualifying Names in the Let clause. You then use Where and Contains to filter the data set, based on the results of the subquery. Finally, the results are output to the console.

Using LINQ to Find Your Documents

User documents are kept in a folder on the Windows Desktop called My Documents. My Documents is one of several folders in Windows known as *special directories*. Using LINQ, let's find the location of My Documents and any Microsoft Word documents that it contains:

```vbnet
Imports System
Imports System.IO
Imports System.Linq

Public Class EntryPoint
    Shared Sub Main()
        Dim MyDocsDir = My.Computer.FileSystem.SpecialDirectories.MyDocuments

        Dim MyDocs = From d In New DirectoryInfo(MyDocsDir).GetFiles() _
            Where d.Extension = ".doc" _
            Order By d.Name _
            Select d.Name, d.Extension

        Console.WriteLine("My Documents is located at: " & MyDocsDir)
        Console.WriteLine()
```

```
        For Each Item In MyDocs
            Console.WriteLine("Document Name: " & Item.Name & ".")
        Next
    End Sub
End Class
```

Executing this example outputs the following to the console on my workstation:

```
My Documents is located at: C:\GJJNF - My Documents

Document Name: Mortgage.doc.
Document Name: Fax Cover Page.doc.
Document Name: First-Class Mail rates.doc.
Document Name: E-mail settings.doc.
Document Name: Letter Head.doc.
Document Name: Media Mail rates.doc.
```

In this example, you import System.IO to use DirectoryInfo. Notice the use of MyDocsDir, retrieved with My.Computer.FileSystem.SpecialDirectories.MyDocuments directly within the query. Next, DirectoryInfo(MyDocsDir).GetFiles() returns an array of FileInfo, as the From clause, and filters the results to return only the Word documents via Where d.Extension = ".doc". Finally, WriteLine outputs the special My Documents directory, as well as its documents, to the console.

Query Evaluation

LINQ implements *deferred evaluation* for queries that will be enumerated via a For . . . Each statement. This means that the query definition, and its execution, is separated. This allows your LINQ query to be reused in another For . . . Each, regardless of any changes in the underlying data. Let's create a deferred evaluation example using the Numbers array:

```
Imports System
Imports System.Linq

Public Class EntryPoint
    Shared Sub Main()
        Dim Numbers() = {1, 2, 3, 4, 5, 6, 7, 8, 9, 10, 11, 12, 13, 14, _
            15, 16, 17, 18, 19, 20, 21, 22, 23, 24, 25, 26, 27, 28, 29, 30, 31, 32, _
            33, 34, 35, 36, 37, 38, 39, 40, 41, 42, 43, 44, 45, 46, 47, 48, 49, 50}

        Dim Query = From x In Numbers _
                    Where x.ToString.Chars(0) = "3" _
                    Select x
```

```vb
        Console.WriteLine("Display original Numbers() that match Where filter.")
        For Each Item In Query
            Console.WriteLine(Item.ToString)
        Next

        For i As Integer = 0 To Numbers.Length - 1
            Numbers(i) += 35
        Next

        Console.WriteLine()
        Console.WriteLine("Display updated Numbers() that match Where filter.")

        For Each Item In Query
            Console.WriteLine(Item.ToString)
        Next
    End Sub
End Class
```

The preceding code outputs the following to the console:

```
Display original Numbers() that match Where filter.
3
30
31
32
33
34
35
36
37
38
39

Display updated Numbers() that match Where filter.
36
37
38
39
```

In the preceding code, you create an integer array, Numbers, and then return those that begin with 3. Next, the array is updated by adding 35 to each element, effectively eliminating all but four numbers. Finally, the query is reused by outputting the four qualifying numbers to the console.

Immediate evaluation occurs when using ToList() and ToArray(). Using these methods executes your query and caches the result. The following code demonstrates immediate evaluation using a Names array:

```
Imports System
Imports System.Linq

Public Class EntryPoint
    Shared Sub Main()
        Dim Names() = {"Jodi", "Charlotte", "James", "Kay"}

        Dim NameArray = (From n In Names _
                    Order By n _
                    Select n).ToArray()

        Console.WriteLine("The names sorted to list.")
        For Each Item In NameArray
            Console.WriteLine(Item)
        Next
        Console.WriteLine()

        Names(1) = "Fabio"

        Console.WriteLine("This uses the cached result, without regard to new name.")
        For Each Item In NameArray
            Console.WriteLine(Item)
        Next
    End Sub
End Class
```

The preceding code outputs the following to the console:

```
The names sorted to list.
Charlotte
James
Jodi
Kay

This uses the cached result, without regard to new name.
Charlotte
James
Jodi
Kay
```

In the preceding example, you create the Names string array to hold four names. Then the ToArray function executes the LINQ query and places the ordered results into NameArray. After outputting the ordered data set to the console, we then change one of the Names to Fabio. Finally, NameArray is output to the console again, demonstrating that the query is not executed again but uses the cached result set.

LINQ to XML

The LINQ to XML in-memory API allows you to read, write, and create XML. Your XML can be treated as a built-in data type, and VB offers two ways to create XML. The first way to work with XML is by using *XML literals*, new in VB 2008. The second method is via the XDocument, XDeclaration, and XElement classes.

In the sections that follow, we will create two XML data sets; one will contain famous trumpet players, while the other will hold the musical genres they were known for.

Genre Data

The genre data contains the name and a unique identifier for each genre the musicians play. In the following examples, we will create the data using an array of genres, XML literals, and XML embedded expressions.

Create an XML Document

Using XML literals allows you to place XML directly into your VB code. You will also use XML *embedded expressions* to place the genres within the XML document. Embedded expressions work similarly to <%= %> in ASP .NET. Let's create the genres:

```
Imports System.Linq

Public Class EntryPoint
    Shared Sub Main()
        Dim Genres() = {"Cool", "Screamin'", "Bebop", "Dixieland", "Classical"}

        Dim Genre_XElements = From Genre In Genres _
                              Select <Genre>
                                         <Name>
                                             <%= Genre %>
                                         </Name>
                                     </Genre>

        Dim Genre_XML = <?xml version="1.0" encoding="utf-8" standalone="yes"?>
                        <Genres>
                            <%= Genre_XElements %>
                        </Genres>

        Console.WriteLine(Genre_XML)
    End Sub
End Class
```

This code will output the following to the console when executed:

```
<Genres>
  <Genre>
    <Name>Cool</Name>
  </Genre>
  <Genre>
    <Name>Screamin'</Name>
  </Genre>
  <Genre>
    <Name>Bebop</Name>
  </Genre>
  <Genre>
    <Name>Dixieland</Name>
  </Genre>
  <Genre>
    <Name>Classical</Name>
  </Genre>
</Genres>
```

In this example, you create an array of Genres to hold the five musical genres. The following LINQ statement uses type inference to create an XElement, while the embedded expression, <%= Genre %>, returns individual genres to the query as it executes. Next, type inference is used again, only this time to create an XDocument. Also in this line of code, <%= Genre_XElements %> is used to place the <Genre> nodes into the document. Referring to elements using < > is an example of an XML *axis property*. Lastly, the genres are output to the console.

Add Elements to an XML Document

Now that you have the genres, let's go about adding the unique identifiers needed to maintain a musician to musician's genre relationship. In this example, you will add five identifiers to the genre XML:

```
Imports System.Linq

Public Class EntryPoint
    Shared Sub Main()
        Dim Genres() = {"Cool", "Screamin'", "Bebop", "Dixieland", "Classical"}
        Dim iCounter = 1

        Dim Genre_XElements = From Genre In Genres _
                              Select <Genre>
                                         <Name>
                                             <%= Genre %>
                                         </Name>
                                     </Genre>
```

```
    Dim Genre_XML = <?xml version="1.0" encoding="utf-8" standalone="yes"?>
                    <Genres>
                        <%= Genre_XElements %>
                    </Genres>

    Dim GenreNames As IEnumerable(Of XElement) = _
        Genre_XML.<Genres>.<Genre>.<Name>

    For Each Item In GenreNames
        Item.AddBeforeSelf(<ID><%= iCounter %></ID>)
        iCounter += 1
    Next

    Console.WriteLine(Genre_XML)
    End Sub
End Class
```

This code will output the following to the console:

```
<Genres>
  <Genre>
    <ID>1</ID>
    <Name>Cool</Name>
  </Genre>
  <Genre>
    <ID>2</ID>
    <Name>Screamin'</Name>
  </Genre>
  <Genre>
    <ID>3</ID>
    <Name>Bebop</Name>
  </Genre>
  <Genre>
    <ID>4</ID>
    <Name>Dixieland</Name>
  </Genre>
  <Genre>
    <ID>5</ID>
    <Name>Classical</Name>
  </Genre>
</Genres>
```

Here, you add a couple of lines of code to the previous example. The `Dim GenreNames` line creates an `IEnumerable(Of XElement)` from the XML at the `Name` node. Iterating through `GenreNames`, the code adds the `ID` just before `Name` by using the `AddBeforeSelf` method. The unique `ID` is created via an incremented `iCounter` and passed to `AddBeforeSelf()` using an embedded expression. Finally, the XML is output to the console.

Save an XML Document

Finally, let's save the XML document to the project directory to be used throughout the rest of this chapter:

```
Imports System.Linq

Public Class EntryPoint
    Shared Sub Main()
        Dim Genres() = {"Cool", "Screamin'", "Bebop", "Dixieland", "Classical"}
        Dim iCounter = 1

        Dim Genre_XElements = From Genre In Genres _
                              Select <Genre>
                                         <Name>
                                            <%= Genre %>
                                         </Name>
                                     </Genre>

        Dim Genre_XML = <?xml version="1.0" encoding="utf-8" standalone="yes"?>
                        <Genres>
                            <%= Genre_XElements %>
                        </Genres>

        Dim GenreNames As IEnumerable(Of XElement) = _
            Genre_XML.<Genres>.<Genre>.<Name>

        For Each Item In GenreNames
            Item.AddBeforeSelf(<ID><%= iCounter %></ID>)
            iCounter += 1
        Next

        Genre_XML.Save("..\..\Genres.xml")
        Console.WriteLine("Genres.xml saved to project directory.")
    End Sub
End Class
```

This code will output the following to the console:

```
Genres.xml saved to project directory.
```

The example creates the musical genres and saves them as Genres.xml in the project directory via the Save method. After executing this example, add Genres.xml to your project. Now that you have the genre data, let's explore the musician data and dig deeper into the LINQ to XML class library.

Musician Data

The musician data set contains the name and a genre identifier for each musician. In the following examples, you will create the data using LINQ to XML classes directly to create and modify an XML document.

Create an XML Document

LINQ to XML offers several classes for this task, such as XDocument, XDeclaration, XElement, and XComment. Let's begin by creating an XML document containing only an XML declaration and a root element:

```
Imports System.Xml.Linq

Public Class EntryPoint
    Shared Sub Main()
        Dim Musicians_XML As New XDocument(New XDeclaration("1.0", "UTF-8", "yes"), _
            New XElement("Musicians", _
            New XComment("This level will hold all the musicians.")))

        Dim SW As New System.IO.StringWriter()
        Musicians_XML.Save(SW)
        Console.WriteLine(SW)
    End Sub
End Class
```

The preceding example will output the following to the console:

```
<?xml version="1.0" encoding="utf-16" standalone="yes"?>
<Musicians>
  <!--This level will hold all the musicians.-->
</Musicians>
```

In this example, you create Musicians_XML by using XDocument and passing three parameters to its constructor: XDeclaration, XElement, and XComment. XDeclaration accepts the standard version, encoding, and standalone attributes. The XElement parameter creates the root element, Musicians, while XComment simply adds a comment to the document. The next two lines of code create a StringWriter and use Save() to write the XML document to SW. Finally, write the XML document to the console.

■**Note** Using Console.WriteLine(Musicians_XML) will output the XML document without its xml declaration, while using StringWriter() outputs the XML document as in the preceding example. In addition, the encoding parameter will be output as utf-16. This is a bug in the current implementation of XDeclaration.

Add Elements to an XML Document

LINQ to XML provides the Add method for adding elements to your XML documents. Let's add a Musician element and five musicians to the XML:

```vb
Imports System.Xml.Linq

Public Class EntryPoint
    Shared Sub Main()
        Dim Musicians_XML As New XDocument(New XDeclaration("1.0", "UTF-8", "yes"), _
            New XElement("Musicians", _
            New XComment("This level will hold all the musicians.")))

        Dim Musician As XElement = Musicians_XML.<Musicians>.First
        Musician.Add(New XElement("Musician", _
            New XComment("This is the level for individual musicians.")))

        Dim Player As XElement = Musicians_XML.<Musicians>.<Musician>.First
        Player.Add(New XElement("Name", "Miles Davis"), New XElement("Genre", 1))

        Musician.Add(New XElement("Musician", _
            New XElement("Name", "Maynard Ferguson"), _
            New XElement("Genre", 2)))

        Musician.Add(New XElement("Musician", _
            New XElement("Name", "Dizzy Gillespie"), _
            New XElement("Genre", 3)))

        Musician.Add(New XElement("Musician", _
            New XElement("Name", "Bix Beiderbecke"), _
            New XElement("Genre", 4)))

        Musician.Add(New XElement("Musician", _
            New XElement("Name", "Maurice Andre"), _
            New XElement("Genre", 5)))

        Dim SW As New System.IO.StringWriter()
        Musicians_XML.Save(SW)
        Console.WriteLine(SW)
    End Sub
End Class
```

The preceding example, when run, outputs the following to the console:

```xml
<?xml version="1.0" encoding="utf-16" standalone="yes"?>
<Musicians>
  <!--This level will hold all the musicians.-->
  <Musician>
```

```
        <!--This is the level for individual musicians.-->
        <Name>Miles Davis</Name>
        <Genre>1</Genre>
      </Musician>
      <Musician>
        <Name>Maynard Ferguson</Name>
        <Genre>2</Genre>
      </Musician>
      <Musician>
        <Name>Dizzy Gillespie</Name>
        <Genre>3</Genre>
      </Musician>
      <Musician>
        <Name>Bix Beiderbecke</Name>
        <Genre>4</Genre>
      </Musician>
      <Musician>
        <Name>Maurice Andre</Name>
        <Genre>5</Genre>
      </Musician>
    </Musicians>
```

In this example, you create an XElement, Musician, by using the First method to find the first <Musicians> tag. Next, you use Add() to create a new Musician element and a comment within <Musicians>. In a similar manner as adding the previous Musician element, you use First to find the first <Musicians><Musician> tag, followed by adding Miles Davis as the first musician.

The next four Add() statements add musicians to the XML. In each case, a new musician is appended at the end of the musicians. Finally, as in the previous example, you use StringWriter(), Save(), and WriteLine() to output the XML document to the console.

Add Elements to a Specific Location in an XML Document

In the last example, you added five musicians to the XML Document by using the Add method. Let's add two more musicians to the document, only this time you will locate a musician within the XML and use the AddAfterSelf method to place new Musician nodes directly after the one you find. Let's add two new musicians to the XML after Bix Beiderbecke:

```
Imports System.Xml.Linq

Public Class EntryPoint
    Shared Sub Main()
        Dim Musicians_XML As New XDocument(New XDeclaration("1.0", "UTF-8", "yes"), _
            New XElement("Musicians", _
            New XComment("This level will hold all the musicians.")))
```

```vb
        Dim Musician As XElement = Musicians_XML.<Musicians>.First
        Musician.Add(New XElement("Musician", _
            New XComment("This is the level for individual musicians.")))

        Dim Player As XElement = Musicians_XML.<Musicians>.<Musician>.First
        Player.Add(New XElement("Name", "Miles Davis"), New XElement("Genre", 1))

        Musician.Add(New XElement("Musician", _
            New XElement("Name", "Maynard Ferguson"), _
            New XElement("Genre", 2)))

        Musician.Add(New XElement("Musician", _
            New XElement("Name", "Dizzy Gillespie"), _
            New XElement("Genre", 3)))

        Musician.Add(New XElement("Musician", _
            New XElement("Name", "Bix Beiderbecke"), _
            New XElement("Genre", 4)))

        Musician.Add(New XElement("Musician", _
            New XElement("Name", "Maurice Andre"), _
            New XElement("Genre", 5)))

        Dim Players As IEnumerable(Of XElement) = _
            Musicians_XML.<Musicians>.<Musician>.<Name>

        For Each Item In Players
            If Item.Value.Equals("Bix Beiderbecke") Then
                Dim GS As New XElement("Musician", _
                    New XElement("Name", "Gerard Schwarz"), _
                    New XElement("Genre", 5))

                Item.Parent.AddAfterSelf(GS)

                Item.Parent.AddAfterSelf(New XElement("Musician", _
                    New XElement("Name", "Louis Armstrong"), _
                    New XElement("Genre", 4)))
            End If
        Next

        Dim SW As New System.IO.StringWriter()
        Musicians_XML.Save(SW)
        Console.WriteLine(SW)
    End Sub
End Class
```

The preceding example, when run, will output the following to the console:

```xml
<?xml version="1.0" encoding="utf-16" standalone="yes"?>
<Musicians>
  <!--This level will hold all the musicians.-->
  <Musician>
    <!--This is the level for individual musicians.-->
    <Name>Miles Davis</Name>
    <Genre>1</Genre>
  </Musician>
  <Musician>
    <Name>Maynard Ferguson</Name>
    <Genre>2</Genre>
  </Musician>
  <Musician>
    <Name>Dizzy Gillespie</Name>
    <Genre>3</Genre>
  </Musician>
  <Musician>
    <Name>Bix Beiderbecke</Name>
    <Genre>4</Genre>
  </Musician>
  <Musician>
    <Name>Louis Armstrong</Name>
    <Genre>4</Genre>
  </Musician>
  <Musician>
    <Name>Gerard Schwarz</Name>
    <Genre>5</Genre>
  </Musician>
  <Musician>
    <Name>Maurice Andre</Name>
    <Genre>5</Genre>
  </Musician>
</Musicians>
```

In this example, you create Players As IEnumerable(Of XElement) from the <Name> node of Musicians_XML. In the following For . . . Each, you look for Bix Beiderbecke in Players. When you find Bix, you add Gerard Schwarz by creating a New XElement and passing it to Item. Parent.AddAfterSelf(). The Parent.AddAfterSelf method places the new XElement directly after Bix by traversing up one level in the XML document, and adding Gerard's node right after Bix's. Next you add Louis Armstrong by passing three new XElement parameters directly to AddAfterSelf(). Finally, output the XML document to the console in the same way as the last example.

Save an XML Document

Finally, let's save the XML document to the project directory to be used throughout the rest of this chapter, along with the Genres.xml you saved earlier:

```vb
Imports System.Xml.Linq

Public Class EntryPoint
    Shared Sub Main()
        Dim Musicians_XML As New XDocument(New XDeclaration("1.0", "UTF-8", "yes"), _
            New XElement("Musicians", _
            New XComment("This level will hold all the musicians.")))

        Dim Musician As XElement = Musicians_XML.<Musicians>.First
        Musician.Add(New XElement("Musician", _
            New XComment("This is the level for individual musicians.")))

        Dim Player As XElement = Musicians_XML.<Musicians>.<Musician>.First
        Player.Add(New XElement("Name", "Miles Davis"), New XElement("Genre", 1))

        Musician.Add(New XElement("Musician", _
            New XElement("Name", "Maynard Ferguson"), _
            New XElement("Genre", 2)))

        Musician.Add(New XElement("Musician", _
            New XElement("Name", "Dizzy Gillespie"), _
            New XElement("Genre", 3)))

        Musician.Add(New XElement("Musician", _
            New XElement("Name", "Bix Beiderbecke"), _
            New XElement("Genre", 4)))

        Musician.Add(New XElement("Musician", _
            New XElement("Name", "Maurice Andre"), _
            New XElement("Genre", 5)))

        Dim Players As IEnumerable(Of XElement) = _
            Musicians_XML.<Musicians>.<Musician>.<Name>

        For Each Item In Players
            If Item.Value.Equals("Bix Beiderbecke") Then
                Dim GS As New XElement("Musician", _
                    New XElement("Name", "Gerard Schwarz"), _
                    New XElement("Genre", 5))
```

```
        Item.Parent.AddAfterSelf(GS)

        Item.Parent.AddAfterSelf(New XElement("Musician", _
            New XElement("Name", "Louis Armstrong"), _
            New XElement("Genre", 4)))
      End If
    Next

    Musicians_XML.Save("..\..\Musicians.xml")
    Console.WriteLine("Musicians.xml saved to project directory.")
  End Sub
End Class
```

This code will output the following to the console:

```
Musicians.xml saved to project directory.
```

The example creates the musicians in the same way as the last example and saves them as Musicians.xml in the project directory via the Save method. After executing this example, add Musicians.xml to your project. With Genres.xml, and Musicians.xml added to your project, you can now explore querying XML with LINQ to XML.

LINQ to XML Queries

Let's create some LINQ to XML queries, revisiting each of the query clauses described in the "LINQ Syntax" section earlier in the chapter. These include From, Select, Distinct, Where, and Join.

From

This example uses the LINQ From clause to return Musicians:

```
Imports System.Linq

Public Class EntryPoint
  Shared Sub Main()
    Dim xml As XDocument = XDocument.Load("..\..\Musicians.xml")

    Dim query = From m In xml.Elements("Musicians").Elements("Musician")

    For Each item In query
      Console.WriteLine(item.Element("Name").Value)
    Next
  End Sub
End Class
```

This code outputs the names of the musicians to the console:

```
Miles Davis
Maynard Ferguson
Dizzy Gillespie
Bix Beiderbecke
Louis Armstrong
Gerard Schwarz
Maurice Andre
```

In this example, the Dim xml As XDocument line of code loads the musician data into memory. The From clause has changed a bit from previous examples. In LINQ to XML, you use Elements() to retrieve node and leaf level data from your XML. In the example, you drill down to the Musician node via the Musicians root node. Finally, to create the output, you use Element("Name").Value to retrieve each musician's name.

Select

This example demonstrates Select usage in LINQ. Here, you will use a Select clause to return the musician's names.

```
Imports System.Linq

Public Class EntryPoint
    Shared Sub Main()
        Dim xml As XDocument = XDocument.Load("..\..\Musicians.xml")

        Dim query = From m In xml.Elements("Musicians").Elements("Musician") _
                        Select m.Element("Name").Value


        For Each item In query
            Console.WriteLine(item)
        Next
    End Sub
End Class
```

This code outputs the following to the console:

```
Miles Davis
Maynard Ferguson
Dizzy Gillespie
Bix Beiderbecke
Louis Armstrong
Gerard Schwarz
Maurice Andre
```

In this example, the `Select` clause contains the reference to `m.Element("Name").Value`, and the `Console.WriteLine` code only need refer to `item`.

Distinct

Using `Distinct` eliminates duplicate values from your return set. In this example, you apply `Distinct` to the genre identifiers in the musician data.

```
Imports System.Linq

Public Class EntryPoint
    Shared Sub Main()
        Dim xml As XDocument = XDocument.Load("..\..\Musicians.xml")

        Dim query = From m In xml.Elements("Musicians").Elements("Musician") _
                        Select m.Element("Genre").Value Distinct

        For Each item In query
            Console.WriteLine(item)
        Next
    End Sub
End Class
```

This code will output the following to the console:

```
1
2
3
4
5
```

In this example, you added `Distinct` to the `Select` clause. Although you have seven musicians in the data set, two of them belong to genre 4, and two of them belong to genre 5. With this being the case, `Distinct` only returned genres 4 and 5 once.

Where

The `Where` clause allows you to filter your data set based on one or more criteria. In this example, you will return the Dixieland musicians.

```
Imports System.Linq

Public Class EntryPoint
    Shared Sub Main()
        Dim xml As XDocument = XDocument.Load("..\..\Musicians.xml")
```

```
    Dim query = From m In xml.Elements("Musicians").Elements("Musician") _
                Where m.Element("Genre").Value = 4 _
                Select m.Element("Name").Value

    For Each item In query
        Console.WriteLine(item)
    Next
  End Sub
End Class
```

This code will output the following to the console:

```
Bix Beiderbecke
Louis Armstrong
```

In this example, `Where m.Element("Genre").Value = 4` filtered the results to return only musicians in genre 4.

Join

The musician and genre data are related by a key. In database terminology, the genre data has an ID that acts as its *primary key*. This means that ID is unique throughout the genre data. Musician, on the other hand, has a *foreign key*, Genre, which points to the musician's genre data. Let's Join the two XML data sets.

```
Imports System.Linq

Public Class EntryPoint
    Shared Sub Main()
        Dim Musicians As XDocument = XDocument.Load("..\..\Musicians.xml")
        Dim Genres As XDocument = XDocument.Load("..\..\Genres.xml")

        Dim MQuery = From M In Musicians.Elements("Musicians").Elements("Musician")
        Dim GQuery = From G In Genres.Elements("Genres").Elements("Genre")

        Dim Query = From M In MQuery _
                    Join G In GQuery On M.Element("Genre").Value _
                    Equals G.Element("ID").Value _
                    Select Musician = M.Element("Name").Value, _
                        Genre = G.Element("Name").Value

        For Each Item In Query
            Console.WriteLine(Item.Musician & " plays " & Item.Genre & " jazz.")
        Next
    End Sub
End Class
```

This code will output the following to the console:

```
Miles Davis plays Cool.
Maynard Ferguson plays Screamin'.
Dizzy Gillespie plays Bebop.
Bix Beiderbecke plays Dixieland.
Louis Armstrong plays Dixieland.
Gerard Schwarz plays Classical.
Maurice Andre plays Classical.
```

In this example, you use both of the XML data sets. You've created MQuery to hold the musician data and GQuery to hold the genres. In both cases, you return all applicable items. The Query line of code uses Join to match each musician to the genre that musician performs.

The Join clause in this example joins MQuery and GQuery on the value of each musician's Genre to the genre's ID. This method of joining data sets is very common in relational database applications, as it enforces the musician-genre relationship and allows for easier maintenance of genre data.

Using LINQ to Create an Excel Spreadsheet

As the final LINQ to XML discussion, let's use LINQ to create an Excel spreadsheet of the musician data. This example requires Excel 2003 or higher to view the finished spreadsheet. If you do not have Excel 2003 or higher, simply comment out the Process.Start code line at the end of the sample. Regardless of which version of Excel you use, you can always view the saved XML in the Visual Studio IDE. On to the example:

```
Imports <xmlns:o="urn:schemas-microsoft-com:office:office">
Imports <xmlns:x="urn:schemas-microsoft-com:office:excel">
Imports <xmlns="urn:schemas-microsoft-com:office:spreadsheet">
Imports <xmlns:ss="urn:schemas-microsoft-com:office:spreadsheet">
Imports System.Linq
Imports System.Xml


Public Class EntryPoint
    Shared Sub Main()
        Dim Musicians As XDocument = XDocument.Load("..\..\Musicians.xml")
        Dim Genres As XDocument = XDocument.Load("..\..\Genres.xml")

        Dim MQuery = From M In Musicians.Elements("Musicians").Elements("Musician")
        Dim GQuery = From G In Genres.Elements("Genres").Elements("Genre")

        Dim Query = From M In MQuery _
                    Join G In GQuery On M.Element("Genre").Value _
                    Equals G.Element("ID").Value _
                    Select _
```

```
            <Row>
                <Cell>
                    <Data ss:Type="String">
                        <%= M.Element("Name").Value %>
                    </Data>
                </Cell>
                <Cell>
                    <Data ss:Type="String">
                        <%= G.Element("Name").Value %>
                    </Data>
                </Cell>
            </Row>

Dim MusiciansExcel = _
<?xml version="1.0"?>
<?mso-application progid="Excel.Sheet"?>
<Workbook xmlns="urn:schemas-microsoft-com:office:spreadsheet"
    xmlns:o="urn:schemas-microsoft-com:office:office"
    xmlns:x="urn:schemas-microsoft-com:office:excel"
    xmlns:ss="urn:schemas-microsoft-com:office:spreadsheet"
    xmlns:html="http://www.w3.org/TR/REC-html40">
    <Styles>
        <Style ss:ID="Default" ss:Name="Normal">
            <Font ss:FontName="Calibri"
                x:Family="Swiss"
                ss:Size="12"/>
        </Style>
        <Style ss:ID="Header">
            <Font ss:FontName="Calibri"
                x:Family="Swiss"
                ss:Size="14"
                ss:Bold="1"/>
        </Style>
    </Styles>
    <Worksheet ss:Name="Sheet1">
        <Table ss:ExpandedColumnCount="2"
            ss:ExpandedRowCount=<%= Query.Count + 1 %>
            x:FullColumns="1"
            x:FullRows="1"
            ss:DefaultRowHeight="15">
            <Row ss:StyleID="Header">
                <Cell><Data ss:Type="String">Musician</Data></Cell>
                <Cell><Data ss:Type="String">Genre</Data></Cell>
            </Row>
            <%= Query %>
        </Table>
    </Worksheet>
</Workbook>
```

```
        MusiciansExcel.Save("MusiciansExcel.xml")
        Process.Start("Excel.exe", "MusiciansExcel.xml")
    End Sub
End Class
```

Running the preceding code will save `MusiciansExcel.xml` and load it into Excel, as shown in Figure 15-1.

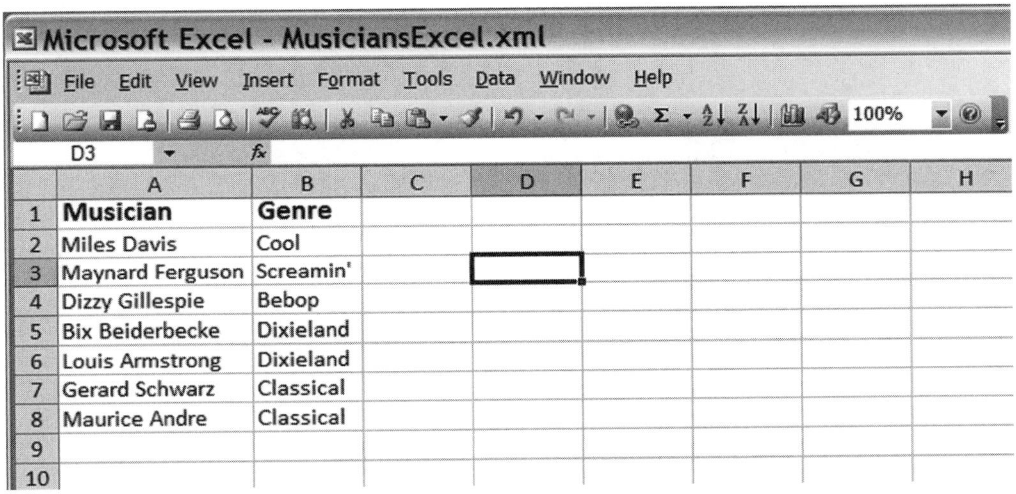

Figure 15-1. *MusiciansExcel.xml viewed in Excel*

In this example, you had added several `Imports` for Office and Excel. `Query` has been updated and now contains row data for the export. The `Select` clause has been totally rewritten; it now contains XML and ASP .NET style placeholders for the individual elements. `MusiciansExcel` holds the XML document, which contains several sections that define how Excel should create the spreadsheet, including `<Workbook>`, `<Styles>`, and `<Worksheet>`. Within the `Table` tag, you use `Query.Count + 1` to define the number of data rows needed by Excel. The first `Row` tag is the header, while `<%= Query %>` appends the rows and cells created by `Query`. Finally, you save `MusiciansExcel.xml` to disk and load it into Excel via `Process.Start`.

LINQ to SQL

LINQ to SQL enables you to use your relational data stores as objects throughout your application. Your RDBMS table structures can now be mapped as standard classes, only these classes will have custom attributes, which identifies them to LINQ. Each class you create will also contain properties that correspond to the columns in a table.

In this section, you will create a Microsoft SQL Server database and two tables, Musician and Genre, to hold data identical to that you used in the "LINQ to XML" section earlier in this chapter. Next, you will create two classes to map the tables to. Finally, we will demonstrate using LINQ to SQL to perform Create, Read, Update, and Delete (CRUD) queries against the two tables.

Musician Data

The musician data set contains the musician's name and genre identifier for each musician you will be working with. The genre data contains the genre name, as well as a unique identifier for the musical genres.

The following database script, which will run in SQL Server 2000/2005, will create the database (AVB2008) and two tables (Musician and Genre), and then load the tables with the needed data. In addition, this script will set the necessary data integrity constraint between Musician and Genre:

```
Use master
GO


If DB_ID (N'AVB2008') IS NOT NULL
    Drop Database AVB2008
GO


Create Database AVB2008
GO


Use AVB2008
Go


Create Table [dbo].[Genre]
(
    [ID]            [int]                   Identity(1, 1),
    [Name]      [Varchar](10)    Not Null
)
Go


Alter Table [dbo].[Genre]       Add Constraint [PK_Genre]
Primary Key Clustered           ([ID] Asc)
Go


Create Table [dbo].[Musician]
(
    [ID]              [int]                   Identity(1, 1),
    [Musician]   [varchar](50)    NOT NULL,
    [Genre]        [int]                   NOT NULL
)
Go


Alter Table [dbo].[Musician]    Add Constraint [PK_Musician]
Primary Key Clustered           ([ID] Asc)
Go
```

```
Alter Table [dbo].[Musician]      Add Constraint [UX_Musician] Unique NonClustered
(
    [Musician] Asc
)
Go

Alter Table [dbo].[Musician]      With Check Add Constraint [FK_Musician_Genre]
Foreign Key ([Genre])               References [dbo].[Genre] ([ID])
Go

Set Nocount On
Go

Insert [dbo].[Genre] ([Name]) Values ('Cool')
Insert [dbo].[Genre] ([Name]) Values ('Screamin''')
Insert [dbo].[Genre] ([Name]) Values ('Bebop')
Insert [dbo].[Genre] ([Name]) Values ('Dixieland')
Insert [dbo].[Genre] ([Name]) Values ('Classical')
Go

Insert [dbo].[Musician] Select 'Miles Davis', 1
Insert [dbo].[Musician] Select 'Maynard Ferguson', 2
Insert [dbo].[Musician] Select 'Dizzy Gillespie', 3
Insert [dbo].[Musician] Select 'Bix Beiderbecke', 4
Insert [dbo].[Musician] Select 'Louis Armstrong', 4
Insert [dbo].[Musician] Select 'Gerard Schwarz', 5
Insert [dbo].[Musician] Select 'Maurice Andre', 5
Go

Select * From [dbo].[Genre]
Select * From [dbo].[Musician]
Go
```

The preceding script, when run in Query Analyzer (SQL 2000) or SQL Server Management Studio (SQL 2005), will output the following to the Results pane:

```
ID          Name
----------- ----------
1           Cool
2           Screamin'
3           Bebop
4           Dixieland
5           Classical
```

ID	Musician	Genre
1	Miles Davis	1
2	Maynard Ferguson	2
3	Dizzy Gillespie	3
4	Bix Beiderbecke	4
5	Louis Armstrong	4
6	Gerard Schwarz	5
7	Maurice Andre	5

In this code, you make the script rerunnable by switching to the master database and checking for the existence of the AVB2008 database via the IF DB_ID statement. If the database does exist, you Drop it. Either way, the Create Database statement creates AVB2008.

Next, you create the tables. The Create Table [dbo].[Genre] statement creates the Genre table with two fields, ID and Name. The ID field is created as an Identity field, which guarantees that each record will have a unique database-assigned value. The Name field is simply a string that can hold up to ten characters. Finally, the Alter Table statement creates a primary key for the Genre table, based on the ID field, in ascending order. This primary key will also be used to ensure that each musician has been assigned a valid genre.

The Musician table is created with three fields, ID, Musician, and Genre. The ID field is the Identity field for this table. The Musician field is a string that can hold up to 50 characters, while Genre is an integer. The first Alter Table statement creates a primary key for the musicians, ensuring that unique names exist in the table. The second Alter Table statement creates a *unique constraint* for the Musician table on the Musician field, which will prevent storing duplicate musician names to the Musician table.

The third Alter Table statement creates a foreign key for the Musician table, which references the ID field of Genre. This is how you enforce the needed *referential integrity*.

The next two sets of Insert statements insert data into the tables. The first set inserts five genres into the Genre table. Notice that you are only populating the Name field directly, as the ID will be assigned by the database. The Musician table will have seven records inserted into it by the next set of Insert statements. As each record is updated, the database enforces referential integrity by validating that the value passed as a genre exists as an ID in the Genre table.

Finally, the two Select statements simply display all records from both tables to the Results pane to validate that the script has executed successfully.

Database/Field Mapping Classes

The next step to undertake in using LINQ to SQL is to map each of your tables to a *mapping class*, or *entity class*. These classes will make LINQ to SQL aware of the structure of your tables. For the tables, you will need two classes: one for Genre and one for Musician.

Genre Class

Create a new class in your project via the Project ➤ Add Class menu and name it Genre. Let's take a look at the definition of the Genre first:

```
Imports System.Linq
Imports System.Data.Linq
Imports System.Data.Linq.Mapping

<Table(Name:="Genre")> _
Public Class Genre
    Private mID As Integer
    Private mName As String

    <Column(DbType:="Int Not Null Identity", Storage:="mID", IsPrimaryKey:=True, _
            Name:="ID", IsDBGenerated:=True)> _
    Public Property ID() As Integer
        Get
            Return Me.mID
        End Get
        Set(ByVal value As Integer)
            Me.mID = value
        End Set
    End Property

    <Column(DbType:="Varchar(10)", Storage:="mName", Name:="Name")> _
    Public Property Name() As String
        Get
            Return Me.mName
        End Get
        Set(ByVal value As String)
            Me.mName = value
        End Set
    End Property
End Class
```

In this class, you begin by importing the needed LINQ namespaces. The Table attribute declares the Name of the table this class will represent, and the two Private fields will be used for data storage. The Column attribute defines a data point, as well as the metadata needed, to LINQ. In the Genre class, you have defined two data points, ID and Name. For ID, you pass the column's metadata by using five properties: DbType, Storage, IsPrimaryKey, Name, and IsDBGenerated. DbType represents the full data type definition needed by your RDBMS. In the case of SQL Server, ID is defined as an Int Not Null Identity field, which is a unique integer value that cannot be Null. The IsDBGenerated property informs LINQ that the underlying value is automatically generated by the RDBMS for each record created. The IsPrimaryKey value of True indicates that this field is being used by the database engine as the table's primary key. Finally, the Name and Storage properties both refer to the data point being stored; Name is the field name in the table, while mID maps to the field in the class.

The second field, Name, is defined via DbType as a Varchar(10). Varchar is a data type that specifies the maximum string length that can be stored in each record. SQL Server stores the actual string length internally on a record-by-record basis.

Musician Class

Now that you have mapped the Genre table to the Genre class, let's map the Musician table to a Musician class. First, create a new class in your project named Musician with the following definition:

```vb
Imports System.Linq
Imports System.Data.Linq
Imports System.Data.Linq.Mapping

<Table(Name:="Musician")> _
Public Class Musician
    Private mID As Integer
    Private mMusician As String
    Private mGenre As Integer

    <Column(DbType:="Int Not Null Identity", Storage:="mID", IsPrimaryKey:=True, _
            Name:="ID", IsDBGenerated:=True)> _
    Public Property ID() As Integer
        Get
            Return Me.mID
        End Get
        Set(ByVal value As Integer)
            Me.mID = value
        End Set
    End Property

    <Column(DbType:="Varchar(50)", Storage:="mMusician", Name:="Musician")> _
    Public Property Musician() As String
        Get
            Return Me.mMusician
        End Get
        Set(ByVal value As String)
            Me.mMusician = value
        End Set
    End Property

    <Column(DbType:="Int", Storage:="mGenre", Name:="Genre")> _
    Public Property Genre() As Integer
        Get
            Return Me.mGenre
        End Get
        Set(ByVal value As Integer)
            Me.mGenre = value
        End Set
    End Property
End Class
```

The Musician class has three Private fields for data storage, mID, mMusician, and mGenre. Looking at the first Column attribute, you can see that the ID column is described identically to the ID column in the Genre table. The Musician column is a Varchar(50), the field name in the table is Musician, and the class member is mMusician. The Genre column is defined as an Int, while the table field is Genre and the class member is mGenre.

Data Context

A data context manages the connection between the classes created previously and your RDBMS. Data contexts generate the actual SQL from a LINQ query, execute it against your RDBMS, and manage the returned or submitted data. To create a data context for the data, you need the following two VB statements:

```
Dim DB_Connection As New String("Data Source=.\SQLEXPRESS;" & _
      "Initial Catalog=AVB2008;Integrated Security=True")
Dim AVB_DataContext As New DataContext(DB_Connection)
```

The DB_Connection line of code creates a *connection string* for the data context. A connection string will contain three sections: Data Source, Initial Catalog, and Integrated Security. Data Source contains the named instance of the SQL Server you're attaching to, while Initial Catalog specifies the database name, and Integrated Security=True indicates that you want the domain credentials to be used to log in to the SQL Server. The next line of code creates the AVB_DataContext data context, using the connection string as a parameter.

Each table you intend to work with can be declared as Table(Of T) using the GetTable method of your DataContext. Using the DataContext created previously, you can create the needed Table collections with the following statements:

```
Dim Musicians As Table(Of Musician) = AVB_DataContext.GetTable(Of Musician)()
Dim Genres As Table(Of Genre) = AVB_DataContext.GetTable(Of Genre)()
```

Finally, DataContext will track changes to your objects until you explicitly ask them to be made to your tables with the SubmitChanges method. If you need to roll back or reject the changes made, you can do so using the RejectChanges method.

LINQ to SQL Database Operations

Let's implement CRUD for the Musician table. Before working through this section, you will need to have created the AVB2008 database and the Musician and Genre tables, loaded the two tables with data, and added the Genre and Musician classes to your project.

Create Musicians

Adding a new Musician can be accomplished in two different ways. The following example will add two musicians to the Musicians table:

```
Imports System

Public Class EntryPoint
    Shared Sub Main()
        Dim DB_Connection As New String("Data Source=.\SQLEXPRESS;" & _
            "Initial Catalog=AVB2008;Integrated Security=True")
        Dim AVB_DataContext As New DataContext(DB_Connection)

        Dim Musicians As Table(Of Musician) = AVB_DataContext.GetTable(Of Musician)()
        Dim Genres As Table(Of Genre) = AVB_DataContext.GetTable(Of Genre)()

        Dim NewMusician = New Musician With {.Musician = "Jon Faddis", .Genre = 2}
        Musicians.Add(NewMusician)

        Musicians.Add(New Musician With {.Musician = "William Chase", .Genre = 2})

        AVB_DataContext.SubmitChanges()

        Dim Query = From m In Musicians _
                    Select m.Musician, m.Genre

        For Each Item In Query
            Console.WriteLine("Musicians Name: " & Item.Musician & _
                              " | Musicians Genre: " & Item.Genre)
        Next
    End Sub
End Class
```

This example, when run, will output the following to the console:

```
Musicians Name: Bix Beiderbecke | Musicians Genre: 4
Musicians Name: Dizzy Gillespie | Musicians Genre: 3
Musicians Name: Gerard Schwarz | Musicians Genre: 5
Musicians Name: Jon Faddis | Musicians Genre: 2
Musicians Name: Louis Armstrong | Musicians Genre: 4
Musicians Name: Maurice Andre | Musicians Genre: 5
Musicians Name: Maynard Ferguson | Musicians Genre: 2
Musicians Name: Miles Davis | Musicians Genre: 1
Musicians Name: William Chase | Musicians Genre: 2
```

In the preceding code, you have added Musicians in two different ways. You added Jon Faddis by first creating a NewMusician, and then passing it to the Add method. Adding William Chase was accomplished by creating a new Musician object directly in the Add() call.

Read Musicians

To implement the read, let's simply use a LINQ to SQL query to validate the existence of the two Musicians added in the last example:

```
Imports System

Public Class EntryPoint
    Shared Sub Main()
        Dim DB_Connection As New String("Data Source=.\SQLEXPRESS;" & _
            "Initial Catalog=AVB2008;Integrated Security=True")
        Dim AVB_DataContext As New DataContext(DB_Connection)

        Dim Musicians As Table(Of Musician) = AVB_DataContext.GetTable(Of Musician)()
        Dim Genres As Table(Of Genre) = AVB_DataContext.GetTable(Of Genre)()

        Dim Query = From m In Musicians _
                    Where m.Musician = "Jon Faddis" Or m.Musician = "William Chase" _
                    Select m.Musician, m.Genre

        For Each Item In Query
            Console.WriteLine("Musicians Name: " & Item.Musician & _
                            " | Musicians Genre: " & Item.Genre)
        Next
    End Sub
End Class
```

This example will output the following to the console when executed:

```
Musicians Name: Jon Faddis | Musicians Genre: 2
Musicians Name: William Chase | Musicians Genre: 2
```

Here, you used a Where clause to find the two musicians that were added to the Musician table in the previous example. After finding them, you output their Musician data to the console.

Update a Musician

Next, you need to update a record in the Musician table, since William Chase is actually known as Bill Chase. The following example will update Bill's record using LINQ:

```
Imports System

Public Class EntryPoint
    Shared Sub Main()
        Dim DB_Connection As New String("Data Source=.\SQLEXPRESS;" & _
            "Initial Catalog=AVB2008;Integrated Security=True")
        Dim AVB_DataContext As New DataContext(DB_Connection)

        Dim Musicians As Table(Of Musician) = AVB_DataContext.GetTable(Of Musician)()
        Dim Genres As Table(Of Genre) = AVB_DataContext.GetTable(Of Genre)()
```

```vb
        Dim BC As Musician = (From j In Musicians _
                              Where j.Musician.Contains("Chase")).Single

        BC.Musician = "Bill Chase"

        AVB_DataContext.SubmitChanges()

        Dim Query = From j In Musicians

        For Each Item In Query
           Console.WriteLine("Musicians Name: " & Item.Musician & _
                             " | Musicians Genre: " & Item.Genre)
        Next
     End Sub
End Class
```

This example will output the following to the console when executed:

```
Musicians Name: Miles Davis | Musicians Genre: 1
Musicians Name: Maynard Ferguson | Musicians Genre: 2
Musicians Name: Dizzy Gillespie | Musicians Genre: 3
Musicians Name: Bix Beiderbecke | Musicians Genre: 4
Musicians Name: Louis Armstrong | Musicians Genre: 4
Musicians Name: Gerard Schwarz | Musicians Genre: 5
Musicians Name: Maurice Andre | Musicians Genre: 5
Musicians Name: Jon Faddis | Musicians Genre: 2
Musicians Name: Bill Chase | Musicians Genre: 2
```

In the preceding example, you created BC As Musician, and used the Single method to return William Chase's record. Updating the data context is done by simple assignment via the BC.Musician = "Bill Chase" statement. After the update to BC, you submit the changes to the RDBMS. Finally, you retrieve the musicians and list them to the console, with William Chase now changed to Bill Chase.

Delete a Musician

In the previous examples, you added two musicians to the Musician table and updated one musician's name. Let's restore the Musician table to its original state by deleting the two musicians previously added:

```vb
Imports System

Public Class EntryPoint
   Shared Sub Main()
      Dim DB_Connection As New String("Data Source=.\SQLEXPRESS;" & _
          "Initial Catalog=AVB2008;Integrated Security=True")
      Dim AVB_DataContext As New DataContext(DB_Connection)
```

```vb
        Dim Musicians As Table(Of Musician) = AVB_DataContext.GetTable(Of Musician)()
        Dim Genres As Table(Of Genre) = AVB_DataContext.GetTable(Of Genre)()

        Dim JF As Musician = (From j In Musicians _
                            Where j.Musician.Contains("Faddis")).Single

        Musicians.Remove(JF)

        AVB_DataContext.SubmitChanges()

        Dim Query = From j In Musicians

        For Each Item In Query
            Console.WriteLine("Musicians Name: " & Item.Musician & _
                            " | Musicians Genre: " & Item.Genre)
        Next
    End Sub
End Class
```

This example will output the following to the console when executed:

```
Musicians Name: Miles Davis | Musicians Genre: 1
Musicians Name: Maynard Ferguson | Musicians Genre: 2
Musicians Name: Dizzy Gillespie | Musicians Genre: 3
Musicians Name: Bix Beiderbecke | Musicians Genre: 4
Musicians Name: Louis Armstrong | Musicians Genre: 4
Musicians Name: Gerard Schwarz | Musicians Genre: 5
Musicians Name: Maurice Andre | Musicians Genre: 5
Musicians Name: Bill Chase | Musicians Genre: 2
```

In the preceding example, you created JF As Musician and returned Jon Faddis' record. Once you retrieved the musician, you deleted him by using the Remove method. After submitting the changes to the RDBMS, you retrieved the musicians and listed them to the console. Jon Faddis is no longer among them.

Review Generated SQL

LINQ to SQL also gives you the ability to review the SQL statement it generates. This debugging tool is available via the Log method. Here's an example of using Log:

```vb
Imports System

Public Class EntryPoint
    Shared Sub Main()
        Dim DB_Connection As New String("Data Source=.\SQLEXPRESS;" & _
            "Initial Catalog=AVB2008;Integrated Security=True")
        Dim AVB_DataContext As New DataContext(DB_Connection)
```

```
      Dim Musicians As Table(Of Musician) = AVB_DataContext.GetTable(Of Musician)()

      Dim Query = From m In Musicians _
                  Where m.Musician = "Jon Faddis" Or m.Musician = "William Chase" _
                  Select m.Musician, m.Genre

      AVB_DataContext.Log = Console.Out

      For Each Item In Query
          Console.WriteLine(Item.Musician & " plays " & Item.Genre & ".")
      Next
    End Sub
End Class
```

The preceding code will output the following to the console when run:

```
SELECT [t0].[Musician], [t0].[Genre]
FROM [Musician] AS [t0]
WHERE ([t0].[Musician] = @p0) OR ([t0].[Musician] = @p1)
-- @p0: Input String (Size = 10; Prec = 0; Scale = 0) [Jon Faddis]
-- @p1: Input String (Size = 13; Prec = 0; Scale = 0) [William Chase]
-- Context: SqlProvider(Sql2005) Model: AttributedMetaModel Build: 3.5.20706.1
```

In the preceding example, you created a LINQ query to select two musicians. Using the Log method, you are able to review the actual Select statement that LINQ will execute on the SQL Server.

Each line in the output that begins with -- is a comment and output as documentation. The first two comments describe the data type, size, and value that will be used in the Where clause, while the last comment gives you general information about your LINQ to SQL environment.

Summary

In this chapter, we introduced you to LINQ, a new set of technologies being implemented with VB 2008. We discussed LINQ in general, extension methods, and Lambda expressions. Next, we explored LINQ to Objects and creating XML Documents. We also looked at LINQ to XML, via a number of examples based on common query operators. Finally, we delved into LINQ to SQL by using the musician and genre data to query and implement CRUD functionality with data classes.

You did it! This chapter concludes your exploration of *Accelerated VB 2008*. We both sincerely hope that you have gained valuable experience and insights into VB by choosing to spend your time with us. Thank you.

APPENDIX A

■ ■ ■

Resources

Books

Abrams, Brad. *.NET Framework Standard Library Annotated Reference, Volumes 1 and 2*. Boston, MA: Addison-Wesley Professional, 2004, 2005.

Allison, Damon, Andy Olson, James Speer. *Visual Basic .NET Class Design Handbook: Coding Effective Classes*. Berkeley, CA: Apress, 2003.

Boehm, Anne. *Murach's Visual Basic 2005*. Fresno, CA: Mike Murach & Associates, 2006.

Booch, Grady. *Object-Oriented Analysis and Design with Applications, Second Edition*. Boston, MA: Addison-Wesley Professional, 1993.

Box, Don, with Chris Sells. *Essential .NET, Volume 1: The Common Language Runtime*. Boston, MA: Addison-Wesley Professional, 2002.

Cwalina, Krzysztof, and Brad Abrams. *Framework Design Guidelines: Conventions, Idioms, and Patterns for Reusable .NET Libraries*. Boston, MA: Addison-Wesley Professional, 2005.

Ecma International. *Standard ECMA-335: Common Language Infrastructure (CLI), Fourth Edition*. Geneva, Switzerland: Ecma International, 2006.

Evjen, Bill, Rockford Lhotka, Billy Hollis, Bill Sheldon, Kent Sharkey, Tim McCarthy, Rama Ramachandran. *Professional VB 2005*. Indianapolis, IN: Wiley Publishing, 2006.

Ferracchiati, Fabio Claudio. *LINQ for VB 2005*. Berkeley, CA: Apress, 2007.

Fischer, Tom, John Slater, Pete Stromquist, Chaur G. Wu. *Professional Design Patterns in VB .NET: Building Adaptable Applications*. Berkeley, CA: Apress, 2002.

Fowler, Martin. *UML Distilled: A Brief Guide to the Standard Object Modeling Language, Third Edition*. Boston, MA: Addison-Wesley Professional, 2003.

Freeman, Elisabeth, and Eric Freeman, with Kathy Sierra and Bert Bates. *Head First Design Patterns*. Sebastopol, CA: O'Reilly Media, 2004.

Gamma, Erich, Richard Helm, Ralph Johnson, and John Vlissides. *Design Patterns: Elements of Reusable Object-Oriented Software*. Boston, MA: Addison-Wesley Professional, 1995.

Griver, Yair Alan, Matthew Arnheiter, Michael Gellis. *Visual Basic Developer's Guide to UML and Design Patterns*. Hoboken, NJ: Sybex, 2000.

Larman, Craig. *Applying UML and Patterns: An Introduction to Object-Oriented Analysis and Design and Iterative Development*. Upper Saddle River, NJ: Prentice Hall PTR, 2004.

Lau, Yun-Tung. *The Art of Objects: Object-Oriented Design and Architecture*. Boston, MA: Addison-Wesley Professional, 2001.

Lhotka, Rockford. *Expert VB 2005 Business Objects, Second Edition*. Berkeley, CA: Apress, 2006.

Liberty, Jesse. *Programming Visual Basic 2005*. Sebastopol, CA: O'Reilly Media, 2005.

Moore, Karl. *Karl Moore's Visual Basic .NET: The Tutorials*. Berkeley, CA: Apress, 2002.

Patrick, Tim, and John Clark Craig. *Visual Basic 2005 Cookbook: Solutions for VB 2005 Programmers*. Sebastopol, CA: O'Reilly Media, 2006.

Richter, Jeffrey. *Applied Microsoft .NET Framework Programming*. Redmond, WA: Microsoft Press, 2002.

Stephens, Rod. *Visual Basic 2005 Programmer's Reference*. Indianapolis, IN: Wiley Publishing, 2005.

Stoecker, Matthew, with Microsoft Corporation. *MCAD/MCSD Self-Paced Training Kit: Developing Windows-Based Applications with Microsoft Visual Basic .NET and Visual C# .NET, Second Edition*. Redmond, CA: Microsoft Press, 2003.

Sutter, Herb. *Exceptional C++: 47 Engineering Puzzles, Programming Problems, and Exception-Safety Solutions*. Boston, MA: Addison-Wesley Professional, 1999.

Troelsen, Andrew. *Pro VB 2005 and the .NET 2.0 Platform*. Berkeley, CA: Apress, 2006.

Yourdon, Edward, and Larry L. Constantine. *Structured Design: Fundamentals of a Discipline of Computer Program and Systems Design*. Upper Saddle River, NJ: Prentice Hall, 1979.

Articles

Kaplan, Michael, and Cathy Wissink. "Custom Cultures: Extend Your Code's Global Reach With New Features In The .NET Framework 2.0." *MSDN Magazine*, October 2005.

Robbins, John. "Unhandled Exceptions and Tracing in the .NET Framework 2.0." *MSDN Magazine*, July 2005.

Schmidt, Douglas C. "Monitor Object: An Object Behavioral Pattern for Concurrent Programming." Department of Computer Science and Engineering, Washington University, St. Louis, MO, April 2005.

Toub, Stephen. "High Availability: Keep Your Code Running with the Reliability Features of the .NET Framework." *MSDN Magazine*, October 2005.

Vermeulen, Allan. "An Asynchronous Design Pattern." *Dr. Dobb's Journal*, June 1996.

Ng, Timothy. "Basic Instincts: Lambda Expressions." *MSDN Magazine*, September, 2007.

Horst, Bill. "Basic Instincts: Type Inference in Visual Basic 2008." *MSDN Magazine*, October 2007.

Web

101 LINQ Samples. http://msdn2.microsoft.com/en-us/vbasic/bb688088.aspx

101 Samples for Visual Basic 2005. http://msdn2.microsoft.com/en-us/vbasic/ms789075.aspx

The Code Project. www.codeproject.com/

Developer.com. www.developer.com/net/vb/

Free Book - Introducing Microsoft Visual Basic 2005 for Developers. http://msdn2.microsoft.com/en-us/vbrun/ms788235.aspx

Visual Basic 2008 Express Edition. `http://msdn2.microsoft.com/en-us/express/future/bb421469.aspx`

VB.Net Heaven. `www.vbdotnetheaven.com/`

Visual Basic Developer Center. `http://msdn2.microsoft.com/en-us/vbasic/default.aspx`

Consuming Unmanaged DLL Functions. `http://msdn2.microsoft.com/en-us/library/26thfadc(vs.90).aspx`

A Closer Look at Platform Invoke. `http://msdn2.microsoft.com/en-us/library/0h9e9t7d(vs.90).aspx`

Code Access Security: When Role-Based Security Isn't Enough. `http://www.devx.com/security/Article/31259/0/page/1`

How to Create an Indexer Property in Visual Basic .NET or in Visual Basic 2005. `http://support.microsoft.com/kb/311323`

How to Demand Permissions by Using Code Access Security. `http://support.microsoft.com/kb/315529`

Code Access Security. `http://msdn2.microsoft.com/en-us/library/930b76w0(VS.90).aspx`

Code Access Permissions. `http://msdn2.microsoft.com/en-us/library/h846e9b3(vs.90).aspx`

Unicode Frequently Asked Questions. `http://unicode.org/faq/utf_bom.html`

Wikipedia, "Regular Expression," `http://en.wikipedia.org/wiki/Regular_expression`, 2007.

Regular Expression Tutorial. `http://www.regular-expressions.info/tutorial.html`

Array Covariance Rules. `http://msdn2.microsoft.com/en-us/library/aa664572(VS.71).aspx`

The LINQ Project. `http://msdn2.microsoft.com/en-us/netframework/aa904594.aspx`

Hooked on LINQ. `http://www.hookedonlinq.com/MainPage.ashx`

Beth Massi, "Sharing the Goodness that is VB: Quickly Import and Export Excel Data with LINQ to XML," `http://blogs.msdn.com/bethmassi/archive/2007/10/30/quickly-import-and-export-excel-data-with-linq-to-xml.aspx`

Douglas Reichard, "Shim Classes," `http://www.ddj.com/cpp/184401200?pgno=5`

Deployment of Managed COM Add-Ins in Office XP. `http://msdn2.microsoft.com/en-us/library/aa164016(office.10).aspx`

■ ■ ■

Running the Examples

This appendix describes the various types of code examples throughout the book and how to run them. It is meant to aid you if you're new to the VB 2008 environment.

Example Types

This book contains three types of code examples: code snippets; classes, structures, and interfaces and console applications.

Code Snippets

A code snippet is a short code sample used to display the syntax of an entire method or single function call. These samples are not meant to be compiled or executed.

Classes, Structures, and Interfaces

These examples contain class, structure, and interface definitions. You build these by using the Class Library project type. Chapter 6 contains several examples that fall into this category.

Console Applications

These examples, built using the Console Application project type, are the most prevalent type of code example in the book. By default, VB creates a `Module1.vb` file with the following stub:

```
Module Module1
    Sub Main()
    End Sub
End Module
```

We recommend that you replace the entire `Module` stub with the example text, which contains a `Public EntryPoint` class and a `Shared Main` method. Next, in your project's Properties page, on the Application tab, set the "Startup object:" to "Sub Main." For examples that require command-line arguments, you can enter these, separated by spaces, in your project's Properties page, on the Debug tab, in the "Command line arguments" input area. Finally, the few samples that discuss globalization require a message box to display the results. You should build and run these examples the same way as other console applications, but you need to add a reference to `System.Windows.Forms` in your project's Properties page, on the References tab.

Running a Console Application via the Debug ➤ Start Without Debugging menu, or the Ctrl+F5 shortcut, will launch the application, displaying each output as needed, then pause with a "Press any key to continue . . ." message when execution is complete.

For a more thorough understanding of an example, place a breakpoint on the first executable line inside Shared Sub Main(), and "Step Into" or "Step Over" each line of code while reviewing the call stack, any variables, and console output.

A Few Words Regarding Modules

If you're an experienced object-oriented developer, the concept of a *module* may seem foreign. The Module construct, which cannot be instantiated, is a feature carried over from Visual Basic 6.0 (VB6) to facilitate migration of those applications to .NET.

A Module, when compiled, is converted to a NotInheritable class with Shared members. These Shared members are available to your entire application, acting like a global variable. This may not be what you desire. Classes, on the other hand, are not automatically Shared.

We consider creating an EntryPoint class, containing a Shared Sub Main method, to be the much better practice for creating object-oriented systems with VB.

Index